Native and Natural

Aspects of the Concepts of 'Right' and 'Freedom' in Irish

Peter McQuillan

CORK UNIVERSITY PRESS
in association with
FIELD DAY

First published in 2004 by
Cork University Press
Crawford Business Park
Crosses Green
Cork
Ireland

© Peter McQuillan 2004

British Library Cataloguing in Publication Data

A CIP catalogue record for this book is available from the British Library.

ISBN 1-85918-364-6

Typesetting by Red Barn Publishing, Skeagh, Skibbereen, Co. Cork

Printed by Betaprint Ltd., Ireland

www.corkuniversitypress.com

LIBRARY
University of Glasgow

CRITICAL CONDITIONS: FIELD DAY ESSAYS AND MONOGRAPHS

Edited by Seamus Deane

1. *The Tree of Liberty*, Kevin Whelan
2. *Transformations in Irish Culture*, Luke Gibbons
3. *Mere Irish and Fíor-Ghael,* Joep Leerssen
4. *Remembrance and Imagination*, Joep Leerssen
5. *Crazy John and the Bishop*, Terry Eagleton
6. *The Keeper's Recital*, Harry White
7. *The Present Lasts a Long Time*, Francis Mulhern
8. *Poets and Politics*, Marc Caball
9. *Ireland After History*, David Lloyd
10. *Ireland's Others*, Elizabeth Butler Cullingford
11. *Circe's Cup*, Clare Carroll
12. *Revival*, P. J. Mathews

I gcuimhne ar m'athair agus ar mo mháthair

CONTENTS

Acknowledgements   ix

1. Introduction   1

2. The Internal and External Dimensions of *Dúchas*   20

3. The Pragmatics of *Dúthaigh* and *Dúchas*   55

4. The Pragmatics of *Dual* and the Habitual   99

5. The Semantics and Syntax of 'Right' and 'Natural' 138

6. Afterword to *Dúchas:* A Vocabulary and Syntax   170
                        of Natural Law?

7. The Irish Idea of 'Freedom'   183

Notes   231

Bibliography   254

Index   267

ACKNOWLEDGEMENTS

This book has been inspired by the challenge of working in an interdisciplinary Irish Studies environment at the University of Notre Dame. I owe a debt of gratitude to all those whose comments, questions and suggestions at various seminar presentations, particularly those of the Friday seminars at Notre Dame, have helped to shape the ideas that have gone into the making of this book. In particular, however, I would like to thank Seamus Deane, Breandan Ó Buachalla, Sarah McKibben and Brian Ó Conchubhair for their close reading of the typescript and for their many helpful comments and corrections. Needless to say, any inaccuracies and imperfections that remain are entirely the author's responsibility. Outside the field of Irish Studies, I am especially grateful to two of my colleagues here at Notre Dame, Susan Blum and Patrick Gaffney, for directing me towards various helpful references in the field of linguistic anthropology; and to Éamonn Ó hÓgáin of the Royal Irish Academy, Dublin, for his helpfulness in allowing me access to that institution's lexicographical data base in Irish.

On a more personal level, I wish to acknowledge the support and encouragement afforded me by my wife, Rachel and two sons, Tom and Jack. This book is dedicated to them and also to the memory of my parents, Felix and Nora. Some debts can never be repaid but I hope that this book would have offered them some reward for the many sacrifices that they made on my behalf.

Finally, I would like to thank Field Day and the staff of Cork University Press for all their help.

1. INTRODUCTION

The main aim of this book is to show how a linguistic, and specifically a linguistic-anthropological, framework might profitably be brought to bear on texts of historical and cultural interest in the Irish language. This method asserts that such texts can only be approached meaningfully in the original language within their own chronological and ideological frame of reference. In a sense, while the book begins as a linguistic-anthropological study, it goes on to include a strong cultural-historical dimension as well. It is hoped, therefore, that it will appeal, in more or less equal measure, to students of Irish culture, language and history alike.

This book is not offered as a textbook of any kind or as an introduction to any branch of linguistic theory. For this reason I have been selective in my exposition of matters linguistic, presenting only what I feel to be absolutely necessary for a non-linguistically oriented readership. To that end, I shall now say something about premises of the discipline known as linguistic anthropology.

Linguistic anthropology and this book

The linguistic-anthropological approach, stated broadly, argues that, while we have an innate ability to acquire language, our ability to *use* language is mediated culturally.[1] Put in such terms, any real understanding of the function of language must make the transition from consideration of phonology, grammar and lexicon to an examination of social and historical practice—in other words, from the formal and structural to the pragmatic dimensions of language. Thus, what Alessandro Duranti calls the 'intricate logic' of linguistic systems has to be apprehended and situated in the context of the activities through which those systems are reproduced.[2] These activities themselves are in turn part of a wider, extra-linguistic context. The relationship between language on the one hand and culture and society on the other is reflexive. As Watkins puts it, language is at once 'the expression of culture and a part of it', and the appreciation of one is therefore essential to an understanding of the other.[3] Not only is language culturally mediated, therefore, but it in its turn mediates historical and cultural experience. In the words of the linguist and anthropologist Edward Sapir, language, particularly through its words, is a symbolic guide and a sensitive index to culture.[4] This theme is taken up in a book by Anna Wierzbicka, *Understanding Cultures through Their Key Words* (1997), in which she compares 'key' words from a variety of languages: English, Russian, Polish, German and Japanese. In Wierzbicka's words,

> Culture-specific words are conceptual tools that reflect a society's past experience of doing and thinking about things in certain ways; and they help perpetuate these ways. As a society changes, these tools, too, may be gradually modified and discarded.[5]

Two of Wierzbicka's analyses stand out, particularly in the present context. The first is her examination of words for 'homeland' or 'native land' in German, Polish and Russian according to the very different cultural and historical resonances that they have in their various languages; the second is her study of words for 'freedom' in Latin, English, Russian, Polish and Japanese. These studies will be taken into account when the relevant lexical items in Irish are discussed. A further purpose of my own study, however, is to argue that linguistic structure *in general,* through its morphology and syntax, is also a powerful tool in the explication of important cultural and ideological concepts. This is discussed in chapters 4 and 5 especially but is also fundamental to aspects of the analysis in other chapters.

In this introductory chapter, I shall say something about the various strands of thought in the linguistic-anthropological tradition that inform the approach to the words being examined in the course of this book. Within this general framework there are two specific aspects of recent research that I wish to emphasize, and in both aspects the name of Michael Silverstein looms large. Firstly, there is the question of the *indexical* nature of linguistic forms, how different aspects of a communicative situation are pragmatically referenced through language use. This can occur in a number of ways. For example, in a community where more than one language is commonly used, the choice of one language over another (code switching) can be indexical of the perceived relationship between speaker and addressee; one of intimacy, familiarity or distance, for instance.[6] In the type of situations to be examined in this particular study we will look at how words, or linguistic signs in general, function as a link between aspects of a current context and a past one. The interpretation of such words tends, therefore, to be specific to the particular context of usage, and interpretation is apt to shift from one context to another. In a sense, then, such words cannot be 'defined', they can only be 'interpreted', as Koselleck et al. put it.[7] The importance of this parameter of indexicality will be especially obvious in our discussion of *dúchas* in chapter 3.

Secondly, we have what Silverstein has called *metalinguistic* or, more specifically, *metapragmatic awareness.* This represents a continuum of speaker awareness of the pragmatics of language or the way in which specific linguistic forms are used. In a classic study that first appeared in 1981, Silverstein adduces a number of parameters by which the degrees of such awareness among native speakers can be calibrated. One of these is the extent to which a linguistic form has unique or unavoidable referentiality; that is to say, can be used to refer to one entity and one only. A proper noun such as 'China', for example, scores highly as uniquely referential and is therefore easily accessible to speaker awareness of its function.[8] Thus, the purely referential or semantic function of such a form also accounts for its pragmatic or communicative function. An example of a linguistic act that is high on the scale of awareness, for example, is the act of my writing at the beginning of this chapter: 'The overall aim of this book is . . .' Here I am functioning at a high level of metapragmatic awareness, glossing, as it were, the linguistic act that I am performing. Conversely, grammatical categories, such as tense and mood endings on a verb, are lower on the scale of awareness. Speakers, apart from specialist linguists and grammarians, tend to be less conscious of such forms, because their usage is largely rule-driven and therefore automatic, being accounted for by the grammatical structure of a language. For example, every well-formed sentence of my text must ordinarily include a verb form that is marked in some way for tense or mood. My use of the word 'must' here is significant, as language use at this lower, grammatical end of the linguistic spectrum tends to be more obligatory in character than at the higher end: however carefully I choose my words, the grammar of the language that I use takes care of so many other aspects of what I write. Thus in typical academic writing an English sentence contains a present tense form. If the subject of that verb is singular, I *must* write either -*s* or -*es* on the end of the verb; if it is plural then I *cannot* add such an ending. In other words, there is no choice in this particular matter, as the grammar of English decides it for me. We can contrast this with the way we refer in everyday usage to one's '*choice* of words', or when we advise people to '*choose* their words carefully', as it were. Grammatical structure, therefore, tends to be reproduced in a more automated or automatic fashion by speakers than lexical items which are generally the object of more conscious deliberation. Purely grammatical elements, because they are generalized over a number of contexts, are less susceptible to speaker awareness than lexical ones. Such limitations on awareness are not tantamount to ignorance, however. If anything, it is precisely because speakers acquire a mastery of the grammatical structure of their language so early that such usage is self-regulating and is indeed a prerequisite of any kind of fluency or communicative competence.[9]

Of considerable importance here are the ideas of one of the founders of linguistic anthropology, Franz Boas.[10] In considering grammatical categories, Boas is in general concerned with *obligatory* categories, the set of which 'determines those aspects of experience that must be expressed'.[11] In drawing attention to the particular value of vocabulary as an index of social and cultural change, Boas's pupil, Sapir, opposes the lexical element of language to the grammatical, a distinction that we have already made above. The former he characterizes as the 'detailed content', the latter as the 'general form' of language.[12] In describing experience, speakers of a given language naturally resort to those linguistic elements that are most readily, most *routinely* available to them in that language. These routine elements are the grammatical categories of a language; and Dan Slobin's recent research, published in 1996, concentrating as it does on the use of such categories among children ranging in age from three to nine, bears out the fact that it is to such routinized categories as a particular grammar provides that speakers most easily have recourse in translating a particular scene into language.[13] This relates directly to what are the most fundamental aspects of the nature of grammar: its automated and obligatory character as outlined above. Speakers of a language, therefore, construe experience *primarily* in terms of the grammatical categories which that language makes available to them. At the very least, as Slobin points out, whatever else grammar does, it directs our attention to such aspects of experience.[14]

Apart from the more automated and obligatory character of grammatical as opposed to lexical elements there is the further question, mentioned above, of the extent to which the semantic-referential and the pragmatic functions of a particular linguistic form coincide. In the case of a form with unique referentiality, the level of coincidence is high. With a grammatical form, however, the degree of convergence may be less marked. For example, if a verb form that describes the repeated occurrence of a situation in past time is used, this is its referential (semantic) function, as in the example *I used to smoke sixty a day*. However, the same form also gives rise to the inference that the situation so described no longer holds at the moment of speaking. Thus, the more purely pragmatic component of the sentence is: *but I no longer do*. In chapter 4 ('The Pragmatics of *Dual* and the Habitual') we will examine the cultural and historical ramifications of the use of precisely this category in Irish, the category known as the habitual past (*aimsir ghnáthchaite*).

What Silverstein's research in this area has tried to do is to set parameters for the degree to which such functional divergences between the semantic and the pragmatic components of meaning either rise to speaker consciousness or are impenetrable to that consciousness. We will return to these parameters later in this chapter, as well as to the relationship between the pragmatic (indexical) and the metapragmatic functions of language and the importance of this relationship for the contents of this book. First, however, I want to take a closer look at the words to be examined.

The words (1): *dúchas*, *dúthaigh* and *dual*

The following is an outline sketch of the words to be examined in chapters 2 to 5. I am not concerned at this point with giving exhaustive definitions, rather with emphasizing the main points of interest (I will say more below about the sources used and their chronology).

Chapter 2 ('The Internal and External Dimensions of *Dúchas*') and chapter 3 ('The Pragmatics of *Dúthaigh* and *Dúchas*'):

> **dúthaigh** (Modern Irish **dúiche**): 1. Hereditary land. 2. Native land, native place, home country.
>
> **dúthchas** (Modern Irish **dúchas**): 1. Hereditary right or claim; birthright, heritage. 2. Native place or country, ancestral home. 3. Kindred affection, natural affinity. 4. Heredity, innate quality, natural bent.

Chapter 4 ('The Pragmatics of *Dual* and the Habitual'):

> **dual** (*substantive used adjectivally with copula*): 1. Native, natural (*do*, to). 2. Proper, fitting. 3. In the natural order of things.
>
> **dualgas:** 1. Natural right, due; customary fee or reward. 2. Duty

Chapter 5 ('The Semantics and Syntax of "Right" and "Natural"'):

> **dlighe(adh)** (Modern Irish **dlí**): 1. Lawful right, due. 2. Tax, tribute.
>
> **díleas:** 1. (as adjective) One's own. 2. Personal property.
>
> **dílse:** 1. Proprietary right. 2. Ownership, property.
>
> **dír:** Due, proper, pertaining (*do,* to).
>
> **díre:** Due, right.

In the introduction to his well-known *Keywords* (1976),[15] Raymond Williams speaks of the five words on which he had originally based his study—*culture, art, class, democracy* and *industry*—as representing what he came to perceive 'as a kind of structure'.[16] I have found this kind of feeling repeated in my own work presented here on the words I have outlined above, all of which are in some way concerned with what is 'right' or 'natural', 'lawful' or 'proper', either by way of hereditary right or sanctioned by custom.

In fact I first came to consider the word *dúchas* in earnest after I had encountered Wierzbicka's discussion of words for 'homeland' in a number of languages.[17] As can be seen from the outline presented above, however, 'native country' is but one of several, apparently diverse, meanings that this word *dúchas* has. To anticipate aspects of the discussion in chapter 2 below ('The Internal and External Dimensions of *Dúchas*'), the default Modern Irish equivalent of 'native land' is *tír dhúchais*, literally 'land of *dúchas*', where *dúchas*, in its genitive case form *d(h)úchais*, stands for a qualifying attribute or quality that marks out the land in question as special in some way. Yet in earlier Irish the simplex *dúchas* is frequently used in this sense of 'native land', not merely as an attributive genitive qualifying another word itself denotative of land in its physical aspect, like *tír*, or *fearann* or *fód*. Thus, in the medieval and early modern periods, *dúchas* signifies the native land both in its material and its symbolic aspects. In the syntax of *tír dhúchais*, however, these two aspects are represented separately and the greater salience of this analytical construction in the modern period tells us something about Irish people's attitudes to their land and its more emotive dimensions in particular historical circumstances, as I will argue in more detail below. Chapter 2 also attempts to suggest what historical relationship obtains between those meanings of *dúchas* that are 'external' in nature (relating to hereditary right and claim: see meaning 1 above) and the more 'internalized' meanings (relating to personal characteristics and traits: see meaning 4 above) and, further, what possible connection exists between either or both of those ranges of meaning and the idea of 'native land' itself.

Chapter 3 ('The Pragmatics of *Dúthaigh* and *Dúchas*') examines closely both *dúchas* and the related term *dúthaigh* (*dúiche*) as they were used during the late sixteenth and early seventeenth centuries in the forging of a new national consciousness between the native Irish and the Gaelicized descendants of the first English colonists of the medieval period in the crucible of Tudor expansionism in Ireland. This essay uses the concept of indexicality introduced briefly above (and see further below) to show how the semiotic structure of these words 'indexes' or pragmatically references such extra-linguistic concerns and developments. The indexical approach stresses the importance of specific contexts for the interpretation of linguistic function.

Chapter 4 ('The Pragmatics of *Dual* and the Habitual') broadens the discussion in two ways. Firstly, our examination of the indexical is continued by an investigation of the pragmatics of the word *dual,* and its derivative *dualgas,* with respect to the relationship between professional poet and patron in Irish society, for example. Secondly, as mentioned above, this chapter also shows that these same pragmatics find a close correspondence in the usage of an entire grammatical category in Irish, that of the *habitual*, which is used to denote the repeated occurrence of an event over an extended period. As has already been mentioned above in our brief exposition of what constitutes linguistic (or metalinguistic) awareness, the implications of such a correspondence are important, both in the similarity and the difference between the nature of linguistic usage and consciousness at both ends of the continuum of meaning, lexical and grammatical. These implications will be examined through a consideration of a number of texts, of the sixteenth and seventeenth centuries especially, in their cultural and historical context. This particular chapter, therefore, demonstrates how the idea of the 'habitual' is pervasive in a number of linguistic domains in Irish, both lexical and grammatical. One aim is to show how the lexical and grammatical expression of what is broadly the same concept can interact to give a certain reading of a text. A further aim is to suggest ways in which such an analysis of habituality in Irish sheds light on the relationship between the more grammaticalized and the more lexicalized components of language in general. In so doing we will be making use of the ideas of Franz Boas on the nature of grammatical meaning and their application by Slobin.

Similar concerns inform the analysis in chapter 5 ('The Semantics and Syntax of "Right" and "Natural" in Irish'), which examines further lexical congeners of *dúchas* within the conceptual domain of what is right, sanctioned by custom (and therefore natural and inevitable). This chapter investigates how linguistic structure at the less conscious grammatical or syntactic end of the linguistic continuum may be considered to act as a reinforcement of ideology as formulated on the more conscious lexical end. This will involve a consideration of the syntax of constructions expressing degrees of the necessity, obligation or appropriateness of a course of action. It will be argued that such constructions can be interpreted as shedding light on the deep semantic structure of words themselves indexical of what is 'right' or 'natural' or 'pre-ordained' in some way. In particular, we will look at a form known as the 'verbal of necessity', an impersonal adjective form like the Latin gerundive which expresses a generalized necessity or obligation, in this context.

As Wierzbicka points out, there are no objective criteria for identifying key words.[18] Such words are those that we feel, often intuitively, will offer unique insights into a given culture and its history. The case for each word has to be made and the strength of that particular case is its own justification however. The idea is to approach key words like *dúchas* and *dual* not simply as individual lexical items but rather as focal points around which entire cultural domains are organized.[19] This can also lead to consideration not only of the words themselves but also of conceptually related collocations, set phrases and grammatical constructions. Consideration of chapters 2 to 5 together draws attention to another parameter adduced by Wierzbicka, that of cultural elaboration, whereby objects and constructs that are central to a given culture may be subject to a proliferation of vocabulary to make finer distinctions and produce more associations within that particular semantic domain. As has already been indicated above, chapter 5 will consider a particular example of such elaboration that affects both lexical and grammatical structure in Irish.

The words (2): *saoirse*

In the preamble to her discussion of words for 'freedom' in a number of languages, Wierzbicka gives the following critique of previous discussions of the subject:

> What is lacking in the philosophical literature is an analysis of 'freedom' and related concepts undertaken from a cross-linguistic perspective— an analysis which would be able to reveal, in a rigorous and methodical way, the similarities and the differences between concepts related to 'freedom' which have been lexically encoded in different languages, and which are often assumed to be simply identical.[20]

Wierzbicka argues here against what she perceives to be a certain bias or presumption that words like English *freedom* can be construed as conterminous with any universal human notion of 'freedom'. This is of course not to dismiss the search for a universalist dimension for the idea of 'freedom'. It is rather that the relation between the universal and the culture-specific dimensions must be reciprocal. A universal core of meaning can be isolated and identified only on the grounds of typological comparison; conversely, the richness of linguistic and cultural diversity can be properly understood only within the context of that universal dimension. Furthermore, a distinction has to be made in discussions of the word *freedom* as it is encoded in the lexicon of English with its various culture-specific Anglophone connotations and the wider philosophical concerns that emerge in individual discussions of 'freedom', where ideas of what is theoretically possible or desirable are involved. In particular, as Wierzbicka argues, it is a gratuitous assumption that what is encoded by English-speakers in the term *freedom* is conterminous with any universal theoretical construct of what 'freedom' entails or (morally speaking) should entail. Words for 'freedom' should be decoded in their own language-specific and culture-specific context.

This is how I approach the Irish word *saoirse* in chapter 7 ('The Irish Idea of "Freedom"'). My purpose is to cross interdisciplinary boundaries, in this instance by putting forward arguments based on considerations of linguistic structure as a means of offering some complementary perspectives on the views of various philosophers, political scientists and historians. In particular I consider the views of Isaiah Berlin and Quentin Skinner in relation to the concept of 'freedom', especially the 'two concepts' (positive 'freedom to' and negative 'freedom from') propounded by Berlin and revised, and to a significant extent refuted, by Skinner.[21] The linguistic framework for discussion is provided by Wierzbicka's comparative analysis of the idea of freedom, and particularly its syntactic realization, in a number of languages—Latin, Russian, Japanese, English and Polish. I shall consider aspects of the development of *saoirse* in the eighteenth and nineteenth centuries under the impact of the rise of nationalism in Ireland, especially in the comparative context of the last two languages listed. What I shall argue is that certain facts of the evolving syntactic behaviour of *saoirse* in Irish, when compared with its equivalent in Polish and contrasted with its equivalent in English, support the arguments of Skinner and undermine those of Berlin on the validity of political, and specifically national, freedom as a separate type. In particular, it will be shown that from a linguistic viewpoint Irish *saoirse* pragmatically references a specifically national and political 'freedom' in a way that English *freedom* does not. At the same time *freedom* and *saoirse* share a more universal dimension, in that they are both examples of what Geoffrey Hughes calls the 'democratization of status words', or an extension of what was once an aristocratic privilege to society at large.[22]

How words point to contexts: indexicality revisited

Having outlined the identity of the linguistic forms to be examined below in some detail, I now want to return to consideration of the linguistic framework in which these are to be set. Mention has been made of the pragmatic-indexical function of language use and it is to this that I wish in the first place to return, especially in relation to *dúchas*. It is precisely in terms of its more abstract, elusive, somehow indefinable essence that we often think of this word *dúchas* in Irish. Consider, for example, the following commentaries on what are essentially the pragmatics of this word (author's translation):

(a) Is minic go mbíonn focail in úsáid againn a nglacaimid leis go dtuigimid a gciall go dtí go n-iarrann duine a mhíniú orainn nó go n-iarrann go n-aistreoimis an focal go teanga eile ionas go dtuigfeadh sé é. Ainneoin ár dtuiscint inmheánach téann sé rite linn focail áirithe a shainmhíniú nó a aistriú go beacht. Focal den chineál seo is ea an focal 'dúchas.' Focal speisialta é a thuigimid níos mó leis an gcroí ná leis an intinn. Focal ar deacair linn míniú cruinn sásúil a thabhairt air. Focal do-aistrithe.[23]

We often use words that we assume we know the meaning of until someone asks us to explain them or to translate them into another language so that they might understand it. Despite our inner understanding we find it difficult to define or accurately translate certain words. The word *dúchas* is a word of this kind. It is a special word that we understand better with the heart than with the mind. A word we find difficult to explain accurately or satisfactorily. An untranslatable word.

(b) 'Dúchas' is one of those terms, often emotive—like 'die Heimat' ('home, homeland, home [native] country') in German, for example—that are difficult to express in translation, carrying as they do many interconnected senses and having a long, language-specific history behind them.[24]

Dúchas here is credited with a certain evocative power, being grasped viscerally rather than intellectually, a linguistic form that, in the terms adduced earlier, poses a challenge to the speaker's own linguistic awareness of meaning and function. Similar considerations are present in the case of the related *dúthaigh* or *dúiche,* although the difficulties there are somewhat fewer. Note, however, how O'Donnell and de Fréine characterize this item in relation to the more generic word *ceantar* 'district'. A *dúiche* is:

ceantar atá níos leithne ná an chomharsanacht, amhail paróiste, nó leathpharóiste b'fhéidir. Baineann seanchas agus dílseacht le dúiche.[25]

a district that it more extensive than the neighbourhood, like a parish or a half-parish perhaps. Local lore and tradition [*seanchas*] and loyalty are associated with a *dúiche*.

This is in contradistinction to the word *ceantar* itself, of which the authors say:

ní bhaineann mothú croí le seo. Gabhann blas neamhphearsanta leis.

there is no heart-felt feeling associated with this. It has an impersonal air.

Williams describes the word *culture* as his 'original difficult word', because of the 'significance of its general and variable usage', as he puts it.[26] In some ways Williams's personal experience with the English word *culture* is replicated by my own experience, as well as that of those authors cited immediately above, with the Irish word *dúchas*. It is this experience of encountering the word *dúchas,* and also *dúthaigh* or *dúiche,* in the context of words denoting 'native land' that has led me in search of some kind of linguistic or semiotic apparatus that will be able to account for this difficulty. I believe that the answer is to be found in a consideration of this *indexical* function of language that I have already mentioned above, to which we now return.

We have already made reference to the two important components of meaning: the semantic or referential function on the one hand and the pragmatic or indexical function on the other. The semantic may be defined as that part of meaning that is relatively predictable and independent of context and that is therefore inherent in linguistic structure itself. The pragmatic, on the other hand, is concerned with language use and its communicative function and is dependent on context for its interpretation. In a number of publications over the past twenty-five years or so Michael Silverstein has drawn attention to these two functions of meaning. The *semantic-referential* function depicts language as a projection of reality or as a form of knowledge, whereas the *pragmatic-indexical* function characterizes language as contextualized, communicative social action.[27] While it is important to remember that language functions in both ways, one of the significant trends in linguistic anthropology in recent times has been to modify what some researchers in the field have seen as certain preconceptions of the primarily semantic-referential nature of meaning in the Western linguistic and philosophical traditions, in particular the idea that meaning consists primarily of matching the linguistic sign to some non-linguistic representation in the external world.[28] However, more detailed study of various ethno-linguistic traditions around the world has revealed that this is a conception of meaning that is by no means universal. In various cultures, usage in context is seen as the 'meaning'. This phenomenon is illustrated notably by the existence in the Australian language Djirbal of two sets of vocabulary for everyday items, the use of one in preference to the other being dictated by specific social and cultural factors.[29] Here meaning is not a matter of word reference or denotation but rather of the pragmatic referencing of kinship relations in a particular social setting. The same type of point is made by Rumsey's comparison of the nature of the direct–indirect speech dichotomy in English, a dualism, or a preoccupation with exact wording as opposed to meaning *per se* that does not exist in many Australian languages, for example.[30]

In such linguistic cultures, meaning tends to be viewed in terms other than those of word reference. In other words, the use of one form over another indexes a particular contextual relationship. In an essay emphasizing the value of linguistics for the study of culture and history, published in 1929, Sapir makes the point that 'the network of cultural patterns of a civilization is *indexed* in the language which expresses that civilization'.[31] In a contemporary text from another continent and from another ideological perspective, Voloshinov describes the word as 'the most sensitive *index* of social changes'.[32] But how exactly are we to understand 'index' and 'indexed' here?

To answer this question, it will be necessary to make a short digression into the nature of the semiotic in language. The origins of the twentieth-century awareness of the importance of the study of signs in language lie with two great contemporaries, the linguist Ferdinand de Saussure[33] and the philosopher Charles Sanders Peirce. In Saussure's view, language was best studied as a closed system or structure (*langue*) consisting of signs whose ultimate value was differential with respect to each other. Each sign has a dyadic structure of 'signifier' (the material aspect of the sign) and 'signified' (the mental or conceptual aspect). The relation between the two aspects of the sign is arbitrary, or based on agreed linguistic convention, and it is for this reason that the true meaning of signs is defined in terms of their difference relative to one another. Hodge and Kress draw attention to the fact that in Saussure's thought language is seen as part of a wider semiotic system from which society, culture and politics are excluded as extra-semiotic phenomena, even though Saussure elsewhere insists that language is a 'social fact'.[34] Saussure thus sets up a dichotomy between 'internal' linguistics (language as a self-contained system) and 'external' linguistics (language as a socially and historically contingent artefact). Having excluded the latter as incapable of scientific treatment, he then progressively narrows the remit of the former by excluding even language-internal historical developments and considerations of the reference of signs (what they refer to in the external world) in favour of their system-internal value (how they are differentiated from other signs). Germane to this procedure was Saussure's fear of chaos in the system of language, which led him to repress the *dynamic* aspects of linguistic reality: the individually, socially and historically contingent facets of language.

Peirce offers a more dynamic conception of the semiotic which stresses the idea of process in the study of meaning. For Peirce the sign is a triadic relation, unlike the dyad posited by Saussure, consisting of the material sign itself and the object it represents. Peirce's triadic type expands Saussure's two functions to three with the addition of the function of 'interpretant', which is, in essence, a further sign or association produced in the mind by the initial sign.[35] This trichotomy is irreducible: all three functions must be present for a sign to function coherently. This addition of the interpretant is crucial, as it introduces a dialogic dimension to semiotics. As E. Valentine Daniel puts it in a study of Tamil vocabulary and concepts that has much influenced my own approach to *dúchas*, 'every semiotic study of however small a cultural aspect must, by definition, remain open and incomplete . . . no polyadic relation has reachable endpoints'.[36] For Peirce, therefore, the construction of meaning is essentially interactive, although he presents it as an element of personal psychology rather than as a social process.

Furthermore, Peirce classified signs into three types: icons, symbols and indexes. An *icon* is a sign that bears some kind of graphic or diagrammatic resemblance to its referent. A *symbol* is a sign whose signification is a matter of convention. Words are symbols in this sense. In English, for example, the sequence 'table' refers to its particular object by such a linguistic convention: there is nothing inherent in the sequence 't-a-b-1-e' that connects it with its referent. This is the semantic-referential aspect of meaning, referred to above, and it rests on the relative fixity or context-independence of meaning. An *index*, on the other hand, relates a sign to an object with regard to contiguity, concurrence or causation; a simple non-linguistic example would be *smoke* as an index of *fire*. What is of greatest interest in the present context is Roman Jakobson's idea of the 'duplex sign' or '*shifter*', that there are certain linguistic signs whose structure is conventional or, in Saussurean terms, 'arbitrary' but whose wider signification is context-dependent or pragmatic.[37] As he himself puts it, 'the general meaning of a shifter cannot be defined without reference to the message'.[38] In semiotic terms, a shifter is therefore both a symbol and an index. This idea has been further elaborated on and applied to cultural linguistic and anthropological contexts by Silverstein and Daniel. Both these scholars stress the indispensable nature of *context* for the interpretation of signs that do not simply *represent* objects (ideas, concepts) but rather presuppose or create them and bring them into a current context. In Duranti's formulation, indexicality is 'a sign-activated connection between an on-going situation and other situations'.[39] Chapter 3, in particular, exploits recent insights into the nature of indexicality in relation to aspects of the history of *dúchas*, while part of the discussion in chapter 4 investigates how the words *dual* and *dualgas* index or pragmatically reference the relationship between professional poet and patron in the medieval and early modern periods.

As his concerns were more epistemological and metaphysical than strictly linguistic, the work of Peirce, unlike that of Saussure, remained peripheral to the study of linguistics until rehabilitated by Roman Jakobson.[40] Since then, Peirce's essentially more pragmatic account of meaning has been of particular importance in the field of linguistic anthropology, the central premise of which, as we have seen, is that the use and the context of use of language is culturally mediated and that language is both embedded in and constitutive of social and cultural practices.[41] Linguistic anthropology is thus a kind of 'cultural linguistics' that studies language as the primary semiotic system among many in the creation of culture.[42] What makes language the most culturally advanced of sign systems is precisely the arbitrary or conventional relation between the linguistic sign and the object it represents. This gives language a particular flexibility and malleability as a culture-forming practice.[43]

Indexicality thus refers to the way in which linguistic forms pragmatically reference particular social, cultural and ultimately historical contexts. As Watkins points out, echoing the views of Sapir and Voloshinov above, it is the lexicon or vocabulary of a language that constitutes the most immediate and direct access to the culture of its speakers, and it is only through philology— the study and interpretation of texts—that historical linguistics can gain access to this material. As Watkins astutely observes, however, philology can be directly compared to pragmatics with regard to methodology: both are concerned with the connection between signs and their context; with their indexical meaning, in other words. From the viewpoint of culture and history, the real task for the linguist is to discover how the linguistic sign makes pragmatic reference to or indexes a cultural domain or domains. This task is a combined linguistic and philological one, what Watkins calls 'the new comparative philology' or 'historical ethno-semantics'.[44] This is the viewpoint that informs my approach to texts in their particular historical contexts in this book.

I feel also that there are correlations to be made here with recent developments in what may be called 'concept history' (*Begriffsgeschichte*), particularly with regard to Koselleck et al.'s monumental *Geschichtliche Grundbegriffe,* published in Germany between 1972 and 1997. Here Koselleck et al. argue for a fundamental distinction between 'word' (*Wort*) and 'concept' (*Begriff*), which is at least analogous to the distinction we have already made between symbol and index: while words may be 'defined,' concepts can only be 'interpreted'.[45] This once again emphasizes the context-contingent nature of meaning in such instances. Further, a word becomes a concept, in Koselleck et al.'s formulation, when it absorbs completely the socio-political context in which and for which it is used.[46]

Before leaving this section, I want to say a brief word about a further linguistic principle that will from time to time inform the approach to syntactic structure. I will mention it here because it represents a metaphorical extension of the semiotic type of 'icon', mentioned above, into the analysis of linguistic structure. Key words represent complex ideas in their own right and are not merely elements in other syntagma. As Hodge and Kress point out, for this very reason they tend to *dominate* the syntax in which they occur.[47] Recent functional approaches to syntactic structure have emphasized the *iconicity* of linguistic structure, the idea being that structural or syntactic relations in language can directly reflect cognitive and psychological processes.[48] This principle will be important in the analysis of both *dúchas,* in chapter 2, and *saoirse,* 'freedom', in chapter 7. In this way the study of words, and indeed of linguistic structure in general, becomes the study of cultural texts. Such considerations precisely are brought to the fore by Williams's engagement with historical semantics in *Keywords*.

Language on language: metapragmatics once again

Having discussed briefly the importance of the pragmatic or indexical function in language, we move to a further consideration of the metapragmatic. This question of the metalinguistic is an important one, since, as Jakobson recognized, without it no consciousness of linguistic form and function would be possible.[49] This whole question of the reflexive use of language—how language is used to communicate about itself and the methodological problems attendant on that fact—has recently been prominent in linguistic anthropology.[50] Language itself (as metalanguage) is the means through which we reflect on and analyse language (as object language). The metalinguistic therefore becomes the bridgehead between the analysis of linguistic structure and the meaningful incorporation of that structure to an account of cultural and historical practice. In a further development of his ideas into the nature of the metalinguistic, Silverstein distinguishes between two separate metapragmatic components: function and discourse. Put simply, 'function' refers to the metapragmatic activity that is *implicit* in everyday interaction and communication (making sense of what people say in context), while 'discourse' represents the *explicit* emphasizing of such activity.[51] Based on Silverstein's discussion, we could perhaps draw up a general model for metapragmatic activity, or that activity which organizes the pragmatic function of language, to include the following components:

1.   Metapragmatic discourse (explicit): emphasizing the metapragmatic function
2.   Metapragmatic function (implicit): interpretation of usage in context
3.   Pragmatics: context-dependent semiotic value
4.   Semantics: context-independent semiotic value

As we shall see in chapter 3 particularly ('The Pragmatics of *Dúthaigh* and *Dúchas*'), without the proper functioning of the metapragmatic component, interpretation of the pragmatic function breaks down. Earlier we mentioned the criterion of unique or unavoidable referentiality as one of Silverstein's parameters of awareness. A further such parameter is what he terms 'relative presupposition'.[52] At the level of metapragmatic function, this entails that the audience shares to a significant degree the knowledge of the specific context in which the speaker uses a particular form and is therefore able to interpret it. In addition, if we reconsider, for example, the two commentaries cited in the previous section on the difficulty of translating the word *dúchas* from Irish into another language, we can observe that, even where such shared cultural knowledge is present, at the more rarefied level of discourse the attempt to explicitly emphasize the sum of these various contextual relations runs into difficulties.

As was already hinted at above, the importance of linguistically imposed limits on awareness is that the degree to which forms are accessible to awareness affects the extent to which they are elaborated on, fashioned and refashioned in ideological terms. As might be expected, and as Silverstein predicts, those items that are more accessible to awareness are more likely to be the objects of conscious deliberation, or 'secondary rationalistic attempt' at explanation, as Boas would have it.[53] Typically, such forms are words. As the case of *dúchas* in Irish will show, however, words with a high indexical content present the greatest challenge to metapragmatic awareness at the lexical end of the spectrum.

A word on linguistic relativity

Before concluding the main exposition of this chapter, a brief word is required on what is often called the 'Boasian tradition' of *linguistic relativity*, after the linguist and anthropologist Franz Boas.[54] As this book is not primarily a comparative study, this concept does not play a central role in much of the ensuing discussion. However, some of the premises associated with it are in the background and occasionally emerge into the open, as in chapter 4 and, particularly, chapter 5. In that chapter, I present evidence that Irish shows a predilection for more non-agentive syntactic structures than English. To make the issue clear, a simple example can be given. Consider the familiar Irish phrase *is maith liom* 'I like', where the logical or semantic first-person subject is coded non-agentively; i.e. as the object of the preposition *le* 'to,' 'with': literally '(it) is good with me'. English, by contrast, codes the subject as a normal agentive subject in the nominative 'I'. The historian Kerby Miller has adduced from such contrasts that speakers of Irish are thus naturally predisposed towards a more passive, fatalistic, less active or agentive world view.[55] In making this argument, he invokes the ideas of Benjamin Lee Whorf that linguistic structure can shape thought and behaviour.[56] As linguistic structure differs from language to language, so too will predispositions supposedly based on that structure. Miller's view will be discussed more fully in chapter 5.

As Duranti points out, the issue of linguistic relativity was the first theoretical concern of the emergent discipline of linguistic anthropology in the early twentieth century in the United States. As he puts it, this concern arose from the coincidence of an idea and a moment. The idea was the close connection between the spirit (*Geist*) of a nation and its language on the one hand, and the world view (*Weltanschauung*) of its speakers on the other, as elaborated by the nineteenth-century German romantic tradition.[57] For Herder, language and thought were mutually dependent, each language having its own irreducible spiritual individuality. These ideas were taken up by von Humboldt, who further emphasized the interdependence of language and national character.[58] The moment was the encounter between European-trained linguists and anthropologists on the one hand and the native languages of North America on the other, which presented radically different structures from those of the Indo-European languages with which these scholars were familiar.[59]

Foremost in this encounter was the German-born Franz Boas who viewed language as an individualist mental construct that imposed an order of classification on experience. Linguistic diversity arose because of the paucity of grammatical categories in language with which to impose such an order on a potentially infinite variety of experience. Thus any given language, for practical reasons, typically highlights only certain salient features of a situation, leaving other aspects unexpressed.[60] Boas thus believed that languages could classify experience but that they do so differently in different cultures. In general, he believed that culture influenced language rather than *vice versa*; but, in his later life, under the influence of his pupil Edward Sapir, he seems to have accepted that language at the *lexical* level at least could shape thought. Language was treated as a universal with regard to core psychological functioning but as culture-specific with regard to historical experience.[61] Grammars of individual languages are therefore different conceptual systems that channel their speakers' attention towards different aspects of reality. This is a corollary of Boas's view of grammatical meaning discussed above: crucially, such classifications may not even rise to consciousness because of the automated nature of grammatical structure.

Sapir developed these ideas of the unconscious in seeing language as a formal, incommensurate but systematic and socially constructed system. The very systematic nature of linguistic structure tends to underline the unconscious nature of linguistic phenomena, as the mind attends to function rather than to form *per se*. In addition, the sheer complexity of such formal arrangement tends to make individual forms impenetrable to folk analysis. The systematic dimension of language also speaks to its automatic, unconscious nature but is also in itself a source of diversity. What speakers of a language tend to do is to naively assume that their language-particular system objectifies reality, whereas in fact there are as many such reconstructions as there are languages.[62]

Three developments or expansions of the idea of linguistic relativity are of particular relevance to the studies in this book. Firstly, Whorf further advanced the idea of the unconscious in language by distinguishing between grammatical categories as either 'overt' or 'covert'. In this way, conceptual distinctions may well be germane to the 'deep' structure of a language without being formally marked on the surface. We can illustrate this distinction simply for the English verb. For every English sentence containing a 3rd sg. present form the verb must be overtly marked by the ending *-s*. Person is therefore an 'overt' category. Transitivity, on the other hand, is covert: there is no formal surface difference between the transitive verb *cook,* for example, and the intransitive *go*. However, the semantic distinction between them can be seen in passivization: *it was being cooked* but not **it was being gone*. Even though transitivity is a covert category in English, it nonetheless contains vital semantic information. Thus the cognitive effects attributable to grammatical structure may not derive from the most 'overt' or most obviously marked grammatical categories but rather from 'covert' ones that work together, as well as with the overt categories, to form a unified psychic complex.

In contrast to Miller's arguments, as we shall see, however, Whorf crucially eschews any *direct* cause and effect between surface linguistic structure and cultural practice. His main concern was the possible relation between habitual thought and behaviour and such 'deep', 'hidden' linguistic structure whereby the habitual mode of thought of the individual is shaped by *analogous* 'fashions of speaking',[63] or what John Lucy terms 'cognitive appropriation' between the structural relations that obtain in various linguistic and, by extension, extra-linguistic domains.[64] In other words, large-scale linguistic patterns produce linguistically conditioned habitual thought and linguistically conditioned features of culture over a long period of coexistence. Whorf thus approached the relation between linguistic structure and other aspects of society and culture in terms of such 'fashions of speaking', which he understood as a complex of semantic features operating at a deep or unconscious level, underlying but cutting across surface linguistic representations such as morphological and syntactic categories and the lexicon.[65] As Duranti puts it, 'Whorf was focusing on how a way of thinking may arise *by analogy* with "fashions of speaking", rather than being a direct mapping of lexical and grammatical structure on to everyday thought and practice."[66] This constitutes in effect what Silverstein terms 'linguistic ideology': 'commonsense' notions shared by speakers of a language about how their language represents the world.[67]

The other two developments are of more recent origin. The second is the research of Slobin into the effects of the particular grammatical categories available in a language on the way in which children learning that language construe their experience of the world—what he calls 'thinking for speaking'. This has already been referred to as representing a return to Boas's ideas on meaning and will play an important part in the discussion in chapter 4. Third is the work of Silverstein on 'awareness,' to which I have referred in the previous section. This, in Whorfian terms, can be seen as an attempt to establish what are the elements of linguistic structure accessible to native-speaker intuition, including the overt and covert categories of a given language.[68] Silverstein builds here on the insights of Boas, Sapir and Whorf into the largely unconscious nature of linguistic usage: what we can see here is, in part, an attempt to more rigorously conceptualize and formulate the Whorfian idea of covert categories or cryptotypes. Thus linguistic categories function along a cline of speaker awareness from the more highly accessible overt categories to the less accessible covert ones. What is particularly important about all this in the present context is that the degree of accessibility affects the extent to which forms are elaborated on, fashioned and refashioned in ideological terms; as might be expected, and as Silverstein predicts, those items that are more accessible to awareness are more likely to be the objects of conscious deliberation.[69]

A vital implication of Silverstein's research is that the basis of this metapragmatic awareness resides in the nature of the linguistic sign itself.[70] Thus there are principled, universally predictable semiotic constraints on native-speaker awareness. There are two independent but interacting vectors here: the universal limits on awareness imposed by linguistic structure on the one hand and the historically and culturally contingent or the culture-specific limits on experience on the other. But because universal limits operate in practice on particular languages, we arrive at language-specific apprehensions of the world and of reality.[71]

Conclusion

In conclusion, I will return briefly to the question of integrating a linguistic model into an account of culture, society and history. A classic dichotomy in the history of linguistic theory, replicating the situation in other branches of the human sciences in general, is the integration of the formal and functional aspects of language use. William Hanks, for example,[72] raises the question of how to incorporate the study of linguistic practice into a general theory of social practice within the context of a discussion of Pierre Bourdieu's concept of the 'habitus'. By habitus is meant a set of socially inculcated, structured and durable dispositions in individuals that are productive and reproductive of habituated activity or 'practice'.[73] Individuals in a given society or culture tend to share this inculcated system, and this is what leads to social cohesion. This is, however, pre-conscious or pre-reflective rather than arising from obedience to laws. The relationship between the concept of dúchas and the question of social and cultural practice will be considered in chapter 6 ('Afterword to Dúchas: A Vocabulary and Syntax of Natural Law?').

It is not sufficient simply to characterize language as a social product; rather it must be shown how linguistic structure itself plays a role in social and cultural processes. What is needed is, in Hanks's words, 'a theory of signification that includes the linguistic system in a non-reductive way'.[74] It seems to me here that Verschueren's working definition of pragmatics provides the context for an integrated, non-reductive approach to the role of language within culture and society. Pragmatics is:

> a general functional (i.e. cognitive, social and cultural) perspective on language and language use aimed at the investigation of dynamic and negotiated meaning generation in interaction. Language use is then viewed as a form of action with real-world consequences and firmly embedded in a context.[75]

The remit of pragmatics is to offer a functional perspective on *all* aspects of linguistic usage and linguistic structure and not merely on certain 'privileged' topics that cannot easily be accommodated under the headings of syntax and semantics. This approach to pragmatics thus integrates the study of language use into the study of human behaviour in general. My own study will repeatedly emphasize the importance of context—here the social, cultural and political changes affecting Irish-speaking society from the sixteenth to the nineteenth centuries—and the ways in which language in its dynamic and interactive aspects both shapes and reflects responses to those developments.

A note on the sources

For chapters 2 to 6, the majority of the sources used date from the Early Modern Irish period, which I divide here, conventionally, into the Classical period

(1200–1600) and the seventeenth to eighteenth centuries. In chapters 3, 4 and 5 in particular the emphasis is on bardic poetry of the late sixteenth to early seventeenth centuries, a time when the traditional Irish order, at the centre of which lay the relationship between the professional poet and his aristocratic patron (see chapter 1 for the pragmatics of *dual* and *dualgas*),[76] was suffering terrible strain under the impact of Tudor conquest and colonization. One poet whose poetry looms large in these chapters is Tadhg Dall Ó hUiginn (died 1591). A reading of the poetry, which reacts to these events, is supplemented by the use of such important prose sources as Céitinn's *Foras Feasa ar Éirinn*, 'The basis for knowledge of Ireland' of the 1630s. As chapters 2 and 7 are more in the nature of an overview than a case study, the chronological span of these essays is somewhat wider. In the essay on *saoirse* especially, examples range from the Old Irish period (conventionally to 900) and Middle Irish period (900–1200) up to the nineteenth and early twentieth centuries.

The periods that are most consistently dealt with in the discussion are the sixteenth and seventeenth centuries in the case of *dúchas* and associated items and the eighteenth and nineteenth centuries in the case of *saoirse*. The reader will note, however, that I make use of two modern dictionaries: Dinneen's *Foclóir Gaedhilge agus Béarla* (1927) and Ó Dónaill's *Foclóir Gaeilge-Béarla* (1977). This is perhaps somewhat tricky from a methodological point of view. My purpose, however, in presenting a synoptic view of these dictionaries' definitions of certain words is simply to give the reader a quick overview of the semantic ranges that will be considered in the ensuing discussion. In the discussion of *dúchas* in chapter 2, the evidence of both dictionaries is conflated for precisely this reason. I have generally chosen these dictionaries, rather than the perhaps more chronologically appropriate Royal Irish Academy dictionary (based mostly on Old and Middle Irish), because they are the most likely to be available to the general reader. It should be noted, however, that in the case of *saoirse* I do draw attention to what I feel are significant differences between Dinneen's and Ó Dónaill's range of definitions. However, as the detailed discussion itself is not based on the evidence of either dictionary *per se,* I do not feel that a discussion of the value of each dictionary as a source is particularly germane. In fact, I do not feel that dictionary-based evidence is central enough to the discussion to warrant any detailed discussion of individual lexicons. Indeed one could argue that part of the sub-text of the entire book is that such evidence should be treated with circumspection, representing, as it does, only the semantic-referential aspect of meaning (see above), or those parts of meaning that can be established relatively independently of a particular context. This risks omitting the pragmatic-indexical dimension of meaning presented in this chapter, which is saturated in specific social, cultural and historical contexts and requires grounding in those contexts.

2. THE INTERNAL AND EXTERNAL DIMENSIONS OF *DÚCHAS*

The main purpose of this chapter is to examine the relationship between the externalized and internalized aspects of the word *dúchas:* on the one hand those aspects that relate more to the socio-political world of hereditary claim and birthright, on the other hand those facets that are more internalized within the subject, such as inherited personal traits and characteristics. In the process I will suggest a possible cognitive-linguistic model to account for the relationship between these two domains of meaning, which will also be considered in relation to the use of *dúchas* and the compound expression *tír dhúchais* to signify Ireland as the native land. This usage is particularly salient in the sixteenth and seventeenth centuries. I will start, however, with the modern lexicography of *dúchas* and proceed to a consideration of certain facts of linguistic structure relating to *dúchas* and its immediate family. This is merely to give the reader a synoptic overview of the range of possible meanings for *dúchas*. The main issues of this chapter will be based on the evidence of texts from an earlier period, principally the sixteenth to the eighteenth centuries.

Dúchas in the Modern Irish lexicon

Let us first take a look at some dictionary definitions, starting with an aggregate of two twentieth-century Irish–English dictionaries: those of Dinneen (1927) and Ó Dónaill (1977).[1] The following semantic clusters emerge for *dúchas*. (The spelling with medial *th* is the older one, as used by Dinneen; I use the modern spelling, as used by Ó Dónaill, in the main text, even when referring to examples with the older spelling.)

(a)   X has something by hereditary right, by birthright:
de réir **dúchais** is reachta   by traditional custom and law
a **dhúchas** agus a dhíre   his birthright and his due

(b)   X has certain family and ancestral connections, which can, however, be rejected or diverged from by an individual, as the second example suggests:

ní dul ó **dhúthchas** duit é   you follow your kind, lit. 'It is no
                                        departing from *dúchas* for you'
níl sé ag tabhairt an **dúthchais** leis   he does not take after his family

(c) X has an inherited natural capacity for or disposition to something:

ba **dhúthchas** dó bheith 'na scoláire	he had an inherited capacity for learning
tá an **droch-dhúthchas** ann	he is fundamentally bad

Note here in (c) the syntax of the preposition *do* 'to', 'for', which generally in this type of sentence indicates something that is external to the subject: *ba dhúthchas dó* is thus literally 'it was *dúchas* for him'. However, in the second example *dúchas* is something that can be explicitly internalized in the subject (preposition *i(n)* 'in', here by the 3rd singular masculine form *ann* 'in him'. So *tá an droch-dhúthchas ann* means literally 'the bad *dúchas* is in him'. I will say more about this distinction and what it involves in its historical context below.

(d) X has an instinct for something:

ag imtheacht lena **dhúthchas**	following his natural bent
bó-**dhúthchas**	a cow's instinct

(e) As a value judgement in aphorisms or proverbs:

is fearr **dúthchas** ná gach aon nídh	inherited qualities are best
is treise **dúthchas** ná oileamhaint	instinct is stronger than education

(f) Denotation of land or place:

bádhach neach le sean-**dúthchas**	everyone loves the old land
ar dhíth a **ndúchais**	deprived of their patrimony

(g) As an attributive genitive:

pobal	**dúthchais**	the home folk
madra	**dúchais**	a mad dog
ball	**dúchais**	a birth mark
tír	**dhúthchais**	native land
teanga	**dhúchais**	native language

These examples show a formidable, and at times apparently arbitrary, range of uses. From a historical point of view, one weakness of dictionaries such as those used here is that they tend to present an aggregate of meanings rather than differentiating chronological stages of usage and development. However, there is a real sense in which modern usage is in some way an aggregate of previous uses according to a people's historical and cultural experience. We may note at this point that certain uses presented above now sound distinctly archaic, in particular those that represent some of the external social and physical dimensions of *dúchas*. These include usages denoting the land itself as a physical entity but also the idea of *dúchas* as representing some kind of quasi-legal claim or entitlement. The sense of these ranges as archaic is confirmed by an early nineteenth-century set of definitions: 'the place of one's birth'; 'an hereditary right'; 'a lawful custom'; also for the derived adjective *dúthchasach*:

'of one's country'; 'natural to one by his family'; 'hereditary'; 'compatriotic'.[2] The structure exhibited by (g) above, where *dúchas* appears as a qualifying genitive *dúchais*, will receive particular attention below, in particular the rise of the expression *tír dhúchais* to mean 'native land', first as an alternative to and eventually as a replacement for the simplex *dúchas* in this same sense.

Dúchas in medieval and early modern Ireland: a semantic field

The following sections will attempt to construct a preliminary *semantic field* for the word *dúchas*. One of the basic insights of structural semantics is that words can be related to one another within what are called 'fields'.[3] According to Saeed, a 'semantic' or 'lexical' field can be defined as a 'group of lexemes which belong to a particular activity or area of specialist knowledge'.[4] For Hughes, such fields contain words or meanings cohering around a particular concept or topic.[5] Each word must therefore be considered in relation to the other words within its field. Lehrer hypothesizes that semantically related words will undergo parallel developments precisely because they are related.[6] Furthermore, she advances two reasons for studying vocabulary in this way. Firstly, it helps in comparing lexical systems between languages; secondly, it helps in understanding the role of *metaphor* in lexical change: that is, the configuration of a lexical set tends to remain intact when it is transferred from one semantic domain to another. It is this second point that will be of greater interest in the present discussion. The whole notion of a semantic field is of structuralist origin, as the meaning of a word is ultimately determined by its place in an overall semantic system or field.[7] For her own part, Wierzbicka half endorses the notion of semantic fields; she insists, however, that words must first be rigorously defined on their own before they can be properly compared with other intuitively related items.[8] Nevertheless, she acknowledges that certain words can form 'more or less natural . . . non-arbitrary groupings'. The aim of what follows in the next three sections is to suggest how such an approach could work in the case of *dúchas*. In conclusion to this preliminary section, however, it is also worth considering at least part of the web of lexical associations that the word *dúchas* gives rise to in Irish in a recent analogical dictionary (author's glosses):

bunús	Relating to people (*daoine*): *breith* 'birth,' *muintir* 'folks,' 'relatives,' *sliocht* 'descent,' *cine* 'race,' *ginealach* 'genealogy'
cosúil	Relating to resemblance (*cosúlacht*): *cúpla* 'couple,' *gaol* 'relation,' *oidhreacht* 'heritage'
eolas	Relating to a source of knowledge (*foinse eolais*): *béaloideas* 'folklore,' *traidisiún* 'tradition'
gaol	Relating to familial relations (*coibhneas teaghlaigh*): *atharthacht* 'paternity,' *fréamhacha gaoil* 'genealogical roots'

meon	Relating to a natural state (*staid nádúrtha*): *carachtar* 'character,' *dearcadh* 'attitude'
nádúr	Relating to a specific nature (*sain-nádúr*): *carachtar* 'character,' *dearcadh* 'attitude,' *spiorad* 'spirit'
oidhreacht	*cultúr* 'culture,' *traidisiún* 'tradition,' *sinsearacht* 'ancestry', *féiniúlacht* 'identity'
tír	*tír dhúchais* 'native land,' *máthairthír* 'motherland,' *athartha* 'fatherland,' *tírghrá* 'patriotism,' *náisiún* 'nation,' *saintréithe* 'defining traits,' *féiniúlacht* 'identity,' *sainiúlacht* 'defining nature,' *cultúr* 'culture,' *sibhialtacht* 'civilization'
tús	Relation to origin (*teacht ann*): *dúchasach—bunús* 'origin,' *breith, saolú* 'birth'[9]

Ó Doibhlin's purpose here is not to be systematic as such, and I do not intend to pursue every one of these connections, but we can see that a number of conceptual domains are encompassed here, both on the individual and the collective level, many of which will be taken up in this and subsequent chapters: *dúchas* as a sense of *origin* (where you come from); of *relations* (to whom and where you belong to); of *heritage* (what is natural to or appropriate for you); of *tradition* (what it tells you about yourself); of *identity* (your country and culture). It will be seen also that *dúchas* operates both within and without the individual, is both external and internal, of which more below.

A lexical family: *dúchas, dúthaigh* and *dú*

As was mentioned in chapter 1, *dúchas* is but one of a family of words, and it is to a consideration of the relationship between the members of this lexical family that we now turn as part of our initial attempt to construct a semantic field. Firstly, let us consider *dúchas* in relation to *dúthaigh* 'native land' or 'native place'. The following is quoted *in extenso* from the twelfth-century text *Cogadh Gaedhel re Gallaibh*, as it creates a meaningful and indeed emotive context for some of the lexical associations to be considered and gives us an idea of the kind of value system within which they operate. Here Brian and Mathghamhain, sons of *Cennedach*, leader of the Dál gCais, are debating the wisdom of engaging the Danes in battle. Mathghamhain wants peace; Brian wants to fight, and he gives his reasons as follows (the relevant lexical items and their English equivalents are emphasized in bold type in the text and translation which is by the author):

> Atbert imorro Brian nirbo coir do-som in ní sin [do radha] uair ba **dúthaig** do éc ocus ba **dúthaig** do Dail Cais uli, uair marb a n-athri ocus a senathri . . . ocus nirbo dual imorro ocus nirbo **duthaig** doib tárna tarcaisin do gabail, uair nir gabsat a n-athri no shenathri sin o neoch ar talmain. Asbert dno nirbo miad menman doib in ferand ro-cosainset a n-athri ocus shenathri. . . a lecun can cath can cliathaig do Gallaib . . . Asbertatar uli . . . ba ferr leo bas ocus éc ocus aeded . . . do agbail ic cosnum sairi a n-athardha ocus a ceneoil . . . Asbert Mathgamain imorro

ba hi comarli ba coir doib do denaib .i. teacht i Casiul na rig . . .; degbir on ar ba he Aeleach Mumhan ocus Temair Lethi Moga. Ba he dna a m[b]unadus ocus **a senducus badein**. Asbert ba fearr a fír catha ocus comlaind sin **inna nduthaig** . . . innas im an ferand forgabala ocus claidim.[10]

Brian said then that he had no right to (say) that since it was **right** for him to die and it was **right** for all the Dál gCais since their fathers and grandfathers had all died . . . and moreover, it was not **right/expected** or **right/natural** for them to take that insult of theirs, because their fathers and grandfathers (ancestors) had never taken that from anyone on earth. He said indeed that it was not honourable for them to give up to foreigners without a battle . . . the land that their fathers and ancestors had earned. They all said that they preferred to die defending the freedom of their fatherland and their people . . . Then Mathgamhain said that the advice they should take was to go to Cashel of the Kings . . .; that was fitting since it was the Aileach of Munster and the Tara of southern Ireland. It was their (place of) origin and their own **ancestral land**. He maintained that their cause was more just in their **native land** . . . than territory taken by conquest and by the sword.

This passage will also loom large in the general scheme of the discussion in chapter 3. First of all we have two members of a family of closely related words in this passage: *dúthaig*, which has the sense of something being 'right', 'fitting', or 'natural', but which also denotes '(native) place', 'land', 'territory'. In addition, we have its abstract formation *ducus* (*dúchas*), with which it often seems to be synonymous. In fact there are several passages in the earlier language where the two appear to be indistinguishable, and perhaps that is the point: the physical, moral and emotive elements of the land as elaborated by this particular lexical family are considered inseparable. This emerges more clearly if I give the translation leaving the Irish words intact (in many of the passages subsequently translated I leave *dúchas* and *dúthaig(h)* untranslated so as not to prejudge any issues):

Brian said then that he had no right to (say) that since it was **dúthaig** for him to die and it was **dúthaig** for the whole of the Dál gCais since their fathers and grandfathers (ancestors) had all died . . . and it was not . . . **dúthaig** for them to take that insult of theirs . . . that was fitting since it (Cashel) was the Aileach of Munster and the Tara of southern Ireland. It was their (place of) origin and their own **sen-duchus**. He said that their cause was more just in their **dúthaig** . . . than territory that had been acquired by the sword.

The wider point here is that the significance of this passage is seriously diminished in translation, because the essential intimate linguistic and therefore *conceptual* or *ideological* connection between the place as heredity or ancestry and the naturalness or rightness to want to defend it is lost: the conventional

English translation would render them as more or less separate or independent concepts. But in Irish this ideological symbiosis is reflected directly, *indexically* and *iconically*, in the lexicon and in the syntactic structure of the language.

There is a further related item, *dú*, which generally means simply 'place' but which also develops the sense of heredity and thus also 'entitlement' and 'what is natural' or 'proper'. This is also the root that gives the Irish word for 'man', 'person', 'earthling', *duine*, and both can be derived from an Indo-European root **ghdhem-* 'earth' as follows, noting in both cases their Greek cognates:

> *(gh)dhó(n)   >   Ir. **dú** 'place'   =   Gk. *chthōn* 'earth'
>
> *(gh)dhonios >   Ir. **duine** 'man', 'person'   =   Gk. *chthonios* 'earthly'[11]

Dú has the sense of (a) 'place', (b) 'native place' and (c) 'entitlement, 'due', as in the following examples from medieval Irish:

(a)   *cuindig **in dú** itáat cuirp na noem*
      Find the place where the saints' bodies are buried

(b)   *Ro gab Herimon in tuascert*   Erimon took the north
      ***dú** dia ciniud,*   a (native) place for his kin,
      Co na sencus, co na sólud,   with their lore and their prosperity,
      co na n-dligud   their rights and entitlements.

(c)   *fersait fáilti móir fri techtaire Mongáin. Ba sí a **dú**.*
      They gave Mongán's emissary a great welcome. That was his due.[12]

Clear cases of (b) do not seem to be particularly well attested. We do, however, find the same predicative use as in the case of *dúthaigh* in the passage above, where *dú* is preceded by the copula *is*: *is dú do* 'it is right/natural for'. This is reflected in O'Clery's *Glossary*, which has the following entry:

> **dú** .i. dúthaig 'becoming'
>
> .i. dual 'proper'[13]

Here *dú* is given the same sense as both *dúthaigh* and *dual*: 'what is right, becoming, natural, proper (for someone)'. It should be noted that (a) *dual* appears collocated with *dúthaigh* in the passage quoted at length above from *Cogadh Gaedhel re Gallaibh* and (b) it is closely associated with both *dú* and *dúchas* in modern collocations:

(a)   **nirbo dual** imorro ocus nirbo **duthaig** doib tárna tarcaisin do gabail
      it was not right/expected or right/natural for them to take that insult of theirs

(b)   *Is é is **dú** agus is **dual/dúchas** dó*
      It's in his very nature

      *Sé an áit is **dual** agus is **dúthchas** dom a bheith ag baile*
      The place that is most natural for me to be is at home[14]

This suggests a configuration as follows:

(i)	place = **dú** ⟶ hereditary place = **dúthaig** ⟶ hereditary right to place = **dúthchas**
(ii)	⟵ ⟵ ⟵
(iii)	⟶ something is 'right'/'natural' for X: is **dú/dúthaig/dúthchas** *do* X ⟶

This lexical family is derived from left to right (*dú* > *dúthaigh* > *dúthchas*) as in (i) in the diagram above; but the important point is that a discrete semantic distinction is not always maintained between them, in the sense that all three, and particularly *dúthaigh* and *dúchas,* can be used to denote 'hereditary or native place'. Furthermore, as we shall below both *dúthaigh* and *dúchas,* but especially the latter, are used in the more abstract sense of 'hereditary claim or entitlement'. This is indicated by the reversed arrows in (ii). This fluidity gives rise to the situation described by (iii), whereby all three words can be used with the verb *is* 'is' in the collocation 'it is right/natural (for someone) to (do X)'. This particular piece of syntax will have great importance in this and the following chapters. We have a common semantic development in each case whereby a moral or value-judgement sense becomes identified with a partic-ular denotation of 'place' as heredity. I will say more below about a possible chronological dimension to the interrelation between the three words, based on the evidence of syntactic structure.

A question that will underlie much of the discussion in this chapter, as well as in the next one, is that of the 'shifting' quality of both *dúchas* and *dúthaigh*. As initial evidence for the 'shifting' quality of the words in question, consider the interchangeability of *dúchas* and *dúthaigh*, which is evident, for example, in the text of a treaty of 1565 between O'Donnell and the Earl of Argyll:

(*a*)   an cís sin do gherradh agas do thogbhail an **duthaig** i Domhnaill uile sa cuigeadh Ulltach ⁊ na thimcheall fa thigerrnas agas **fa dhuthchas** i Dhomhnaill fein agas o Domhnaill da thógbail sin agas da íocc le neart Miccailin AGAS fos ata dfiachaibh ar ON Domhnaill agas ar a shliocht cúig céd buánna do chunnmhail gach en bliadhna **na dhúthaigh** an Érinn don iarrla sin.[15]

and to levy and raise that tribute in the whole lands of O'Donnell in the province of Ulster and thereabout within his lordship and within O'Donnell's own patrimony, and O'Donnell shall with the help of Mac Cailin raise and pay that tribute AND further it is incumbent on O'Don-nell and on his descendants to maintain every year in his patrimony in Ireland for the use of the Earl . . . five hundred billeted soldiers.

(*b*)   Mac Cailin fo chomhnamh agas do cuideachagh le On Domhnaill fa **dhuthaig** ⁊ fa thigerrnas athar ⁊ senathar i Dhomhnaill do chur ar a laimh ⁊ fa smacht ⁊ fa umhlacht do go fheadh nearta an iarrla sin.

Mac Cailin shall with all his strength succour and assist O'Donnell in the putting into his possession and under his control and into obedience to him of his own, his father's and his grandfather's land and lordship.

On the other hand, examples can be found, especially from the seventeenth century onwards, where *dúthaigh* and *dúchas* form a semantic contrast of some kind. In the following example, from the late seventeenth century, the North Connacht poet Seán Ó Gadhra laments one Brian Ó hUiginn in a poem, 'Truagh ceas na gcarad anocht', (Pity the plight of friends tonight). The poet speaks of his subject's relationship with the land of Tyrawley in Co. Mayo:

Tír Amhalghaidh na dtreas dte mar bhfuil **dúthchas bhar ndúithche**[16]	Tyrawley of the keen battles where resides the *dúchas* of your *dúiche* (*dúthaigh*)

Here *dúchas* is what gives the *dúthaigh* its rationale or justification, that quality that makes the native land a place apart from any other. This quality of *dúchas* can thus be abstracted from its material realization of *dúthaigh*. In many earlier sources, as in the passage from *Cogadh Gaedhel re Gallaibh* and the text of the O'Donnell–Argyll treaty, on the other hand, the more physical and more symbolic aspects of the land are treated or 'packaged' as one. This issue is of great importance and will be resumed in more detail below.

Here we can get a sense of what Sapir means by saying that language is 'a symbolic guide to culture'[17] and we find ourselves very much in the weft and warp of the Irish ideology of 'place'. We see also how some of Wierzbicka's 'key word' criteria apply: the vocabulary of place is salient in that it is extremely evocative. A further function of this symbolism is that such lexemes receive a high level of *elaboration*; that is, the basic idea they encode gives rise to more and more cultural associations in speakers' minds. The following section presents some further possibilities for consideration in relation to *dúchas*.

A wider semantic field for *dúchas* (1): 'external' dimensions

It should be noted first that *dúchas* also has a much less common derivational antonym *andúthchas,* as used by the sixteenth-century poet Tadhg Dall Ó hUiginn in a poem 'Fada cóir Fhódla ar Albain' ('Long has Ireland a claim on Scotland'). Note in particular the association between *andúchas* or 'non-*dúchas*' and foreignness, which, as we shall see, particularly in chapter 3, presents a salient context for the use of *dúchas* in the sixteenth and seventeenth centuries in particular:

Créad fa dtiobhradh clann Cholla, ar son ar fhás eatorra, tar magh mbarrúrchas mBanbha	Why should the children of Colla for whatever arose between them render allegiance to a strange foreign land

tal **d'andúthchas** allmhardha?[18]	Rather than to Banbha's plain of bright-waving crops?

The same poet uses *andúthchas* in the attributive genitive construction in another poem 'Tógaibh eadrad is Éire' ('Raise the veil from Ireland'):

Mac an cheannaighe ód-chluin sin	On hearing that, the merchant's son
gabhthar leis grádha gaisgidh	took orders of chivalry
téid don bharrúrthais deirg dhuinn	he departed from the rosy maiden of the soft, shining hair
re **ceird n-andúthchais** d'fhoghluim.[19]	to learn a calling of *andúchas* (a strange calling).

The formal distinction between *andúchas* and its corresponding genitive *andúchais* is important and prefigures a more detailed discussion below in relation to the word *dúchas* and its own genitive *duchais*. It may be noted in passing that the antonym *andúchas* is now largely obsolete in Irish. Firstly, however, I want to present some other candidates for inclusion in the semantic field of *dúchas*. Since almost all of these will be taken up in more detail in subsequent chapters, I will do no more than outline some possible relations here.

(1) *Dúchas and ceart:* In the following passage from Céitinn's *Foras Feasa ar Éirinn*, note the relevance of Fitzstephen's foreignness in the contrast drawn between *dúchas* and *ceart*, which is defined in the Royal Irish Academy's *Dictionary of the Irish Language* (henceforth *DIL*) as 'right; claim; entitlement; justice' (cf. Latin *certus*).[20] As we shall see in chapter 3, this sheds light on an important poem of the 1570s, Tadhg Dall Ó hUiginn's 'Fearann cloidhimh críoch Bhanbha' ('The land of Ireland is sword land').[21] Here Ruaidhrí Ó Conchobhair finds that neither Mac Murchadha, the high king of Leinster, nor Fitzstephen, his English ally, are willing to engage him in battle. He requests that the latter leave the country, as he will not fight for the right (*ceart*) to be there, nor has he any hereditary entitlement (*dúchas*) to it:

(*a*)   nach raibhe **ceart ná dúthchas** aige ar bheith innte[22]
        as he had neither right nor *dúchas* to be there

The next item is a modern example of the survival of this association:

(*b*)   ó cheart is ó **dhúthchas**
        by right and by birthright

The disjunctive *ná* 'or,' 'nor', in the first passage in particular suggests that *ceart* and *dúchas* are being distinguished and that *dúchas* may be subsumed under *ceart* as a particular kind of 'right', (i.e. 'birthright'). The following example, also from the early seventeenth century, invokes similar considerations:

Ó dearor gur dhealbhuis chraoibh	Since it is said that you have formed the branches
ríshliocht Gaoidhiol do gach taoibh	of descent of the Gaelic kings from every side
's go n-abra acht amháin Dál gCais	and you mention that everyone save the Dál gCais
gur chaillsiod **ceart an dúthchois**.[23]	has lost the right of *dúchas* (birthright).

(2) *Dúchas* and *dúal:* The passage from Céitinn in (1) above continues as follows. Note the relationship and distinction between *dúchas* and *dual,* where the latter is something that is 'natural' but imposed from without rather than residing within. Thus in the following passage, what is *dual* to Diarmaid as king of Leinster is that which is sanctioned by the custom and practice pertaining to the traditional claim of the high king of Ireland on Leinster, rather than residing in birthright, as in the case of Diarmaid's own claim to the province of Leinster, which is his *dúchas*. (DIL for *dúal:* 'native, hereditary; natural to; belonging to by right or descent; that which is fitting'.)[24] Peace is concluded between Mac Murchadha and Conchobhair, therefore, in the following terms:

> Cúigeadh Laighin do léigeadh do Dhiarmaid, amhail **fá dúthchas** dó; agus d'fhiachaibh ar Dhiarmaid umhla is dísle do choimhéad do Ruaidhrí amhail fá **dual** do gach rígh dá mbíodh ar Laighnibh do dhéanamh do ríoghaibh Éireann.

> Diarmaid was left the province of Leinster as was *dúchas* for him; and Diarmaid was obliged to submit to and remain loyal to Ruaidhrí as had (always) been *dual* to every king of Leinster to submit to the kings of Ireland.

As we have seen above, *dual* is particularly closely associated with the members of the *dú-dúthaigh-dúchas* family in its predicative use with the copula, examples of which have already been given. There is a further formation from *dual,* the abstract noun *dualgas:*

> fios filleadh don duine don ionad ba **rí-dhualgas**[25]

> tidings of one returning by royal right

As an abstract noun in Modern Irish, *dualgas* acquires the salient sense of external force or obligation ('duty', as it is usually glossed) being *imposed*, as opposed to the more internalized dimensions of *dúchas*. Both *dual* and *dualgas* will be taken up in detail in chapter 4.

(3) *Dúchas* and *folaidecht:* DIL defines *folaidecht* as 'lineage, descent'. In the following passages, (*a*) from the sixteenth century and (*b*) from the twelfth, the relation between *dúchas* and blood line is made tellingly clear. Excerpt (*a*), from *Betha Colaim Chille* ('The Life of Colmcille') refers to Colm Cille's remorseful

abrogation of the high-kingship of Ireland which was his birthright *o duthcas* ⁊ *o folaidhecht* 'by right of birth and blood':

(a)   ⁊ gor threig C.c. righacht Erind fair; oir fa **dual** do o duthcas ⁊ o **folaid-hecht** hi.[26]

The semantics and pragmatics of *dual* will also be taken up in chapter 4; but note here how, as with *ceart* above, *dúchas* appears as a particular kind of subset of what is *dual*. For our earlier extract we return to the twelfth-century *Cogadh Gaedhel re Gallaibh*, where we have already noted the repeated emphasis on the exemplar of one's ancestors, 'fathers' and 'grandfathers'. Later in the same text the same point is reiterated when Mac Giolla Phádraig of Ossory makes a claim on the Dál gCais for which there is no hereditary basis, while that of the men of Desmond is accepted because they were of the same blood (*ba hionann fuil dóib ocus do Dal cCais*):

(b)   Is annsin asbert mac Briain conárbh iongnadh mac Maoilmhuaidh ocus Desmhumha d'iarraidh braighdedh ocus a sealaigheachta ar Dal cCais óir ba hionann fuil dóib ocus do Dal cCais; ocus rob iongnadh leo Mac Giolla Patraicc d'iarraidh na sealaigheachta **nar dhuthchas dó** d'fágbáil.[27]

It was then that the son of Brian said that it was no surprise that the son of Maolmhuaidh and the men of Desmond were seeking hostages and a share of the kingship from the Dál gCais, as they were of the same blood; but they were amazed that Mac Giolla Phádraig was seeking a share of the kingship which was not *dúchas* to him to obtain.

Here the prepositional phrase (*nar dhuthchas dó*) conveys clearly the idea of a person's hereditary right (or not) and once again that it was not *dúchas* to Mac Giolla Phádraig to receive a share of the kingship, because he was not related by blood to the Dál gCais. Note again the 'predicative' syntax here—copula (here in the past negative form *nar*) plus *dúchas* plus the preposition *do* 'for', 'to'—which will be discussed in detail in chapter 5. In fact in both this section (3) and the last (2) *dúchas* shows the same syntax that we have already considered above in relation to *dúthaigh*:

Verb FA / NAR	**D(H)ÚTHCHAS**	**Preposition DÓ**

The connections of *dúchas* with genealogy and lineage are strong, as can be inferred from virtually every example given thus far. In the poem 'Druididh suas a chuaine an chaointe' ('Be silent you lamenting bands') (c. 1640, an elegy for Éamonn Fionn Mac Piarais, variously attributed to Seathrún Céitinn and Pádraigín Haicéad) we have this association of *dúchas* with genealogy, tradition, heredity and sense of origin:

Ní áirmhim ceangal gach sleachta dár shíol me	I don't recount every familial connection whence I came
ná dlúitheagar **dúthchais** mo dhaoine	nor the intricate weft of my people's *dúchas*
le cianaibh do liathnuimhir líne	since antiquity like an unbroken lineage
do shinsearaibh thionsgnaimh an taoisigh.[28]	from the original ancestors of our leader.

We see again the association of *dúchas* with *sinsir* 'ancestors' (*do shinsearaibh*) in the last line. We will consider below an early example of *dúchas* in the context of an eleventh-century parody of the idea of genealogy. This general connection with genealogy and lineage is very important for modern developments, as will be seen below.

(4) *Dúchas* and *dligheadh:* In the following, again from Céitinn, the Irish have been much discomfited by the Viking presence. *DIL* defines *dliged* as 'law; duty; prerogative; tribute'. The editor of this passage has taken *na dúthchasa* as genitive and translated it 'of the country'; this would be the only example known to me of *dúchas* as a feminine noun. I have instead taken *na* as standing for the disjunctive *(io)ná* '(n)or'.[29] The result of the Viking presence is that the native order has broken down:

> gan file gan feallsamh gan oirfideach ag leanamhain **dlighidh na dúthchasa**
>
> neither poet nor wise man nor musician observing law or custom

In both *dligheadh* and *dúchas* here there is a sense of what is right or sanctioned by custom or tradition.

(5) *Dúchas* and *díre: DIL* defines *díre* as '(i) honour price; (ii) penalty; (iii) one's due or right'. In the following example the king is being assured of general support among the men of Ireland, because he has treated each according to their status. In this extract from a late thirteenth- or early fourteenth-century text, *dúchas* has very much the sense of heredity as a principle of social order, of getting what is one's due or birthright:

> . . . nár léigis uasal a n-inadhaibh ísil, ná daor a flaithes flatha, ná cam do chaithem re cóir, acht gach nech for **a díre ⁊ for a dúthchas**.[30]
>
> . . . because you have not allowed the high-born to descend to lowly places, nor base elements to aspire to kingship, nor injustice to be used against what is right, but (have treated) everyone according to his due and his *dúchas*.

In this connection it is worth recalling the set phrase given from Ó Dónaill's dictionary above: *a dhúchas agus a **dhíre*** 'his birthright and his due', (for which see further chapter 5).

(6) *Dúchas* and *athartha*: Note in the following extract the association of *dúchas* with *athartha,* the *DIL* definition of which is 'fatherland; patrimony; native land' (cf. Latin *patria*):

> Is trúaighe lim iná sin gach ní tiucfus doib as sin .i. ferg Dé ar son a ndrochgnímartha fen indus go scrisfuither as **a ndutchus** ˥ as a n-athardha fen iad fa glentaib Erind le nert ˥ le tren echtrand ˥ allmurach.[31]

> I regret more than that everything that will come on them from that, i.e. the anger of God for their own evil acts, with the result that they shall be driven from their *dúchas* and their patrimony around the valleys of Ireland by the power and strength of aliens and foreigners.

Here *dúchas* and *athardha* would appear to be largely synonymous—*dúchas* as 'native land' in the sense of 'inheritance'. However, in view of the semantic field of inheritance constructed above, it should be noted that *dúchas* is not the term used in the Old Irish laws to denote 'inheritance' or 'patrimony'. The word used there is *orbae*, for which the *DIL* definition is 'patrimony; heritage; real estate':

> Tri orbai rannaiter fíad chomarbaib: orba drúith ˥ orba dásachtaig ˥ orba sin.[32]

> Three inheritances that are divided among the inheritors: the inheritance of an imbecile, of a lunatic, and of an old man.

This suggests that *dúchas* is more part of the socio-cultural sphere than of the legal sphere.[33] I will say a little more about this aspect in chapter 6, while the relationship of *athartha* to both *dúchas* and *dúthaigh* will be resumed in chapter 3.

We find that *dúchas* before and during the seventeenth century collocates particularly with words that are denotative of aspects of '(birth)right', 'entitlement', 'heredity' and 'descent'. An extension of this would appear to be its use in a less than purely abstract sense to refer to the native land itself. We will investigate this connection further in a wider European context in chapter 3, but it is to the more internalized dimensions of *dúchas* that we now turn.

A wider semantic field for *dúchas* (2): 'internal' dimensions

From the seventeenth century on we find more and more examples of *dúchas* in the more internalized sense of a personal trait, instinct or habitual mode of behaviour. An example comes from the seventeenth-century prose satire *Pairlement Chloinne Tomáis* (PCT), where a member of the arriviste Clann Tomáis is given the following advice:

> Léig díot, a bhráthair, na bearta as **dúthchus** duit do theacht tríot, óir do-chuadar cách amach oruinn.[34]

> Give up, brother, the tricks that are *dúchas* (come naturally) to you, for everyone has got wise to us.

One thing worth drawing attention to here is the phrase *do theacht tríot* 'to come through you'. Literally, the entire sentence reads 'give up the tricks that are natural to you *to come through you*'; that is stop allowing them to come (out) through you, which presupposes that the same traits are somehow *internalized*. Another early seventeenth-century example of the same idea comes from a very different text, Aodh Mac Aingil's tract on the sacrament of confession, published in Louvain in 1616. Speaking of the sin of pride as manifested by Luther's behaviour, he has this to say:

> Táinig **dúthchas** an uabhair tríd, ⁊ mar nár fhulaing Lucifer Dia féin do bheith ós a chionn ar neamh, níor éidir lena mhac mhallachdach Luteir an Bráthair Preisdiur d'fhulang do chor ós a chionn féin ar talamh.[35]

> The inherited instinct for arrogance *came through him,* because, just as Lucifer had not suffered even God to be above him in Heaven, so his accursed son Luther could not bear Brother Prestor being placed above him on earth.

Crucially, the description of pride (*uabhar*) as *dúchas* or an inherited trait is predicated on Luther's putative genetic relationship with the Devil, but equally important is the syntax: *dúchas* is something that comes out from within. Compare the popular contemporary proverb:

> Briseann an dúchas **trí shúile an chait/fríd na crúba**
> *Dúchas* breaks out through the cat's eyes/through the hooves

This is unlike any of the other examples we have considered: *dúchas* here stands for inherited *personal* characteristics, which are manifested by 'breaking through' from the 'inside'. This is a sense that becomes salient in the modern period. Elsewhere in the PCT text already cited we find the following evaluation of Clann Tomáis:

> imirt agas ól as tréighthe do chlannuibh lábánach san aimsir si . . . Tugabhuir bhur **gceárda dúthchais** ar mhalairt .i. ionnracus ar ghuid ⁊ ar ól cannuighe.[36]

> gambling and drunkenness are the characteristics of the progeny of churls these days . . . You have exchanged your native crafts: honesty for robbery and the drinking of galley-pots.

Here the *ceárda dúthchais* 'native crafts' (for more on the context in which this expression is used see chapter 3) are equated with character traits (*tréighthe*). I present briefly below some examples from the seventeenth to the nineteenth centuries in which the use of *dúchas* has such an internalized dimension:

(1) *Dúchas* and *dúil*: Ó Dónaill's dictionary gives the following range of meanings for *dúil*: 'desire, fondness, liking; expectation, hope'. A similar use of *dúchas* is found in Dáibhí Ó Bruadair's famous poem 'Caithréim Thaidhg', 'The triumph of Tadhg' (c. 1688), which celebrates the reversal of fortune that Catholics enjoyed in Ireland after the accession of King James II in 1685. Here

he says, in reply to and in support of a poem already composed celebrating this upsurge in Irish Catholic fortunes:

A mhic Uí Dhálaigh is sásta an bheatha dhuit	O descendant of Dálach, 'tis a real good job for you
beith is breith ar reic na haiste sin	the existence and chance of reciting that poetry
fhoillsigheas gur díomhaoin bheith dearbhtha	which proves how false it is to rely upon
do bheartaibh saobha an tsaoghail mhalartaigh	the bewildering tricks played by the fickle world
Beart díobh nár bhreathnuigheas ó baisteadh mé	None of these tricks have I seen since my baptism
is mó do thógaibh ceo dom aigne	that raised from my mind the mists more effectively
is tug mo dhúil óm **dhúthchas** anmhain	and cause my desires to desist from my *dúchas*
ná suim céille an scéil do chanaise.37	than the sum of the sense of the story you sang now.

In another poem, Ó Bruadair characterizes the English conquest of Ireland as a consequence of God's anger at the sinfulness of the Irish. Accordingly, the fact of English success has nothing to do with their particular *dúchas* or natural instinct for heroic endeavour, or, as he phrases it,

Ní dúil a los dúthchais i mbeartaibh árda38	No natural instinct (*dúchas*) in such men for noble deeds

Interestingly, *dúchas* is again collocated with *dúil*, literally 'It is no desire for heroic deeds on account of *dúchas*' where *dúchas* is seen as the basis for *dúil* 'desire'.

(2) *Dúchas* and *fuinneamh*: Ó Dónaill defines *fuinneamh* as 'energy; force, vigour; pep, spirit'. The following extract is from a poem in the late seventeenth- or early eighteenth-century prose text *Párliament na mBan*:

D'úrnuighthibh bíodh **dúthchus** is fuinniomh ad chroidhe
is í an úmhlacht do stiúrfaig chuige sin sínn
bíodh sgrúda ⁊ cúram aguibh chum guídhe
is dábhúr ccumhdach biaidh dúthracht is taramuin Chríost.39

When praying have ***dúchas*** and energy in your heart
it is humility that will guide us to that
be zealous and diligent with respect to prayer
and the goodness and sanctuary of Christ will protect you.

(3) *Dúchas* v. *cinnteacht*: Ó Dónaill gives as one of the meanings of *cinnteacht*

'stinginess.' In one of his poems Aogán Ó Rathaille lauds in traditional style the generosity of one Domhnall Ó Donnchadha:

Cé tá re sealad faoi Ghallaibh ag áitreabh	Though for the past while living among foreigners
Níor fhoghlaim uatha cruas na cráidhteacht	he has learned from them neither hardness nor miserliness
Níl cinnteacht 'na chroidhe ná cáim air	there is no stinginess in his heart nor defect
acht **dúthchas** maith a shean ag fás leis.[40]	but the good *dúchas* of his ancestors grows with him.

Here the 'good *dúchas*' is opposed to negative character traits such as stinginess, callousness and coldness. Note once again, however, the explicit connection with ancestry (*dúchas maith a shean*).

(4) *Dúchas* and *tallann*: Ó Dónaill gives as the range of *tallann* 'talent, gift; impulsive spirit, impulse, fit'. The following extract is from a poem by the nineteenth-century Armagh scribe and poet Art Mac Bionaid:

Dá measfaí tallann (is ní áirím **dúchas**),	If talent were assessed, never mind *dúchas*,
Chuirfeadh an prionsa ciúin seo an báire.[41]	this quiet prince would win the day.

In each of these instances *dúchas* is associated with some inner or innate dimension of the individual personality: 'desire', 'energy', 'generosity' and 'talent'.

Given the nature of the evidence it can often be extremely difficult, if not impossible, to reconstruct a historical picture of the relation between the more external and internalized aspects of *dúchas* at the micro-level. One possible approach we have already suggested is the application of structuralist principles in the construction and analysis of semantic fields.[42] Hughes constructs a typical semantic field diagrammatically along two axes—synchronic and diachronic—which we could adapt for *dúchas*, as in the diagram overleaf.[43] A diagrammatic presentation of this kind would suggest two things. Firstly, there is a chronological progression on the one hand from, let us say, more aristocratically inflected meanings of birthright and hereditary claim in the early modern period to more protean meanings of a later period, which have to do more with personal traits and characteristics (*tréithe*). Secondly, there is a shift in linguistic register from 'high' to 'low' (needless to say these are not meant here to be value terms). These two dimensions, the historical and the sociolinguistic, can be fairly easily correlated. Hughes speaks here of the 'democratization of status words'.[44] In a related vein, C. S. Lewis talks of the moralization of status words, whereby terms associated with status and qualifications based on birthright have a tendency to become generalized as descriptions of character.[45]

SYNCHRONIC			
		High register	
	ceart	*	
	dual	*	
	dligheadh	*	
	díre	*	
	folaidheacht	*	
	athartha	*	
DIACHRONIC	**Archaism**	**(dúchas)**	**Neologism**
- -			
		*	
		*	*'tréithe'*
		*	*dúil*
		*	*fuinneamh*
		*	*tallann*
		*	
		Low register	

When we compare earlier and later uses of the word *dúchas*, what we find in general terms is what I would call an internalization of meaning. I will try to place what I mean by this term in a wider context later in this chapter. For the moment, the following remarks will suffice. In the earlier period the more salient use of *dúchas* relates primarily to the external social and physical world, as representing a hereditary right to the land (social) or the land itself (physical). In the contemporary language, on the other hand, *dúchas* emphasizes more the internalized or personalized ideological world: it belongs to each individual within but also to the community as an aggregate of those individuals. This is latent in the earlier language also, but it is now far more prominent than before. The same process can be seen in the development of the predicative and attributive use of *dúthaig* from the noun 'land', 'hereditary land' (physical-social external) which evolves the meanings 'right', 'natural (for)' (moral, internal).

At this point, however, I have to enter a couple of caveats. Firstly, from a philological viewpoint it is axiomatic in historical linguistics that the first attestation of a change in a text is not the change itself. Secondly, we must consider the socio-linguistic consideration of the nature of our sources: until well into the modern period the literature reflects the social and political aspirations of a certain class or caste. It may be that the more 'aristocratic' bias of *dúchas* in the earlier period is due to that fact, obscuring a more protean reality in other

registers of the language. Indeed, even within that higher register more internalized senses can be found. Here are some examples from the bardic poetry
of the early modern period:

Tugadh dhuid ó **dhúthchas t'athar**   Thou hast inherited from thy
                                          father

—dot uabhar ní hadhbhar coisg!—   —and this will not lessen thy
                                          pride—

cneas tana mar an aol, a Éamoinn,   fair skin, white as lime,
mala chaol ós réallainn roisg.[46]   and a thin eyebrow over a star-
                                          bright eye.

Consider the following extract from a poem composed by the early thirteenth
century poet Muireadhach Albanach Ó Dálaigh for one Murchadh, son of
Brian Dall and a descendant of Brian Bóramha:

Tomhais cia mise, a Mhurchaidh;   Guess who I am, o Murchadh
maith do **dhúthchas** deaghurchair;   thou art born to good casting
do chinn t'athair ar aithne   thy father surpassed in
                                         discernment
ar na cathaibh córaighthe.[47]   the marshalled battalions.

Here the connection between inborn traits and heredity is apparent. From the
seventeenth century we have the last two quatrains of a poem by Muiris mac
Briain Óig Uí Mhaolchonaire dedicated to Calbhach Rua Ó Domhnaill, who
settled in Connacht in the post-Cromwellian period. These quatrains are
addressed to Calbhach's wife, Eibhlín Nic Shuibhne. The final one reads:

Beannacht uaim tre dhúthracht dhi   A blessing from me to her with
                                          fealty
fialbhean do shaoirfhréimh Shuibhni   the generous woman of the free
                                          stock of Suibhne
ben gan aonolc as ferr foss   woman without evil, best in
                                          calmness,
do mheall daonnocht ón **dúthchos**.[48]   who coaxed humanity from
                                          nature.

In a number of sixteenth- and seventeenth-century sources we have the phrase
dúthchas re, which occurs in the sense of 'a natural instinct, inclination or talent *for* something', as in (*a*) a poem for Cú Chonnacht Mag Uidhir
(1566–1589) by Cú Choigcríche Ó Cléirigh entitled 'Urra ac oighreacht
Éiremhóin', ('The heritage of Éiremhón has a surety') and in (*b*) one of the
early seventeenth-century poems entitled 'Iomarbháigh na bhFileadh' ('The
Contention of the Bards'):

(*a*)   Tuc cách cúl red thegmháilsi   Everyone has refused to meet you
        tú gan ágh is aigmhéile   you are the most terrible in combat
        a mhic shúlghlas Shiobháine   O blue-eyed son of Siobhán
        do **dhúthchas re** daghthréighibh.[49]   you have inherited good traits.

(b)   a hucht druadh dá n-iarradh neart   If Fiacha should seek power by
                                                 means of druids
        do b'fhiú a **dhúthchas re**   it would have been worthy of his
            draoidheacht   *dúchas* for wizardry.

        Dúthchas re gaisceadh a Aodh   Your *dúchas* (inherited bent) for
                                                 heroic deeds, Aodh,
        atá agaibh as bhar ngaol.[50]   that you acquired from your
                                                 relations.

There is also the evidence of *dúchas* in proverbs, those repositories of aphoristic knowledge, or 'informal tradition'.[51] One of the proverbs recorded by Mac Adam in the nineteenth century, 'Is treise dúchas ná oiliúint', is still current today and is already found in a sixteenth-century text, *Eachtra Uilliam*:

> as dual don dúthchas dialladh re 'roile gion go mbeith fios a chéile aca, mar adeir an senfhocal go sonnradhach: 'treisi an **dúthchas** ná an oileamhain'.[52]

> it is natural for those of common stock to resemble each other though unaware of the relationship. As the proverb says: instinct is stronger than upbringing.

A further aphorism, moreover, is buried in the passage quoted above in the phrase 'as dual don dúthchas dialladh re'roile', which is to be found in its original form in another seventeenth-century source:

> Dialladh duine re a **dhúthchas**[53]

> Let each one follow his natural bent

The evidence of proverbial sayings in particular would suggest that such 'internalized' meanings were well established in the language by the seventeenth century at least, and indeed we have encountered much earlier examples of the same phenomenon. However, older meanings of words often never quite disappear and *dúchas* could still be found until recently in at least one variety of Irish with the meaning 'place'. The following example from Uíbh Ráthach in Co. Kerry refers to a cow that had to be sold as it kept wandering back to its original habitat or *dúchas*:

> Chuirtí ruchall féna dhá chois tosaigh agus chuireadh sí dhi treasna an chnoic . . . agus ní stadadh sí go mbuineadh sí a **dúchas** amach arís.[54]

> A spancel would be put under her two feet and she would take off over the hills . . . and she wouldn't stop till she reached her *dúchas* ('home') again.

However, the *general* shift in salience of meaning from more external to more internal in the modern period is certainly tenable. As already suggested, this whole process is amenable to a more universalist interpretation. Further consideration of these questions will be deferred until an important piece of syntax has been examined: the use of *dúchas* as an attributive genitive in the form *d(h)úchais*.

Further to *dúchas* as a 'quality': use of the genitive *dúchais*

In many earlier sources we find a close association between *dúchas* and the land itself, where the native land is signified in both its physical and its symbolic aspects. We have already seen examples of this usage above, notably in the twelfth-century passage from *Cogadh Gaedhel re Gallaibh*. This usage is particularly noticeable in the literature of the sixteenth and seventeenth centuries as the Tudor conquest of Ireland takes effect and the Irish diaspora in Europe produces the first exile poetry of the modern period. This poetry taps into a vein of Renaissance patriotism as we shall see in chapter 3 in particular. This is not to claim that these associations necessarily *arise* at this particular time but rather that they come to the fore in reflecting social and historical realities. As this is to form a large part of the discussion in chapter 3, I will not labour the point here. However, I will briefly give one example from the pen of Uilliam Nuinsean (William Nugent, son of the Baron of Delvin in Co. Westmeath).

Two famous poems of exile have come down to us from Nuinsean written after 1571, when he had gone to study at Oxford. In the poem 'Fada i n-éagmais Inse Fáil' the poet talks longingly of the physical beauty of Ireland, which he contrasts with the misery he feels at being in England. He concludes:

Gibé uaibh do bheath a-bhus,	Whoever of you who happens to be here
dá roiche a-rís dá **dhúthchus**,	if he reaches again his *dúchas*
fearr ós chách do-chím a chor:	I see his state as better than anyone's:
go bráth ó' thír ní thiogfadh.[55]	never would he leave his land.

Here *dúchas* again seems to denote the land itself, as is shown by the fact that it is governed by the verb *roich* 'reach'. More remarkable, however, is the use of the word *dúchas* in the first stanza:

Fada i n-éagmais Inse Fáil	A long time absent from Ireland
i Saxaibh (dia do dhiombáidh):	in England enough cause for dejection
sia an bhliadhain ó Bhanbha a-bhus	away from Ireland the year seems longer here
('s labhra dhiamhuir **ar ndúthchus**).	it's a mysterious saying: 'our *dúchas*'.

Note again here the beginnings of the 'subjectification' or 'internalization' of meaning already adduced above in this stanza, where *dúchas* seems to lose at least some of its connection with the external and concrete and becomes something ineffable yet ever-present, in that it informs habitual behaviour and conventional perception, here literally the sense of how time passes.

Increasingly, in fact, from the early seventeenth century on we find the use of *dúchas* to denote the physical entity of the land itself being replaced by a noun phrase in which the head or governing noun is itself denotative of the land, with the genitive of *dúchas* (*dúchais*) used in an attributive or associative function. In this section I present some examples of this before going on to their analysis below. We can see in Nuinsean's poem a metalinguistic awareness of the abstract or elusive quality of *dúchas*, and, as we have already seen, we have increasing evidence from the seventeenth century onwards that the internalized personal dimensions of *dúchas* are becoming more significant, presumably as a concomitant of the disappearance of the Irish aristocratic order during that century. A further consequence of this development is the growing prominence of a more analytical piece of syntax for which Nuinsean's other famous poem of exile, 'Diombáidh triall ó thulchaibh Fáil', ('Dejection to leave the hills of Ireland') provides an examplar. Here the phrase *domhan dúthchais* 'native world', literally 'world of *dúchas*', occurs:

Dá bhfaomhadh Dia damh tar m'ais	If God were to permit me once again
rochtain **dom dhomhan dúthchais**	to reach my world of *dúchas*
ó Ghallaibh ní ghéabhainn dol	from foreigners I would take no invite
go clannaibh séaghainn Saxon.[56]	to the noble families of England.

Here *dúchas* appears as an attributive genitive, which functions as an adjective: it describes an attribute of the land rather than denoting the physical entity of the land itself, prefiguring its general usage in modern Irish, most commonly the phrase *tír dhúchais* 'native land'. The syntax of this construction can be presented diagrammatically:

Physical designation of 'land': e.g. **fearann**	Attributive genitive **d(h)úchais**

In fact, in many sources of the early modern period we find both the simplex *dúchas* and the more analytical construction, e.g. *tír dhúchais*, used side by side:

(*a*)   'Is fearr **dúthchas** iná gach ní,' ar Fearghus, 'uair ní haoibhinn do neoch maitheas dá mhéad muna fhaice a **dhúthchas**.'

'A native land is better than anything,' said Fearghus, 'for no excellence, however great, is delightful to one unless one sees one's native land.'

(*b*)   Atá . . . Fearghus do theacht chugainn la teachtaireacht as ár **dtír dhúthchais féin** le síoth.

Namely . . . that Fearghus should come to us with a message of peace from our native land.[57]

In a political poem of the 1580s, to be considered in more detail in chapter 3, 'Dia libh a Laochraidh Gaoidhiol', ('God with you, warriors of the Gaels') we have the association of the simplex *dúchas* 'native land' with *oireacht* 'patrimony', 'assembly' and its opposition to *eachtruinn* 'foreigners':

(*a*) Crádh liom eachtruinn dá bhfógra, It kills me that foreigners have outlawed

rioghradh Fhódla 's a n-oireacht the kings of Fódla and their assemblies,

's nách goirthior dhíobh 'na **ndúthchus** and that all they are now called in their homeland

acht ceithearn chúthail choilleadh.[58] are shifty woodland bandits.

However, in this same poem we find the expression *fearann dúthchais* as an equivalent to the simplex, where it is spoken of in the same breath as 'the land of your ancestors' (*talamh bhar sinnsear*):

(*b*) Déntar libh coinghleic calma, Wage war like valorous wolves
a bhuidhion armghlan fhaoiltioch, you blessed band of the shining arms

fá cheann **bhar bhfearuinn** on behalf of your land of
dúthchais, *dúchas*,
puirt úrghoirt innsi Gaoidhiol. the fresh fields of the island of the Gael.

In fact the same two terms are still found in the work of the late eighteenth- and early nineteenth-century poet Mícheál Óg Ó Longáin:

(*a*) Deinidh go subhach a Ghaela Rejoice and make merry, you Gaels,

tá an chabhair ag téacht gan mhoill . . . help is coming without delay . . .

de shúil go bhfaicfinn saor sibh in the hope that I may see you free

in bhur **ndúchas** féin arís. in your own *dúchas* again.

(*b*) is Gallabhúir do dhíbirt and to banish the foreigners
as **fearann dúchais** díleas from the dear native land
ár sinsear go deo[59] of our ancestors for ever.

In sixteenth- and seventeenth-century sources we also find the following alternatives to *dúchas* as a designation of 'native land':

(1) *Fonn dúthchasa*: In the following excerpt, from Céitinn's *Trí Bior-Ghaoithe an Bháis*, ('The three shafts of Death')[60], note also the persistent use of *dúthaigh*, particularly in reference to Heaven as everyone's *dúthaigh*, 'native place' or 'inheritance'. Note further its equivalence to *fonn dúthchasa* 'native soil', which in this passage translates the Latin *solum natale*:

An seiseadh hadhbhar fá ndligheann duine gul do dhéanamh, tré iomad fuinn nó mianghusa do bheith ar neach ré dul ar neamh, is **dúthaigh** dá gach aon-duine. Óir is follus go mbí mian ar gach neach, triall **dá dhúthaigh féin**, mar thuigthear a briathraibh Óibhid, mar a n-abair: *Nescio qua natale solum dulcedine cunctos ducit, et immemores non sinit esse sui:* 'Ní feas damh, ar sé, créad an mhilse bhíos **san bhfonn ndúthchasa**, ag tarraing na n-uile, ┐ nach léigeann dóibh bheith neamhchuimhneach orra féin.' As na briathraibh se Óibhid is iontuigthe go mbí dúil ag gach neach '**na dhúthaigh féin** ┐ go mbí súil tar a ais aige ré triall innte as a **dheóraidheacht**.[61]

The sixth reason that a person is entitled to weep is having excessive desire and ambition to go to Heaven, everyone's *dúthaigh*. Since it is obvious that everyone wants to go to his own *dúthaigh*, as can be understood from Ovid's words where he says . . . 'I do not know what sweetness is in the native land of **dúchas** which attracts everyone and does not allow them to be forgetful of themselves.' From these words of Ovid it is understood that everyone desires his own *dúthaigh* and wants to go back there out of his exile.

The opposition in this passage between a sense of *dúchas* and the idea of 'exile' is one we shall encounter again, especially in chapter 3.

(2) *Athartha dúchais*: In an earlier example we saw *dúchas* juxtaposed with the word *athartha* 'fatherland', 'patria'. In fact *dúchas* can also be used after *athartha* as an attributive genitive, as occurs notably in the sixteenth-century *Betha Colaim Chille*:

> Et togaim fos an bas sin d'faghail a n-oilethre suthain a bfhecmais mo tíri ┐ mo talaimh ┐ **m'athardha duthcais fen**.[62]

> And I elect moreover to die in permanent exile from my country and my land and my own native fatherland.

(3) *Tír dhúchais*: This becomes the default expression for 'native land' in Modern Irish. We have already seen an early modern example above; a further example is found in Céitinn on the theme of spiritual exile:

> An treas adhbhar doilgheasa bhíos ag an anam i n-ifreann tré bheith ar díbirt ┐ ar deóraidheacht i gcoigrích ifrinn i gcéin óna chrích bhunaidh ┐ **óna athardha** dhílis .i. flaitheas Dé . . . arna gcor ar athchur ┐ ar ionnarbadh ann **óna dtír dhúthchais** ┐ óna gcathair chomhnuighthe féin .i. flaitheas Dé.[63]

> The third reason that the soul in Hell has for grief is that it has been expelled and exiled to Hell's foreign land far away from its land of origin and from its dear fatherland . . . having been banished from their [the souls'] native land and their own city of abode, that is, God's kingdom.

Note here the identification of *tír dhúchais* with *athartha* 'fatherland,' 'patria', and its opposition once again to the foreign element, this time in its physical dimension of *coigrí(o)ch*, as well as in the state of exile as above. Typically, the most evocative use of the attributive genitive is in the modern collocation with *tír* 'country' to mean 'native land', as in the following nineteenth-century history by the Armagh scribe and poet Art Mac Bionaid *Comhrac na nGael agus na nGall le chéile* ('The struggle of the Gaels against the foreigners') in an address attributed to Hugh O'Donnell on the eve of battle:

> An tse a thuitfidhis, tuitfidh se go glormhur a' trod air son an cheart, air son libeartaigh agus air son a **thir-dhuchas**.[64]

> Whoever should fall, he shall fall gloriously fighting for what is right, for liberty and for his native land.

The difference between the use of the simplex and the analytical construction to denote the 'native land' is that in the latter case *dúchas* no longer serves as the denotation of the land itself but rather as an attribute of the land: the native land's latent qualities of being subject to a hereditary right are abstracted and ultimately internalized. The denotative use of *dúchas* comes increasingly into competition with the expressions of the type *tír dhúchais* from the seventeenth century onwards. In fact by the nineteenth and early twentieth centuries the phrase *tír dhúchais* is firmly established as the default expression for 'native land' as in the following quotations from (a) the nineteenth-century Meath poet Aodh Mac Domhnaill and (b) Patrick Pearse:

(*a*)   Uch! A Éirinn a rúin, a **thír dhúchais** mo chairde[65]

Och, Ireland my sweetheart, O native land of my friends!

(*b*)   Is mora dhuit, a **thír ár ndúchais**! Go mairirse go bráth![66]

Hail to our native land! May you endure for ever!

Note the syntactic variation in (*b*), which is literally 'O land of our *dúchas*'. We can compare this with the more usual *ár dtír dhúchais* 'our native land', literally 'our land of *dúchas*' (as in the extract from the early modern 'Deirdre' story above) and note the flexibility or elasticity of the syntax with the different placement of the possessive 'our' in each instance.

I would argue that it is precisely in this elasticity that the key to the meaningfulness, culturally and historically, of this piece of syntax lies. Here there arises the question of the tension within *dúchas* between what can and cannot be taken away; in other words, the relation between the naturally given and the culturally and historically contingent. (For the type of metaphorical transference involved here, see the discussion of the word *dual* in chapter 4.) The important point is the *conceptualization* of the native land as something that cannot be taken. In other words, to refer to Ireland as your *dúchas* is to say that it is, in effect, as inalienable from you as inherited personal characteristics. However, in real life, as the Irish people discovered to their cost in the seventeenth and eighteenth centuries, the land could be, and indeed was, largely taken away. My argument here is that, as a corollary of this development, we have the rise of a more dissociative and analytical syntax for *dúchas* in the form *tír dhúchais*, literally 'land of *dúchas*'. This can be illustrated diagrammatically as follows. In the first instance the material and symbolic aspects of the native land are indexed by the one sign, *dúchas*. In the alternative configuration, however, the material (*tír*) and symbolic (*dúchas*) aspects are separated, and each is presented as a different sign:

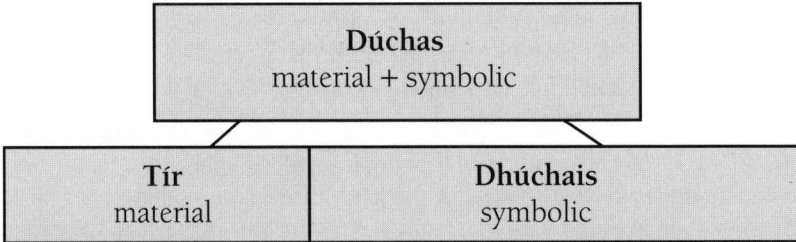

Dúchas
material + symbolic

Tír	Dhúchais
material	symbolic

This is a case of what is called diagrammatic iconicity, whereby a direct relationship is posited between conceptual structure and linguistic structure. It is as if Irish-speakers are saying: the land as a physical and material entity (*tír*) may well be taken from us, but the ideology of the native land and our identification with it (*dúchas*) cannot. The claim is not that this analytical syntax arises in the seventeenth and eighteenth centuries—there are examples of it from the fifteenth century at least—but it does seem to acquire added salience after the sweeping socio-economic and cultural changes of this period. In contemporary Irish it has in effect supplanted the simplex as the expression for 'native land'. Kerby Miller's analysis of *dúchas* as an 'unusually strong' attachment to the native place fails to take this essential syntactic development into account.[67] Apart from raising the question of how unusual the strength of this attachment is or was (chapter 3 will have some brief discussion on this), it fails to account for developments in the syntax of *dúchas,* in particular the rise of this more analytical syntax as a *dynamic* conception of all that the native land and its associations entail.

However, as already mentioned above, *dúchas* as a simplex form does survive alongside the analytical form. In this connection it is interesting to note that it frequently has definite connotations of loss or exile and of regret for that loss in the eighteenth and nineteenth centuries. The following excerpts, (*a*) and (*b*), from the eighteenth-century writer Seán Ó Neachtain associate the loss of *dúchas* with exile, an association we have seen with Céitinn's writings above. The comparison in (*a*) is between the exile of Irish and of the Israelites, a common analogy in the seventeenth and eighteenth centuries. The analogy will be taken up again in chapter 3. The other excerpts also refer to contexts of exile: (*c*) is from the eighteenth-century poet Eoghan Rua Ó Súilleabháin; (*d*) is from a poem written in the Caribbean in the 1860s, while (*e*) is taken from an address by Daniel O'Connell to the Catholic Association in Dublin in 1824 against the dangers of secret societies:

(*a*) Agus mar ba híad an cine Iúdaighe clann Dé . . . gur tuga leaga an-mhór dhóibh nár tuga do dhrong ar bhioth oile acht dona Gaodhuil amháin . . . Óir d'imigh a gcreideamh agus **a ndúthchas** uatha ⁊ gí gur imigh **a ndúthchas** ó chlanna Gaodhuil, tá a gcreideamh ar marthuinn acu . . . Agus arís, a Dhía Mhóir na Glóire, goir abhaile chum **dúthchais a sinnsir** do chlann dhílis Ghaodhuldha.

And because the Jewish people were the Children of God . . . they were greatly oppressed in a way that no other people were except the Irish . . . since their religion and their native land were lost to them, and although the Irish lost their land, their faith endures . . . And again, O great God of glory, summon your dear Irish children home to the native land of their ancestors.

(*b*) is iongnadh liom nach bhfóirionn tú ar na Gaedhil bhochta tá fagháil bháis don ghorta agus a maoin agus a bhfunn, a **ndúthchus** agus na huile eile dá gceart ag Gaill, re ar díbreadh a sean agus a sinsior le feill agus le inghreama.

It amazes me that you do not help the poor Irish who are dying of famine, while their wealth and land, their inheritance and all their other entitlements are in the hands of the English, by whom were banished their ancestors through treachery and persecution.

(*c*) I Sacsaibh na séad i gcéin óm **dhúthchas**.

In England of the treasures far from my homeland.

(*d*)
Bhínnse im' stéig bhocht le teas na gréine	I used to be parched by the heat of the sun
Ag séideadh piléar dhíom lem' namhaid ó dheas—	spraying bullets at my enemy in the south
Agus tar éis gach aon ní ní thug Dia saor mé	And after all that God did not release me
Aríst go hÉire, **mo dhúchas ceart**.	back to Ireland, my true homeland.

(*e*) Nac iomda duine is eolach dhuin nach air thuill air chor ar bith e do seolaidh na dhibirtheach ona **dhúthchas**.

How many innocent persons have we known to suffer transportation? (lit. 'to have been sent as exiles from their native land').[68]

Once again, in (*a*) and (*b*) we see the virtually inescapable connection between *dúchas* and ancestry (*sean; sinnsear*). Historical shifts in meaning can thus be viewed as shifts in the salience of certain meanings over others, even though older, more archaic meanings may well survive in the background for long periods, to be evoked and re-evoked whenever necessary.[69]

Further to the external and internal dimensions of *dúchas*

One way to address this question of the internal and external dimensions of *dúchas* and their possible historical relationship is to re-examine the overall configuration of the *dú*-based family of words considered earlier. For ease of exposition I present in summary fashion the historical aggregate of the meanings of (i) *dú*, (ii) *dúiche* (*dúthaigh*) and (iii) *dúchas*.

(i)   1. *Lit:* Place, patrimony, inheritance, due
       2. (*Used as adjective with copula*) Native, natural; proper, fitting (*do*, to)

(ii)   1. Hereditary land
       2. Native land, native place, home country
       3. Land, estate
       4. Region, territory; district, locality, countryside

(iii) 1. Hereditary right or claim; birthright, heritage; ancestral estate, patrimony

       2. Native place or country, ancestral home; traditional connection

       3. Kindred affection, natural affinity

       4. Heredity, innate quality, natural bent

       5. Natural wild state: wildness, madness

       6. (gs. as a.) Inherited, inherent, innate, native

I have highlighted the more abstract and internalized senses by which *dúchas* is usually differentiated from the other two items. The important senses for the purposes of the present discussion are (iii) 4 and 6, and it can be seen, indeed we have already seen, that meaning 6 is actually 4 used attributively or adjectivally (i.e. *dúchais*). In fact there is syntactic evidence for a process of increasing abstraction here, proceeding from (i) the basic etymon *dú* to (iii) the most abstract form, *dúchas*. As the older spelling *dúthchas* with the medial *-th-* clearly shows, this is based is on the form *dúthaigh* with the addition of the abstract suffix *-as*. So in general terms *dúchas* must originally have meant something like 'the quality associated with and derived from the *dúthaigh* or native place.' But the focus of *dúchas* is on heredity as transmitted by ancestry. This double association presupposes a substantive and reciprocal relationship between the native place and the people whose native place it is. Let me outline the relevant linguistic evidence here:

(1) We have already seen evidence of the syntax *is dú/dúthaigh/dúchas do* (X), which can be roughly glossed 'it is right / natural for (X)', in accordance with an ethical code that is indexically and iconically linked to the symbolic aspects of the native land. Here is a further example where we have two instances, one each of *dú* and *dúthaigh,* in short succession, from an early seventeenth-century text *Beatha Aodha Ruaidh Uí Dhomhnaill* ('The Life of Red Hugh O'Donnell'):

andar la gach aon díobh **ba dó buddéin ba dú** cendus ⁊ tigernus an tíre. Don-angatar-sidhe ó bhiug co mór fo ghairm Uí Domhnaill iar ttocht do don tir ⁊ **ba dúthaigh doibh** cia no thiestais.[70]

each one believed that the leadership and lordship of the country was due to himself. They arrived, from small to great, at the behest of Ó Domhnaill and it was right and proper that they should all come.

The earliest example of this transition from the idea of 'place' to the notion of 'right' or 'entitlement' in any member of this lexical family features *dú*, perhaps not surprisingly, as this is the basic etymon. An example occurs in an early eighth-century law text, *Bretha Nemed Toísech*:

dligthius **dú** do airig ard fichit sét sernar.[71]

the *aire ard* is entitled to, as his due, twenty *séts* which are ordained.

Here *dú* denotes not 'place' but a right or entitlement that originally evolves through a sense of that place but which is then generalized to mean a 'natural' right or due. We have seen the same sense in the case of *dúchas* above, but it is also attested in the case of *dúthaigh*, as in the following twelfth-century example:

ro cóirged cach nech **ar duthaig** a athar ⁊ a tshenathar.[72]

everyone was arranged according to what was due his father and grandfather.

(2) We have already considered in some detail the syntax of *tír dhúchais*. However, we also find as a variant *tír dhúthaigh* or *tír dhúiche* in the same sense of 'native land'. Thus the same reciprocity exists between the land itself as *dúthaigh* and the special qualities associated with that denotation as exists with *dúchas*. This finds expression in linguistic structure, although the collocation with *dúchas* is much more common. Examples from the late Middle and early Modern Irish periods include:

(*a*)   Atai-si ar ndul **ad thir dhuthaigh**.

You are going to your native country.

(*b*)   ráncatar síar . . . co Tír nAmalgaid .i. a **fhlesca fírdúiche** fén.

they went west . . . to Tír nAmalgaid, that is, their own native domain.[73]

Significantly, however, *dú* is excluded from this kind of syntax, which would suggest that the relevant meaning of *dú* 'native place' was becoming, or had already become, obsolete by the time this syntax evolved, some time in the medieval period.

We therefore have a kind of historical progression if we combine (1) and (2) here (where the asterisk indicates that the particular construction is not attested) (see overleaf):

To complete this rough historical progression we can adduce the additional *semantic* range of *dúchas* as opposed to the other two lexemes in question,

HISTORICAL PROGRESSION

>   >   >   >   >   >

Is dú/dúthaigh/dúchas do	Tír dhúthaigh/ dhúiche/ dhúchais
	*Tír dhú

which involves more 'internal' meanings. While it may be argued that most of the attested senses of *dúchas* are 'internal' to the extent that they presuppose a connection to the past by blood and by birth, it is clear that some are more internalized, relatively speaking, than others. I am referring here to those meanings that relate to personal traits and characteristics and that lack the more externalized socio-cultural, ideological and even political dimensions that are expressed primarily by ranges 1 and 2 above. These ranges include the idea of birthright which is then extended to encompass one of the most salient material dimensions of that right—the native land itself.

It is this whole question of *internalization* or *subjectivization* of meaning that I wish to pursue here within a more general framework. In recent times the work of several scholars has shown that the transfer of meaning from less to more abstract domains is a recognizable, cognitively motivated feature of language.[74] Consider the following sets of examples from Sweetser, who argues that we possess a 'multi-leveled cultural understanding of language and thought' that enables us to transfer semantic structure metaphorically from one area of experience to another.[75] A particularly clear example is the pervasive connection between verbs of sense perception and verbs of knowledge and intellect, where verbs of seeing and hearing (external, physical) become verbs of knowing and obeying, respectively (internal, mental), and verbs of touching (external) become verbs of emotion (internal):

(a)   IE *weid-* 'see'   Gk *eidon* 'see' > Gk perf. *oida* 'know' lit. 'I have seen'
                                (cf. Engl. *idea*)
                                Lat. *video* 'I see' v. Irish *fios* 'knowledge'

(b)   IE *k'leu-s* 'hear'   (i) Gk *kluō*; Irish *cluinim* 'I hear' (also Ir. *cluas* 'ear')
                                (ii) Engl. *listen*; Russ. *slusat'* 'listen'
                                (iii) Danish *lystre*; Russ. *slusat's'a* 'obey'

The direction here is primarily physical > mental or concrete > abstract. Traugott identifies a similar general semantic path of development from 'meanings based in the external described situation > meanings based in the internal (evaluative/perceptual/cognitive) described situation'.[76] Sweetser adduces further evidence from various domains of language use for this process of 'subjectivization' or 'internalization' of meaning, showing, for example, that it can be applied to various clause types as well as to lexical items.

If we take grammatical structure seriously we may note the kinds of structures in which *dúchas* commonly occurs. Of principal interest here is the fact that *duchas* in Modern Irish is something that can be *in* you, which is a clear iconic linguistic reflection of the semantic development—the internalization of the external—at issue here:

(a) Tá sé **mar dhúthchas ionnat** an chaint a bheith agat.

  It is as *dúchas in* you to be chatty.

Note, however, that the alternative with *duit* is also given, reflecting the older syntax and semantics:

  Tá sé **mar dhúthchas dhuit** an chaint a bheith agat.

  It is as *dúchas for* you to be chatty.

(b) Is millteanach a' **dúthchas** fairrge atá **sna** Sasanaigh.

  The English really have the sea in their blood.[77]

In fact this syntax of internalization is already found in Ó Bruadair in the seventeenth century; and I have found a further example from the late eighteenth-century Clare poet Tomás Ó Míocháin:

(c) Donnchadh an Chúil atá **dúthchas** feardha **ann**.

  Donnchadh an Chúil with his natural manliness (lit. 'the virile *dúchas* is in him).

(d) an prionsa den tsaorcheap '**nar** [= inar] **dhúchas** an ríshlat.

  the prince of the noble stock in whom the royal sceptre is *dúchas*.[78]

Again the principle here is one of *iconicity* or the idea that conceptual relations are reflected directly in grammatical structure.[79] As Haiman puts it, 'linguistic forms are frequently the way they are because, like diagrams, they resemble the conceptual structure they are used to convey'.[80] We also have the following variations on a theme, which give a sense of the internal and ineluctable dimensions of *dúchas*:

  Briseann an **dúchas** trí shúile an chait / fríd na crúba
  Dúchas breaks (out) through the cat's eyes / though the hooves

  Cad a dhéanfadh cat ach luch a mharú?
  What (else) would a cat do but kill a mouse?

  An rud atá *sa* chat bíonn sé *sa* phisín.
  What's *in the* cat is *in the* kitten.

This syntax of *dúchas* as internal to the subject represents the culmination of a lengthy historical process that reaches its greatest intensity with the social, cultural and political dislocations of the modern period in Ireland.

I recall here the extract given in chapter 1 from Éilis Ní Thiarnaigh's essay on the relationship between *dúchas* and spiritual life, where we find a metapragmatic equivalent for this syntactic structure of 'internalization': *dúchas* is 'a special word that we understand more with the heart than with the mind' (*Focal speisialta é a thuigimid níos mó leis an gcroí ná leis an intinn*), a word we find difficult to explain 'despite our inner understanding' (*ainneoin ár dtuiscint inmheánach*). We can see here that *dúchas* has a certain evocative power, being grasped more intuitively than intellectually. But here we have also a cognitive parallel to the grammaticalized internalization discussed above in semantic terms: *dúchas* is part of our internalized understanding.

In many of the early examples it is not always easy to tell whether *dúchas* has primarily a more external signification, in that entitlement is a simple fact of hereditary right, or whether it rests on an appreciation of the more internalized personal characteristics that fit one for a particular office or position. In the following example we have a brief prose extract after a poem dedicated to the poet Fland mac Lonáin (fl. 890) from his mother, Laitheocc Láidheach ingen Laighnecháin, herself a poet, in which the scribe comments:

> Fland mac Lonáin . . . ar **dúthchus** a máthar do dhechaidh sidhe re héiccsi.[81]

> Fland mac Lonáin . . . on account of his mother's *dúchas* he followed the poetic calling.

So the art of poetry is Flann's by birthright, and this is the idea conveyed here by *dúchas*. Yet it seems to me that *dúchas* is somewhat ambivalent between the more 'external' idea of an inherited entitlement (to be, or to consider oneself, a poet) and the more internalized one of inherited gifts or talent. Similar considerations arise with the earliest attestation of the word *dúchas* that I have found, the ninth-century 'speculum principis' of *Tecosca Cormaic*:

> 'A húi Chuind, a Chormaic . . . cid asa ngaibther flaithemnas for túathaib ⁊ chlandaib ⁊ chenélaib?' 'Ní hansa . . . A feib chrotha ⁊ cheneóil ⁊ érgnai, a gáis ⁊ ordan ⁊ eslabrai ⁊ indraccus, a feib **dúthchusa** ⁊ airlabhra, a nirt imgona ⁊ sochraite gaibther'.[82]

> 'O grandson of Conn, O Cormac . . . whence is chieftaincy taken over tribes, and clans, and races?' 'Not hard to tell . . . By virtue of shape and race and knowledge, through wisdom and rank and liberality and honesty, by virtue of *dúchas* [hereditary right] and eloquence, by the strength of fighting and an army it is taken.'

Once again, the question is whether *dúchas* here really refers to a 'hereditary right', as the editor would have it, or to more of a personal qualification for office in the form of inherited characteristics.

A further example in a poem from the eleventh-century prose text, *Aislinge Meic Con Glinne*, a satire on the greed and gluttony of the clergy, is of special interest, as it represents a parody of the whole idea that underlies *dúchas,* that of ancestry, genealogy and the tracing of one's descent:

Bennach dún a chlérig	Greet us, O cleric
a chlí chloth co comgne	you renowned prop of native learning
mac Midbuilce mela	son of the Honey Pot
meic Bela, Meic Bloince	son of Meat Juice, son of Grease
Maith do **duthchus** degbid	Good is your *dúchas* for good food
is milis re tengaid.[83]	it is sweet to the tongue.

This instance is particularly interesting, because it is precisely the more protean and internalized sense of *dúchas* that is being used to lampoon the 'higher', more aristocratic function, and this is all the more significant because the example is relatively early in date. These examples further emphasize the 'shifting' or 'fluid' quality of *dúchas* as a concept, a theme that will be taken up in the next chapter.

Conclusion

As we have seen, *dúchas* is the abstract noun built on *dúthaigh* with an abstract suffix *-as*. Such is the symbiotic relationship between right to place and the place itself that the meanings of *dúthaigh* and *dúchas* frequently overlap, as indeed both words do with the most basic etymon of the family, *dú*. The meaning of 'native place' becomes especially prominent in the case of *dúchas* in the sixteenth and early seventeeth centuries for social, cultural and political reasons. This is followed in the seventeenth and eighteenth centuries by a general process of abstraction or generalization of meaning, which again reflects socio-cultural and political realities. When we compare the use of the modern '*dúchas*' with the earlier '*dúthchas*', what we find in general is a progressive internalization of meaning: in the earlier period usage relates primarily to the external social and physical world, *dúchas* as representing a hereditary right to the land (social) or the land itself (physical). In the contemporary language, on the other hand, *dúchas* emphasizes more the internalized or personalized ideological world: it belongs to each individual within but also to the community as an aggregate of those individuals. This is latent in the earlier language also but is now far more salient than before. It is tempting to suggest that the greater abstraction and subjectivization of *dúchas* over the last three centuries is symbolic of loss of control by the Irish people over the physical entity of the land itself. It also seems reasonable to connect the loss of salience of the idea of hereditary right or entitlement with the demise of the old Irish aristocracy in the seventeenth century and the concomitant rise of individualism and an entrepreneurial middle class (see further chapter 3). This can be tied in with more general processes of change that were afoot in Europe at large at this time, namely the transition from feudalism to capitalism. Hughes speaks here of the *democratization* of status words, while Lewis refers to their *moralization*, whereby they come to stand for character traits and values that can be attributed to any individual. In fact much of the 'tension' in the history of *dúchas* is generated by this external–internal dynamic between socio-cultural meanings and internal or personal meanings. What the tension revolves around is this: which aspects of inheritance, of lineage and genealogy are inalienable, and which can be appropriated by others? The question is posed in an acute form in the seventeenth and eighteenth centuries with the use of *dúchas* to signify both the material and the emotive aspects of the 'native land'. As we have seen, since the seventeenth century a more transparent, more analytical syntax of the 'native land' has come to the fore in Irish and has progressively ousted the older simplex *dúchas* in this meaning.

The question of the historical relationship between the internal and external senses of *dúchas* is a difficult one. While the two senses have co-existed since the medieval period, there is evidence that the more internal sense or senses have become more significant in the modern period. As has been argued, this internalization has found clear syntactic expression in Modern Irish. However, it cannot be maintained that there has been a straightforward 'internalization of meaning' in the course of the history of *dúchas*, as the word shows signs of this 'shifting' quality—from external to internal—at all periods of the language. Aspects of this shifting quality in a particular historical context will be examined more closely in chapter 3. Even the evidence of folk wisdom as expressed in proverbs shows a certain tension between the imputed immutability of one's *dúchas* and the possibility of deviating from it. Compare, for example, two proverbs and their variants as given by O'Rahilly.[84] The first is a Scottish variant of the well-known proverb already cited above concerning the primacy of *dúchas* over education, while the second occurs in an early seventeenth-century text (see also above):

(*a*)   Is **buaine** dùthchas na oilean.

   Dúchas is more permanent / enduring than education.

(*b*)   Dialladh duine re a **dhúthchas**.

   Let each one follow his natural bent.

A third example entertains the possibility of deviation:

(*c*)   Minic ná deaghaidh bó le **bó dhúthchais**.[85]

   Often a cow does not take after its breed.

It should be noted that *dúchas* can refer to non-animate natural phenomena, although this usage is less common. Take, for example, the following seventeenth-century examples from Ó Bruadair referring (*a*) to the natural propensity of streams to flow and (*b*) to the enduring nature of precious stones:

(*a*)   ré fostadh a fuairshreabh i n-aghaidh **a ndúthchais**

   damming up its cool streams against their natural tendency

(b)   adamant .i. clocha buadh . . . óir an t-arm sa bhonn ria a mbeanann ní
        dia **ndúthchas** bithbhrigh sáidhte ┐ síorthollta do ghréas aige.[86]

        adamant, that is, precious stones . . . for the implement which partakes
        in any way of their nature ever possesses constant efficacy in thrusting
        and perpetual piercing.

As an example of the contestability of the notion of *dúchas* in the cultural
sphere, however, consider the contrasting views of Seosamh Mac Grianna, the
twentieth-century writer and Breandán Ó Doibhlin literary critic and profes-
sor of French at Maynooth on the importance of *dúchas* in modern literature
in Irish, the first two extracts being from an essay by Mac Grianna published
in 1936:

(a)   Más cóir dúinn dóchas a bheith againn go mbeidh Éire saor, ní lúide is
        cóir dúinn a bheith ag dúil go mbeidh sí Gaelach. Is beag is fiú an
        chraobh gan an bhláth: níl inti ach brosna agus is dual di a bheith ina
        chual chonnaidh a dhófar . . .

        If we should hope that Ireland will be free, we should no less wish it to
        be Gaelic. The branch is hardly worth anything without the flower: it is
        nothing but firewood as a bundle that will burn.

(b)   An chéad rud atá riachtanach an tseanlitíocht a chur i gcló, agus litriú
        an lae inniu uirthi, agus gan míniu ar bith i mBéarla uirthi . . . Sa dóigh
        atá orainn fá láthair tá an **cainteoir dúchais** féin i gcontúirt é a mhilleadh
        le Galltacht gach aon nóiméad sa lá.[87]

        The first thing that is necessary is to print the old literature, and in
        modern spelling, with no explanation of it in English . . . The way we
        are now even the native speaker is in danger of contaminating it with
        Englishness every minute of the day.

Note here the idea of 'pollution', one's *dúchas* as something corruptible by foreignness. A somewhat more nuanced treatment is given in the following passages by Ó Doibhlin:

(c)   . . . d'fhéadfaí a rá i dtaobh **nóisean an dúchais** i litríocht Ghaeilge na
        haoise seo go raibh dearcadh fealsúnta taobh thiar de a ba chúis le tean-
        nas nó le coimhlint áirithe in intinn na scríbhneoirí, agus nár tángthas
        ar aon réiteach sásúil ar an fhadhb . . . Is é Seán Ó Ríordáin is íogaire
        agus is meabhraí a léirigh an droch-choinsias a fhéadann **idéal an**
        dúchais a bhunú sa Ghaeilgeoir . . .

        . . . it could be said about the notion of *dúchas* in the Irish-language
        literature of this century that it was the philosophical outlook behind it
        that engendered tension or a certain conflict in writers' minds, and that
        no satisfactory resolution of the problem has been found. It is Seán Ó
        Ríordáin who has most sensitively and perceptively shown the guilty
        conscience that the ideal of dúchas gives rise to in the Irish-speaker . . .

(d)   Tá faitíos orm gurb é **perfectionnisme an dúchais** fé ndeara cuid den leochaileacht seo. Ní ar an **dúchas** ann féin is ceart an milleán a chur, ach ar an dearcadh diúltach sin nach ligfeadh aon nuaíocht, aon bhreis saibhris ina chomhair.[88]

I fear that it is the 'perfectionnisme' of *dúchas* that is responsible for some of this fragility. It is not *dúchas* itself that is to be blamed but that negative mentality that would not allow any innovation, any enrichment to affect it.

The two sets of passages would appear to be almost diametrically opposed, the former stressing the 'in-cultural' aspects of *dúchas*, the need to restore older 'untainted' modes from within the tradition, the latter emphasizing the need for open-endedness and diversity in the modern world. Ó Doibhlinn criticizes a certain unrealistic attitude towards *dúchas*—a too tradition-based approach that underplays its regenerative and innovative aspects. In fact a similar debate about the nature of *dúchas*, though rather different in its particular cultural and historical milieu, can be read between the lines of certain late sixteenth- and early seventeenth-century texts, as will be argued in chapter 3. Very much in the spirit of Mac Grianna's comments above is the observation below from a remarkable recent book, *Dúchas na Gaeilge* by Maolmhaodhóg Ó Ruairc, which concerns itself with many aspects of the 'genius' of Irish, asserting and affirming in particular what distinguishes it idiomatically and conceptually from English. The author says in his introduction:

Tá an Ghaeilge truaillithe ag éirim an Bhéarla.[89]

Irish has been contaminated by the 'spirit' of English.

Questions are raised here about how *dúchas* itself is to be apprehended: is it inalienable and immutable, or malleable and regenerative; can it be appropriated and re-appropriated? The following chapter will attempt to provide some answers to this question by looking at a specific historical context.

3. THE PRAGMATICS OF *DÚTHAIGH* AND *DÚCHAS*

The purpose of this chapter is to take a close look at both *dúthaigh* (*dúiche*) and *dúchas* as they were used during the late sixteenth and early seventeenth centuries and to show how their semiotic structure pragmatically references certain non-linguistic developments, especially the Irish reaction to English expansionism during this period. To provide the desired framework for the discussion I shall be drawing on the work of Silverstein and Daniel on the *indexicality* of linguistic signs.[1]

The concepts of *dú*, *dúthaigh* and *dúchas* once more

To set the frame for discussion for this present chapter I give once again the summary of definitions given by Ó Dónaill of these three closely related words: (i) *dú*, (ii) *dúiche* (*dúthaigh*) and (iii) *dúchas* (*dúthchas*).[2] On this occasion, however, I am emphasizing somewhat different aspects (for *dúiche* and *dúchas* again I give the more historical spellings in parentheses):

(i)   1. *Lit:* Place, patrimony, inheritance, due

      2. (*Used as an adjective with copula*) Native, natural; proper, fitting (*do*, to)

(ii) **1. Hereditary land**
2. Native land, native place, home country

     3. Land, estate

     4. Region, territory; district, locality, countryside

(iii) **1. Hereditary right or claim; birthright, heritage; ancestral estate, patrimony**
2. Native place or country, ancestral home; traditional connection

     3. Kindred affection, natural affinity

     4. Heredity, innate quality, natural bent

     5. Natural wild state; wildness, madness

     6. (Genitive singular as adjective) Inherited, inherent, innate, native

As we saw in chapter 2, the basic etymon of this family, *dú*, is derived directly from the Indo-European word for 'earth', and there is a certain progression of abstraction from (i) to (iii) in the definitions presented above. As the most abstract member of the family, *dúchas* in particular is characterized by a distinctly 'fluid' range of meanings. However, this 'shifting' quality applies to both *dú* and *dúthaigh* as well. One semantic domain that is historically central to all three words is the idea of 'place' or 'land', especially viewed as 'inheritance' or 'patrimony'. As we can see, it is in the ranges highlighted above that *dúthaigh* and *dúchas* are contiguous, and it is precisely these ranges of meaning that will be the focus of the present discussion. For both words there is a rough historical progression from senses 1 and 2 to the other meanings, which have tended to become more prominent since the seventeenth century. This means that the two words have tended to diverge in their prototypically central meanings since the period in question in ways that will be central to my argument, and I will refer briefly again to this divergence below.

We also saw that this lexical family is built up derivationally from (i) to (iii); but the point is that a discrete semantic distinction is not maintained between the individual members. In addition we considered the fact that each of the family members participates in the following syntagm:

Is *dú/dúthaigh/dúchas* do X

which has the general sense of 'It is right/natural/fitting for X (to).' It seems likely that we are dealing here with a linguistic family that expressly configures a certain ideology, associated at its base with the idea of 'place' or a special kind of 'place'. It is the nature of one aspect of that ideology that I wish to examine in this chapter: the use of both *dúthaigh* and *dúchas* to establish various co-ordinates of collective identity in early modern Ireland.

In chapter 1 above I discussed the nature of the *indexical* in language and its importance for this study. As we saw, in terms of the Peircean semiotic, an index relates a sign to an object according to contiguity, concurrence or causation. In Duranti's formulation, indexicality is 'a sign-activated connection between an on-going situation and other situations'.[3] This is the *pragmatic* aspect of meaning, and it is in such terms that I will argue that the conventional linguistic signs *dúthaigh* and *dúchas* are best understood as 'shifters' or context-dependent signs that index various pragmatic domains.[4] It is precisely this pragmatic area of dependence on context that can often have a chronological dimension. Consider one example given by Dinneen for *dúchas* in his dictionary and the translation he gives with it:

Is fearr **dúthchas** ná gach aon nídh.[5]

Inherited qualities are best (lit. '*dúchas* is better than everything').

For a speaker of Modern Irish this translation is entirely unexceptionable. However, let us look at the phrase in its fifteenth-century context. This is the

'Deirdre' story (*Oidheadh Chloinne Uisnigh*), where Fearghus, Naoise and his brothers find themselves in exile in Scotland. Part of this passage was already given in chapter 2:

> 'Is fearr **dúthchas** iná gach ní,' ar Fearghus, 'uair ní haoibhinn do neoch maitheas dá mhéad muna fhaice a **dhuthchas**.' 'Is fíor sin,' ar Naoise, 'dóigh is annsa leam péin Éire iná Alba, gé madh mó do mhaith Alban do-ghéabhainn.'[6]

> 'A native land is better than anything,' said Fearghus, 'for no excellence, however great, is delightful to one unless one sees one's native land.' 'That is true,' said Naoise, 'for Ireland is dearer to me than Scotland, though I should get more of Scotland's goods.'

In context we can see that the modern default interpretation cannot apply in a purely referential sense; this is clinched by Fearghus talking about 'seeing' his *dúchas* as a material entity. However, as was argued in the previous chapter, Naoise's response indicates that *dúchas* embodies more than the merely material, including also the symbolic aspects of the native land.

'*Báidh nádúrtha an dúthchais*': Ireland's Spanish connection

The following example, on the other hand, gives us, potentially, a different situation. The text is a letter from Domhnall Ó Súilleabháin Béirre to the King of Spain, written in Kinsale in December 1601. The term in the first passage translates fairly naturally as 'native land' or 'patrimony', which is how Ó Cuív renders it in his recent edition of the text.[7] The English translations given below are more or less contemporary with the original however.[8] There is also a contemporary Spanish translation, which will be dealt with presently. In this first passage, Ó Súilleabháin is appealing for aid:

(*a*) a n-aghuidh ar n-eascarad atá ag múchadh an chreideimh Chatoilica go diabhluidhe, ag básughadh ar n-uaisle go díbhfheargach, ⁊ ag santughadh **ar ndúthchais** go haindlightheach.[9]

> against our Enemies that seek to overwhelme and extinguish the Catholike faith diabolically, put to death our Chieftaines tyrannously, coveting our Lands and Livings unlawfully.

At the beginning of the letter there is a much more revealing passage which I give first in its shorter and then its longer contexts:

(*b*) Atá riamh . . . go follas dá hshíordhearbhadh eadrainne na hÉireannaigh nách fuil aonní amháin as neartmhuire oibrigheas inar ccroidhthibh do thuar ⁊ do bhreith ar ngrádha ⁊ ar n-inmhuine iná **báidh nádúrtha an dúthchais** ⁊ cuimhniughadh an charadraidh bhíos do g[h]náth ar ar n-aire . . .

> It hath beene ever . . . manifestly proued by daily experience among us

the Irish, that there is nothing worketh more forcibly in our hearts, to winne, and to draw our loue and affection, then [than] naturall inclination to our Progeny and Ofspring, and the memoriall of the friendship, which sticketh still in our minds . . .

Here Ó Cuív again takes *dúchas* as 'patrimony', translating *báidh nádúrtha an dúthchais* as 'the natural fondness for our patrimony', which is again unobjectionable as far as it goes. However, the translation 'native land' or 'patrimony' may turn out to require further unpacking through contextualization. Let us take the wider context:

(c)   . . . Ar mbheith dúinne, príomhGhaoighuil na hÉireann, cían ó hshoin ar ttarr[a]ng ar bphréimhe ⁊ ar **mbunadhuis** ó threibh ord[h]ruic fhíorúasal na nEasbáinneach .i. ó Mhíleadh . . . do réir fhiadhnuise ar seinleabhur seanchuis, ar ngég ngeinealuigh, ar starthuidh ⁊ ar ccroiniceadh.

Wee the meere Irish (the chief Gaelic people of Ireland) long sithence deriving our roote and originall from the famous and noble race of the Spaniards: *Viz.* from Milecius . . . by the testimony of our old ancient bookes of antiquities, our Petigrees, our Histories, and our Cronicles.[10]

The general thrust of the passage is the idea of the common descent of the Irish people from their ancestor Míl of Spain. The earliest efforts to articulate this common consciousness are in the seventh century, when it first takes shape as part of the challenge to integrate native Irish traditions within the framework of Christianity as the origin legend of humankind in general.[11] Thus Ireland's Spanish connection is established. A passage from *Annála Ríoghachta Érenn* (also known as 'The Annals of the Four Masters') gives us a more immediate context. Aodh Ó Domhnaill, following the defeat at Kinsale, resolves to seek help from Spain on the advice of Ó Néill, on the grounds that Philip III was most likely to rally in defence of the Catholic faith in Ireland (*dar cenn an chreidimh catolice Rómhanaigh*), but also because of the traditional affinity that existed between the Spanish and the Irish due to their common origin:

araill ele **tria na bháidh fri Gaoidhealaibh** ar a t-tocht cétus do ghabháil Ereann as in Spainn amhail as follas isin leabhar dianidh ainm in Leabhar Gabhala.[12]

through his affinity with the Irish, seeing as they had come from Spain to take Ireland, as is clear from the book called 'The Book of the Taking'.

Note that, significantly for the letter under discussion, once again the word *báidh* (modern *bá*) is used to describe this feeling of mutual affection, which is here reciprocated by the Spanish. Further to the use of *báidh* and its derivatives in this context of *dúchas,* another contemporary text (early seventeenth century) gives what looks like a proverb or proverb-type expression as follows:

Bádhach neach ré **shean-dhúthchas**.[13]

Everyone is fond of his native land.

Clearly *báidh* and *bádhach* were feelings easily evoked by consideration of the idea of *dúchas* in seventeenth-century Ireland. However, the connection to be examined more closely here is that between *dúchas* and *bunadhus* (modern *bunús*) 'origin', which Ó Cuív translates here as 'foundation'. To investigate this relation further we can look once again at part of the passage from the twelfth-century account of the war of the Irish against the Vikings that was quoted extensively in chapter 2. The point that was established there and that the present discussion will reinforce in a number of directions is that this passage is a veritable goldmine for the ancient Irish ideology of 'native place' and the right to that place. The relevant excerpt here concerns the rationale posed by the Dál gCais for leaving Thomond and returning to Cashel, the seat of the high-kingship of Munster, to wage war on the Vikings.[14] The reason for the return to Cashel was that

Ba he dna a **m[b]unadus** ocus a **senducus** badein.[15]

It was their place of origin and their own ancestral *dúchas*.

It is this connection between *dúchas* and a sense of origin that I wish to pursue further now by resuming consideration of Ó Súilleabháin Béirre's letter. A possible key is offered by the different treatment of the crucial phrase *báidh nádúrtha an dúthchais* in the English and Spanish translations. The contemporary English translation 'progeny and offspring' is a curious one and appears to show some misunderstanding: the associations of *dúchas* are with ancestry and not progeny, as we have already seen. What is also curious is that in the contemporary Spanish translation *dúchas* is left untranslated and the phrase *báidh nádúrtha an dúthchais* is simply rendered 'amor natural'. This somewhat erratic treatment suggests that the original phrase is not a simple matter, especially when it is compared with the relative ease of translating the phrase *ag sanntughadh ar ndúthchais* later in the text, where *dúchas* is rendered in English as 'lands and livings' and in Spanish as 'bienas y rentas'. It seems that the 'difficulty' in this passage from Ó Súilleabháin Béirre's letter lies precisely in the indexical nature of *dúchas*, the way the word points to particular aspects of a present context and links it to other contexts—again, in Duranti's formulation, 'a sign-activated connection between an on-going situation and other situations'.[16] Inevitably such contexts, as here, tend to be both culturally specific and historically contingent, which makes for a certain incommensurability between cultures with regard to translation. Indexical signs are literally, etymologically, signs that 'point' in the direction of a particular social and cultural context. Indexical function in this sense is, of course, germane to all language use, and it is therefore important to distinguish degrees of indexicality. For example, if I indicate 'this table' then usually in such a context the object is readily available perceptually. Where such ostensive definition is not possible, however, or where the use of a word is such that it invokes, for example, a past context where perception is not so immediately available, the scope of indexical semiosis is potentially much greater. What Ó Súilleabháin Béirre does here is to use the indexical properties of *dúchas* as a pointer towards contextually relevant cultural co-ordinates of national identity: in this case the 'Milesian' connection of a shared racial origin with the Spanish, which is of course contextually highly appropriate. This is the performative aspect of indexicality in the creation and formulation of identity. But such a creative act requires what Gumperz calls *contextualization cues*, the acquisition of which is both permitted and constrained by cultural and ideological forces.[17] I am arguing here that *dúchas* in the passage quoted above is such a 'cue' that implies and requires culture-specific knowledge for its interpretation, which is why both the English and Spanish translators 'fail' in this instance.

In addition, a further association of *bunadhus* as 'place of origin', 'native land' with the idea of 'fatherland' (*athartha*), occurs in the seventeenth-century text known as 'The Flight of the Earls', where *bunadhus* could almost be interchanged with *dúchas*:

> Innissit gur do chríchoibh Lochlann **a mbunadhus** go rapsat ag térnódh tar aiss ón Spáinn go a **n-atharrdha** badéin.[18]

> They told them that they were natives of Lochlainn [Scandinavia] and that they were returning from Spain to their own country.

In fact the same close association occurs in the twelfth-century passage from the *Cogadh Gaedel re Gallaibh* above, which formed the context of the discussion of *dúchas* and *bunadhus*:

> Asbertatar uli . . . ba fearr leo bas ocus éc ocus aeded . . . do agbail ic cosnum sairi a n-athardha ocus a ceneoil.[19]

> They all said . . . that they preferred to die defending the freedom of their fatherland and their people.

This word *athartha* 'fatherland,' 'patria' (cf. *athair* 'father'), is another one that assumes great importance in the sixteenth and seventeenth centuries; it will be discussed below in connection with the general European revival of patriotism in the sixteenth century.[20]

'Dia libh a laochruidh Ghaoidhiol':
Gaelic Irish nationalism in the 1580s

The idea of *bunadhus* 'origin' or 'place of origin' has given us our first co-ordinate of *dúchas* in the early modern period. It is now time to investigate a second 'sign-activated connection' or cultural co-ordinate of *dúchas*. This is indexed in the passage from the twelfth-century *Cogadh Gaedhel re Gallaibh*, where Cashel is considered a good place to fight, as it is *Temair Lethi Moga* 'the Tara of the southern half of Ireland':

Asbert Mathgamain imorro ba hi comarli ba coir doib do denaib .i. teacht i Casiul na rig . . . degbir on ar ba he . . . **Temair Lethi Moga**. Ba he dna a m[b]unadus ocus a senducus badein.[21]

Then Mathgamhain said that the advice they should take was go to Cashel of the Kings . . . that was fitting since it was . . . the Tara of southern Ireland. It was their (place of) origin and their own ancestral *dúchas*.

We are dealing here with the association of *dúchas* with symbolic sites, in this case Cashel and Tara, in traditional Irish ideology. As is well known, there are four provinces in modern Ireland: Connacht, Leinster, Munster and Ulster. However, the word for a province is *cúige* (Old Irish *cóiced*), which means literally 'a fifth', presupposing the existence at some point of a further province, which has since disappeared. As Rees and Rees point out, there are two variants of this tradition, the first being that there were two Munsters (east and west).[22] In what becomes the dominant tradition, however, as embodied by *Lebor Gabála Érenn,* ('The Book of the Taking of Ireland')[23] the missing fifth province is that of *Midhe* (modern counties Meath and Westmeath), which etymologically means 'middle' (< *Medion* 'middle', cognate with Latin *medium*). Céitinn's account of the establishment of this middle province by the king Tuathal Téachtmhar is revealing about its symbolic and ideological importance.[24] According to Céitinn, Tuathal established Midhe by taking a piece of land from each of the other four provinces. Moreover, he built a fort on each of the four pieces of land and each one of these forts is associated with a particular province: Teamhair (Tara) with Leinster, Uisneach with Connacht, Tailtiu with Ulster and Tlachtga with Munster. In this way the real significance of Midhe is realized: it represents in microcosmic form the underlying unity of the four existing provinces whereby the new fifth presupposes and depends on the existence of the other four. As Rees and Rees further point out, the division of the world into four quarters with a central fifth is also attested in Indian and Chinese cosmographies, where again the organic unity of four parts is realized in a fifth that is a microcosm of the other four.[25]

Moreover, they adduce a further telling parallel. Just as Midhe is the fifth province, which a Middle Irish text associates explicitly with the notion of kingship and sovereignty,[26] so the Milesian or Gaelic invasion in the traditional scheme of the *Lebor Gabála Érenn* is the fifth and culminating invasion that establishes the political dispensation of early Ireland. Just as the Milesian connection was our first cultural co-ordinate above, so this idea of the symbolic centre is the second one, and both express the underlying cultural unity of the Gaelic Irish.

This latter idea finds especially cogent expression in various poems of the sixteenth and seventeenth centuries, which show a preoccupation with the loss of this symbolic centre. As well as the symbolic centre of Midhe, each of the other four provinces had its own capital, such as Cruachain in Connacht and Cashel in Munster, which had many features in common with the four central sites already mentioned: they were built on hills and were burial mounds dedicated to their founders, who were invariably female figures. Assemblies were held at these centres, and participation guaranteed the well-being and prosperity of the kingdom. Mac Cana speaks here of the cult of the centre in Irish, indeed in Celtic, ideology,[27] and, as we shall see, references to Tara, Tailtiu, Cashel and Cruachain are used to evoke this cult of the centre in the poetry to be discussed below.

Perhaps the clearest statement of the importance of the symbolic centre occurs in one of Tadhg Dall Ó hUiginn's most highly charged political poems, the one addressed to Brian na Múrtha Ó Ruairc.[28] The poem's essential message is contained in its title, 'D'Fhior Chogaidh Comhailtear Síothcháin', ('To the man of war peace is observed'), the implication being that only bellicosity can secure peace and respect from the English. In Caball's view it was probably composed around 1588, after Ó Ruairc had incurred the displeasure of Sir Richard Bingham, president of Connacht, for assisting survivors of the Spanish Armada in the north-west.[29] This poem to Ó Ruairc is a full-blooded appeal to Gaelic Irish racial pride born of a long historical and cultural awareness. At the heart of Tadhg Dall's appeal to Ó Ruairc is the fact that the English hold the dead centre (*glémheadhón*) of Ireland, while the Irish are banished to the periphery (*dá gcur i gciomhsaibh*):

Siad dá gcur i gciomhsaibh Banbha,	They are being thrust onto the outskirts of Ireland
buidhne Ghall 'na glémheadhón.[30]	whilst regiments of foreigners are in the centre.

Mac Cana has identified the significance of these lines in accordance with traditional Irish ideology: 'the foreigner has established himself at the sacred spot which symbolises the unity of the country'.[31] Naturally it is precisely there that the apocalyptic struggle will have to be fought and won, the battle for Tara, Tailtiu and the River Boyne, and all traces of the foreign presence obliterated before the Gaels emerge triumphant (note that the overriding concern is not with the administrative centre of Dublin):

(a)	Déantar leision láimh re Tailltin	Beside Taílte let great towers
	túir mhóra do mhionchuma;	be pulverized by him
	sgriostar leis go bruinne mbrátha	let him sweep utterly away
	a muille a n-átha a n-iothlunna.	their mills, their kilns, their granaries.

The poet then turns his attention to the fifth province of *Midhe* and the Boyne, historically one of the divisions between the north and south of the country:

(b)	Foileóchthar leó learga Midhe	The slopes of Meath will be covered by them
	ré méid na gcreach gcathardha	with the vastness of the spoils from the cities
	budh iomdha slighe um Bóinn	the powerful cunning host will

mbreacgloin	make many a road
'gon bhróin neartmhair nathardha.	about the bright-trouted Boyne

(c) Líonfaidhear do linntibh corcra — The land of Meath will be flooded

clár Midhe ón dá mhearghasraidh, — with ruddy pools from the two vigorous bands

go n-éirghe fuil ós na formnaibh — until the blood rises above the shoulders

san mhuigh thonnghloin Teamhrach sain. — on that bright-surfaced plain of Tara

Muidhfidh ainnséin ar fhóir Saxan — Then will the Saxon tribe be vanquished

ré síol Ghaoidhil ghéirreannaigh, — by the seed of the keen-weaponed Gaels

nách bia do shíor ón ágh d'fhógra — so that there will be from proclamation of war

ós chlár Fhódla acht Éireannaigh.[32] — none save Irishmen over the land of Ireland.

Although the poem is addressed to Ó Ruairc of west Bréifne, the argument is presented in national terms: as the poet says, all Ireland will embark on war under his leadership (*leis ón tuinn chalaidh go' chéile, raghaidh Éire ar aon-chogadh*). Note also the use of *Éireannaigh* in the last line, a term whose inclusive and exclusive dimensions will be discussed in the next section. In any case, quite apart from the various references to 'Ireland' and 'Irish' in various guises, the fact that the poet centres his argument (literally) on the old symbolic and cultural unity of Ireland clinches the argument for a national dimension.

Although neither of the terms *dúthaigh* or *dúchas* is used in this poem, they occur in others of roughly the same period that are concerned with the same theme of how Ireland must be re-appropriated from foreign domination and control. One such poem, already cited in chapter 2, is 'Dia Libh a Laochruidh Ghaoidhiol', ('God with you, warriors of the Gaels!') by Aonghus Ó Dálaigh[33] dating from the 1580s. This poem is found in the *duanaire* or poem book of Fiacha mac Aodha Ó Broin, who joined Viscount Baltinglass in revolt in 1580 at the time of the second Desmond rebellion in Munster. Bradshaw identifies the political context as the growth of English colonialist aggression in south Leinster after the 1550s and 1560s, which, coupled with the defeat of the Kildare Fitzgeralds, enabled the rise of the O'Byrnes, especially the Col Raghnaill branch, of which Fiacha was a member.[34] According to Bradshaw, some of the poems in this poem book give evidence of new concerns among the poets: the traditional medieval theme of the glorification of the local dynast is now set in a national, not a local, context, and it is not the aggrandisement of the dynasty itself but rather its role in rejuvenating the national cause, the Irish race and nation, that is to the forefront. Interestingly, as Bradshaw points out, this is not yet the Catholic 'faith and fatherland' nationalism of the seventeenth century, already prefigured in Ó hUiginn's poem discussed below, but rather a type of ethnic Gaelic nationalism, which is evidenced by the first line:

Dia libh, a laochruidh Gaoidhiol![35]   God with you, warriors of the
Gaels!

The poet begins by exhorting the native Irish to avoid cowardice by reminding them of their pedigree in battle; the second stanza reinforces the national import of the message, which extends to the whole of the Gaelic Irish nation (*puirt úrghoirt innsi Gaoidhiol*): to defend and reclaim the native land (*bhar bhfearuinn dúthchais*). The importance of this emphasis on a putative 'Gaelic' component has already been discussed:

fá cheann **bhar bhfearuinn dúthchais**, on behalf of your native land,
puirt úrghoirt innsi Gaoidhiol[36]   the fresh fields of the island of
the Gaels.

The national theme continues in the following stanza, where the warriors of the Gaels are advised not to shirk battle if they wish to press their claim to the whole of Ireland. The poet further reminds them that, though they are banished to the periphery, vigilance is one of their primary allies. Note also the equivalence of *fearann dúchais* (for the syntax of which see chapter 2) and *fearann bhar sinnsear* 'the land of your ancestors', recalling the twelfth-century compound *sendúchus* above:

ag seilg troda ar fhéin eachtrann   hunting down the foreign
troop
'gá bhfuil **fearann bhar sinnsear**.[37]   that holds the lands of your
ancestors.

The poet then evokes a series of symbolic sites to which the Irish have been slow to press their claim (*agra*): we have the invocation of Tara (*Lios Teamhra*), Cashel, the seat of the high-kingship of Munster, Cruachain, the equivalent of Cashel in the western province of Connacht, and Tailte (Old Irish *Tailtiu*), which tradition associates with Ulster, as we have seen:

Mó as mall gur hagradh libh-si   You seem the more slow to
claim
Magh Life ná lios Teamhra   the plain of the Liffey or the
fort of Tara
ná Caisiol na sreabh nuaghlan   or Cashel of the ever clear
streams
ná míonchlár Cruachna Meadhbha.   or the smooth plain of Maeve's
Cruachain.

Is díoth cuimhne, a chlann.   It is loss of memory, O children
Míleadh . . .   of Míl . . .
. . . tug oirbh gan agra Tailtean.[38]   that has made you relinquish
your claim to Tailte.

We thus have a further example of the symbolic centre already discussed in this previous section. Note also in the following extract the identification of the expression *dúchas* with *fearunn dúthchais* (lit. 'land of *dúchas*') as above and its association with *oireacht* 'patrimony', 'assembly'. All these are opposed to the idea of *eachtruinn* 'foreigners' and also conceptually to the idea of outlawry in the following passage cited earlier:

Crádh liom eachtruinn dá bhfógra,	It kills me that foreigners have outlawed
ríoghradh Fhódla 's a n-oireacht	the kings of Fódla and their assemblies,
's nách goirthior dhíobh **'na ndúthchus**	and that all they are now called in their
acht ceithearn chúthail choilleadh.[39]	homeland are shifty woodland bandits.

There is further evidence of this opposition between *dúchas* and banditry in a contemporary proverb that appears in an early seventeenth-century poem of Scottish provenance—a cautionary poem that counsels prudence to a Highland chief after his sons have been taken captive by the Lowland Privy Council:

An senfhocal, a chúl chas: 'cothuigh go dían fad **dhúthchas**'	The maxim, curly-haired one: 'take good care of your inheritance,'
a thobar fial na bhfileadh, 's ná hiarr cogadh coillidheadh'.[40]	—generous fountain of poets— 'and do not seek the warfare of outlaws'.

Thus *dúchas* is identified with the centre of the social order, as opposed to outlaw elements of the periphery. Other poems of the period contrast this idea of the centre with the injustice of exile, and it is to one such text that we can now turn.

In a poem apparently composed in response to the Plantation of Ulster, 'Mo Thruaighe mar Táid Gaoidhil',[41] Fear Flatha Ó Gnímh (1602–c.1640) gives considerable attention to the violation of the physical aspects of the Irish landscape; its whole balance and fundamental rationale has been destroyed by the English and Scottish planters. A remarkable feature of Ó Gnímh's poem is its focus on the cultural dislocation that has occurred as a result of the Ulster Plantation, and in particular on the physical and material aspects of this dislocation:

Treóid Ghall i gcluaintibh a gcean.	The foreign herds in the meadows of their kine
túir aolta i n-áit a bhfoirgneadh,	lime-washed towers instead of their old houses;
margaidh uatha in gach oirear,	they have set up a market in every border area,
cruacha ar ardaibh aonaigheadh	and stacks of grain on the hillsides of assemblies.

Ní aithneann inis Logha   The island of Lugh recognizes
ní dá faithchibh fonnmhara,   nothing of its pleasant fields;
cnuic dhlaoiréidhe i ndiaidh a n-air;   lush-covered hills have been
                                         ploughed;
biaidh saoirÉire 'na Saxain.[42]'   noble Ireland will be another
                                         England.

Alienation takes the form of non-recognition. Thus Banbha, their foster-mother and the personification of Ireland, no longer recognizes the Irish as her own children. The Irish are consequently exiles in their own land ('na ndro-ing dheórata):

Is í an drong dhligheas d'aithne   To the island of Conn, it's the
                                         people
d'inis Chuinn is comhaithghe;   that it should recognize who are
                                         foreigners;
ní Goill is aoighidh aca,   it is not the English they
                                         consider strangers,
Gaoidhil 'na ndroing dheórata.[43]   the Irish are as an exiled troop.

The plight of the Irish is compared to the predicament of both the Trojans and the Chosen People of Israel. Note again the references to symbolic sites: Tara, Tailte and the River Boyne:

Mar lucht na Traoi ar n-a toghail   Like the people of Troy after its
                                         destruction
dá ndíchleith i ndíothrabhaibh   hiding in the wilderness
fian Teamhra a-táid ó Thailtin,   Tara's army is gone from Tailte
a bhfáid sealbha seachaintir   their native lands are given up.

Cosmhail re Cloinn Isra-hél   Like the children of Israel
thoir san Éighipt ar éidréan   in the east in feeble exile in
                                         Egypt,
Mic Mhíleadh um Bhóinn a-bhus   are the sons of Míl here about
                                         the Boyne,
ag síneadh dhóibh ó a ndúthchas.[44]   wandering away from their
                                         dúchas.

The loss of dúchas here is the retreat from the Boyne, the loss of Tara and Tailte. Note particularly the reference to the Irish as feeble exiles in their own land; later in the poem Ó Gnímh asks if the Irish will much longer be in exile. We shall see further below that the idea of dúchas is elsewhere found at this period contrasted with the theme of exile or situated within a context of exile. Once again, the last two lines here make explicit the 'Milesian' connection discussed above. Earlier in the poem Ó Gnímh had already spoken of the Irish as under the oppression of a foreign army, and he makes reference to the dire possibility that Ireland will become another England. Here dúchas is the focal point of a sense of loss or alienation.

As has been stated above, the poet concentrates on the material and symbolic desecration that has occurred as the result of plantation. This theme is echoed in another poem of the same period, 'Cáit ar ghabhadar Gaoidhil' attributed to Lochlainn Ó Dálaigh:

Roinnid f eatorra féin,	They divide it up amongst themselves
an chríoch-sa chloinne saoir Néill,	this territory of the children of noble Niall
gan phoinn do mhoigh lachtmhair Fhloinn	without a jot of Flann's milky plain
nach bhfoil 'na acraibh agoinn.	that we don't find becoming mere 'acres'.
. . . Cóir a ttuiriomh—tarrthaidh sinn	We have witnessed egregious changes
iomlaoid éaxamhla ar Éirinn,	upon Ireland—it is right to bewail them
'n a mbiadh iongnadh riomh roimhe	which would have been wondrous at any previous time
fa fhiadh lionnghlan Laoghaire.	upon the sparkling-watered land of Laoghaire.
Tarramar—trom an pudhar— Puirt oireachais d'fhásughadh,	Heavy is the shame! We have witnessed seats of government being made desolate
na torchoirthe ag searg a sreibh, dorchfhoithre sealg 'na sráidibh.	the produce wasting in a stream dark thickets of the chase become thoroughfares.
. . . Aonuighe a n-áitibh sealga, sealga ar slighthibh suaitheanda, creasa tar fhaithche d'fhál air	Assemblies in places of hunting hunts upon illustrious streets belts of the hedges of cultivation over the plain's face
gan dál ghraifne fá a ngruadhaibh.[45]	without a meet over its cheeks.

The poetry of this period reacts to events, such as the Plantation of Ulster, the importance of which transcend the merely local. The alleged national scope or 'proto-nationalist' nature of such poetry has been contested, for example by Dunne,[46] who rejects any analysis in terms of a historiography that would seek antecedents for the nationalism of the nineteenth and twentieth centuries in this earlier material. In discussing Dunne's views, Gibbons makes the point that the amorphous and decentralized nature of Irish society was actually its strength against Tudor expansionism, the paradigm being one of native resistance to the concentration of power in the centre.[47] Significantly, Gibbons entitles his discussion 'identity without a centre'. Yet the texts we

have been considering show a marked preoccupation with a *symbolic* or ideological centre, which we can perhaps situate in the context of what Cohn,
in a discussion of regionalism in India, calls a 'symbol pool' of associations.[48]
This symbolic pool can consist of various types of cultural and historical artefact, from literature on the one hand to religious shrines and important land-
marks on the other. A significant concomitant of this symbolism is the fact
that regions are defined according to their centre rather than their boundary
or periphery.

The Rees brothers also make a telling analogy between the organization of
the provinces and the sequence of invasions as detailed in *Lebor Gabála Érenn*,
the crucial one being between the fifth province, 'Midhe', and the fifth or
'Gaelic' invasion of the sons of Míl as the final piece in the political puzzle: it
was the Milesians who gave Tara its name, and it is *Midhe* that is associated
with the mythological function of kingship, as set out, for example, in the Middle Irish text known as 'The Settling of the Manor of Tara', which defines the
extent and the attributes of each of the five provinces.[49] While the historical
record suggests that the idea of a *de facto* political high-kingship is a relatively
late one, nevertheless the idea of a 'fifth' presupposes an underlying unity as
argued here, the reflex of an old cosmographic schema. Indeed, as Mac Cana
points out, the propaganda associated with the high-kingship depends for any
effect it might have on the persistence and pervasiveness of this *idea* of an
underlying unity, which receives reinforcement at various junctures in the
medieval period—critically for example at the time of the Viking invasions,
when the obstinate resistance staged by the Uí Néill dynasties invoked precisely the idea of the Tara high-kingship as a focal point of such resistance.[50]
In addition, Ó Corráin argues that the Irish learned classes were preoccupied
with the consciousness of themselves as a larger 'natio' and that, moreover, by
the eleventh and twelfth centuries there were increasing attempts to convert
that consciousness to more tangible political reality.[51] As Ó Corráin observes,
this consciousness, based on the same origin legend, informs the main corpus
of genealogies and also aspects of the legal corpus from an early period, and
we have already considered how it could still be evoked in a very pragmatic
way in a seventeenth-century context.[52]

What we have here, therefore, is a classic disparity between political and
cultural-symbolic realities; indeed scholars of other societies have stressed the
inverse relation that often seems to obtain between the two. Cultural homo-
geneity may render centralized political structures irrelevant and otiose; in fact
Fortes and Evans-Pritchard argue that 'bonds of utilitarian interest between
individuals and between groups are not as strong as the bonds implied in common attachment to mystical symbols'.[53]

As Mac Cana points out, the main harbingers of this idea of Irish unity in
the medieval period were the hereditary, professional poets—attached to a
local patron but with unrivalled freedom of movement throughout Ireland.[54]
The topos of unity is frequently used as a rather conventional device in the

medieval period, but, as Mac Cana and others more recently have pointed out, it acquires a more urgent relevance after the middle of the sixteenth century. Political disunity was tolerable as long as shared cultural values and ideology were paramount; it is when these latter come under threat in the late sixteenth and early seventeenth centuries that the 'cult of the centre', the symbolic centre, acquires added cogency.

'Fearann cloidhimh críoch Bhanbha': native Irish and Old English in the sixteenth century

The passage from Ó Súilleabháin Béirre's letter to Philip III of Spain, discussed above, contains a further contextualization cue of the importance of national identity in seventeenth-century Ireland. We may note an apparent terminological distinction where he uses two different national designations: (*a*) *Éireannaigh*, translated into English as 'Irish', and (*b*) *(príomh)G(h)aioghuil na hÉireann* 'the meere Irish' or 'native' Irish (Ó Cuív: 'the chief Gaelic people of Ireland'):

(*a*) Atá riamh . . . dá hshíordhearbhadh eadrainne na **hÉireannaigh**

   It hath beene ever . . . manifestly proued . . . among us the Irish

(*b*) Ar mbheith dúinne, **príomhGhaoighuil na hÉireann**, cían ó hshoin ar ttarr[a]ng ar bphréimhe ⁊ ar mbunadhuis ó threibh ord[h]ruic fhíorúasal na nEasbáinneach .i. ó Mhíleadh.

   Wee *the meere Irish* long sithence deriving our roote and originall from the famous and noble race of the Spaniards: viz. from Milecius.[55]

Ó Buachalla discusses succinctly the background to this terminological difference.[56] The words *Éireannach* and Gaedheal (*Gael*) were originally used synonymously. Later in the medieval period the term *Éireannach* came to include all the inhabitants of Ireland; this is its semantic range in the annals of the fifteenth and sixteenth centuries. The early seventeenth century, on the other hand, sees the formation of a detente between Gaelic Irish and Old English to produce the emergent Irish nation, founded on the common confessional identity of Counter-Reformation Catholicism. At this point *Éireannach* acquires an exclusive element: those not of the Catholic faith are excluded.

Caball has argued that an early example of this new national understanding is a poem by Tadhg Dall Ó hUiginn, 'Fearann Cloidhimh Críoch Bhanbha', ('The land of Ireland is sword land'), addressed to MacWilliam Burke in the 1570s.[57] Before we consider Ó hUiginn's poem in detail, let us retrace our steps with regard to some of the relevant terms. We have already considered the following passage from the twelfth century *Cogadh Gaedhel re Gallaibh* with the expression *fíor gcatha* 'just cause' (literally 'truth of battle'). The import of the passage is that this justice is guaranteed when defending the native land (*dúthaigh* or *dúchas*) but not where the antithetical *fearann cloidhimh* 'sword land' is concerned:

> Asbert ba fearr a **fír catha** ocus comlaind sin inna **nduthaig** . . . innas im **an ferand forgabala ocus claidim**.[58]

> He said that their cause ('battle truth') was more just in their native land . . . than territory taken by conquest and by the sword.

Some four centuries later the same language is being used in sixteenth-century Ireland in the cause of 'faith and fatherland' against the heretic Queen Elizabeth I. Three letters have survived in Irish by the leader of the Desmond resistance of the 1570s, James Fitzmaurice Fitzgerald, written to various gallowglass leaders in Munster as in the following to Aisdunn Mac Domhnaill (18 July 1579):

> Agus is coruide dho theacht, is maith an **fíor gcatha** atá aguinn hi n-aghaidh ár námhud .i. sinne ag cosnamh ár gcreidimh ⁊ **ár ndúthaighe**, agus iad san ag cur an chreidimh ar gcúl ⁊ ar tí **ár nduthaidhe féin** do bhuain dínne; sinne ar an bhfírinne ⁊ iad-san ar an mbréig . . .[59]

> And it is the more right to come, because we have a just war against our enemies, i.e. we are defending our religion and our native country, and they are setting aside the faith and about to take our own native land from us; we are on the side of truth, they are on the side of falsehood.

This expression *ag cosnamh ár gcreidimh agus ár ndúthaighe* is something of a stock phrase in Fitzmaurice Fitzgerald's correspondence. In a recent study of aspects of the political ideology of this period in Irish sources, Mac Craith concludes that the use of *dúthaigh* in such contexts shows that the focus cannot be entirely a national or nationalist one.[60] This point will be taken up below. The more significant ideological development that takes place in the sixteenth century, however, concerns the perceived relationship between *dúthaigh* and *fearann cloidhimh*, and for this we will turn to Ó hUiginn's poem, which is roughly contemporary with the letters of Fitzgerald.

First, however, further light is shed on the idea of *fearann cloidhimh* by a passage in the *Leabhar Muimhneach*, which, like the original passage from *Cogadh Gaedhel re Gallaibh* above, has relevance to the putative relationship of the Dál gCais to the kingship of Cashel. The high king of Munster, Feidhlimidh Mac Criomhthainn, has set about securing hostages and pledges in the usual manner from the various kings of Munster, who refuse, however, to submit to him unless he first demand hostages from the Dál gCais (*clanna Luighdheach*). However, as Feidhlimidh points out to them, he does not have the same entitlement to hostages from them, and the reason is as follows:

> ní raibhe fearann cathaoire Caisil fa chlannaibh Luighdheach amhail do bhí futhaibhsean acht **feronn forgabhála cloidhimh** fri ré cian.[61]

> The clanna Luighdheach did not inhabit the lands of Cashel's seat as they did but rather conquered sword land since ancient times.

Here *fearann cloidhimh* is opposed to *fearann cathaoire* and is in effect outside
the king's jurisdiction for that reason. When Feidhlimidh leads the men of
Munster on a hosting to secure hostages from the Dál gCais, they are met with
precisely that same response: not only was the king of Cashel not entitled to
hostages but it was an act of tyranny (*anfhlaithes*) for him to seek them:

> dáigh ní thug athair ná seanathair dá dtáinig rompa géill do rígh do
> ríoghaibh Éireann riamh, óir **ferann forgabhála is cloidhimh** bhaoi
> futhaibh; agus níorbha do chóigedh Mumhan é; agus níor dhligh neach
> ní dhíobh.[62]

> since none of their ancestors before them had given hostages to any king
> of the kings of Ireland, as the land they inhabited was sword land and
> conquered territory and did not belong to the province of Munster; and
> nobody was entitled to anything from them.

In other words, the *fearann cloidhimh* stands outside the expression of the underlying unity inherent in the word *cóigeadh* (*cúige*), as discussed above. We may
remember also the passage from *Cogadh Gaedhel re Gallaibh* above where the Dál
gCais had maintained that their cause would be more just defending Cashel as
their *dúthaigh* than any *fearann cloidhimh ocus forgabhála* that they might have
acquired. In fact this is very much part of the particular context here as well: the
Dál gCais are aggrieved that they have been deprived of their *cert comhd-
húthchasa,* their 'right of joint sovereignty', to the kingship of Cashel:

> Agus ní cúis uma ndlighfidhe ní dhíobh .i. **cert comhdhúthchasa** Caisil
> fria ré tríochad ríogh gan chóir ná chert ná sealuighecht do chomhall
> dóibh uime.[63]

> And this was not a reason why they should owe anything: the right of
> the joint inheritance of Cashel which for the duration of the reigns of
> thirty kings had been denied them without justice or right or alternation.

The question of this verb *dligh* and its relationship to *dúchas* will be taken up
in a later chapter.

A further view is given on the relationship between the use of force and
the question of 'right', as embodied by both *dúthaigh* and *dúchas,* in a fascinating early fifteenth-century poem by Tuathal Ó hUiginn, 'Do Roinneadh
Ríghe Connacht', ('The kingdom of Connachta has been divided').[64] The poem
is addressed to Eoghan Ó Raghallaigh, lord of Bréifne from 1418 to 1449,
whom the poet urges to end the partition of Connacht by seizing Cruachain,
the ancient seat of the high-kingship of the province and by rejecting English
law, as epitomized here by the acquisition and acceptance of land by way of
charter (*cairt*).[65] His address to Ó Raghallaigh is therefore not simply about the
physical re-appropriation of land but is much more a rejection of the entire
rationale that underlies an alien legal system, symbolized by the *cairt ainbhfine*
or 'foreign charter', the recognition of which amounts to a betrayal of the
native Irish heritage:

(a) Cairt ainbhfine ar Inis Fáil   What does it matter to the son of
                                                   Seán
     cá meisde do mhac Sea-áin?   that there is a foreign charter to
                                                   Inis Fáil?
     sa chartaigh má déaghthar dhi   If you look at Éire herself she and
                                                   all her acres
     léaghthar 'n-a hacraibh Éire   are to be found named in that
                                                   charter.

     Gach Gall aca lenab áil   Every Gall who wants
     sealbh an oiléinse d'fhagháil   possession of the island
     cairt ó rígh Shagsan do shir   asks a charter for it from the King
                                                   of the Saxons
     le a ngabhsan tír Airt Éinfhir.   with which he takes over the land
                                                   of Art Aoinfhear.

(b) Sliocht na gcéidfhear dá bhfuil féin   No man of the race of Míl
     ní leanann—is lorg soiléir—   is to be successor of the race of
                                                   the ancients
     rádh cairte dá gcuire i seadh   of whose blood he is—this is
                                                   clear—
     duine do mhaicne Míleadh.[66]   if he pays heed to the language of
                                                   the charter.

In anticipation of the arguments to be used by Tadhg Dall Ó hUiginn almost
two centuries later (see below), the poet draws the necessary moral. Since the
Gaelic Irish seized the land of Ireland from the Tuatha Dé Danann by force,
they recognize one kind of charter only to the *dúthaigh,* which is the valour to
take the land at the point of a sword or spear. In fact, since the days of the
Túatha Dé Danann, Ireland has never been taken except by force:

(b) Síol Féilim ó shoin nír shir   Ever since then Féilim's race
     troigh d'Éirinn acht ar éigin.   have never taken land except by
                                                   force.

(c) Cairt eile ní iarrfa sibh   Thou shalt seek no other charter
     acht tú ar thoradh do ghaisgidh;   except thy own reliance on thy
                                                   gallantry:
     léim fa ghaoibh géara dod ghuin   to charge against the sharp spears
                                                   that pierce thee
     séala dhaoibh ar do **dhúthaigh**.   is thy true charter to thy land.

     An chraoiseach leathan sa láimh   The sharp spear in thy hand
     's an colg a ceardcha Bholcáin   the blade from Volcan's smithy
     madh faigse hí budh hí an tsleagh   the spear if it be nearer thee—
     is í do chairtse an cloidheamh.   the sword is thy charter.

(*d*)   Cairt eile thógbhus tusa   Another charter shalt thou raise
                                                         aloft

         dá dtig táth do **dhúthchasa**   a charter that will unite all thy
                                                         native land

         tógbha sgiath i nglotain gháidh   thou shalt raise up thy spear in
                                                         the face of danger

         docair dá thriath a thógbháil.[67]   even its lord can hardly lift it.

In other words, native Irish ideology gives seizure by force its imprimatur. Earlier in the poem Ó hUiginn makes it plain that Ó Raghallaigh's true inheritance (*dúthaigh fhíre*) is the high-kingship of Connacht as symbolized by the ancient royal stronghold of Cruachain:

(*f*)   **Dúthaigh fhíre** hí don fhior,   The true country of the hero
         Cruacha caithir a sinnsior,   is Cruacha his ancestor's fort
         ní ghairfe mé acht deoradh dhe   if Eoghan remains in Bréifne
         Eoghan dá mbé sa Bhréifne.[68]   I can only call him an exile.

Finally, the poet reveals the reason for Eoghan's reluctance to stake his claim to his heritage:

(*g*)   Fian Gall do ghabháil treise   The seizing of power by the Goill
                                                         (foreigners)
         ar mínleach na Midheise.   over the plain of Midhe.

Note the contrast implied here between the true native land (*dúthaigh fhíre*) and *deoradh* 'exile', which prefigures the conceptual opposition between *dúchas* and the injustice of exile found in Ó Gnímh's seventeenth-century poem discussed above. Once again we have both Cruachain and Midhe as symbolic centres that need to be reclaimed.

As we see here, physical force is one of the unifying elements of the *dúchas* (*táth do dhúthchusa*). Furthermore, in light of the consideration given above to the expression *fearann cloidhimh* ('sword land') and its putative opposition to the 'native' place (or *dúthaigh/dúchas*), the phrase *is í do chairtse an cloidheamh* 'the sword is thy charter' is an interesting one, as indeed the sword is now the charter to the *dúchas* (*cairt dá dtig táth do dhúthchasa* 'charter that will unite all thy native land') and not just an instrument of brutal force. In a sense the antithetical relationship between inherited land and conquered land is stood on its head in a way that anticipates Tadhg Dall Ó hUiginn's poem of the late sixteenth century. Ó hUiginn begins his poem by saying that Ireland is nothing but sword land, thus acknowledging the claim of the strongest to its territory;[69] and the way in which he hammers on the ideas of *ceart* and *cóir*, both meaning 'right' or 'just claim', and elaborates on their relationship to the use of force (*neart, éigean*), is noteworthy:

         Fearann cloidhimh críoch   The land of Banbha is but sword
               Bhanbha,   land,
         bíoth slán cháich fá chomhardha   let all be defied to show

go bhfuil d'oighreacht ar Fhiadh bhFáil

acht foirneart gliadh dá gabháil.

that any can inherit the Land of Fál

save by conquest by force of battle.

Ní fhuil cóir uirre ag aoinfhear—
críoch shuaitheanta shean Ghaoidheal
bheith fa neart an té is treise—

is é ceart na críchese.

No one man has any claim to
the shining land of the ancient Gaels:
to be under the power of the strongest
is the law of this country.

Ní fhuil do cheart ar chrích bhFáil
ag Macaibh Míleadh Easbáin,
's ní bhí ag gach gabháil dár gheabh,

acht sí d'fhagháil ar éigean.[70]

There is no right to the land of Fál
on the part of Sons of Míl of Spain
nor on the part of any other conquest
except to take her by force.

The poet then recounts how Ireland was conquered by various waves of invaders. In the mythico-historical scheme of *Lebor Gabála Érenn* the fifth and final wave is represented by the Gaels,[71] but, in a significant anticipation of Céitinn's *Foras Feasa ar Éirinn* of the 1630s, the poet extends the scheme to include the Anglo-Normans and their descendants and issues a refutation to those who impute foreignness to them.[72] Note that the word used here for foreigners is once again *deóraidh* 'non-natives' or 'exiles'; we shall have reason to consider this item again later:

Gi bé adéaradh gur deóraidh

Búrcaigh na mbeart n-inleóghain—
faghar d'fhuil Ghaoidhil nó Ghoill

nách bhfuil 'na aoighidh agoinn.

Whoever says that they are foreigners
the Burkes of the lion-like deeds
let one be found of the blood of Gael or Gall
who is not a guest among us.

Gi bé adeir nách dleaghar dháibh

a gcuid féin d'Éirinn d'fhagháil
cia san ghurt bhraonnuaidhe bhinn
nách lucht aonuaire d'Éirinn?

Whoever says that they do not deserve
to receive their share of Ireland
who in the sweet dewy field
are more than visitors to Ireland?

Gé adeirdís sliocht Ghaoidhil Ghlais
coimhighthe le cloinn Séarlais—

clocha toinighthe bheann mBreagh—
coimhighthe an dream adeireadh.[73]

Though the descendants of Gaoidheal Glas
used to call the children of Charles foreigners
set stones of Banbha's hills
they were foreigners who used to say that.

For Leerssen, this poem is to be placed firmly in the context of 'cultural frater-
nization' between the descendants of what he calls the 'Hiberno-Normans' and
the native Irish,[74] both equally threatened by the growing aggressiveness of the
Tudor monarchy in Ireland, rather than read as a cynical betrayal of the Irish
cause, as Dunne had interpreted it.[75] Similarly, Caball sees the poem as evidence of the tension afflicting the native Irish literati in the face of English
expansionism in the 1570s and an effort on Ó hUiginn's part to formulate a
sense of shared national identity between the two groups.[76] As indicated above,
this involved rehabilitating the Gaelicized descendants of the Anglo-Normans,
bringing them in from the margins of the formalized medieval Irish world view.
In other words, the Burkes and their peers represent in fact a sixth wave of
invaders to be grafted onto the Milesian schema: as Caball remarks, this accommodation was to assume great importance by the beginning of the seventeenth
century in the hands of Céitinn in particular. The poem continues:

Dul uatha ag Éirinn ní fhuil	Ireland cannot escape from them
deich mbliadhna ar cheithre chéadaibh	for four centuries and ten years
atá an tír thiormarsaidh thais	has the warm, ancient, humid land
fa fhionnghasraidh shíl Shéarlais.	been under the fair warriors of the seed of Charles.
Is siad féin is uaisle d'fhuil;	It is they who are noblest in blood
iad is fhearr fhuair an **dúthaigh**;	they who have best won the heritage
díobh is doibheanta **Bóinn Bhreagh**	from them the *Bregian Boyne* cannot be taken
oireachta dan cóir creideamh.	nobles to whom homage is fitting.
Ní thiocfa 's ní tháinig riamh—	There will not be, nor has there ever been,
an chlann do chin ó Uilliam—	a line equal in power to the race
fine ar chumhachtaibh 'na gcruth	that sprang from William
cumhachtaigh **Thighe Teamhrach**.[77]	rulers of the *Dwelling of Tara*.

Here Ó hUiginn makes the most telling use of the word *dúthaigh* and its associations to bring his argument full circle: if all of Ireland is *fearann cloidhimh*,
based on the Gaelic origin legend, it is also the *dúthaigh*, the claim to which is
based on longevity of tenure; as Caball points out, the legitimacy of the Burkes
in Ireland is predicated on a long and venerable occupation of their land (*Dul
uatha ag Éirinn ní fhuil | deich mbliadhna ar cheithre chéadaibh*) and a nobility for
which they deserve credence (*oireachta dan cóir creideamh*).[78] The remit of the
concept of *dúthaigh* is indexed here by the references to the Boyne and Tara,
where we are again at the symbolic centre as opposed to any geopolitical

allusions to the Burkes' own territory in Tyrawley, Co. Mayo. This, it seems to me, represents a bold ideological leap compared with the passage considered above from the twelfth-century 'Cogadh Gaedhel re Gallaibh', which posits a more or less antithetical relation between *fearann cloidhimh* and *dúthaigh* based on the criterion of the 'just cause' (*fíor gcatha*).

Aside from its dedication to MacWilliam Burke, the poem also bears a dedication to the native Irish chief O'Donnell, as follows:

Conn Ó Domhnaill, Dia dhá dhíon	Conn O'Donnell, may God protect him
géag bhuadhach d'fhuil na n-airdríogh;	Precious scion of the race of the high kings
fear gan mhaothchroidhe um cheann gcean	a man without lack of courage in exploits
ceann na laochroidhe ó Lithfear.[79]	leader of the warriors from Lifford.

Caball draws attention to this 'simple but meaningful gesture' in the context of the poem's presentation of the descendants of both Gael and Anglo-Norman as heirs to the land of Ireland.[80] It seems to me that the additional dedication of this poem to O'Donnell in particular has a possible further significance, however. The evidence for this contention is taken from Lughaidh Ó Cléirigh's *Beatha Aodha Ruaidh Uí Dhomhnaill*, a work of political propaganda on behalf of the O'Donnells in which their claim to historical dominion over the MacWilliam Burkes is asserted.[81] On more than one occasion we are reminded of the foreignness of the Burkes, how they had originated in France and gone to England, whence they had come to Ireland and seized the land of Tyrawley (*Tír nAmhalgadha*) in Co. Mayo from its rightful indigenous inhabitants (*na tuatha diarbho toich*):

> Ba sain ceinél ro aitreibh í an ionbaidh sin ⁊ na tuatha diarbho toich ó chéin mháir. Búrcaigh slondadh an cheneoil rotus-n-aitreb an tan sin. Ba do Fhrancaibh a **mbunadh**chenél ⁊ a criochaibh Saxan . . . ro chedghabhsat an chrioch.[82]

> The people who lived in it at that time were distinct from the people to whom it had rightfully belonged in antiquity. Burke was the name of the family who inhabited it at that time. Their origin was French and it was from England . . . that they had first taken possession of the land.

Note in particular the association of the Burkes with a French (or Norman) as opposed to a 'Spanish' (i.e. native Irish) origin and the characterization of this connection in terms of *bunadh,* the same term that underlies *bunadhus,* as discussed above. This particular text contains further references to the perceived otherness of the Burkes among Gaelic Irish society of the north and west of Ireland, in addition to their claimed subordination to the O'Donnells:

> Do-thaot ann tra Mac Uilliam Burc Teaboitt m Uateir Chiotaigh ⁊ **cenib do Ghoidelaibh dhó** ba duthaig dfhior a ionaid cia no thíosadh úair

> batar a shinnsir riamh . . . fo chíos do Chenel cConaill *m* Néill ónd úair
> ro gabsatt na Burcaigh for fhoirb Amalgadha *m* Fiachrach.[83]

> There came also Tibbot, the Mac William Burke, son of Walter Ciotach,
> *and though he was not of the Gaels*, it was right for his deputy to come, as
> his ancestors . . . had always been subject to Cineal Chonaill, ever since
> the Burkes had occupied the land of Amhalgadh mac Fiachach.

Finally, an entry for 1580 in *Annála Ríoghachta Éireann* may reflect the existence of a certain dissatisfaction at MacWilliam Burke's lack of bellicosity and his tendency to collaborate with the authorities:

> Mac Uilliam Búrc . . . nó chonccnadh do gnáth lásan b-prionnsa do écc[84]

> MacWilliam Burke . . . who always assisted the sovereign, died

In the poem under discussion, Ó hUiginn seems to be addressing his message of accommodation to O'Donnell and prevailing native Irish attitudes in the north-west of Ireland as much as to MacWilliam Burke himself.

There is a further important point to consider here in relation to the use of *dúthaigh* and its attendant symbolism. Here the Burkes are associated with the great symbolic site of Tara, the ideological focus of the high-kingship of Ireland but an area with which they have no direct historical or geographical connection and to which they have no realistic political claim. The use of *dúthaigh* here is again a contextualization cue to a wider cultural and ideological reality, the fuller importance of which will be discussed in the next section. It is thus what Cohn in another context calls a 'symbol pool' of associations.[85] As was argued above on the basis of the passage from the twelfth-century *Cogadh Gaedhel re Gallaibh*, I believe that in the case of *dúthaigh* we are dealing with a designation for place that is primarily symbolic rather than spatial, political or geographical in orientation.

Ó hUiginn's poem raises the question of the criteria of both inclusivity and exclusivity with regard to the accommodation of 'newcomers'. In a similar vein an interesting passage in Céitinn's *Foras Feasa ar Éirinn*, expands on the general relation between *ceart*—'right', 'claim', 'entitlement' (*DIL*)—and *dúchas* and should be closely considered in view of the emphasis placed by Ó hUiginn on the former term (along with the largely synonymous *cóir*) as an agent of legitimization.[86] The context is given by the events of 1169 in which Diarmaid Mac Murchadha, king of Leinster, and his Anglo-Norman ally Robert Fitzstephen face the advancing king of Connacht and aspiring high king of Ireland, Ruaidhrí Ó Conchobhair, and are reluctant to engage him in battle.[87] The upshot is that Ruaidhrí requests Fitzstephen to leave Ireland on the following grounds:

(*a*)   nach raibhe **ceart ná dúthchas** aige ar bheith innte

    as he had neither right nor *dúchas* to be there

Peace is eventually concluded as follows:

(b)   Cúigeadh Laighin do léigeadh do Dhiarmaid **amhail fá dúthchas dó;**
agus d'fhiachaibh ar Dhiarmaid umhla is dísle do choimhéad do
Ruaidhrí **amhail fá dual do gach rígh** *dá* mbíodh ar Laighnibh do
dhéanamh do ríoghaibh Éireann.

Diarmaid was left the province of Leinster as was *dúchas* for him; and
Diarmaid was obliged to submit to and remain loyal to Ruaidhrí as had
[always] been *dual* to every king of Leinster to submit to the kings of
Ireland.

Here *dúchas* occurs disjunctively (cf. *ná* 'nor') with the more general term *ceart*,
and the relevant point of contrast here appears to be the issue of indigenous-
ness as opposed to foreignness: Diarmaid's birthright gives him the kingship
of Leinster as his *dúchas* or hereditary right, while his subordination in turn to
Ó Conchobhair is dictated by what is *dual,* a term to be discussed in detail in
chapter 4 but that may by roughly glossed here as 'established custom'.
Fitzstephen, however, is on all counts excluded from any kind of right or
claim, and it is therefore worthwhile in the present context examining further
Céitinn's attitude to Fitzstephen as expressed elsewhere in his history. Céitinn
characterizes Fitzstephen as one of five evil leaders of the Norman conquest
who had visited more destruction and violence on Ireland than there had been
in the previous two centuries combined.[88] This treachery and tyranny is contrasted, however, with those other leaders of the Norman invasion (*gabháltas
Gall*) who did much good in Ireland by respecting native traditions and by
becoming acculturated to them over time.[89] The former group significantly left
no heirs or descendants; the latter, on the other hand, prospered in Ireland
and Céitinn expressly includes the Burkes among their number. Elsewhere
Céitinn makes a distinction between the idea of a pagan conquest (*gabháltas
pagánta*) and a Christian conquest (*gabháltas Críostamhail*), characterizing the
pagan conquest as one that shows no respect for native tradition and that in
fact exterminates the original inhabitants and obliterates their language as part
of the act of appropriation.[90] The Christian conquest, on the other hand, is
content to accept the submission of the original inhabitants and to introduce
new settlers from the metropolis to co-exist peacefully alongside them.

As Bradshaw points out,[91] it is possible to put Céitinn's ideological position here in a wider European context of the contemporary debates on the
nature and legitimacy of conquest in the Americas.[92] Céitinn's notion of the
pagan conquest accords with the views of Sepúlveda, for example, that the
indigenous inhabitants might legitimately be conquered and enslaved, while
his notion of the Christian conquest tallies with the ideas of de las Casas that
native inhabitants have certain rights of dominion (*dominium*) based on
natural law. More recently, Clare Carroll has shown that the arguments
employed by Pilib Ó Súilleabháin Béirre in his Latin history of 1621 are based
on a Suárezian interpretation of such natural law concepts as *dominium* and
consuetudo or 'custom', and it is interesting to consider this latter term in the

light of Céitinn's use of *dual* in the passage quoted above.[93] Ó hUiginn's poem addressed to MacWilliam Burke argues for an acknowledgment of the right of those inhabitants of Ireland historically marginal to the Gaelic Irish society who had remained in long and successful occupation of the land of Ireland. This is reminiscent of the *praescriptio longi temporis* of natural law which in effect turns a *dominium de facto* into a *dominium de iure*. In other words, the continuing successful existence of a claim constitutes its own (retrospective) legitimacy; and this is the basis of Burke's entitlement (*ceart*) to the '*dúthaigh*'.[94] In fact it is no accident that an Irish proverb still current expressly links the concept of *dúthaigh* or *dúiche* with the idea of permanence:

> Is buan fear ina **dhúiche**.
>
> A man endures in his native land.[95]

It is this idea of permanence that is crucial to Ó hUiginn's argument above.

Among Céitinn's catalogue of the Norman leaders who did good in Ireland, and whose descendants had therefore continued to thrive, are also the Nugents, or *Nuinnsionnaigh*. Another interesting dimension to *dúchas* at this period arises in the poetry of Nuinsean, of Old English stock and not of the hereditary Gaelic Irish bardic tradition. He nevertheless composes poetry in the syllabic metres of the professional poets. Nuinsean's poetry offers a fascinatingly different view of the idea of *dúchas* as available in the 1570s, a version that, although less politically fraught or freighted perhaps than the instances discussed up to now, is nevertheless compatible with them and arguably constitutes an enrichment of them. Two famous poems of exile have come down to us from Nuinsean written after 1571, when he had gone to study at Oxford. In these two poems he taps into a contemporary strain of Renaissance patriotism, the rediscovery of the Classical idea of the *patria*, the simple love of the native land.

In the poem 'Fada i n-Éagmais Inse Fáil', ('A long time absent from Ireland'), the poet talks longingly of the physical and cultural attractions of Ireland. These he contrasts with the misery he feels at being domiciled in England.[96] The poem gives a beautiful sense of Bradshaw's characterization of sixteenth-century patriotism as 'inward-looking and protective' rather than 'aggressively expansionist'.[97] I will begin the consideration of this poem by giving the first and last stanzas, as the occurrence of *dúchas* in each of them serves to frame the poem's content:

Fada i n-éagmais inse Fáil	A long time absent from Ireland
i Saxaibh (dia do dhiombáidh):	in England enough cause for dejection
sia an bhliadhain ó Bhanbha a-bhus	away from Ireland the year seems longer here
('s labhra dhiamhuir **ar ndúthchus**).	it's a mysterious saying: 'our *dúchas*'.

Gibé uaibh do bheath a-bhus,	Whoever of you who happens to be here
dá roiche a-rís **dá dhúthchus**,	if he reaches again his *dúchas*
fearr ós chách do-chím a chor:	I see his state as better than anyone's:
go bráth ó' thír ní thiogfadh.	never would he leave his land.

In the final stanza *dúchas* can reasonably be translated as 'homeland', 'native land'; but note in the first stanza on the other hand Nuinsean's own recognition of the shifting indexical quality of *dúchas* in the line 'it's a mysterious saying our *dúchas*': it is a quality that makes the time seem longer when he is absent from it. Having devoted considerable attention to describing the beauty and prosperity of Ireland, Nuinsean then refers to the poets of Ireland as *filidh cláir Ghall a's Ghaoidheal* 'the poets of that land where Gaill (foreigners) and Gaels live', a reference that represents precisely the accommodation between Gaelic Irish and Old English that was adumbrated in Ó hUiginn's poem in political terms above.

Elliott speaks of 'the increasingly confident use in sixteenth-century Europe of the words *patria* and *patrie*'.[98] In the same vein Caball speaks of the 'burgeoning sense of patriotism' evident in Nuinsean's poems, whereby the poet uses his experience of foreign culture to set in relief those aspects of Ireland that he regards as characteristic and determinate of identity.[99] Simms refers to a 'new concept of patriotism' in Nuinsean's poems, spawned by the Renaissance and Counter-Reformation,[100] while both Mac Craith and Caball also connect the evolution of the exile genre—a genre that Nuinsean was among the first to cultivate—to the Renaissance rediscovery of the idea of *patria*, which is as much inclusive of people and culture as of territory.[101] In Nuinsean's poem the idea of *dúchas* forms the pragmatic essence of this patriotism in both its more material and its more elusive, emotive and subjective aspects. However, the impression should not be given that such a version of patriotism was the preserve of the Old English at this period. In a poem composed in Rome in the late sixteenth century, 'A Fhir Théid go Fiadh bhFuinidh', Maol Mhuire Ó hUiginn, archbishop of Tuam in the years 1586 to 1590 and brother of the more famous poet Tadhg Dall Ó hUiginn, envies a companion about to set off on a journey home to Ireland:

A fhir théid go Fiadh bhFuinidh,	O man who goes to the land of Ireland
mo-chean toisg dá dtriallfaidhir!	happy the reason for your journey
críoch naomhda thirmlinnte the	blessed warm land of dried up lakes (?)
maordha an fhirminte uaiste.[102]	noble the sky above her.

After an idealized discussion of the merits and delights of Ireland, the poet chastises the Irish for their sinfulness and arrogance:

Fuilngidh Día **dúthaigh** a sean	God suffers the *dúthaigh* of their ancestors
tré anuabhar Mac Míleadh,	through the trumped-up pride of the sons of Míl
tír ainglidhe fá n iadh tonn,	angelic land enclosed by the wave
fá rian ainbhfine eachtrann.[103]	to be under the rein of foreign oppression.

As Caball points out, this poem is noteworthy for its treatment of a theme that is to become a commonplace rationalization of the Irish Catholic predicament in the seventeenth century: the Irish people are suffering the wrath of God for their trumped-up arrogance and sinfulness and resemble the Israelites in exile in Egypt.[104] There is a strong 'faith and fatherland' dimension to this poem,[105] which is also evidenced by the use of the term *athartha* 'fatherland' (cf. Latin *patria*), which, from Ó hUiginn's vantage point on the Continent, clearly connotes Ireland as a whole. Moreover, *dúthaigh* and *dúchas* are again explicitly contrasted with the manifestation of foreignness, here *ainbhfine eachtrann* 'the evil race of foreigners'. Significantly in the present context, by focusing on the native land itself Nuinsean engenders what Bradshaw describes as 'a common bond that made for internal unity and a value that could be shared with members of other racial groups and nationalities'.[106]

It is onto the model of the Milesian origin legend and the idea of the 'fifth fifth', as symbolizing the unity of the other four parts, that the descendants of the twelfth-century English in Ireland are grafted as the sixth, and final, wave of invasions.[107] The words *dúthaigh* and *dúchas* index a particular pragmatic domain of cultural unity in early modern Ireland. Although this is based on the native Irish ideas of descent from Míl and the establishment of a symbolic centre of kingship and sovereignty around Midhe—'the Middle', or the fifth that unites the other four parts of Ireland by being a microcosm of them—we see it being extended to those elements of Irish society that have the *praescriptio longi temporis* of a successful, 'Christian' occupation of the country. It is this pragmatic function and its extension that raise these concepts out of the purely local or dynastic. This extension has its wider synchronic and international counterpart in the Renaissance rediscovery of the idea of *patria* in sixteenth-century Europe.

The concepts of *dúthaigh, dúchas* and *athardha*

Before turning to a further aspect of *dúchas* that becomes salient in the seventeenth century, there is another word to be examined briefly in this context of sixteenth-century patriotism. In the stanza immediately following the one quoted from Maolmhuire Ó hUiginn's poem above we find *dúchas* used as an equivalent of *dúthaigh* but also juxtaposed with the word *athardha* 'patria,' 'fatherland':

Gan fhágbáil oirir Bhanbha	Not to leave the shores of Ireland
gan anmhain ón **athardha**	not to remain from the fatherland
mo-chean lén héidear é a-nois	happy the one who can manage it now
gan tréigean Dé ná a **dhúthchais**.[108]	not to forsake his God or his *dúchas.*

Here we have the language of an ideology of 'faith' (*gan tréigean Dé*) and 'fatherland' (*athardha* and *dúthchas*). There is, in fact, a considerable overlap in the sources of this period between the terms *dúchas* and *dúthaigh* on the one hand and the term *athartha* on the other. In the following extracts we may note again the apparent similarity between the uses of *dúthaigh* and *athartha*. This is from a source already cited above, *Beatha Aodha Ruaidh Uí Dhomhnaill*, in which Aodh Ruadh Ó Domhnaill is making a circuit through north Connacht, restoring to their territory those who have distanced themselves from the English. This is to culminate in the bestowal of the headship of the MacWilliam Burkes on Tibbot Burke and the restoration of his patrimony (*dúthaigh*):

(a)   ase do deachaidh cettus cuga-som for athchur ⁊ ionnarbadh asa thir ⁊ do rairrngert dho **co ttiobradh ina duthaig doridhisi**

it was he who had first come to him, having been expelled from his lands, and he had promised him that he would re-install him in his patrimony again

(b)   ***Do rat-somh*** dana Ó Ruairc ⁊ Mac Diarmata ***ina n-atharda*** iarna n-iondarbadh la Gallaibh.[109]

Besides, he brought Ó Ruairc and Mac Diarmada back into their patrimony after they had been expelled by the foreigners.

Note that here the similarity between (a) and (b) extends to the entire syntagm used: (i) a form of the verb 'give' or 'bring' (*tabhair*) that governs (ii) a prepositional phrase with *i* 'into'. In the sixteenth-century life of St Colm Cille we find that *dúchas* as denotative of the land is also closely identified with the word *athartha* 'fatherland', 'patria':

Is truaighe lim iná sin gach ní tiucfus doib as sin .i. ferg Dé ar son a ndrochgnimartha fen indus go scrisfuither **as a ndutcus ⁊ as a n-athardha fen** iad fa glentaib Erind le nert ⁊ le tren echtrand ⁊ allmurach.[110]

I regret more than that everything that will come on them from that, i.e. the anger of God for their own evil acts, with the result that they shall be driven from their own inheritance and patrimony around the valleys of Ireland by the power and strength of aliens and foreigners.

As the issue here is 'patrimony' or 'inheritance', it is often difficult to say outside the immediate context whether these words are intended to have local or national scope. This continues to be so even when, as with both *dúchas* and *dúthaigh*, *athartha* is explicitly contrasted with the notion of foreignness, from which it has to be protected:

> Ro badh do mhóirsgélaibh Gaoidhel oidheadh an Bhriain h-ísin, uair ní thainicc dia bhunadh freimh ó chein mháir neach no dearsccaighfedh dhe . . . **ag imdhíten a athardha ar ainffine eachtrand**.[111]

> The death of this Brian was one of the great stories of the Irish, for there had not been for a long time any one of his stock who surpassed him . . . in defending his native land against foreign adventurers.

In this context of defending one's patrimony, a common collocation current in the 1580s is the collocation of *dúchas* with *díon* 'protecting', as in the following example:

> Goin san ghoin is creach san chreich   He inflicted wound for
> wound, raid for raid
> . . . do-níodh ag díon **a dhúthchais**.[112]   . . . in defending his *dúchas*.

As we have seen on more than one occasion in the case of *dúchas*, the opposition between *athardha dhílis badhdhéin* 'one's own patria' and foreign oppression (*ainffine ettrócar echtronn*) is notable, as in the following extract, where Aodh Ruadh Ó Domhnaill is depicted as the Irish Messiah:

> Acht chena uair narbho lainn la Dia an dilghenn ⁊ an droichdhiach do ratsat Goill for lucht na criche ina **n-athardha dílis badhdhéin** dus-fucc lais an macthairngertach morghlondach . . . dia soeradh ar an **ainffine n-ettrócar n-echtronn**.[113]

> but besides, since the destruction and evil acts inflicted by the English on the inhabitants of the country in their own beloved native land were displeasing to God, he brought the valorous, prophesied lad . . . to free them from the unmerciful foreign rabble.

In addition, the word *dúthaigh* is frequently accompanied by *dílis*, used in the sense 'inalienable', 'indefeasible', i.e. 'own', and also by the reflexive *féin* 'own':

(a)   Geallais Diarmaid . . . Loch Garman is an dá thriúcha céad fá goire dhi mar **dhúthaigh dhílis** go bráth do Roibeard Mac Stiabhna.

   Diarmaid promised . . . Wexford and the two cantreds nearest to it to Robert Fitzstephen, as his own territory in perpetuity.

(b)   A chomhuirle dhóibh gan síth do dhénamh le feruibh Sasan acht re liberti coinnséis, agus **a nduthaidhe féin** don Egluis Catoilici.[114]

   His advice to them was not to make peace with the English except in return for liberty of conscience and [the restoration of] its land to the Catholic Church.

Further evidence of the 'special' associations of *dúthaigh* comes from its use to refer to Heaven as everyone's *dúthaigh*, and here the sense of inheritance is particularly significant:

> Smaoineimoid go fhoilemid san saoghal so inar n-oilirtheachuibh agus inar ndibiorthachuibh agus gurab ar Neaomh atá **ár nduthaidh fhirin-neach**.[115]

> We think that we are in this world as pilgrims and exiles and that it is in Heaven that our true inheritance is.

In the devotional writings of Céitinn also we find (*a*) *dúthaigh* and (*b*) *tír dhúchais* and *athardha* used with reference to Heaven. Note also the recurrence of associations and oppositions discussed above for *dúchas* and *dúthaigh*: the opposition to exile (*deóraidheacht*) and foreignness (here *coigríoch*; see also chapter 2):[116]

(*a*) An seiseadh hadhbhar fá ndligheann duine gul do dhéanamh, tré iomad fuinn nó mianghusa do bheith ar neach ré dul ar neamh, is **dúthaigh** dá gach aon-duine. Óir is follus go mbí mian ar gach neach, triall **dá dhúthaigh féin**, mar thuigthear a briathraibh Óibhid, mar a n-abair: *Nescio qua natale solum dulcedine cunctos ducit, et immemores non sinit esse sui:* 'Ní feas damh, ar sé, créad an mhilse bhíos **san bhfonn ndúthchasa**, ag tarraing na n-uile, ⁊ nach léigeann dóibh bheith neamhchuimhneach orra féin.' As na briathraibh se Óibhid is iontuigthe go mbí dúil ag gach neach 'na **dhúthaigh** féin ⁊ go mbí súil tar a ais aige ré triall innte as a **dheóraidheacht**.

The sixth reason that a person is entitled to weep is having excessive desire and ambition to go to heaven, everyone's *dúthaigh*. Since it is obvious that everyone wants to go to his own *dúthaigh*, as can be understood from Ovid's words where he says . . . 'I do not know what sweetness is in the native land which attracts everyone and does not allow them to be forgetful of themselves.' From these words of Ovid it is understood that everyone desires his own *dúthaigh* and wants to go back there out of his exile.

(*b*) An treas adhbhar doilgheasa bhíos ag an anam i n-ifreann tré bheith ar díbirt ⁊ ar deóraidheacht i gcoigrích ifrinn i gcéin óna chrích bhunaidh ⁊ **óna athardha dhílis** .i. flaitheas Dé . . . arna gcor ar athchur ⁊ ar ionnarbadh ann **óna dtír dhúthchais** ⁊ óna gcathair chomhnuighthe féin .i. flaitheas Dé.

The third reason that the soul in hell has for grief is that it has been expelled and exiled to hell's foreign land far away from its land of origin and from its dear fatherland . . . having been banished from their [the souls'] native land and their own city of abode, that is, God's kingdom.

Perhaps the most notable use of the word *athartha* at this period occurs in Ó Cléirigh's biography of Aodh Ruadh Ó Domhnaill, particularly in the phrase *iris agus athartha* 'faith and fatherland'.[117] The same kind of phrase occurs with *athartha* also, as in the following obituaries for Rudhraighe Ó Domhnaill, who died in 1608 in Rome, and Aodh Ó Néill (Hugh O'Neill), who died in 1616 in the same city:

(a)　ro badh meinic i m-beirn bhaoghail **ag imdhíden a irsi, & a athardha**

　　　he had often exposed himself to danger, defending his faith and father-land

(b)　Tighearna coccthach . . . **ag díden a irsi, & a athardha**

　　　a belligerent lord . . . defending his faith and fatherland[118]

This appears to repeat the sentiments expressed by Fitzmaurice Fitzgerald in the 1570s with a different terminology. One of these letters (to Aisdunn Mac Domhnaill) has already been quoted; the following is to another gallowglass leader, Raghnall Mac Colla, dated 31 July 1579:

Comhairligh gach aon dod cháirdibh lenab feirdi cathughudh **ar son a gcreidimh ⁊ a ndúthaighe** ná ór no airgead no iad le chéile dfághuil ar son a dtuarusduil, teacht dom innsuidhe-si.[119]

Advise every one of your friends who likes fighting for his religion and his country better than for gold and silver, or who wishes to obtain them all as their wages, to come to me.

Here *creideamh agus dúthaigh* anticipates the later phrase *iris agus athardha* 'faith and fatherland'. Mac Craith, in discussing the three letters of Fitzmaurice Fitzgerald referred to above, naturally draws attention to this central aspect of his crusade: religion and native soil. With regard to the word *dúthaigh* as used in these letters, he points out that it covers a wide span of meanings, from regional to national ('ó cheantar dúchais go tír dhúchais'). Furthermore, he argues that the year 1579 is far too early for the Irish leaders to have fully developed the ideas of faith and fatherland ('creideamh agus athartha'). His conclusion is that it is much safer ('i bhfad níos stuama') to give *dúthaigh* a more local significance in Fitzgerald's letters.[120] What is especially interesting here is Mac Craith's contrastive analysis of Fitzmaurice Fitzgerald's letters written in English where he talks about defending 'God's honour, the health of our country, and for the restoring of the Catholic religion again'; 'the common good and weal of this noble Ireland'; 'our dear country'; 'zeal for God's honour and their own country'. Mac Craith concludes that Fitzgerald shows a much more acutely developed national sense in his English letters, where he is addressing the Old English rather than the native Irish, and that this heightened sense is predicated on the nature of his audience. The background to this assumption has been described by Morgan[121] and Bradshaw[122] as the rise of patriotism, first among the Old English of the Pale in the 1550s. Catholic exiles on the Continent wedded this patriotism to the tenets of the Counter-Reformation in sixteenth-century Ireland and thus was 'faith and fatherland' nationalism born—the type of nationalism promoted by Aodh Ó Néill in the cause of national unity.

In Mac Craith's analysis this nationalism does not find expression in Irish-language sources until after Ó Néill's death, not, in fact, until Lughaidh Ó Cléirigh's biography of Aodh Ruadh Ó Domhnaill, written some time between 1616 and 1632. There, however, the phrase *creidiomh agus dúthaigh* has been replaced by *iris agus athartha* 'faith and fatherland', and Mac Craith sees this change as significant, describing it as a 'great leap':

> is mór an léim atá déanta ón bhfocal *dúthaigh* mar atá sé ag Séamus Mac Muiris Mac Gearailt go dtí an focal *athartha* a úsáideann Lughaidh Ó Cléirigh.[123]
>
> it is a great leap from the word *dúthaigh* as James Fitzmaurice Fitzgerald has it to the word *athartha* that Lughaidh Ó Cléirigh uses.

It seems to me, however, that, based on the totality of evidence for both *dúthaigh* and *dúchas* and bearing in mind the shifting, indexical and pragmatic nature of these forms, we can at least admit the possibility that *dúthaigh* no less than *dúchas* is a shifter—a sign characterized more by its pragmatic essence than by its semantic-referential denotations. It is in the light of such sign-activated symbolism that Mac Craith's discussion of the use of *dúthaigh* in the letters of Fitzmaurice Fitzgerald should be considered, and perhaps modified. If indeed, as I contend, we are dealing with a pragmatic construct here, this offers another view on the question of whether such words have a national or merely a local significance. To give this question a wider context, I now consider briefly some relevant comparative evidence from a culture that is chronologically, geographically and linguistically far removed from Irish-speaking Ireland in the sixteenth century.

A comparative framework: the Tamil concepts of *ūr* and *nātu*

On account of similarities in their semiotic structure, a possible point of contact here for Irish *dúthaigh* and *dúchas* is Valentine Daniel's discussion of the Tamil concepts of *ūr* 'village' and *nātu* 'country' and their relation to the Sanskrit-derived terms *kirāmam* and *dēsh*.[124] In distinguishing between the former, indigenous terms on the one hand and the latter, borrowed terms on the other, he draws on the distinction made by Silverstein between essential pragmatic and semantic-referential meaning.[125] Both *ūr* and *nātu* are contextually defined: both terms are 'person-centric' and change with the cognitive and spatial orientation of the speaker.[126] In general terms, the *ūr* is a named territory inhabited by people believed to share in the substance of its soil. Within its broad definition, however, *ūr* is a 'shifter' and refers to a territory or piece of territory to which the speaker orients himself or herself at a given time, for example:

1.   If you normally go to the post office on a Wednesday at three o'clock, that is your *ūr* at that given time.
2.   Your *ūr* can also be a foreign country in which you happen to live at a particular time.
3.   A distinction can be made between *ūr* in this sense and the *conta ūr*, or the place where the relation with the soil is the most intimate and inalienable.
4.   Perhaps the most common use of *ūr* is to refer to the local village.

The word *nātu,* 'country', 'nation', is again contextually defined: it can be (*a*) all of India, (*b*) the state of Tamil Nadu, (*c*) the ancestral Tamil lands, or (*d*) the immediate locale.

The nature of these terms can best be understood if they are compared with their Sanskrit-derived equivalents for 'village' and 'country', both of which are administrative and geographico-political concepts. Thus in contrast to the range of possibilities inherent in the word *nātu,* in the case of *tēcam* (< Sanskrit *dēsh*) the only possibility for a Tamil is 'India.' In the case of *ūr* as against *kirāmam,* the former is typically not defined by a linear boundary but rather by what Cohn calls a 'symbol pool' (shrines, important roads). Typically the definition of the *ūr* starts from the centre, that of the *kirāmam* from the periphery. Daniel established this distinction largely on the basis of how people would draw maps: *kirāmam* maps simply delineated the extent of the territory with respect to other territories; *ūr* maps, on the other hand, contained much more local detail and history.

The relationship between the *ūr* and the people who inhabit it is seen as a transformative one, in that the soil substance of the *ūr* and its people mix in a reciprocal way. Daniel's conclusion is that the *ūr* is 'a fluid sign with fluid thresholds'. His analysis of these two Tamil lexemes bears out the issues of meaning involved. In the semantic-referential mode there are two equivalent items for 'village', *ūr* and *kirāmam.* Closer observation of context, however, reveals two distinct symbolic systems. In Silverstein's terms, the argument is for a pragmatic grammar, where meaning is a function of, among other things, the relation of speaker and audience, the location and time of discourse. The search, as in the case of *dúchas* and *dúthaigh,* is for clues to the pervasiveness of a symbolic construct as Daniel has it.

In other words, multiple significations and interpretations are potentially present at the same time, and the specification of a particular meaning is dependent on the particular context of usage. The first question here is: how do the pragmatics of indexicality affect the interpretation of *dúthaigh* and *dúchas* with respect to other designations of (*a*) land (*tír, fearann* and *críoch*) and (*b*) native land (*athartha*).

I have proposed that *dúthaigh* and *dúchas* are 'shifters' (Silverstein) or 'fluid signs' (Daniel); that is, their essential meaning is pragmatic rather than simply semantic-representational, as with other words denotative of land. Their signification, especially that of *dúchas*, shifts with context, depending on the spatial and cognitive orientation of the speaker—from local to national, from concrete to abstract and from personal to collective. As designations of land or territory or place they thus represent 'symbol pools', in Cohn's terms, rather than bounded physical entities. There are particular structural and syntactic arguments that can be adduced in support of this thesis:

(1) Syntacticized use with the copula *is* and the preposition *do* is confined to *dúthaigh* and *dúchas*: *Is dú/dúthaigh/dúchas do*, the interchangeability of which suggest on an indexical level the reciprocal substantive relation between place and the moral code of human behaviour. To rehearse this particular structure, we have the twelfth-century passage already cited in chapter 2:

> Atbert imorro Brian nirbo coir do-som in ní sin [do rabha] uair ba **dúthaig** do éc ocus ba **dúthaig** do Dail Cais uli, uair marb a n-athri ocus a senathri . . . ocus nirbo **dual** imorro ocus nirbo **duthaig** doib tárna tar-caisin sin do gabail.[127]

This ideological symbiosis is reflected directly in the structure of Irish, and this symbiotic relationship persists to the present day. The proof of this is lin-guistic: the word *fearann*, for example, could never be substituted for *dúthaigh* in the phrase *ba duthaig do* 'it was right for him'. This restriction applies to all other designations of land in Irish outside the *dú* family. Note the impossibil-ity of the following:

> *Is é is **fearann/tír/críoch** do

But also   *Is é is **athartha** do

What this clearly shows is that the lexical family of *dú, dúthaigh* and *dúchas* when used to refer to 'land' does not represent the idea of land in a purely semantic and referential sense but is rather indexical of certain key features of land or particular kinds of land in a more pragmatic sense.

(2) The use as attributive genitive with other designations of land is proper to *dúthaigh* and *dúchas* only; that is, the existence of doublets such as *tír dhúthaigh* or *tír dhúiche* on the one hand and the much more common *tír dhúchais* on the other. Here *dúthaigh* or *dúiche* is used attributively to denote a quality that is associated with a particular land, as was discussed in chapter 2.

(3) Another aspect of the relationship between *dúthaigh* and other words deno-tative of land is the apparent constraint on the use of descriptive or adjectival modifiers denoting the physical or natural aspects of landscape with *dúthaigh* and *dúchas*. Below are some examples, mostly from works already considered:

(*a*)   an **tír** chraobhach chruithneachtach this land of branches and of
                                                            wheat

tír na sreabh gorm ngoirmealtach	land of the blue bird-haunted clear streams
tír ainglidhe fá n-iadh tonn	angelic land enclosed by the wave
críoch naomhda	blessed land

(b) **dúthaigh** a sean — the land of their ancestors
chum **dúthchais** a sinnsir — to the land of their ancestors
sean**duthchus** — ancestral land
dúthaigh fhíre — true country

(b) **dúthaigh** a sean	the land of their ancestors
chum **dúthchais** a sinnsir	to the land of their ancestors
sean**duthchus**	ancestral land
dúthaigh fhíre	true country

There are significant differences here in the types of adjectival and attributive complements that the different designations can govern: *tír* and *críoch* are the most free as regards possible adjectival complements and therefore the most neutral with respect to physical or natural descriptions; *fearann* is more likely to refer to types of territorial demarcation; while both *dúthaigh* or *dúchas* and *athartha* are the most restricted. *Athartha* also shows a similar semantic range of both 'inheritance' and its material embodiment.

The arguments are primarily linguistic in nature and with this in mind it might be helpful to get an overview of the semantic range of these items from Ó Dónaill,[128] comparing also the kinds of lexical associations that *dúiche* and *dúthaigh* give rise to compared with such words as *tír, críoch* and *fearann*:

dúiche fine	the ancestral land of the family
dúiche ár n-aithreacha agus ár seanaithreacha	land of our fathers and forefathers
mo thír **dhúiche**	my native country
dúiche thalaimh	an estate of land
an **dúiche** máguaird	the surrounding country
Molann gach aon duine a **dhúiche**	everyone praises or values his homeland
Is buan fear ina **dhúiche**	a man is solid in his homeland

For the first proverb given above we also have the nineteenth-century variant:

Molaidh gach duine a **dhúthchas**.[129]

Everybody praises his native land.

Note again the strong connection between *dúthaigh* and the familial and the ancestral, which recalls *dúthaigh a sean* and *senducus* from above. All the words of the *dú* family have this abstract possibility, which does not belong to more purely semantic-referential designations for land or territory. The more concrete and physical denotations for such words will be apparent from the following examples, based again on Ó Dónaill:

fearann cairte	charter land

fearann eaglaise	church land
fearann pósta	dowry land
críocha na tíre	the boundaries of the country
críoch fhearainn	headland, margins of a field
críocha an domhain	the countries of the world
pobal/rialtas na **tíre**	the people/government of the country
an **tír** máguaird	the surrounding country
ar muir is ar **tír**	on land and on sea

Thus *dúthaigh* and *dúchas,* even as a territorial designation ('homeland'), are not so much a geographical-political concept as a symbolic one of context-dependent associations (landscape, culture, history and personal ties).

This evidence speaks for the greater abstract quality of the lexemes in question: the land itself is seen as a material embodiment of a principle, while that principle is abstracted from the sense of land as one's own or native place. Thus we posit the same kind of relationship as Daniel does for Tamil culture: a substantive reciprocal relation between the land and its people, which is reflected both in linguistic structure itself and in contextual elusiveness as 'shifters'.

In seventeenth-century sources there are clear references to *dúthaigh* as meaning Ireland as a whole. A notable example is from the preface of Theobald Stapleton's bilingual catechism (Irish and Latin) of 1639, where he discusses the need to cultivate Irish as a national means of expression:

> nach foil ar Riocht no Herean (**mo dhuthe nadurtha**) ni as riochtanasuidh na an Teagasc Criostuidhe dho bheith ar eolas aca ionna Tteangain **nduchais nadurtha féin** ionnas go dtuigidis go soleir í féin agus a chioll.[130]
>
> that the Kingdom of Ireland (my natural *dúthaigh*) has no greater need than that everyone should know the Catechism in their own natural native language that they might understand it and its meaning clearly.

The use of the word *nádúrtha* is interesting here, as it appears to contrast with the way in which *dúthaigh* is collocated with the adjective *fírinneach* 'real, truthful' in the passage from the same work by Stapleton cited above to refer to 'Heaven'. In the passage immediately above, *dúthaigh* clearly refers to Ireland, indeed to the 'kingdom' of Ireland. We have a further reference of this kind from a letter of 1642 concerning the death of Aodh Ó Domhnaill, son of Ruairí, who died in the service of the King of Spain. Note the parallel phrases, which are emphasized:

> do iarr a ched le congnamh dfhaghail no gan a fhaghail ⁊ **a léigean dá dhúthaigh**. Et as amhlaidh do conncas don Rígh ⁊ dá chomhairle gan **a léigean go hÉrinn**.[131]

he requested his leave to get help or not to get it and to be allowed [to return] to his native land. The king and his council decided not to allow him [to go] to Ireland.

However, this word still occurs in seventeenth-century texts with a more local frame of reference, as in the following extract from a life of Declan in which the saint's own *dúthaigh* is contrasted with the rest of Ireland:

> tuccattar iatt fein ettar anam agus chorp do Día agus do Déclán. Agus do cenglattar íad féin fo chuing agus fo riaghail dó, agus do cumhdaighedh leis **ina duthaig fein sna Déisibh** . . . agus ni hedh amhain ina duthaig féin acht i ttíribh ele Ereann fo cuairt.[132]

> they gave themselves body and soul to God and to Declan. And they bound themselves under his yoke and his rule, and they were sheltered by him in his native place in the Decies . . . and not only in his own native place but in all the other lands of Ireland.

Both *dúthaigh* and *dúchas,* as we have seen, activate a more contemporary connection to an ideology of patriotism, the Renaissance humanist notion of *patria*—the devotion to an idealized community, whether on a local or a national scale.[133] As both seem to shift according to the spatial or cognitive orientation of the speaker, it is noteworthy that the most salient examples of *dúthaigh* and *dúchas* as carrying a national reference occur in contexts of exile. Annalistic references, on the other hand, are more likely to have a more local interpretation, as is unambiguously the case in the following:

> tarla doibh-sidhe beith i ccampa i **ndúthaigh Uí Mhechair** i n-Uíbh Cairín.[134]

> they happened to be in camp in O'Meagher's country in Ikerrin.

In addition, *dúthaigh* appears in a number of early seventeenth-century sources apparently divested of its symbolism, where it is to be translated merely as 'estate'. Accordingly, we have the following from the text of a letter written in 1631 concerning the well-known German planter Matthew de Renzy, who had acquired lands in the midlands of Ireland. When he visited Ireland he was so taken with the beauty of the place that he decided to settle:

> do chinn ar anmhain san iath agus fearann fíorálainn do cheannach ar a chuid ionnmhusa agus airgid agus do rinne amhlaidh, ór **do cheannaigh duthaigh mór** a nDealbhna McCochlain . . . **do cheannaigh fós duthaigh mor** a nDruinn.[135]

> he determined to stay in the country and with his wealth to buy a fine estate. And so he did, for he bought a great territory in Dealbhna meic Cochlain . . . He also bought a large estate in Druinn.

Here a *dúthaigh* is simply a piece of land in a commercial sense, in the same way that *fearann* is in the same passage and hence the interchangeable use of the two terms. Similar in its usage is the following extract from *Annála Ríoghachta Éireann*:

> Asseadh airecc ro thionchoiscc a ainshén do Dhiarmait, Iarla Des-
> mumhan do thairbert don Presidens, & d'Iarla Tuadhmumhan dar cenn
> ionnmais, & edala, & **ar shaoirsi, & ar shochar dúthaighe**.[136]

> The solution which his ill fortune indicated to Diarmaid was to hand
> over the Earl of Desmond to the President and the Earl of Thomond in
> return for wealth and property and the liberty and profits of an estate.

It should be noted that this 'demystification' of the idea of *dúthaigh* continues
in the contemporary language, where the common Munster expression *sa
dúthaigh* means simply 'in the area' or 'in the locality'.

It is probably for reasons such as these that *dúthaigh* and *dúchas* do not
develop as political expressions of the emerging confessional nationalism of
the seventeenth century. Both concepts particularly *dúchas*, are too protean in
their semantic-pragmatic ranges. In other words, both *dúthaigh* and *dúchas*
may have been perceived as too 'fluid'; it is also interesting that since the seventeenth century the words have increasingly diverged in accordance with the
way one would have expected them to be originally differentiated, *dúchas* having the more abstract range, *dúthaigh* or *dúiche* much more a territorial designation. One key is perhaps to be found in Ó Gnímh's poem above: if *dúchas* is
a person-centric symbol pool rather than a geographical-political demarcation,
what is to be done when those symbols are taken away? It is then that *dúchas*
becomes 'internalized' in Irish as argued in chapter 2.

Another key is provided by the emergence in the early seventeenth century
of the word 'nation', Irish *náision* in the writings of the Louvain school—a
clearer, more internationally recognized sign, more of a *tabula rasa* in Irish
terms and instantly comprehensible in the world of international propaganda
and diplomacy.[137] The earliest example of the word occurs in Ó Cianáin's *Flight
of the Earls* (1609):

> Arna mhárach trá. 30. Octobriss ticc mac Uí Néill, corenéil na nEirin-
> nach chuca go mbuidhin ndermhair ndeighinnill do chaiptínibh, do
> dhaoinibh uaissle do Spáinneachaibh agas d'Eirinnchaibh ⁊ do **gach
> nasion archena** dia mbátor.[138]

> The next day, the thirtieth of October, O'Neill's son, the Colonel of the
> Irish [regiment], came to them with a large well-equipped company of
> captains and of noblemen, Spanish and Irish and of every other nation.

The earliest consistent use of the term is in Mac Aingil's tract on the sacrament
of Confession, *Scathán Shacramuinte na hAithridhe*[139]:

(*a*)   Bíd leabhráin mar so ag **gach náision Chatoilic eili** ⁊ atáid do riach-
danas ar an **náision dá bhfuilmídne** go speisialta.

Every other Catholic nation has such books, and they are especially
required by the nation to which we belong.

(*b*)   ní fhuair aoinrégión don Chríosduidheachd an phriuiléid si .i. bheith saor ón uili eiriceachd, achd Éiri amháin ⁊ a hinghean ionmhuin Alba résan aimsir si, mar scríobhuid ughdair óirdheirce **náision eili**.

No other region of Christendom received this privilege, i.e. to be free from every heresy, except Ireland and her dear daughter Scotland before this time, as the renowned authors of other nations record.

(c)   Dá ndéindís fós fir Éirionn uile rún ar mhalairt creidimh do-ghéntaoi aca . . . ní dhiongnadh na talta eili rún air, achd do bhíadh sgríobhtha a sdairibh **iomad náision**, mar atá aca gurab é Pádraig tug chum creidimh sinn.

Even if the men of Ireland were to convert secretly . . . the other lands would not keep it secret, but rather it would be written in the histories of many nations, just as it is that Patrick brought us into the faith.

The most interesting feature of this usage is that the Irish are one nation among many and this seems to be the consciousness that it principally embodies.[140] Note particularly the telling juxtaposition between 'our nation', 'the nation to which we belong' and 'every (other) nation'.

In fact the protean nature of *dúchas* becomes accentuated in the modern period, although that could be as much a question of sources and registers of language as of absolute chronology. This should be set in the kind of context presented above for the 1570s and 80s, with *dúthaigh* and *dúchas* arguably invoking a more resonantly 'Gaelic' ideology than the more neutral *ceart* as in Céitinn. It is noteworthy in this connection that other, more neutral and all-embracing terms, such as *athardha*, were tried (cf. *iris agus athardha*). Since both *dúthaigh* and *dúchas* are 'shifters', which pragmatically index central areas of the domain of Irish cultural and ideological unity, they proved unsuitable as a means for advancing Ireland's case in international terms.

'Na bearta as dúthchas duit': social change in early modern Ireland

The late sixteenth and early seventeenth centuries also saw great social and economic change in Ireland. In particular, the traditional Irish lordship and the medieval pattern of familial landownership was increasingly undermined by the cumulative effect of plantation, administrative centralization, the enactment of common law and the advent of individual proprietors. An invaluable Irish-language source for this period is the satirical text *Pairlement Chloinne Tomáis*, and our final set of examples will be based on a consideration of that text.[141] Caball argues that the traditional interpretation of this text as an upper-class satire on the rural agricultural class has obscured its true inspiration and focus;[142] its historical remit is rather the lampooning of an emergent, increasingly Anglicized entrepreneurial class of *nouveaux riches,* an upwardly mobile agrarian middle class that the author claims has consolidated its prosperity in the aftermath of the Nine Years' War of 1592–1601.[143] According to the text, the origins of 'Clann Tomáis', or family of Thomas, lay in the fact that St Patrick had permitted Tomás, although descended from a serpent, to remain in Ireland, as he was human on his mother's side. He then laid down strict ordinances for governing their demeanour towards the nobility.[144] By the sixteenth to seventeenth century, however, Clann Tomáis were sending their children to school,[145] espousing English common law,[146] embracing the English language,[147] being irreligious[148] and making matches beyond their station. The first section of the text includes a speech by their leader, Murchadh Ó Multuaiscirt, which lays down the code of conduct prescribed for Clann Tomáis: to unite against the aristocracy in a policy of careful social and economic advancement and to abandon their uncultivated ways:

> Léigidh dhíbh, a bhráithreacha . . . bhur gcótuidhe croicinn . . . Léigidh dhíbh fós bhur mbéasa brocacha brúideamhla.[149]

> Leave off, brothers, your leather coats . . . Leave off also your filthy brutish ways.

The last third of the text is concerned with the 'parliament' convened by Clann Tomáis in Co. Kerry in 1632. The session has just begun when it is interrupted by the approach of Labhrás Ó Lándornáin from Co. Limerick, who informs the parliament that countless members of Clann Tomáis have been sentenced to hanging by various courts of law throughout the south of Ireland for offences of theft and robbery (*déanamh gada agas foghla*). This surprises Clann Tomáis only to the extent that, although they steal land because it is expensive, the blame for such depredations has traditionally been assigned to the 'idle nobility, the minor nobility and scroungers among the tail-end of noble families' (*uaisle díomhaoine, leathdhaoine uaisle ⁊ sgramuiridhe d'iarmhur folanna uaisle*). When one of their number advances this opinion, however, Labhrás informs him that the game is up and advises Clann Tomáis to renounce the violence and theft that are second nature to them. Note how the phraseology echoes that of the quotation given immediately above (except that now it is singular: *léig díot, a bhráthair,* for plural *léigidh dhíbh a bhráithreacha*):

> Léig díot, a bhráthair, na bearta **as dúthchus duit** do theacht tríot, óir do-chuadar cách amach oruinn, ⁊ do fríth fiaghnuise ⁊ fionna-chomharthuighe ar n-uilc.[150]

> Give up, brother, the tricks that are *dúchas* [come naturally] to you, for everyone has found us out, and evidence and certain proof of our wrongdoing have been found.

In chapter 2 we drew attention to this aspect of the internalization of *dúchas* as something that 'comes out through you from within you', in particular in the well-known proverb *Briseann an dúchas trí shúile an chait* ('*Dúchas* breaks out through the cat's eyes'.) After two further visitors have taken their leave of the parliament and urged Clann Tomáis to wind up its business, the 'prophet of Clan Thomas' (*fáidh Chloinne Tomáis*), Brian Brúideamhail, states that it is simply not in their nature to do so. Significant again here is the depiction of *dúchas* in terms of character traits (here *tréighthe*):

> Ní dual dóibh críoch mhath do chor orra . . . óir broid agas goid agas bréaga, tunáth, tnúth agas tuaisgiort, míchreidiomh, mírún ⁊ míchráb- hadh, éitheach, imirt agas ól as tréighthe do chlannuibh lábánach san aimsir si . . . Tugabhuir **bhur gceárda dúthchais** ar mhalairt .i. ionnra- cus ar ghuid agus ar ól cannuighe, umhlacht ⁊ lábántacht ar mhórdháil agus ⁊ ar stámur, bhur gcríochnumhlacht ⁊ bhur bfhuadar ar ól píopuidhe tobaca.[151]

> It isn't natural for them to complete it . . . for harshness, lying, secret mur- der, envy, coarseness, irreligion, malice, impiety, perjury, gambling and drunkenness are the characteristics of the progeny of churls these days . . . You have exchanged your native crafts: honesty for robbery and the drinking of galley-pots, humility and serfdom for swaggering and inso- lence, your thoroughness and energy for the smoking of tobacco pipes.

Brian concludes by urging Clann Tomáis to return to its former honest and servile demeanour, in other words to return to their *cearda dúthchais*. This phrase also occurs among the bardic elite at this period. By the beginning of the seventeenth century the downfall of the hereditary bardic order is one of the main themes of the poetry. One of the most famous Ulster practitioners of his time, Fear Flatha Ó Gnímh, addresses the following poem to one of the Magennises of Down, where the issue is very much the demise of what was part of hereditary right for the poets:

Mairg do-chuaidh re **ceird ndúthchais**:	Alas for him who has followed his family profession
rug ar Bhanbha mbarrúrthais	it has befallen Banbha of the fresh soft surface
nach dualghas athar is fhearr i n-achadh fhuarghlas Éireann.	that in Ireland's cool green field one's father's natural calling is not the best.
Do héirgheadh dhóibh thuaidh is teas	It has come to them from north and south
nach bí ar breith don ord éigeas	that the poetic order cannot speak
labhairt ar oigdhe a n-aithreadh: malairt oibre ionnsaighthear.[152]	of their fathers' produce: let us set about a change of work.

In the same way Ó Gnímh's contemporary Mathghamhain Ó hIfearnáin laments the change in artistic fashion: the craft of their ancestors no longer has what is *dual* or 'natural' to it:

A mhic ná mebhraig éigsi cerd do shen rót ró-thréig-si	Son don't even think of poetry abandon the craft of your ancestors before you

tús anóra gér **dual** di	though it really should have pride of place
fa tuar ansógha in éigsi.[153]	poetry has been a cause of misery.

Note the equivalence here of *cerd do shen* 'the craft of your ancestors' and Ó Gnímh's *re ceird ndúthchais* 'hereditary profession' and the equivalence of both to *dualghas athar* 'a father's natural calling'. Thus the phrase *ceird dhúthchais* or *cearda dúthchais* becomes in a sense a crystallization of social and economic change in early seventeenth-century Ireland: viewed with regret by the poets themselves and as the subject of cutting satire by their apologists. These two poems will be discussed in more detail in chapter 5.

In his discussion of the relation between semantic and social change in English, Hughes sees the dissolution of feudalism and the concomitant rise of capitalist exchange and ideas of a new equality as one of the decisive transformations—a manifestation of growing bourgeois pragmatism whereby erstwhile terms of privilege become the new vocabulary of self-advancement.[154] This process ultimately internalizes such concepts in the individual and means that they are within the attainment of everyone. We can relate the increased significance of this use of *dúchas* in the seventeenth century to analogous processes in the community of Irish-speakers, in particular an increase in the relative social flexibility of an *arriviste* entrepreneurial middle class.

Conclusions

We can conceive of the words *dúchas* and *dúthaigh* as indexes that pragmatically reference cultural and ideological domains of meaning. These words act as contextualization cues; to borrow Silverstein's metaphor, we can think of them as semiotic arrows that index various co-ordinates of national identity in early modern Ireland.[155] Such co-ordinates are those of origin (*bunadhus*) and the symbolic centre (*Midhe* 'the middle or fifth fifth' and *Teamhair* 'Tara'). We found that these are already present in the twelfth-century *Cogadh Gaedhel re Gallaibh*. The ideological innovation of the sixteenth century is their extension to those elements of Irish society living in Ireland for some four hundred years but traditionally marginal to native Irish society.

In this discussion I have repeatedly emphasized the *pragmatic* aspects of the words *dúchas* and *dúthaigh*. We can recall here Verschueren's formulation of the role of pragmatics in linguistics, given above in chapter 1, as providing 'a general functional (i.e. cognitive, social and cultural) perspective . . . aimed at the investigation of dynamic and negotiated meaning generation in interaction . . . firmly embedded in a context'.[156] Our own study has repeatedly emphasized the importance of context—here the social, cultural and political changes affecting Irish-speaking society in the sixteenth and seventeenth centuries—and the ways in which language in its dynamic and interactive aspects both shapes and reflects responses to those developments. In the case of *dúthaigh* and *dúchas* we have seen how meaning is in fact both socially and interculturally 'negotiable' and how the indexical function of language both presupposes certain contexts and creates new ones.

In conclusion, as has been argued both *dúthaigh* and *dúchas* are 'shifters', which pragmatically index important areas of the domain of Irish cultural and social identity. During the period under discussion this pragmatic essence has both a centripetal dimension, in the extension of the concepts of *dúchas* and *dúthaigh* to make them inclusive of a wider Irish national identity, and a centrifugal one, in the democratization and internalization of *dúchas* with the demise of the native Irish aristocracy and the rise of individualism in the seventeenth century. Because class, social or cultural grouping, is generally not conterminous with the speech community as a whole, we have here what Voloshinov calls 'the social multi-accentuality of the sign': the same words spoken with different social and cultural accents.[157] Experience is not merely reflected, therefore, but also refracted by language.

Postscript: Further comparanda for *dúchas* as 'native land'

When we are in search of comparanda for *dúchas,* it is interesting that it is in some ways more revealing to go to southern Asia, to the *ūr* and *nátu* of Tamil culture, than to many of the European cultures in closer proximity. With regard to the three languages surveyed by Wierzbicka—German, Polish and Russian—all show features in the designation for homeland that are compatible with the idea of *dúchas,* although *dúchas* has a pragmatic essence, or greater underlying shifting quality.[158] Both German *Vaterland* and Polish *ojczyzna* ('fatherland') are etymologically connected to the word for 'father' in each language. Wierzbicka argues that German *Vaterland* has strong connotations of the superordinate paternal authority, with its concomitant sense of a moral national duty, an externally imposed imperative to defend it. On the other hand, the Polish word is given a more 'maternal' interpretation, despite its etymology, of a beloved mother for whom one would willingly sacrifice oneself, more of an internal or subjective imperative. Note that this association with the self-sacrificing mother-figure obtains, despite the etymology from *ojciec* 'father'; note also the connection with the plural *ojcowie* 'fathers' (i.e. 'ancestors'). The word is attested from the sixteenth century onwards, but only in the nineteenth century does it acquire its modern cultural significance, linked to the word *naród* 'nation'. Wierzbicka remarks that it is specifically not identified with the state but places the emphasis on the centrality of culture and tradition, as in the emotive adjective *ojczysty*. The word *ojczyzna* originally had a strong emotional component, like German *Heimat*, and is closely linked in the sense of being a place of origin or birth. The adjective *ojczysty* is closely connected to culture and tradition: note the following collocations, where it functions like the attributive genitive *dúchais*:

jezyk ojczysty   native language

kraj ojczysty	native land
dzieje ojczyste	past history of one's country

It also emphasized the collective, so that *ziemia ojczyzta* is 'native land' in its shared national perspective, as opposed to *ziemia rodzinna* 'land of birth' from the individual point of view (like *Heimat*). This latter word is clearly cognate with the Russian *rodina* 'native land', a word that carries less of a moral imperative than either *Vaterland* or *ojczyzna*. As with the latter, the association of *rodina* is again maternal, but here it is a good beneficent mother rather than the suffering one. As a designation of 'homeland', Wierzbicka argues that *rodina* has a more concrete everyday sense than its German or Polish equivalent: you can go home to your *rodina*. The stem *rod-* is rich in further lexical associations:

(a) **rod** genus, type, kind, race, generation, birth

(b) **rodít'** bear, give birth; **rodít'sya** be born, arise, grow
     rodít'el'i parents

(c) **rodína** native land **rodínka** birthmark (cf. Irish *ball dúchais*)
     rodnóy native

(d) **ródstvenn'ik** relations **rodslóvnaya** family tree
     rodonatchál'n'ik ancestor

(e) **rodník** spring

In addition, German has the word *Heimat*, which, in contradistinction to *Vaterland,* is the 'sentimental' subordinate unique place associated with a happy childhood—a place but not necessarily a country, big enough to be a collective but small enough to have 'human measure'. As Wierzbicka remarks, this element of nostalgia no doubt reflects the reality of German life after 1871, when close-knit communities were being swallowed by larger units. As we have seen, both *dúthaigh* and *dúchas* can vacillate between the two senses.

Benedict Anderson comments on the general nature of the vocabulary of patriotism by noting its close associations with 'the vocabulary of kinship (motherland, *Vaterland, patria*) or that of home (*heimat* or *tanah air* "earth and water", the phrase for the Indonesians' native archipelago.') He further points out that such vocabulary tends to reinforce both the natural and the involuntary aspects of the tie that one feels towards one's 'nation' or 'native land'.[159] As we have seen, the Irish word *athar-tha* belongs in this category and, furthermore, *dúchas* fits easily into this frame of analysis, with its associations of blood line, ancestry and hereditary right, as well as its more internalized senses of inborn character and inherent nature. These complementary aspects of what is natural and involuntary or beyond human agency will play a large part in our further discussion of *dúchas* and related words in the chapters that follow.

4. THE PRAGMATICS OF *DUAL* AND THE HABITUAL

This chapter has two main aims: firstly, an examination of the word *dual* and its derivative *dualgas* in relation to aspects of *dúchas* already discussed in previous chapters and secondly, an investigation of a possible correlation between the lexical and grammatical ends of the linguistic spectrum of meaning. In particular we will examine the possibility that ideology formulated at the more reflective and conscious end of the spectrum—the lexicon—might be reinforced by the expression of similar concepts at the more automated, grammatical end. It is here that Silverstein's examination of the relationship between speakers' use of language (pragmatics) and their ability to consciously rationalize such usage (metapragmatics), discussed in chapter 1, is of importance. These implications will be examined through a consideration of a number of texts from the sixteenth and seventeenth centuries in their cultural and historical context.

Dual, dualgas and dúchas

As with *dúchas* in chapter 2, I begin by presenting an aggregate of historical meanings of both *dual* and its derivative *dualgas* from Ó Dónaill:[1]

(1)   *Dual*

> 1. Native, natural (*do*, to)
> 2. Proper, fitting
> 3. In the natural order of things; fated; possible

(2)   *Dualgas*

> 1. Natural right, due; customary fee or reward
> 2. Duty

One comparison that can be made immediately is between both the semantics and the syntax of *dual* and *dú*. From the semantic viewpoint both have the meaning 'native', 'natural', 'proper', 'fitting', but this is closely bound up with the kind of syntactic structure in which these two lexical items most commonly appear, as we have seen in chapters 2 and 3[2]:

> Is é is **dú** agus is **dual** dó
>
> It's in his very nature

This type of syntactic structure will recur continually in the present chapter and will receive a detailed consideration in chapter 5. Furthermore, the derivative *dualgas* stands in a relation to its basic etymon *dual* comparable to that between *dúchas* and *dú,* already considered in chapter 2. In other words, both *dualgas* and *dúchas* embody a particular realization or manifestation of the semantic and pragmatic content of the basic etymon as an abstract right or entitlement. This is characterized as 'natural' or 'expected' in a general sense in the case of *dualgas*, as more specifically 'hereditary' in the case of *dúchas*. We shall return to a more detailed consideration of *dualgas* below. At this point, *dual* and *dúchas* can be profitably compared and contrasted from their use in proverbs and aphorisms. The particular examples that follow are taken from the nineteenth-century collection by Robert MacAdam made in east Ulster. We can start with his examples of *dual*. The first four examples fall into the same syntactic pattern: *Cha dual X gan Y* 'X is not *dual* without Y':

(*a*)   Cha **dual** toit gan teine 's cha **dual** teine gan daoine.

There is not usually smoke without fire, nor fire without people.

(*b*)   Cha **dual** grian gan scáile.

There's not usually sunshine without shadow.

(*c*)   Cha **dual** Satharn gan ghrian 's cha **dual** Domhnach gan aifrionn.

It's not usual for Saturday to be without sunshine, nor a Sunday without Mass.

(*d*)   Cha **dual** sagart gan chléireach 's cha **dual** Domhnach gan aifrionn.

It's not usual for a priest to be without a clerk, nor a Sunday without Mass.[3]

In cases such as these, *dual* is indexing what is a product of either natural or cultural forces. The first two proverbs are instances of the former: no smoke without fire, no sun without shade. The latter two, however, refer to phenomena that are culturally contingent, as in no Sunday without Mass. This I take to be another example of a conceptual transference from the realm of nature to the domain of culture, such as has already been discussed for aspects of *dúchas* in chapter 2. What is *dual* therefore is *presumed* or *expected* to be an inevitable, natural or usual outcome, whether this presumption is derived from observation of nature or deducible from custom or habit. Subjective evaluations of situations can thus be made on the basis of such observations and presumptions, as in the following Co. Donegal example:

Shíl mé nár **dhual** don mhaidin a theacht choíche.[4]

I thought the morning was destined never to come.

There is thus a certain grey area between what is merely 'habitual' and what is more 'generic' or 'nomic' or law-like; but the important point is that aspects of life that are in fact culturally and historically contingent can be conceptualized as if they had the inevitability of natural phenomena. Thus the relationship with one's native land is conceptualized as being as inherently natural as an inherited character trait. A further example of *dual* given by MacAdam concerns this idea of genetic inheritance discussed already in the case of *dúchas*.

> Budh **dual** do laogh an fhiaidh rith a bheith aige.[5]
>
> It's natural for the fawn of a deer to have fleetness.

With this proverb we can directly compare the following familiar one with *dúchas*:

> Thug sé ó **dhúchas** é mar thug a mhuc a rútáil.[6]
>
> He got it from nature as the pig got rooting (in the ground).

One thing that emerges from consideration of the *dual* proverbs, however, is the sense that B is not only the observed customary outcome of A but that *it could not be otherwise*. Smoke has to occur as the result of fire, shade is an inevitable concomitant of sunshine, while under normal circumstances a fawn can hardly *avoid* inheriting fleetness. This aspect of *dual* is perhaps clearest in those areas that involve an overlap with heredity or *dúchas*. This means that both *dual* and *dúchas* have an appearance of inevitability, which takes them beyond the realm of the 'merely' habitual or customary, a question to which we will return below. This sense of inevitability is further borne out by consideration of the following proverb variants where, as an equivalent to the familiar Irish form (*a*), O'Rahilly also gives a Scottish variant (*b*)[7]:

(*a*)   Cad do dhéanfadh mac an chait acht luch do mharbhadh?

What else would the cat's son do but kill a mouse?

(*b*)   Bu **dual** do mhac a' chait an luch ithe.

It is natural for the cat's son to eat the mouse.

One proverb in MacAdam's collection reads like a paraphrase of both of these, the very familiar one already discussed in other contexts:

> Briseann an **dúchas** tre shúilibh a chait.[8]
>
> The natural disposition of the cat bursts out through its eyes.

Further close examples of *dual* and *dúchas* appear almost as paraphrases of one another where the idea of heredity is involved, as in the common expression *is dual athar dó é* 'like father like son', literally 'it is the *dual* of his father to him':

> Tá ceol maith ag Donnchadh agus ba **dual** athar dó sin.[9]
>
> Donnchadh plays music well as you'd expect from his father.

For *dúchas* Mac Maoláin has the following:

Tá an ceol inti ó dhúchas.

The music is in her blood (lit. in her from *dúchas*).

This latter expression Mac Maoláin himself glosses as *bhí an ceol ag a muintir roimpi* 'her people before her were musical'. Here again we see issues of nature, of heredity, of what cannot be otherwise. Both *dual* and *dúchas* represent natural states that are genetically transmitted and therefore beyond human agency; we will discuss the *syntax* of this idea in particular in chapter 5. A wider distinction that is relevant here is that *dúchas* is the means or genetic mechanism by which what is *dual* is transmitted.

We find earlier examples of *dual* in the medieval and early modern periods expressing the same idea of an outcome as due to nature or accepted practice:[10]

(*a*)   Ua **dual** am deigrith don fir sin o mathair.

Good running was hereditary to him from his mother.

(*b*)   Gan ghort ní **dual** deaghbhranar.

Without a field there can be no good tillage.

This sense of inevitability can also be put to humorous use. In the following early modern tale a jester (*clesaide*) is performing his repertory of tricks, one of which consists of releasing a pup, a hare and a servant boy from one bag and a young woman from another and sending them up a silk rope. The woman has instructions that the dog should not harm the hare. Suspiciously, there follows a long period of silence, and the jester expresses his fears:

> 'Is ecal lim,' ar sé, 'co bfuil drochchor gá dhénam ann sút tuas ocus má tá ní rachaid cen dígail.' 'Crét sin,' ar Tadhg Ó Cellaig. 'Atá,' ar in clesaide, 'co mbiadh in chú ac ithe in gerrfiaid ocus in gilla ac dul chum na mná.' 'Bud **dual** sin féin,' ar Tadg. Tairrngios in tsnáithe iarsin ocus fuair in gilla itir dá chois na mná ocus in chú ac creim chnám in gerrfiaid.[11]

> 'I'm afraid,' he said, 'that there is mischief afoot up there and if there is it won't go unpunished.' 'What might that be?' asked Tadhg Ó Cellaig. 'Well,' said the trickster, 'that the dog might be eating the hare and the young lad having his way with the woman.' 'That would only be natural,' said Tadhg. He pulled in the rope after that and found the young man between the woman's legs and the dog gnawing the hare's bones.

The use of the word *féin* gives *dual* a somewhat caustic edge here. *Bud dual sin féin* is as much as to say '*even* that might happen' or '*even* that would be expected'. In other words, nature takes its course, or, 'what *else* would you expect?' In his collection of Irish epigrams, O'Rahilly cites the following quatrain:

Tarraing nádúra ní **dual**   It is not *dual* to extract the nature

as an ngual do bhíos go dubh	from the coal that is black
gé go ndearnais geal é iné	though you made it bright yesterday
atá 'na ghual féin iniu.[12]	it is still coal today.

It is not permitted by nature to extract the essence from the coal. The first line, however, has an interesting variant, which appears to say the opposite: *Tarraing nádúra* **as** *dual* 'It is *dual* to extract the nature'. This seems to imply that it is natural to *try* to extract the essence, or to give the appearance of extracting it. There is again the same 'tension' in these variants between the 'law-like' or immutable side of nature on the one hand and the human-made or customary on the other. The semantics of *dual* can be resolved into the following description: an event or state A is known by repeated observation or perception to consistently produce an event or state B; B is therefore expected from or predicated on the basis of A. As we shall see, this correlation between what is expected on the basis of what is previously known is central to the pragmatics of habituality.

However, at this point I would like to return to a more detailed consideration of the relationship between *dual* and *dúchas*. As we saw in chapter 2, the proverb *briseann an dúchas trí shúile an chait* indexes the internalization of *dúchas*, which 'breaks out' from within the individual, as in the case of 'through the cat's eyes'. This internalization is particularly salient in Modern Irish, as we have already seen, but is not characteristic of the typical use of *dual*, which occurs almost exclusively in predicative function with the verb 'to be' (*is*), even where issues of heredity are concerned. Thus to return to our proverb above, *Budh dual do laogh an fhiaidh rith a bheith aige*, we can analyse the *dual* component as follows:

Budh	dual	do laogh an fhiaidh	rith a bheith aige
would be	*dual*	for (the) calf of the deer	running to have

Thus *dual* stands outside the main predicate and appears indeed to regulate its content from this vantage point on the outside. This very syntax of *dual* in its rigidity and pervasiveness offers us an important clue here. In cases of conceptual overlap, that is, where issues of heredity are involved, *dúchas* can be taken as subordinate to, or a particular manifestation of, what is a more general regulatory principle of nature and custom: that which is *dual*. That this is also the case historically can be verified from a number of examples. In the first example, from a sixteenth-century translation of the English romance *William of Palerne*, (*Eachtra Uilliam*) this relationship is presented explicitly:

Agas fós dá mbeith fios sgéul agadsa nó aige fén, as maith fuair an ridire anaithnidh úd an chríoch sa do chosnumh ⁊ feidhm ⁊ fíorchongnamh do thabhairt las an mbanríoghain úd, óir dlighidh gach mac mínréir a mháthar, dóigh as **dual don dúthchas** dialladh re'roile gion go mbeith fios a chéile aca, mar adeir an seanfhocal go sonnradhach: treisi an dúthchas ná an oileamhain.[13]

And if you but knew the truth of the matter and if he but knew, that unknown knight did well to protect this land and give service and succour to its queen. For every son owes implicit obedience to his mother and it is natural for those of common stock to resemble each other though unaware of the relationship. As the proverb says: instinct is stronger than upbringing.

As we saw in chapter 2, a large part of the force of this passage derives from the use of two proverbs or aphorisms: *dúchas* is stronger than education (*oileamhain*) and 'people follow their hereditary instincts' (*diallaid daoine re a ndúthchus*). It is the following of those instincts, one's *dúchas* in other words, that is *dual* here: the context is that the eponymous hero William has arrived back in Sicily, having spent his life in exile. He is described at first as *an ridire anaithnidh* 'the unknown knight', until his identity is revealed to the ruling king of Sicily and the queen, who is in fact William's mother. In the passage above, the king's son is explaining to his father why it was *dual* or 'natural' for him to have acted as he did in protecting the land and serving its queen, even though unaware of his relation to her. Here again *dual* gives the sense of a force that is beyond human agency: in fact the particular agency of *dual* here is *dúchas* itself. This sense of *dúchas* as the agent of *dual* is also present in the following passage, though the syntax is different:

Nír iadsat ocus nir comraicseat fa aen duine reme riam, frem a fodhla finechais mar do iadsat fán ard-flaith hUa nAinmirech, uair is iatso na **dual-ghnimartha duchusa** ris ar diallustar Domnall a cuisib cairdiusa ocus a cosmailecht cheneoil na n-oirech ⁊ na n-uasalaithrech.[14]

There met not, and there united not in any one person before, such distinguished genealogical branches as met in the monarch grandson of Ainmire; for the following were the ancestral hereditary characteristics which he derived from his consanguinity with and descent from the chiefs and noble fathers.

In other words, the hero's deeds (*gnímartha*) are deeds that are *dual* (*dual-ghnímartha*) precisely on account of his heredity (*dúchas*) and the natural, expected outcome of this particular heredity.

I now wish to return to a couple of passages that were first presented in chapter 2. Firstly, we have already considered a passage from Céitinn's *Foras Feasa ar Éirinn* where *dúchas* in the sense of a hereditary right to something occurs disjunctively with *ceart,* a more general term of right or entitlement. We found that Fitzstephen's foreignness and Céitinn's attitude to him as one of the five tyrannical Norman leaders was at the heart of his being denied any entitlement to the land of Ireland (see chapter 3). A few lines later a different attitude is expressed towards Fitzstephen's native Irish ally Diarmaid Mac Murchadha, king of Leinster, after peace has been made between Mac Murchadha and the aspiring high-king of Ireland, Ruaidhrí Ó Conchobhair:

Cúigeadh Laighin do léigeadh do Dhiarmaid amhail fá **dúthchas** dó; agus d'fhiachaibh ar Dhiarmaid umhla is dísle do choimhéad do Ruaidhrí amhail fá **dual** do gach rígh dá mbíodh ar Laighnibh do dhéanamh do ríoghaibh Éireann.[15]

Diarmaid was left the province of Leinster as was *duchas* for him; and Diarmaid was obliged to submit to and remain loyal to Ruaidhrí as had [always] been *dual* to every king of Leinster to submit to the kings of Ireland.

We have already drawn attention to the nature of the syntax in which both *dual* and *dúchas* are implicated in this passage in chapter 2. As was argued in chapter 3, Diarmaid's birthright gives him the kingship of Leinster as his *dúchas* or hereditary right, while his subordination in turn to Ó Conchobhair is dictated by what is *dual,* which may by roughly glossed here as 'established custom'. Thus we have the distinction between *dual,* something that is presented as natural and inevitable but that *can be* imposed from without rather than residing within, as opposed to the more purely internal aspects of *dúchas.* This sense of a more internalized dimension to *dúchas* is heightened where it is conjoined with *folaidecht* 'lineage', 'descent' (from *fuil* 'blood'), and both are subsumed under an overarching concept of *dual*; in another passage already briefly considered in chapter 2 from *Betha Colaim Chille,* an angel intervenes in a dispute between Colm Cille and one Ciarán, son of the wright (*mac an tshaeir*), in the former's favour by pointing out to the latter that, whereas he had only had to sacrifice his life as an artisan to follow God, Colm Cille had made a more exalted sacrifice:

⁊ nar treicc se ar Dia acht an culaidh tshaírse sin do bi ga athair ⁊ gor treig C.c. righacht Erind air; oir **fa dual** do o duthcas ⁊ o folaidhecht hi.[16]

While he [Ciarán] had abandoned nothing for God except the labouring suit that his father had had, Colm Cille had given up the kingship of Ireland on his account; for the kingship was due to him from *dúchas* and blood line.

In the following passage, *dual* appears almost as an alternative to *ceart* in the passage from Céitinn above:

Cuireas Néid mhac Saidhin íar sin draoíghthe fíre focail-cheart d'agallamh Rígh na hÁisia, gá rádh leis nár cheart agus nár chothrom an fochain catha do bhí aige; agas fós nach raibhe **dúal nó dúthchas** aige ó shean nó ó shinnsir lé cíoscháin an mhagha sin.[17]

Néid mac Saidhin sent truth-speaking druids to address the King of Asia telling him that his pretext for battle was neither right nor fair; and, moreover, that he had neither *dual* nor *dúchas* by virtue of ancestry or forebears to the tax and tribute of that plain.

In other contexts where *dúchas* or *dúthaigh* signify the native place, *dual* can also be used to partially paraphrase this sense:[18]

(a)   'Cidh as **duthaig** duit?' . . . 'Ríghi Tuath mBreg . . . as **dual** damh'

'What is your *dúthaig?*' . . . 'the kingdom of the Tuath mBreg . . . is *dual* to me'

(b)   Ca crich is **dual** dit?

What country is *dual* to you?

(c)   Cia an chríoch . . . as **dúthchas** duit?

What is the territory . . . that is *dúchas* to you?

From these examples the native or hereditary land can either be designated as the *dúthaigh* or paraphrased as *an chríoch is dual/dúchas do* (X) 'the land that is *dual* or *dúchas* to (X)'.

The semantics and pragmatics of *dualgas*

Another particular representation of what is *dual* is found in its derivative *dualgas,* which has the variants *dualas* and *dualchas.* We can summarize the historical range of *dualgas* succinctly from Ó Dónaill as (i) 'natural right, due; customary fee or reward' and (ii) 'duty'. Of prime interest here is the relationship between the two senses of *dualgas:* one's 'due' or 'entitlement' on the one hand and one's 'duty' or 'obligation' on the other are opposite sides of the same coin, or two complementary aspects of the same reflexive process. In other words, *dualgas* is what is both 'due to' and 'due from'. This type of reciprocity has many manifestations in early Indo-European societies, as Benveniste[19] and Watkins[20] point out. One important manifestation of the reciprocity of relations is the relationship between patron and poet, so important in medieval Irish society. In fact Watkins demonstrates that precisely within this particular domain in Old Irish this process of reciprocity and exchange is reflected indexically and iconically in the following pairs (*dúan—dúas* and *clú—cnú*):[21]

Conferred by poet	Conferred by patron
dúan 'poem'	*dúas* 'recompense'
clú 'fame'	*cnú* lit. 'nut' = 'jewel', 'trinket', 'reward'

It is not clear whether or not *dual* and *dualgas* can also be related to the root that gives *duan,* but in any case my contention is that the semantics of *dualgas* cannot be determined without reference to both the indexical nature of its relation to this kind of reciprocity and also its relation to the basic etymon *dual.* To try to illustrate what I mean, I shall look at a few examples from medieval and early modern sources. First, however, it should be noted that, as with *dual* above *dualgas* and *dúthaigh* may alternate where the latter is used in its abstract sense of entitlement. The following parallel passages from *Acallam na Senórach* relate to the order of guests at the Tech Midchuarta. Each guest is to be seated according to social and hereditary rank; note that their entitlement (*dualgas* or *dúthaigh*) is derived from that of their fathers and grandfathers once again. It is interesting to compare the wording of the two recensions; and we have a similar usage in other medieval texts:

(*a*) (As a aithle sin táncatar rompa i Temraig ocus táinic Cormac i tech mór midchuarta ocus) do córaiged gach nech ar **dualgas** a athar ⁊ senathar ann

(*b*) ro córiged cach nech ar **duthaig** a athar ⁊ a tshenathar

(After that they came to Tara and Cormac came into the great ale house and) everyone was arranged according to what was due his father and grandfather

(*c*) a righa ⁊ a thoisigh diaidh a ndiaidh do réir a **ndualgus**.[22]

his kings and chiefs one by one according to their due.

Clearly both *dúthaigh* and *dualgas* here signify an 'entitlement', or something that is 'due to' someone by virtue of their status. As indicated above, however, the word *dualgas* indexes the entire reciprocal domain of what is *dual* in the process of exchange and so can signify, in context, more of an obligation than an entitlement. This gives rise to the Modern Irish sense of 'duty', which of course is right or entitlement viewed from the other side, as in the following two examples from the seventeenth and eighteenth centuries, respectively, (*a*) Ó Bruadair's lament for Séamus do (*sic*) Barra and (*b*) Donlevy's Catechism,[23] while (*c*), taken from the Irish version of Daniel O'Connell's address to the Catholic Association in 1824, gives the typical modern sense of 'duty' or 'obligation':[24]

(*a*) **Dualgus** do thuamadh óm aithribh   To sing thy dirge is my ancestral duty;

nach tréigim geadh tréith mo chabhair   I shan't neglect, although my aid be feeble,

bheith do ghnáth i láimh 's i labhairt   To be in word and act forever faithful

le cuain ríoghdha Tighe Molaige.   To the royal tribe of Teach Molaige.

(*b*) Gan smuaineadh air Dhía nó air an **dualgas** a dlighthear dhó

Without thinking of God or the entitlement/obligation that he is owed

(*c*) Asé ar ttuairim go bhfuil sé ceangailte orrainn mar **dhualgas** sibh do chómhairliughadh.

We deem it a duty we owe to you to put you on your guard.

The reciprocal or reflexive nature of the process is evident from a comparison of (*a*) and (*b*) above. To take the second one, *dualgas* from the divine viewpoint is a right or entitlement, from the human viewpoint a duty or obligation. The same can be said of the following passage, where Diarmaid Mac Murchadha and his ally Fitzstephen combine forces with Maurice

Fitzgerald to extract revenge for the injustices that the inhabitants of Dublin have inflicted on Mac Murchadha's kingdom (*gach aindlighe da ndearnsad lucht Átha Cliath air féin*). Leaving Fitzstephen behind, he proceeds with Fizgerald to plunder Dublin (*d'argain Átha Cliath*). When the citizens of Dublin learn of this they resolve to appease the king of Leinster by sending him gold and silver:

> do ghealladar go dtiubhraidís gach ceart ⁊ gach **dualgas** da raibhe ag Mac Murchadha orra roimhe sin dó.[25]

> they pledged that they would give Mac Murchadha every right and due that they had owed him before that.

Again from Mac Murchadha's viewpoint we speak of a 'due', from the viewpoint of the inhabitants of the city of a duty or imposition.

In the relation of poet to patron, *dualgas* features in the sense of 'payment' or 'remuneration' for a poem. Here the domain of what is *dual* is again indexed in the sense that it is *dual* that the poet confer honour on his patron and in his turn be correspondingly rewarded. In a poem of protest from the late sixteenth century, 'Créd fúarais oram a Áoidh', an Ulster poet, Maolmuire Mac Con Uladh Mhic an Bhaird, complains to the O'Donnell, Aodh Rua Ó Domhnaill, that he has failed to meet his obligations to the poet as his patron; in particular that he has failed to provide him with suitable retinue and patrimony.[26] The poem is replete with the language of obligation, entitlement and indebtedness. After enquiring of his patron what he might have done to offend him, Mac Con Uladh continues by asking whether it is because of the poet's place of origin, the patron's acquaintance or lack of acquaintance with the poet, or rather some defect in the poem itself:

gé 'táoi **ag béin a dúalais di**,	or is it that you found a blemish in my poetry
nó an béim úarais ar mh'éigsi?[27]	that you are withholding its due from me?

Here *dúalas* is the entitlement due to the poet on account of his poem, and that is what is being withheld. The verb *dlighidh* and its derivatives are also very important in the poem in the context of this entire semantic domain of what is 'right', 'natural', 'expected' and will be considered in more detail in chapter 5.

In the following stanza the poet laments his lack of a retinue (*lucht leanamhna*), and the next stanzas place a particular emphasis on the idea of *cóir*, which recalls the ideological sphere of Tadhg Dall Ó hUiginn's poem to MacWilliam Burke discussed in chapter 3. Note also the language of right and entitlement as expressed here by two parts of the verb *dlighidh* 'owes', 'is owed': past tense *dhluigh* and the adjectival *dleacht* 'lawful', 'legitimate':

A hí Dhomhnaill, níor **dhluigh dhuibh**	O O'Donnell, you had no right

cur énfhocal am aghaidh	to voice any opposition to me
fán lucht leanamhna as **dleacht** dún;	regarding the retinue to which I am entitled;
neart na healadhna ar n-iompúdh.	Art's prerogative has been over-turned
Éccóir duit dol am aghaidh	It was unjust of you to go against me
am **chóir** trá sul tángabhair.[28]	in my claim, rather than to accede (?).

In a fashion reminiscent of Tadhg Dall Ó hUiginn's poem, considered in chapter 3, the poet continues to hammer on the idea of the 'right' (*cóir*) that has been withdrawn from him. Here we have *cóir* in the general sense of 'justice', 'fair play', of which *dualas* or *dualgas* is a specific aspect, while another dimension of this general entitlement is again *dúchas*:

Gan tabhairt **mo dhúalghais** damh	Who knows but your reason
cá fios dúinn nach é h'adhbhar	for withholding my right from me is to wait
nó go mbeinn inghill n-anma.	until such time as I should be worthy of a title
's go ndingninn eirr mh'ealadhna.[29]	and should complete the last stage of my art.

Note again in the following stanza the use of the verb *dlighidh*, here in the autonomous or non-agentive (roughly speaking, 'passive') form, where the logical subject is governed by the preposition *do* (see chapter 5 for a discussion of this syntax):

Ó tá **ar ndúthchas** fád dheirc mhoill	Since my patrimony is under your jurisdiction,
dlighthear dhuitsi, a Í Dhomhnuill,	you are obliged, o O'Donnell,
cur leam nó go n-aghar é	to support me until I receive it,
a thamhan as fhearr úirchré.	o tree sprung from the finest soil.

As the editor himself points out, the specific nature of the poet's complaint remains in some doubt, precisely because of the range of application of both *dual(g)as* and *dúchas*. This lack of specificity applies to the terms *cóir* and *inmhe* as used in this poem as well.[30] The idea of hereditary property applies to *inmhe* as well as to *dúchas*. In other words, all these items may refer to traditional rights and entitlements in general or to possessions, property in particular.

In various other poems of the period we have complaints from poets deprived of their *dúchas*. For example, the same poet in another poem addressed to Aodh Ruadh Ó Domhnaill while the latter was captive in Dublin in the period preceding 1592, 'Iomchair Th'Atuirse, a Aodh Ruaidh', ('Carry your grief, Red Hugh') bemoans the chaotic state of Tír Chonaill, in particular the fact that the poets are without their patrimony:

Atáid th'éigis is t'ollaimh
do thaoisigh, do thearmannaigh

i dtalmhaibh nár **dhúthchais** dáibh

ó dhamhraidh chúlchais Chruacháin.[31]

Your poets and your *ollamhs*
your leaders, your church tenants

are in lands that are not *dúchas* for them

from the curly-haired stags of Cruachán.

A similar protest at the loss or withholding of inheritance is found in the works of Maolmuire's kinsman Fearghal Óg Mac an Bhaird:

Buain a dhúthchais do dhuine
ní breath ríogh do Rudhroidhe

is liom-sa a chogar ó chiort

ionnsa m'obadh óm oidhreacht.[32]

Taking his *dúchas* from one
that is not a judgement from Rudhroighe befitting a king

an audience with him is mine by right

it is difficult to deny me my inheritance.

In similar terms, two leading poets of the early seventeenth century, Fear Flatha Ó Gnímh and Mathghamhain Ó hIfearnáin, lament the decline in the prestige of poets and the status of the hereditary bardic order precisely as representing the denial of what is *dual* or *dualgas*. These poems have been referred to already in chapter 3 and will be discussed at greater length in chapter 5:

(*a*) Mairg do-chuaidh re ceird ndúth-
       chais:
       rug ar Bhanbha mbarrúrthais

       nach **dualghas** athar is fhearr
       i n-achadh fhuarghlas Éireann.

Alas for him who has
followed his family profession
it has befallen Banbha of the fresh soft surface

that in Ireland's cool green field
one's father's natural calling is not the best.

(*b*) A mhic ná mebhraig éigsi

       cerd do shen rót ró-thréig-si

       tús anóra gér **dual** di

       fa tuar anshógha in éigsi.[33]

Son, don't even think about poetry
abandon the craft of your ancestors before you
though it really should have pride of place
poetry has been a cause of misery.

In view of the usage of *dualgas* considered above in relation to such poems of complaint on the part of the hereditary poets, the early seventeenth-century *Pairlement Chloinne Tomáis* offers a succinct commentary on the premises that underlie these poems of protest. One of the members of the low-born Clann Tomáis offers this advice to his son:

Ná grádhaig an t-aos uasal,
is ná tabhair **dualgus** don éigse,

Do not love the aristocracy,
do not give payment to the poets,

ná héist re foghar orgán,	do not listen to the sounds of organs
's ná creid comhrádh cléire.[34]	and do not trust the talk of priests.

Elsewhere in the same text we are told that St. Patrick laid down strict ordinances for governing the behaviour of Clann Tomáis towards the nobility, whom they were obliged to serve. By the reign of Brian Bóramha's grandson Muircheartach, however, they were renouncing their obligations and would work only for pay:

> gur léigeadar dhíobh aodhaireacht ná treabhaireacht do dhéanamh do neach ar bith acht dóibh féin amháin, muna bfhaghadaois págha nó **dualgus**.[35]

> they had given up herding and ploughing for anyone except themselves only, unless they got pay or wages.

To redress this situation, Muircheartach calls an assembly of 'all those who had understanding and authoritative knowledge of the law and history' (*lucht eolais agas ughdarráis a dlighe agas a seanchus*), who roundly condemn the presumption of Clann Tomáis. The passage above is interesting in its juxtaposition of the older 'aristocratic' term *dualgas*, with its connotations of an ordained, reciprocal entitlement and obligation, with the relatively recent loanword *páigh* 'pay'. Perhaps this is to expose the mercenary, mercantile and entrepreneurial nature of Clann Tomáis, though I cannot be sure if this juxtaposition is deliberately satirical. Nonetheless, it seems likely that there is some wit attached to the juxtaposition of the two words here.

We shall return to the poetry of this period in due course; but some more examples to illustrate the pragmatic nature of *dualgas* are in order here. The first text to consider is a Middle Irish poem found in the *Metrical Dindshenchus* entitled 'Slige Dala'. This is a poem on the origin and discovery of the five great Irish roads of tradition, the road of the title being the great south-western road from Tara in the east to Ossory in the south. The poet begins by asking:

Senchas cía lín non-iarfaig	What company asks us the legend
sliged Dala dag-bríathraig[36]	of the Road of Dalo the affable

He then proceeds with his *senchas*: how Dalo arrived from Scythia with his wife, Cre, his fellow-warrior Canann and his wife Caire. It is made clear that, although the road derives its name from Dalo, its *senchas* does not end there. Of Caire in particular the poet relates:

ic dún Chairin cét costud	at Dún Cairin of a hundred feastings
fúair éc ocus imfhostud	she met death and surcease
Is í sin a fodail fhír	This is her just portion
iar scur monair is mígním,	after ceasing from effort and ill-doings,

| feib fúair tria munigud mass | as through her fair confidence she gained |
| a sudigud, a senchass.[37] | her dwelling place with its story. |

Thus Caire herself is part of the road's *senchas*. The history of Slige Dala turns out to be something of a preamble to the *senchas* of the five roads in general, for the narration of which the poet announces his credentials:

Tathum buidin do brethaib,	I have an array of judgements,
do chuirib, do chóem-srethaib;	of melodies and staves in order fair;
fail lim dliged is damna,	I have legal lore and matter for song,
senchas sliged sóer-Banba.[38]	even the story of the roads of noble Banba.

The poet then proceeds to relate the manner in which the various roads were found one by one and by whom. Finally he sums up and in fact draws a parallel between the process of the roads' discovery and his own 'discovery' of their *senchas*:

Is amlaid-sin fo-frítha	In this wise were discovered
na sligthi, na sen-chrícha,	the roads, the ancient mearings,
mar fhúarus a mbunad mbrass,	as I found their high origin,
a **ndúalus**, a ndind-shenchas.[39]	their traditional rights, their local legends.

Here the editor gives the translation as 'traditional rights', but there is little in the poem to suggest that rights are involved here. In fact *dúalus* here is to be contextualized with both *bunad* 'origin' and *senchas* 'historical knowledge', two concepts that have already been discussed in relation to *dúchas* in chapter 3. In like fashion we can say that *dualas* here pragmatically references or indexes a sense of origin and history. In fact, in reference to the roads it can simply be taken as 'everything that is *dual* to them'—everything that accrues to them or belongs to them, in this case their origin and history.

In a sixteenth-century poem on the efficacy of Christ's sacrifice on the cross, 'Fiu a bheatha bás tighearna' ('The Lord's death is as valuable as his life'), the Westmeath poet Diarmuid Ó Cobhthaigh speaks of Christ's commitment to humankind and the manner in which his sacrifice was predestined. Note the use of *dual* here again in what appears to be a proverbial expression:

Do dhearg tuar bhos mbairrleabhar,	The Lord, when fastened to the cross
—gan ghort ní **dual** deaghbhranar—	ploughed up the lea of His slender-fingered hands;
rí re clár do do cuibhrigheadh;	every good lea must be ploughed;
do bhí a ndán i ndearnabhar.	what You did do was ordained.

Leanbh cígh do dhruim **dhualasa**	The darling son to prove his dutiful love
a cígh do bhuing beofhrasa	poured forth torrents of living blood from his breast
guais sreabh chorcra an chíoghasa	dangerous for men is that purple stream
rompa gan fhear n-eolasa.[40]	if they have no pilot to guide them.

The translation of *dualas* offered here, 'dutiful love', indexes the reference not only to everything Christ had done as being *a ndán* 'in store', 'destined', but also to his 'good will' (*daghumhla*) in saving humanity:

Síoth dá thaobh dhóibh daing-nighidh	He uses His kinship with the Virgin
a ghaol re hóigh d'airrdheanaibh,	to give visible proof to men of His pardon;
rí 'n-a fhuilngidh anmhuirir	the Lord who is the support of a great family [the world],
fuilngidh ar thrí tairrngeadhaibh.[41]	he supports them on three nails.

Here Christ's *dualas*—his duty—is both what is expected of and pre-ordained for him.

In all cases of *dualgas* considered above, the interpretation is pragmatic, in that *dualgas* in any given context must always be referred back to the underlying sense of what is *dual*, both 'to' and 'from' those referred to, and interpreted accordingly. Both words are employed as part of the pro-Stuart or Jacobite rhetoric of the seventeenth and eighteenth centuries. In employing the trope of the true king as wedded to the land of Ireland, one eighteenth-century poet describes the Stuart Pretender as *céile dual na Banban,* the only spouse that is *dual* or 'natural' for Ireland.[42] Compare this with the welcome accorded King James I by Fearghal Óg Mac an Bhaird in 1603, 'Trí coróna i gcairt Shéamáis' ('Three crowns in James' charter'), where the closely related term *dú* (see chapter 2) is used to describe the same relation of king married to the land:

Fada a-tá i dtairngire duit	It has been a long time stated in prophecy
críoch Sagsan—is iul orrdhruic;	that England should be yours—this is common knowledge
duit is **dú** Éire amhlaidh	likewise you are entitled to Ireland
is tú a céile ar chomhardhaibh.[43]	by all appearances you are her true husband.

Likewise Tomás Ó Míocháin more than a century and a half later can use both *dual* and *dúchas* to account for the right of the Stuarts to the kingdom of Ireland:

(*a*)	an tí dar dhleathach **dual** do an bhuan-tslat 's a chor[óin]	to one to whom is lawful and *dual* the eternal sceptre and the crown

(b)   an prionsa den tsaorcheap 'nar   the prince of the noble stock in
      dhúchas an ríshlat   whom the royal sceptre is *dúchas*
      Is an fionnbhile fíordhlitheach   and the fair, legitimate, wandering
         fánach   scion
      Do thuirling i réimfhlaitheas raon-   who descended into the extensive
         mhar a shinsir   sovereign kingdom of his
                                                 ancestors
      In Éirinn faoi shaoire na Cásca.[44]   Into Ireland by holy day of Easter.

Note once again how in both instances *dual* and *dúchas* are in close association with derivatives of the *dligh* lexical family (*dlitheach, dleathach*) mentioned
above. In the same way, the right of the Stuart derives in Irish terms from the
natural right inherent in *dualgas* as in the poetry of (a) Seán Ó Neachtain and
(b) Aogán Ó Rathaille:

(a)   Díbirt is fuadradh, luathscrios is léan
      ar mhaoin, ar chuallacht, ar bhualach, ar thréad
      na ndaoine tá ag fuagradh 's ag ruagan an té
      is **rí ceart ó dhualgas 's ón uaisle** darb é.

      Expulsion and vagrancy, destruction and affliction
      on the wealth, the companies, the cattle and the herds
      of those who are outlawing and banishing the one
      who is the true king from *dualgas* and nobility.

(b)   Fios fiosach dom d'inis, is ise go fíor-uaigneach
      fios filleadh don duine don ionad ba **rí-dhualgas**
      fios milleadh na droinge chuir eisean ar rinnruagairt
      's fios eile ná cuirfead im laoithibh le fíor-uamhan.[45]

      True tidings she revealed to me, most forlorn
      tidings of one returning by royal right (*dualgas*)
      tidings of the crew ruined who drive him out
      and tidings I keep from my poem for sheer fear.

In both poems there is an antithetical relationship between the rhyming (*rí*)-
dualgas and *ruagan* (Ó Neachtain) and (*rinn*)*ruagairt* (Ó Rathaille) both meaning 'banishing', 'banishment'. Given the messianic nature of much Jacobite
poetry, both in Ireland and Scotland, it is perhaps not irrelevant here to hark
back to the devotional dimensions of *dualgas* as standing for Christ's sacrifice,
as discussed earlier in relation to Ó Cobhthaigh's poem.

   From the evidence surveyed thus far we can summarize the semantics and
pragmatics of *dual* and *dualgas* as follows. The relationship between two states
of affairs, A and B, is *dual* in that B is seen as a natural reflex or product of A.
This implies that any time A obtains, B may be expected. This conclusion is
arrived at through observation of a causal relation, *more than once over an
extended period,* which occurs either as a natural or a cultural phenomenon: it is

known that A has produced B and is therefore *expected* to produce it on all subsequent occasions. These premises are carried over to the derivative *dualgas*. We have seen a number of examples where *dualgas* can be said to have something of the 'shifting' or indexical quality of *dúchas*, even if not to quite the same extent. In the same connection, before moving on to consider the grammatical expression of what is expected on the basis of what is known, or the 'habitual', it is worth noting the following examples of the use of *dualchas*, the Scottish equivalent of Irish *dualgas*. The first is from the dictionary of Edward Dwelly, while the second is from an eighteenth-century Jacobite text that complains of the high taxes imposed on Scotland by the descendants of William of Orange:

(a)   'S e do **dhualchas** a bhi duineil[46]

      It is your (hereditary) nature to be manly

(b)   gun chus againn fuaight riu an **dualchas** no'n dáimh[47]

      with us having little in common with them in hereditary nature or kinship

Here *dualchas* is virtually indistinguishable from Irish *dúchas* (or indeed from Scottish *dùthchas*). For a final, and very different, example, in the Old Irish legal tract on possession and liability concerning the keeping of bees we find the following judgement:

> fintiu griain i mbechbrethaib is sí-ede fo-choslea derbfhine ar is í derbfhine i mbechbrethaib tír bes-da nesam foda-loing.[48]

> the kindred share of land in bee-judgements is the one which the *derbfhine* takes, for the *derbfhine* in bee-judgements is the holding which is nearest to them [and] which supports them.

To this the following commentary is appended:

> ata **duthcus** don [fh]ine a **dualgus** ind fearaind isna beachaib do reir na mbreath.

> the kin has a right to the bees in virtue of the land according to the judgements.

This in its turn is reminiscent of the examples discussed above of the relationship between *dual* and *dúchas*, where the latter is seen as the instrument or agency of the former. Here *dúchas* is the hereditary right of the kin group, which arises as a consequence of (*a dualgas*) possession of the land.

Habituality in the Irish verb

I have emphasized above those components of the semantic description of *dual* and *dualgas* that are also crucial in relation to the *grammatical* expression of habituality, which will be examined in this section. Modern Irish makes the following category distinctions in the finite verb:

(i)   **An aimsir láithreach** (present tense) which indicates the present moment: e.g. *feicim anois iad* 'I see them now'.

(ii) **An aimsir chaite** (past tense): a point in past time: e.g. *rith sé* 'he ran'.

(iii) **An aimsir fháistineach** (future tense): a point in future time: e.g. *tiocfaidh Somhairle anocht* 'Somhairle will come tonight'.[49]

These categories perform the *deictic* function of tense, which is that of placing a situation in past, present or future time relative to the moment of speech. In addition there are two other categories described as tenses:[50]

(iv) **An aimsir ghnáthchaite** (past habitual tense): an indefinite number of points in past time: *thagadh an galtán gach lá anuraidh* 'the steamer used to come every day last year'

(v)   **An aimsir ghnáthláithreach** (present habitual tense): an indefinite number of points in past *and future* time: *tagann an galtán gach lá* 'the steamer comes every day'.

As is apparent from the terminology employed in (iv) and (v), these categories are in some way elaborations on (ii) and (i), respectively. The key to this elaboration lies in the nature of the common term *gnáth*, which may be translated as 'usual' or 'customary'. We shall return to a more detailed consideration of this term in its various historical dimensions below. Thus (iv) codes a situation that was usually or habitually the case in past time, while (v) characterizes a situation as usually the case in a timeless sense (note the characterization above 'an indefinite number of points in past *and future* time'). As Ó Siadhail points out, and as we will see in more detail below, the distinction between 'habitual' and 'non-habitual' is clearly marked only in the past tense and in the present tense of the verb 'to be'.[51] Let us take the latter case first. The form of the non-habitual present *(a)tá* can be used to indicate that a state of affairs is either (*a*) occurring at the present moment or (*b*) continuous:

(*a*)   **Tá** sé ag obair anseo **anois díreach**.   He is working here right now.

(*b*)   **Tá** sé ag obair anseo **seasta**.   He works/is working here permanently.[52]

On the other hand, the habitual *bíonn* presupposes a succession or repetition of different occasions on which a given situation applies, as signalled by the types of temporal adverbs that are its concomitant: *de ghnáth* 'usually', *uaireanta* 'sometimes', *gach lá* 'every day' and *go minic* 'often'; for example:

> **Bíonn** sé ag obair anseo **de ghnáth/uaireanta/gach lá/go minic/ó am go ham**.
>
> He works here usually/sometimes/every day/often/from time to time.

As already indicated this aspectual distinction is much more explicit and pervasive in the past, where it affects every verb. The distinction here is between (*a*) a state of affairs that can be described as one specific, discrete occurrence at a particular time and that is rendered by the simple past tense and (*b*) one that again involves repetition over a period and that is expressed by the habitual past:

(*a*)   **Chuaigh** sé abhaile ar a hocht   He went home at eight last night
     aréir

(*b*)   **Théadh** sé abhaile ar an mbus   He always went home on the bus
     i gcónaí[53]

As we have noted, the term used to denote the habitual function is the prefix *gnáth-*, as in *gnáthláithreach* (habitual present) and *gnáthchaite* (habitual past). In addition, the adverb that most generically defines the function of the habitual is *de ghnáth* 'usually', 'ordinarily'. We can now examine the implications of this word *gnáth* itself and its derivative adjective *gnách*, older spelling *gnáthach*. Let us take a look at a few proverbs, as we did for *dual* above, this time from Mícheál Óg Ó Longáin's nineteenth-century collection:

> Ní **gnáthach** caonnach ar an gcloich bhíonn a' síorchorruighe
>
> It is not usual for a stone that is constantly moving to have moss (a rolling stone gathers no moss)
>
> Ní **gnáth** fear náireach éadálach
>
> It is not usual for a modest man to be wealthy
>
> Ní **gnáth** cosnamh iar ndíth tighearna
>
> It is not usual to sustain a fight once the leader is dead
>
> Ní **gnáth** ár gan élóidhtheach
>
> It is not usual to have a battle without survivors (cf. English 'It's a hard battle where none escapes')
>
> Is **gnáth** sealbh ar gach síoriasacht
>
> It is usual for every perpetual loan to grant possession[53]

We can see that these examples bear more than a passing resemblance to the proverbs containing *dual* given above. In structure, we have by and large a common pattern where 'X' is the lexical variable *dual* or *gnáth*:

Ní/Is	**X** = dual/gnách	A *gan* B

A is/is not X without B

As we saw above, *dual* itself frequently translates as 'usual' or 'customary'; there is thus at least a certain overlap. One thing that differentiates many of the *dual* proverbs, however, is the sense that B is not only the customary outcome of A but that *it could not be otherwise*. As we saw earlier in this chapter smoke has to occur as the result of fire, shade is an inevitable concomitant of sunshine, while under normal circumstances a fawn can hardly *avoid* inheriting fleetness. As we have seen, this aspect of *dual* is perhaps clearest in those areas that involve an overlap with heredity or *dúchas*. With *gnáth* we appear to have a more casual or circumstantial relation between A and B, although one that nevertheless normally obtains. In fact this is, arguably, intrinsically so with some of the *dual* examples that deal with culturally rather than naturally contingent phenomena: no Sunday without Mass, for example. In general, however, we have to posit an additional semantic-pragmatic component for *dual* as involving a sense of inevitability. This point will be pursued further in chapter 5, where we will consider the syntax of both *dual* and *gnách* in greater detail.

What interests us here primarily is the possibility of making a link between the words *gnáth* and *dual* as *lexicalicizations* of habituality on the one hand and present and habitual past (or 'imperfect') categories as its *grammaticalization* on the other. With this in mind we can return to the first two of Ó Longáin's proverbs above—(*a*) *Ní gnáthach caonnach ar an gcloich bhíonn a' síorchorruighe* and (*b*) *Ní gnáth fear náireach éadálach*—and consider some of the variants of these given by O'Rahilly:

(*a*)   Ní **thagann** caonnach ar chloich reatha

     Ní **bhailígheann** an chloch reatha cúnach

     Ní **ghabhann** cloch reatha caonnach[55]

In each case the highlighted form characterized by the ending -(*e*)*ann* is the present habitual, which here performs essentially the same semantic function as *gnáth*(*ach*). This is not to say that the present forms are identical with the use of *gnáth*, rather that they are strongly compatible with it. Similarly, for (*b*) we have the analogous proverb:

(*b*)   Ní **fhaghann** sagart balbh beatha

     A mute priest does not get a livelihood[56]

Similar paraphrases would also account for the habitual dimensions of *dual*, for example **Ní/Cha bhíonn toit gan teine*, 'There's no smoke without fire'.

In a succinct analysis of the semantics and pragmatics of habituality, Skerrett analyses sentences expressing habitual actions in accordance with a set of implications to which they give rise and that render the use of habitual-marked categories appropriate.[57] He gives as his examples the following two sentences, where the first contains the present and the second contains the past habitual form of the verb *bligh* 'milk':

(*a*)   **Bligheann** Seán an bhó   Seán milks the cow

(*b*)   **Bhligheadh** Seán an bhó   Seán used to milk the cow

The essential point is that habitual-marked sentences imply a more complex state of mind than non-habitual ones. This becomes clear when the sentences above are compared with (*c*) their simple past and (*d*) their future tense equivalents:

(*c*)   **Bhligh** Seán an bhó   Seán milked the cow

(*d*)   **Blighfidh** Seán an bhó   Seán will milk the cow

Sentence (*c*) simply makes a report that on some specific occasion in the past the action in question took place. Sentence (*d*) makes a prediction that on some specific occasion in the future the action will take place. The habitual sentences, on the other hand, appear to combine aspects of report and prediction without corresponding to either, the implications of which Skerrett schematizes as follows.[58] For any time X it is

> KNOWN: that event S has occurred at times previous to X with frequency i (i > 1)
>
> EXPECTED: that event S will occur at times subsequent to X with frequency i (i > 1)

If X is concurrent with the time of utterance, PRESENT

If X is previous to the time of utterance, PAST

As Skerrett puts it, 'the speaker reports a complex state of mind, in that he has made a judgement based on knowledge and expectation, of the normality of an event'.[59] It is worth emphasizing again, after Comrie, that this presupposes an event that is 'characteristic of an extended period of time'. This idea of extension is crucial; thus *he stood up and coughed five times* does not count as habitual.[60] This is strongly reminiscent of the analysis given above for the two lexical items *gnáth* and *dual*, bearing in mind that the latter has a further component of perceived inevitability. Thus the semantics and pragmatics of the **expected** that follow from the **known** are a common underlying basis for both specific lexical items and grammatical categories: we can talk here in both cases of the *pragmatics of habituality*. There is the further inference or *implicature* with the habitual past that the situation described no longer holds. The pragmatics of habituality will be taken up in a particular historical context below.

The obligatory nature of habituality in Irish

Consider the following example from Céitinn's *Foras Feasa ar Éirinn* as an instance of how this contrast between simple and habitual past shapes a narrative. Céitinn in his history tells us of the mythical king Ughaine Mór, who had twenty-five children. Each of them would make a circuit of Ireland in succession, so that eventually they exhausted the country's resources exacting tribute and feasting as they went. When the king's subjects objected, it was decided to divide Ireland into twenty-five parts, one part for each of his children, so that none would be a burden to any of the others and this division became a fiscal and administrative one. Note the telling aspectual contrast all through this passage (simple past in bold; habitual past in bold capitals):

> **do bhádar** cúigear ar fhichid do chloinn ag an Ughaine (*had*) sin . . . Agus an tan **DO BEIRTHÍ** saorchuairt Éireann leo (*went*), mar a **mBÍODH** mac díobh anocht (*stayed*), **DO BHÍODH** (*stayed*) an mac oile amárach ann . . . ionnus gach taobh 'n-a **dTUGDAOIS** aghaidh (*directed their steps*) go **gCAITHTÍ** leo (*they exhausted*) a **mBÍODH** do bhiadh is do lón ann. Agus mar **thugadar** fir Éireann sin dá n-aire (*observed*) **do chuadar** (*they went*) do cheisneamh an dochair sin . . . is é ní ar ar **chinneadar** (*agreed*) leath ar leath Éire do roinn i gcúig rannaibh fichead . . . Agus is do réir na ronna soin **DO TÓGTHAOI** (*used to be paid*) cíoschána ⅂ dualgais da gach rígh **da raibhe** (*reigned*) ar Éirinn feadh trí céad bliadhan.[61]

I will defer a complete translation of this passage, in order to emphasize certain features of its grammatical structure and the way in which that structure helps to shape discourse structure. In the case of the simple past, two focal usages can be identified here. The translations of the verbs in the passage are those of the editor. Firstly, both the first and last lines contain examples of the verb 'to be' (*do bhádar* and *dá raibhe*). With this verb the simple past often indicates *continuousness*: thus *gach rígh da raibhe ar Éirinn* 'every king that (ever) was (ruled) over Ireland', conceiving the succession as an unbroken line. In addition, the fact that Ughaine had twenty-five children, for example, is expressed by the non-habitual form, even though it cannot be represented *punctually* along the time axis. In the case of other non-stative verbs, on the other hand, as in the middle segment beginning *Agus mar a thugadar,* the simple past in each case indicates the attainment of an end-point to a single, discrete occurrence, or an event that is closed over its frame.[62] However, forms must be marked as habitual (here in capital letters), where the intention is to convey the idea of an act that has taken place repeatedly over what is to be understood as an extended period (here the various circuits of Ireland and their consequences; also the levying of tribute on the basis of the division of Ireland into twenty-five parts). The difference between habitual and non-habitual in Irish is that the latter represents one discrete closure over the event frame, even over an extended period, while the former does not.[63] Now it is illuminating to compare this segmentation of past time with the editor's perfectly idiomatic (and accurate) English rendition of the Irish verbs marked for the habitual above. Of the six such verbs directly translated by them, five are glossed by the English simple past tense. However, it may be noted again, by virtue of the gloss 'used to be paid' below, that English does indeed have a device for signalling habituality. Indeed English (like Irish) has more than one. Note how the following alternative translations of a section of the passage would read if we were to treat the marking of habituality in English in the same obligatory way as it is done in Irish. There are two ways to do this, by (a) the circumlocution *used to* and (b) the otherwise conditional form *would:*

(a)   And when they **used to go** on a free circuit around Ireland, where one of the sons **used to be** at night, the other one **used to be** tomorrow . . . so that wherever they **used to direct** their steps they **used to consume** all the food in the area.

(b)   And when they **would go** on a free circuit around Ireland, where one of the sons **would be** at night, the other one **would be** tomorrow . . . that wherever they **would direct** their steps they **would consume** all the food in the area.

The first alternative in particular, which represents the standard means of rendering past habituality in English, sounds distinctly irksome and un-idiomatic—in fact it positively grates on a native speaker of that language. The second is somewhat less irritating and indeed may have something of a rhetorical effect.

In the following passage the connection between the grammatical category 'habitual' and its underlying semantic prime *gnáth* is quite explicit:

Agus an tan **DO SHUIDHEADH** Brian n-a shuidhe ríogh is é rí Mumhan **DO SHUIDHEADH** ar a dheasláimh; *amhail fá ghnáth* ris gach rígh d'fhuil Éireamhóin ríogha Uladh do chur ar a ndeasláimh.[64]

And when Brian sat in his king's seat it was the king of Munster that used to sit by his right hand, *as was the accustomed practice* (gnáth) with all the kings of the descendants of Éireamhón to put the kings of Ulster on their right-hand side.

The crucial point here is that the expression of habituality in Irish is *obligatory* in a way that it is not in English, and that this obligatoriness has important ramifications for the *rhetorical style* of the language.[65] It is this question of rhetorical style that I wish to pursue in the following section by looking in detail at a couple of texts in their particular historical and cultural milieu.

A historical context for habituality: some sixteenth- and seventeenth-century poems

As Slobin points out, a rhetorical style has a greater general effect than simply directing attention to the semantic content of whatever forms the grammar provides: there are consequences for what is 'said' and 'unsaid' in any given language. What I want to do here is to suggest some ways in which this works with the habitual past in Irish and how that might assist us in the hermeneutics of reading texts in their particular context. As a necessary preliminary we might consider what aspects of the meaning of the habitual past are more pragmatic or inferential, as against those that are more semantic or directly referential. We may take a simple English example for illustrative purposes, 'John used to smoke sixty a day'. From the point of view of semantic content, the proposition states that, over some extended period in the past, it was John's habit to smoke sixty (cigarettes) a day. What is equally important here, however, is the pragmatic inference or implicature to which this statement gives rise; namely, that the situation described no longer holds at the moment of speaking. The difference between these referential and inferential facets of meaning can be illustrated by a test of negation: semantic content is contradicted by negation ('John didn't used to . . .' invalidates the original proposition) whereas negation of the pragmatic inference allows the original to stand ('John used to . .. and still does in fact'). Thus the use of the habitual past has consequences, as Slobin would have it, in terms of what is 'said' and 'unsaid'. As a further preliminary to approaching textual examples, let us remember too the 'obligatory' or more 'automated' nature of the habitual past in Irish than in, say, English.

Our first example is a poem that pursues a theme that is common at the end of the sixteenth and beginning of the seventeenth century: namely, that the hereditary order of poets is no longer receiving the deference it regards as its due. In this chapter we have already looked at such a poem by Maolmuire Mac Con Uladh expressing the poet's expectation of a reciprocal relation with his patron, which is indexed by the term *dualgas,* itself derived from ideas of what is *dual* or naturally, inevitably right. With this poem we can compare further a poem by his more famous kinsman Fearghal Óg Mac an Bhaird, 'Fuarus Iongnadh a Fhir Chumainn', composed while he was in exile in Spain in the first years of the seventeenth century and addressed to Flaithrí Ó Maolchonaire, Archbishop of Tuam and founder of St Anthony's College in Louvain.[66] The opening of the poem in particular is noteworthy for its contrast between what to the poet is a breach of custom (what is therefore *iongnadh,* literally *in + gnáth* or 'not *gnáth*', see above) and what the poet feels is due (what is therefore *dual*):

Fúarus **IONGNADH** a fhir chumainn	I have found a marvel, my friend
cádhus úatha ní fhúair mé	no reverence have I found from people
na daoine dar **DHÚAL** ar n-ionramh	to whom it were fitting to wait on me;
as úar náoidhe an **t-IONGNADH** é.	it is a cold new marvel.
Meisi folamh, féch nach diongna,	That I'm empty: see if this is a thing to mark,
's daoine dáora ar nár **DHÚAL** gean	while base folk, unworthy of regard,
sunna ón Spáin ag agháil ionnmhuis	are here receiving riches from Spain
a n-anáir chláir bhionnghlais Bhreagh.	in honour of the sweet, green plain of Bregha.

Nír bheag let athair mar **IONGNADH**	Thy father would have held it no small wonder
gan m'ana ag fás, foirfe an coll,	that my possessions grow not, complete is the ruin,
is toice ag fás ag mac moghadh	while a serf's son finds his riches growing,
a shlat dár fhás toradh trom.[67]	O thou branch from which has grown rich fruit.

Thus here what is *iongnadh* 'wondrous', 'marvellous', in a negative sense of course, offends the expectation of what is *dual* or ineluctably right or natural, 'fitting'. Some of the grammatical or structural reflexes of this situation are worth noting in this poem. Note how a concomitant of what is 'unexpected' and 'new' (*iongnadh*) in the first stanza is the use of the simple past form *fúarus/ní fhúair* with what amounts to the force of an English perfect 'I have found/not found'. Such a form, in both languages, can be used for 'present time' effect to indicate the continuing or present relevance of a past event, which is most certainly the case here: the poet has made what is (for him) a shocking discovery, which continues to disturb him greatly. A further concomitant of this 'present' context is the use of the progressive to refer to people 'receiving wealth': *ag agháil ionnmhuis*. In sharp contrast we may note one of the final stanzas, where the poet remembers the glory of former days:

Mag Aonghusa, aigneadh faoilidh,	Magennis of the joyous nature
fáilte **GHNÁTH DO-GHEIBHINN** úadh,	constant welcome I was wont to get from him
DO BHÍODH a thoil ar tí a dáilte,	his love was always ready to be bestowed
nírbh í soin an fháilte fhúar.[68]	that was no cold welcome.

Here *gnáth* is used as an adjective qualifying the noun *fáilte* 'welcome' and has as its corollary the use of the past habitual *do-gheibhinn* (from the same verb as the simple past *fúarus* above). In this way the grammatical structure of Irish, the obligatory nature of the distinction in the expression of the two kinds of past, reinforces the poet's sense of the more conscious contrast made at the *lexical* level of what was once *gnáth* and is now *iongnadh*. This brief analysis on the linguistic level squares well with Caball's assessment of the importance of this poem in the context of the relationship between the poet, Mac an Bhaird, and his patron, Ó Maolchonaire: the former the 'purveyor of a venerable corporate ethos', the latter a European scholar of significance and friend of Philip III of Spain. In this context the poem emerges as a *cri de cœur* from one Irish scholar to another.[69]

This contrast between two kinds of past—what has latterly become the case against what used to be the case—we find in other poems of this period. In another of his more notable political poems, 'T'aire Riot a Riocaird Óig', Tadhg Dall Ó hUiginn addresses Riocard Óg Búrc of the MacWilliam Burkes on the inadvisability of assuming an English title in preference to his familiar native one.[70] As Caball notes, the immediate political background to the poem is uncertain.[71] What is not disputed, however, is Ó hUiginn's horror of the idea of Riocard Óg assuming an English title. Tadhg Dall frames his poem around his concerns about the implications of such an acceptance for Burke within his own territory. Both the terms *dúthaigh* and *athardha* 'patrimony' are used as the poet attempts to hammer home the ramifications of a foreign title (*ainm allmhardha*) in relation to those terms: even if Riocard were to receive the overlordship of all Ireland, it would do him no good should he renounce his original name:

Dá bhfaghthá ceannus Chláir Fhloinn	Didst thou get the headship of Flann's plain
níorbh fhiú dhuit a dhreach shéaghoinn,	it would not advantage thee, thou gallant form
ainm allmhardha dá rádh ruibh	in thy native place
fa chlár ndagh Bhanbha id **dhúthaigh**.	to reign over Banbha by a foreign title.
Crosmaoidne h'iomlaoid anma	In the name of poetry we forbid thee
ort a hucht na healadhna;	to change thy title
cóir car an athanma ar ais	thou shouldst renounce the new appellation
suil rabh **h'athardha** it éagmais.[72]	rather than lose thy patrimony.

Put simply, the adoption of a foreign title means the loss of everything: his authority, support and wealth. As Caball puts it, 'the poet is saying that Ricard's title has underwritten his patrimony, emblematic as it was of the sanctioned integrity of his overlordship in the family territories'.[73]

The word used to characterize this original title is *gnáth,* used here adjectivally. This usage again has the past habitual as its concomitant, which is then contrasted with a string of 'perfects' or pasts of recent occurrence or present relevance:

Mar sin nár dhealoighthe dhoit	Ever thus it were not for thee to part
ret **ainm nGNÁTH**, red ghníomh n-ordhruic	from thy wonted title, thy well-known deeds
ris gach mbuaidh **dá mBÍOTH** oraibh	with every triumph that thou hadst of old
ós uaidh fríoth a bhfuarabhair.	since from it was got all that thou didst win.
A mheic Riocaird, a rún tais,	O son of Richard, gentle of heart,
an t-ainm iasachta **uarais**,	as for the foreign title thou hast got
níor **thárraidh** tú dá tharbha	never didst thou gain any advantage

nár **sháraigh** clú an chéadanma.[74]   that the fame of the former title
                                             did not outdo.

The simple past, as used in the second of these stanzas, again concerns itself
with more recent events: the implications of having accepted a foreign title are
viewed from the point of view of their continuing relevance. Similarly, the form
a bhfuarabhair that concludes the first stanza can be translated 'all that you
have (ever) got (of fame)'. This, however, is the result of events that are coded
past habitual: *gach mbuaidh dá mbíoth oraibh,* all those victories earned repeatedly over a long period. It should be further noted that the editor translates
this as 'every triumph that thou hadst *of old*'. The emphasis here stems from
the fact that the Irish text contains no item that corresponds directly to this
English phrase 'of old'. Yet the translation seizes on an important *pragmatic*
aspect of the use of the past habitual, which is the inference or *implicature* that
the event or events so described no longer hold at the time of speaking and
belong to a past that is therefore seen as psychologically remote. This contrastive use of the past habitual with the simple past as a perfect continues
throughout the poem:

(a) A **nDÉANDAOIS** ar ndaoine riamh   Any offences that our people
     do chiontaibh ar Chloinn Uilliam,   ever used to commit against
                                          Clanwilliam

     dúin **DO BHÍODH** eineaclann ann,   ours would be the honour price
                                          therefore

     a ghríobh meidhealtrom Manann.   thou powerfully attended
                                          champion of Man.

     Mar **DO-NÍDÍS** romhaibh riamh   Even as the fragrant blossoms
     sgotha cumhra Clann Uilliam   of Clanwilliam ever did
     déana, a choillbhile bheann   do thou, O forest tree of Bregia's
        mBreagh   height,
     um cheann oirbhire t'fhileadh.   about thy poet's reproach.

(b) **Do-rinnis** malairt mheallta   Thou madest a deceptive bargain
     d'iomlaoid ar nách inleanta,   an exchange not to be persisted in,
     a sduagh caithréimeach cnuic   thou triumphant champion
        Bhreagh,   of Bregia's hill,
     aithmhéileach duit a dhéineamh.[75] thou shalt regret the deed.

Similarly, here the non-habitual past *do-rinnis* means 'you have made', an
action with continuing consequences. Having recited a parable for the edifi-
cation of his patron, the poet resumes his theme by focusing again on the act
that continues to have consequences:

     Do dháilis, a chruth corcra,   Thou gavest, ruddy-faced
                                          form,

     ainm síor ar ainm n-iasachta   an abiding name for a temporary
                                          one

a námha chnuic bhaillbhric Bhreagh	O fighter of Bregia's gaily-tinged hill
dob aimhghlic dhuit a dhéineamh	that was an imprudent deed of thine
Dob fhiú a **dtárrais** ó thosaigh	All that you have obtained from the start
don mhionn oirdhreic anmasoin	from that renowned jewel of a name was worth enough
a chlaochládh nár dhéanta dhuit,	that thou shouldest not displace it
a réalta ó chaomhChlár Chormuic	star from Cormac's noble plain

Tugais ris id Riocard Óg	With it, as Richard Óg
i n-aois naoidheanta i n-allód	in youthful days long ago
seal is tarbhaighe **tug** fear	thou hadst as profitable a time as ever man had
ar fhud ghlanmhaighe Ghaoi- dheal.[76]	throughout the bright plain of the Gael.

As the poet reminisces on a litany of past glories, he switches again to the habitual past:

DO CAITHTÍ leat eacht oile	Of yore thou wouldst spend a day
lá ag argoin bhruaich Bhóroimhe,	ravaging the shores of Bóromha
lá fán mBúill dtirmshreabhaigh dtais,	a day by the soft shallow streams of the Boyle
lá ag inbhearaibh bhrúigh Bhearnais.[77]	a day by the flats of Bearnas.

But then another shift to the non-habitual brings the events described closer to home again (i.e. *you have explored*):

Comhmór **do cuairtaigheadh** libh	Equally didest thou explore
bruaich Fhorbhair, imle Sligigh	the brinks of Forbhar, the borders of Sligo
uatha soin go Cruachain Choinn	from them as far as Croghan of Conn
'só Chruachain soir go Sionuinn.[78]	and from Croghan eastwards to the Shannon.

Given the insistence that the Irish and English titles are incompatible the contrast between habitual and non-habitual aspects is a telling grammatical reflex of this incompatibility. We find the same type of aspectual contrast between the two kinds of past in Eochaidh Ó hEodhasa's poem 'Ionmholta Malairt Bhisigh' ('A change for the better is praiseworthy'), composed around 1603, 'welcoming' in a somewhat whimsical and ironic fashion the change in literary tastes at the end of the sixteenth century that sees the rise of a less convoluted, less arcane style of poetry.[79] In this poem the simple past again has the force of a 'perfect' of current relevance, while conversely the past habitual carries the implicature of an event or situation that no longer obtains:

Le dorchacht na ngrés snoighthe	By the obscurity of carven ornament
DO BHÍNNSE ag tuilliodh gráine:	I used to earn disgust
fa hí ughachta mhóráin	many protested that
nár **dhíol** roghráidh ar ndáinne.	my verse was unworthy of favour.
Beag nach **BRISIODH** mo chroidhe	Every poem I composed hitherto
gach dán roimhe dá **gCUMAINN**:	used to almost break my heart
is mór an t-adhbhar sláinte	it is a great cause of health
an nós so **táinig** chugainn.[80]	this new fashion that has come to us.

The poems considered above are particularly telling in their specific cultural and historical context of the threat posed to the native bardic order in the late sixteenth and early seventeenth centuries. The grammatical expression of the habitual past is part of their overall rhetorical effect. The Irish-speaker not only *may* express in an overt grammatical fashion the distinction between past situations that have repeatedly occurred over an extended period in the past (and are thus *gnáth* and even *dual*) and past events that are continuous and, more poignantly in many cases, have continuing relevance: he *must* do so. This obligation is part of and informs the rhetorical style of the language.

We find the same kind of issues in Ó Bruadair's poetry, on both the national and the personal levels, from later in the seventeenth century. In the poem 'Créacht Do Dháil Mé im Arthach Galair' ('A wound has made me a repository of sickness'), the poet describes the aftermath of the Cromwellian settlement of the 1650s and notes with particular distaste the advent of English planters in increasing numbers. This he contrasts with an Ireland of a 'Golden Age', which is naturally depicted in terms of the habitual past, where Deirdre and the great female figures of the mythical past reside. This situation is contrasted with an offensive present and the prospect of an equally distasteful future:

(*a*)	Ag so an bhuidhean, gidh scíosmhar a aithris,	This is the gang though I hate to name them
	bhias 'na gcomhnaidhe i mótaidhibh geala,	who will live in bright motte and bailey
	Gúidí Húc is Múdar Hammer	Goody Hook and Mother Hammer
	Róibín Sál is fádur Salm.	Robin Saul and Father Psalm.
(*b*)	Mar a **mBÍODH** Déirdre an ghléghein ghartha,	Where once lived Deirdre the bright-born daughter
	Éimhear na gciabh 's a Liath Mhacha,	the long-haired Eimhear and the Grey of Macha

mar a **mBÍODH** Aoibheall taoibh na craige
is banntracht chuana Tuatha Dé Danann.

where Aoibheall lived in her rocky mansion
and the elegant ladies of Dé Danann.

(c)   Mar a **mBÍODH** dámhscol báird is reacaigh,
cleasaidheacht rinnce, fíonta is fleadha.[81]

There were schools of dancers and of poets
intricate dances, gastronomic pleasures.

Once again the habitual past contrasts rhetorically with the simple past, which indicates an event whose consequences are still felt, in this case the defeat of the Irish:

. . . Och dul na féinne úd fá úir leacaigh
is é **do ró bhris** Fódla bheannach.[82]

O the going of those soldiers into graveyards
has split the hills of this old nation.

The same contrast applies in poems of a more purely 'personal' nature, as in for example, Ó Bruadair's lament for the decline in his social status as a poet: 'Is mairg nár chrean re maitheas saolta' ('Pity the man who didn't tie up some worldly goods'). The poet again contrasts the old with the new, and the contrast finds its grammatical expression in the opposition of (a) habitual and (b) simple past:

(a)   **DO BHEANNACHADH** damh an bhean 's a céile cneis

. . . **DO GHABHAINN** isteach is amach gan éad i dtigh

The wife would (= used to) salute me and so would her mate

. . . I could come and go (= used to) in a house with no jealousy

(b)   **D'athruigh** 'na ndearcaibh dath mo néimhe anois

. . . ó **shearg** mo lacht re hais na caomhdhruinge[83]

According to them I've changed my colours

. . . My milk has dried up as far as they're concerned

To conclude this section I return to the lexical end of the linguistic continuum of meaning. In many other poems of the seventeenth century the deleterious consequences of the Flight of the Earls and the subsequent Plantation of Ulster are described in terms of what is *iongnadh* and not *dual:*

Anocht as uaigneach Éire
do bheir fógra a firfhréimhe
gruaidhe a fear sa fionnbhan fliuch

treabh is **IONGNADH** go huaigneach.

Lonely is Ireland tonight:
the outlawry of her native stock
fills with tears the cheeks of her men and fair women:

that the land should be desolate is unusual.

. . . Gan gáire fa ghníomhraibh leinbh	No laughter at children's play:
cosg ar cheól glas ar Ghaoidheilg	an end to music: Gaelic is silenced:
meic ríogh mar nár **DHUAL** don dream	sons of kings unhonoured:
gan luadh ar fhíon nó aithfreann.[84]	no mention of wine-feast or of Mass.

Similarly, the poem 'Cáit ar Ghabhadar Gaoidhil' ('Where have the Gaels gone?') also concerns itself with what is *iongnadh,* in this case the aftermath of the Plantation of Ulster:

IONGNADH leam créad a ccor-san,	I marvel at what can be their condition,
laoich na longphort solusghlan;	the heroes of the bright pure fortresses:
fuaras bruidhne Banbha Cuinn	I have found the mansions of Conn's Ireland,
bruidhne a h-adhbha 's ní fhaghuim.	but I cannot find the companies of her halls.
. . . Cóir a ttuiriomh—tarrthaidh sinn	We have witnessed egregious changes upon Ireland
iomlaoid éaxamhla ar Éirinn,	—it is right to enumerate them—
'n a mbiadh **IONGNADH** riamh roimhe	which would have been wondrous at any previous time
fa fhiadh lionnghlan Laoghaire.[85]	upon the sparkling-watered land of Laoghaire.

In a bitter poem by Céitinn, what has latterly become *gnáth* is actually contrasted with what is inherently *dual.* The theme is a familiar one in seventeenth-century poetry, that of the prostitution of Ireland:

A Bhanbha bhog-omh dhona dhuaibhseach,	O sad, lonesome, gloomy Ireland
is tú an bhean gan fachuin uaille	you are the woman without cause for pride
GNÁTH mar iarsma id dhiadh buaidhreadh	distress is a common remainder in your wake
is creidhm i n-uidhe gach laoi dod nuachar	and fretting in the course of every day for your husband
Do-chím-se, a mhalartach racht-muiseach ruaireach,	I see, you faithless, conceited, whore
gur tréigeadh leat, gidh beart nar **DHUAL** duit,	that you have abandoned, though a deed not *dual* for you,
an dream **d'fhuiling go minic** a dtuargain	the people who have often endured a pounding

> d'fhaobharaibh lann nglas dteann is   from blades of grey steel and hard
> cruaidhshleagh.[86]   spears.

All things being equal, the congruence of *gnáth* and *dual* presupposes that all is well with the world. If it is not, what was formerly alien and repellent (*iong-nadh*) can quickly become the new dispensation (*gnáth*).

Conclusion: The relation between grammar and lexicon

In the previous section we have been concerned with examining the expression of habituality, both in its more lexical and its more grammatical aspects. The important distinction between the two dimensions lies in the more automated and obligatory nature of grammatical expression, as well as its more generalized content. Lexical choices, on the other hand, tend to be made more consciously.

As a result, lexical choices operate at a higher level of *metapragmatic awareness*[87] than grammatical choices; but the two types in fact operate along a historical cline or continuum along which lexical meaning is generalized to produce grammatical function. One basic principle in the evolution of grammatical structure is that words that begin as having a specific lexical content can, over time and through usage, lose the specific nature of that content and be used in more generalized functions. In other words, a lexical item can become a grammatical one. This process is known as *grammaticalization*, and its effects can be illustrated within the domain of habituality in Irish. This general question of the obligatory nature of grammatical forms brings us to a more detailed consideration of the relation between lexicon and grammar. The point that will be pursued is that grammatical structure, being more a part of the speaker's routinized sub-consciousness as well as being obligatory in nature, may well act as reinforcing agent for meanings and concepts that are expressed more explicitly in the lexicon. It is important to note that this obligatory nature applies as much to written as to spoken language—the contrast between habitual and non-habitual aspects of Irish is mandatory, no matter which medium is employed.

The function of grammar can be appreciated by considering the role it plays in the evolution of 'new' languages, such as creoles. The central question here is, why does grammatical structure evolve at all, since various pidgin languages, for example, show that speakers can communicate with largely lexical and paralinguistic strategies. An important work in this regard is Labov's study of the evolution of obligatory grammatical tense markers in Hawaiian Creole.[88] A *pidgin* is a language with no native speakers, one that evolves among speakers of substrate languages in contact with a superstrate language or dialect. In general, such a language has little or no grammatical marking and is characterized by slow and deliberate delivery. If, however, a succeeding generation acquires this pidginized language as its native language it becomes a *creole* and shows different evolutionary characteristics. It is an observed feature of pidgins that, when nativized as creoles, they show a rapid progression towards grammatical forms such as definite articles, relative clauses and tense-mood-aspect forms, and that this correlates with a marked increase in speed and fluency of delivery.[89] It is within this context that Labov locates the development of obligatory tense markers. As he points out, this evolution cannot be said to constitute a logical or semantic improvement on the previous state, nevertheless grammatical forms appear to serve a number of pragmatic and psycholinguistic needs, as speakers with native fluency make more expressive and communicative demands of their language. The evolution of obligatory grammatical markers is related to economy of effort, to the ease of processing information in discourse situations. As such markers are automatic, they enable other aspects of the message to be foregrounded in the hearer's mind. Thus the obligatory and automated nature of grammatical structure is, in a sense, its most important defining feature.

As Lehmann puts it, 'The grammaticalization of a sign detracts from its autonomy.'[90] The routinization of older forms is eventually felt to be inimical to the expressive and communicative needs of language, and the solution is to replace older forms with newer, 'more expressive' ones.[91] It is for such reasons that Haiman refers to grammaticalization as 'habituation', which results 'when individual words and collocations are frequently repeated'.[92] Similarly, Hagège speaks of grammar in terms of its obligatory and mechanical character,[93] while Sankoff has described the evolution of grammatical structure as a transition from *ad hoc* spur-of-the-moment communicative strategies to grammatical rules governing usage.[93] In fact, linguistic change can be construed in terms of a renewal of the expressive element in language by its speakers. Such changes as we have been describing are ascribed to 'linguistic creativity' by Lehmann, because speakers, as he puts it, 'do not want to express themselves the same way they did yesterday, and in particular not the same way that someone else did yesterday'.[95] The search, therefore, is for originality and expressiveness; but because the grammatical choices available in a language at any given time are constrained for practical and functional reasons, speakers continually find new ways of saying the same thing as the old way becomes routine and commonplace. This gives rise to the idea of a linguistic cycle, and the drive towards expressivity makes it unidirectional, that is, always from less to more expressive.

We can see this cyclical dimension at work in the historical evolution of the expression of habituality in Irish, to which we now return. The expression of the semantic-pragmatic domain of habituality could be given the following, at least partial, characterization according to its lexical and grammatical components:

Lexical Components:	*dual* 'native', 'natural'
	gnáth 'custom'
	de ghnáth 'usually'
	gnách 'usual', 'customary'
Grammatical Components:	Past Habitual of any verb 'used to . . .'
	Present Habitual of verb *bi-* 'is usually'

It should be remembered that the central lexical term here is *gnáth*, and that the semantic characterization of *dual* contains an additional element of inevitability. Indeed an immediate consideration of the relation between the lexical and grammatical expressions of habituality is pertinent in the case of Modern Irish, in the sense that many contemporary Ulster dialects have replaced the grammaticalized past habitual category with a more lexically based construction containing one of the lexical characterizations of habituality par excellence: *gnách* (*gnáth* + *ach*). Thus the Irish linguistic atlas for the English sentence 'He used to come' has (*a*) the inflected past habitual for all dialects except Mid and North Donegal and Co. Tyrone, where (*b*) the periphrastic construction *ba ghnách leis a theacht* is used[95]:

(*a*) **Grammatical:**	**Thagadh / thigeadh** sé
(*b*) **Lexical:**	Ba **ghnách** leis a theacht
	lit. 'It was *gnách* for him to come'

I highlight here the contrast between the specific lexical content of *ba ghnách leis* with the more generalized grammatical expression of habituality in the inflected form. Here habituality has two components: (i) lenited form (*thag-/thig-*) of the present stem (*tag-/tig-*) and (ii) 'irrealis' ending *-(e)adh* (an ending that signifies unreality or non-actuality). The generalized nature of this marking is reinforced by the fact that both components are features that are shared by the conditional mood, the *would* form in Irish. While the putative relation between the habitual past and the conditional mood is beyond the scope of this discussion, it is worth taking a brief look at the general classification of the Irish verb by the native grammarians of the late medieval to early modern period to see what light it sheds on the present discussion.

The main conceptual distinction made is that between so-called 'full' and 'half' categories, as follows.[97] The two 'full' or main categories are the simple past and the future tense; the two 'half' or functionally derived categories based on them are the habitual past and the conditional mood (otherwise known as the secondary future), respectively. The relationship between the simple and habitual past is the pragmatic function of *deimhnioghadh* 'affirming' (i.e. that an event has taken place), while that between future and conditional is *fáistine* 'prediction' (lit. 'prophecy'). These relationships can be presented diagrammatically as follows:

SIMPLE PAST	FUTURE
Láindeimhnioghadh	**Lánfháistine**
('full-affirming')	('(full-)prophecy')
HABITUAL PAST	CONDITIONAL

Leithdeimhnioghadh	**Leathfháistine**
('half-affirming')	('half-prophecy')

In his eighteenth-century Irish grammar Mac Curtin explains the term *lei-thdeimhnioghadh* as follows: 'semi-affirmative, or half affirmation   by reason that it doth not positively affirm any thing to have been done',[98] and Ó hEod-hasa clarifies the point further in his own grammar of a century previously: 'semi-affirmation or imperfect past tense because it does not simply affirm that something was done but rather that it is [was?] wont to happen'.[99] For this reason, the imperfect or past habitual 'half-asserts', in that it reports not the occurrence of a particular situation but rather both the knowledge and expectation of its repeated occurrence over a period in the past. It is this generic or non-specific nature that leads Fleischman to associate habituals with irrealis or non-actual modality,[100] and it is interesting to read the native Irish term *lei-thdeimhnioghadh* in this light: where situations are indefinite as regards the number of occurrences and the time of occurrence they can be regarded as extending over possible worlds.[101] On the other hand, the simple past reports 'that an event has occurred . . . at some specific time' in the past.[102] It therefore identifies more strongly with realis or actual modality and is pragmatically more 'fully' asserted as *láindeimhnioghadh*. The analysis of the medieval grammarians into 'full' and 'half' categories receives striking confirmation from the observation of Wagner, who noted in the course of his fieldwork for his linguistic atlas the propensity of Irish-speakers, when solicited for the forms of particular verbs, to give the simple past (preterite) or future tense forms initially and to produce the other forms based on the present stem—that is, the habitual categories of present and past—only on further examination. This led him to the conclusion that preterite and future forms are foremost in the linguistic consciousness of Irish-speakers. His remarks are worth quoting in full (my translation from the original German with added emphasis):

> The essence of the finite verb in Irish became clear to me in the course of my dialectological fieldwork. I noticed that speakers, whenever I asked them for the forms of a particular verb, usually answered initially with the forms of the future and past tenses and only gave the forms of the present or past habitual after closer questioning. I concluded from this that future and past tenses are *in the foreground of the Irish linguistic consciousness* [emphasis added] and that the forms based on the present stem (i.e. including the past habitual) are functionally derived categories.[103]

The pragmatic distinction made in Irish between the 'full' and 'half' modes thus cuts across more conventional semantic distinctions of tense, aspect and mood: 'full assertion' is the perfective past tense, while 'half assertion' is the habitual past, 'full prediction' is the future tense, while 'half prediction' is the conditional mood. I believe that the contexts considered above for this use of the habitual past in contradistinction to the simple past, offer a real cultural

and historical slant on the idea of *leithdeimhnioghadh* that is the native characterization of the past habitual.

In the putative relation of the lexical to the grammatical we are raising the
question of speaker consciousness or awareness, which brings us back to the
work of Silverstein. Of particular interest here is the extent to which forms
performing a pragmatic or communicative function are susceptible to speakers' *metapragmatic* awareness of their function.[104] One parameter that Silverstein establishes is that the level of speaker awareness of a particular form is
proportionate to the extent to which that form is unambiguously referential,
or has a unique referent.[105] High on this scale of referentiality are proper
nouns, followed by other lexical items such as common nouns and verbal
roots.[106] It is here, of course, that we find the items *dual* and *gnáth*. Such root
forms are the linguistic elements most open to conscious speaker awareness
and thus analysis and manipulation of their semantic content generally. However, other components of language are more routinized and automated, more
a matter of habit and practice, and are therefore less susceptible to awareness:
grammatical markers, markers for tense, mood and aspect in verbs, for example, and phonological segments. Yet it is precisely the *obligatory* nature of such
markers that is of interest here: how can we make a meaningful correlation
between obligatoriness and low linguistic awareness?

Although the overtly comparative dimension in most of this book's chapters is small, the comparison made above between the obligatory nature of the
grammatical expression of the habitual in Irish as against its more optional
nature in English, together with the concomitant effects that this situation has
for the rhetorical style of each language, does raise the question of *linguistic relativity*, discussed briefly in chapter 1. The main tenet of this idea is that the
differences between the grammatical and the lexical structures of languages
represent different conceptual systems, which cause the speakers of those languages to attend to different facets of experience.[107]

It is here that recent research by Slobin, already referred to, is of value.
Addressing the whole tradition of linguistic relativity from von Humboldt to
Whorf, Slobin reformulates the parameters within which this question can be
made more tangible by returning to the ideas of Boas on grammatical meaning.
Instead of talking of a putative relation between 'thought' and 'language' in the
abstract, as it were, he proposes a more pragmatically oriented, dynamic formulation of the relation between 'thinking' and 'speaking' or, more accurately,
'thinking *for* speaking'. The question here is, in construing a particular experience of the world, what are the aspects of that experience that speakers of a given
language *must* express in that language?[108] This is less a matter of language as
constitutive of a particular, culture-specific 'world view' or of habitual modes of
thought than it is of linguistic categories shaping the dynamics of actual communication in specific situations. What Slobin's analysis shows is a less abstract
characterization than the type of analysis favoured by Whorf, but it constructs
a more tangible reality: the fact that, in describing experience, speakers of a given

language naturally resort to those linguistic elements that are most readily, most *routinely*, available to them in that language. These routine elements are *grammatical categories* and Slobin's research, concentrating as it does on the use of grammatical categories among children from the ages of three to nine, bears out the fact that it is to such routinized categories as a particular grammar provides that speakers most easily have recourse in translating a particular scene into language. This relates directly to what is perhaps the most fundamental aspect of the nature of grammar: its automated character. Other linguistic components, such as the lexical, tend to be more optional in nature. As Slobin notes, 'Each [language] is a subjective orientation to the world of human experience and this orientation affects the ways in which *we think while speaking*.'[109]

Speakers of a language, therefore, construe experience primarily in terms of the grammatical categories that the particular language makes available to them. What makes Slobin's reformulation more convincing, however, is the fact that languages may not be consistent in agreeing with or diverging from one another among a number of semantic domains. Irish and English, for example, may diverge on the obligatory nature of the expression of habituality but agree on the expression of progressivity, as compared with other European languages.[110] This naturally gives one pause for thought before making general claims about how either Irish or English codes a *particular world view* with respect to other languages. Similarly, in the case under discussion here it seems legitimate to claim that Irish accords a certain importance to the expectation of the normality of events based on knowledge of their habitual occurrence. This expectation finds expression on both the lexical and the grammatical level. Quite how much further this can be taken is difficult to say. As a number of scholars have pointed out, one of the great difficulties in the way of investigating the Whorfian hypothesis is the difficulty of correlating linguistic categorization and non-linguistic behaviour in any convincing and systematic way.[111]

Habituality from a typological perspective

I now wish to place the discussion of habituality in Irish in a wider typological perspective by referring briefly to two recent studies of aspect from a cross-linguistic perspective. Dahl defines habituality as the quantification of a situation over a set of occasions given either explicitly (by means of a qualifying adverb) or by context.[112] In fact he states of the habitual in general: 'cases where HAB [habitual] is typically used are those in which the adverb *usually* is possible in English'. On the past habitual in particular, he observes that this term is being used 'as a label for categories which are mainly used for habitual sentences with past time reference and are not analyzable as consisting of HAB [habitual] or HABG [habitual-generic] combined with a regular past tense'.[112] Significantly, Dahl comments on the 'low text frequency of this category'. Furthermore, Bybee, Perkins and Pagliuca, in their typological survey of between

75 and 100 languages, make a similar observation on the relative infrequency of specific, overt grammatical morphemes denoting 'habitual' as opposed to other aspectual distinctions of similar specificity such as progressive or anterior (perfect).[113] The expression of habituality tends strongly to be asymmetrical with respect to tense, with habitual meaning much more likely to be overtly expressed in the past than in the present, where it arises as a default interpretation from a more general imperfective sense.[115] This, as we have seen, is the case for Irish also, with one striking exception in the present: the stative verb 'to be', which distinguishes habitual *bíonn* from non-habitual or actual *tá*.

The relative infrequency of the overt, grammatical expression of habituality in the world's languages suggests that there is perhaps something particularly distinctive, if not unique, in this Irish 'fashion of speaking' or, as I might paraphrase Slobin, 'fashion of thinking for speaking'. In addition, we might also draw attention to another observation of Bybee et al. Commenting on the lexical sources of grammatical expressions for habituality in languages, they make two pertinent observations.[116] Firstly, the lexical meaning of the item used to express habituality is very close to the grammatical meaning of habitual, as in the case of English *use,* now current only in reference to past time as *used to.* One of the primary meanings of this verb when first borrowed into English from Old French was 'to follow a usage or custom'. Secondly, a lexical source for the grammatical meaning *habitual* that is attested more than once is a verb 'to know'; thus in Haitian Creole the verb *kône* 'to know' (from French *connaître*) means in its shortened form *kôn* 'be used to'. Both these points can be applied to the Irish case of *gnáth* above. As we have seen, its semantics are those of the grammatical habitual, and in fact it serves as the prototypical qualifying adverbial of habituality. From an etymological point of view, it is the Indo-European root 'to know'.[117] From this derive a number of well-known words in various languages: English *know, can,* German *kunst* 'art', 'craft', Latin *(g)noscere* 'to know', Greek *gnōmōn* 'judge', as well as *gnōstos,* the source of English 'gnostic'. The Irish form *gnáth* and the corresponding noun *gnás* 'custom', 'usage', are discussed by Greene,[118] and we will discuss other derivations from this root in Chapter 6. The pragmatics of *gnáth* in Irish thus index an entire domain of knowledge and the expectation of the normality of an event that is built on it.

Conclusion

In considering grammatical categories Boas was in general concerned with *obligatory* categories, the set of which 'determines those aspects of experience that *must* be expressed.'[119] At the very least, as Slobin points out,[120] whatever else grammar does it directs our attention to such aspects of experience. For Boas each situation to be construed consists of a 'complete concept' or 'mental image'.[121] Because of the observed relative paucity of grammatical categories in the world's languages, compared with vocabulary items, different languages select different aspects of the complete image. It is here, of course, that languages show great diversity. As we have seen, grammatical structure forces the speaker of Irish when construing a situation with past time reference to distinguish the habitual occurrence of that event from a single, discrete occurrence in a way that does not apply to the English-speaker. This applies for the Irish-speaker to any such situation in the past in a quite automatic fashion. On the other hand, lexical items such as *dual* and *gnáth*, while they express similar concepts, operate much more selectively.

The idea of what is *gnáth* or 'usual' is at the prototype centre of habituality in Irish. The word *dual* shares this common semantics but brings a further 'generic' or 'law-like' character of apparent inevitability to bear, even though it cannot always be absolutely distinguished from *gnáth*. At the heart of this there is a common semantic and pragmatic basis: what is 'known' as valid over an extended period becomes 'expected'. This is lexicalized in both *gnáth* and *dual* and grammaticalized in two ways: (*a*) the formal opposition of simple past and habitual past and (*b*) the opposition in the present tense of the verb 'to be' between habitual *bí-* and non-habitual *tá*. Finally, the semantic-pragmatic issues discussed find a particularly poignant cultural and historical resonance in the poetry of the late sixteenth and seventeenth centuries.

5. THE SEMANTICS AND SYNTAX OF 'RIGHT' AND 'NATURAL'

As with chapter 4, the goal of this chapter is twofold. Firstly, it examines a number of words not previously considered in any detail in terms of their relationship with the lexical items already analysed, in particular with *dúchas*. Secondly, this chapter shares a common theme with the previous one, namely an investigation into how linguistic structure at the less conscious grammatical or syntactic end of the linguistic continuum may be considered to act as a reinforcement of ideology as formulated on the more conscious lexical end. What this will involve is a consideration of the syntax of constructions expressing degrees of necessity, obligation or appropriateness of a course of action and the way in which such constructions can be interpreted as shedding light on the deep semantic structure of words themselves denotative of what is 'right' or 'natural' or 'pre-ordained' in some way. Once again the texts to be considered are from the sixteenth and seventeenth centuries.

Initially we need to examine briefly the more conscious articulations of such ideology and I will begin as usual by presenting some summary definitions based on Ó Dónaill,[1] in order to give an overall sense of the contemporary and historical ranges of these words: (i) *dligheadh*, (ii) *dílis*, (iii) *díleas*, (iv) *dílse*, (v) *dír* and (vi) *díre*. I give only those meanings that are especially germane:

(i)   Lawful right, due; tax, tribute

(ii)   Own; proper (*do*, to)

(iii)   Personal property

(iv)   Proprietary right; ownership, property

(v)   Due, proper, pertaining (*do*, to)

(vi)   Due, right

Clearly, (ii) to (iv) form a group or family on their own based on *dílis*, as do (v) and (vi), based on *dír*. Once again we can note the prominence of the idea of what is 'due', 'proper', 'natural' or 'one's own'. I now consider each of these items briefly, including in each case examples that suggest how they relate to the idea of *dúchas* and, to a lesser extent, *dual*, already discussed, before placing them in a broader syntactic framework, which takes the following form:

VERB **IS**	LEXICAL VARIABLE	PREPOSITION **DO**
'is'	e.g. *dú/dúthaigh/dúchas/dual*	'to' 'for'

Examples of this type of syntax have already been considered in the case of both the *dú-* and the *dual-* families in chapters 2 to 4 and will recur with the other lexical items considered in this chapter. Firstly, however, we need to examine in some detail the semantics and pragmatics of the words in question, notably *dligheadh,* the complex based on *díleas,* and *díre.*

What is lawful and due: *dligeadh* (Old Irish *dliged* Modern Irish *dlí*)

The *DIL* defines Old Irish *dliged* as 'law; duty; prerogative; tribute'. The early Modern Irish form is *dligheadh* (genitive *dlighidh*), as in the following passage from Céitinn, where he describes the disruption that the Viking presence has caused to every level of Irish society, material and intellectual: there is a Viking king over every cantred in Ireland, the Irish are prohibited from wearing their own style of clothing, and their forts and churches are under occupation. Accordingly, the learned classes have suffered (this example was quoted in chapter 2):

> gan file gan feallsamh gan oirfideach ag leanamhain **dlighidh na dúthchasa**[2]
>
> neither poet nor wise man nor musician observing law or custom

These items occur elsewhere collocated with the verb *lean* 'follow', 'adhere to'. Passage (*a*) bears a striking resemblance to the preceding in describing the disagreeable regime to which Munster was subject under the Vikings.[3] In (*b*) note the occurrence of the phrase *nach dúthcha dhaoiph-se* ('that it is not right for you'), which contains a further derivative of *dúthaigh,* again in the sense 'right' or 'natural':

(*a*)   gan feallsaim gan filid gan oirfidigh ag leanmhain **dlighidh na duthchusa** a n-deigh-righ tar grain na n-garbh-Lochlannach

  neither men of wisdom nor poets nor musicians following the law or natural custom of their good kings on account of the enmity of the crude Norsemen

(*b*)   fós atá ní eile ann, .i. **nach dúthcha dhaoiph-sí** a teachtadh nó teanng-habháil do tháoibh chiníl nó clann-mhaicne iná dhamh-sa **dá leantaoi dligheadh nó dúthchus**[4]

there is something else: that it is not more right for you to possess and hold it fast on account of race or descent than for me, if *dligheadh* or *dúchas* were to be followed

The three examples that have been quoted are from seventeenth- and eighteenth-century sources. A very similar collocation is in fact attested in a much earlier source, the eleventh-century *Lebor na Cert* 'The Book of Rights', which is devoted in the main to setting out the rights and entitlements of the kings of Cashel:

Dligead ocus fodail na tuarostal sin beós andso ó ríg Caisil do rígaib tuath ⁊ mór-thuath iar sochar a forba ⁊ a ceneóil, a feib **dligid** ⁊ **dúchasa**, ⁊ ar sochar grád ⁊ dílmaine.[5]

This is the just duty and division of those stipends from the king of Cashel to the kings and territories according to the revenue of their land and kindred, by virtue of claim and heritage according to the benefit of rank and nobility.

We can see here how the idea of what constitutes correct practice and procedure—the social order—resides at least partly in what is *dúchas* and also what is *dligheadh*. Let us concentrate on two culturally important and mutually dependent meanings of *dligheadh*. Firstly, *dligheadh* signifies 'what is right or due *to* someone; due, right, prerogative'.[6] In the Middle Irish saga *Fled Dúin na nGed* there is an incident reminiscent of the traditional Celtic motif of a contest among warriors for the champion's portion in the banqueting hall. A stranger is advised not to break any bone with the marrow on it, as that portion is traditionally reserved for a particular youth of the household, whose *dliged* it therefore is (*a*); the stranger disregards this advice and the youth rises up in anger (*b*)

(*a*)   As-bert an filid fris-[s]ium ria ndul isin dún, dia tuctha cnáim smeara for méis ina fiadnaisi, cena bladad co bráth, ar atá a teglach in rig oglach diana **dligeadh** cech cnáim im a téit smir . . . 'Maith sin' ol se . . .

Before entering the palace the poet had told him if a bone should be brought on a dish in his presence, not to attempt breaking it for there was a youth in the king's household to whom every marrow bone was due . . . 'That is good,' said the other . . .

(*b*)   Innister don laech ucud diarba **dlighed** an smior a ní sin. At-raig sein suas co feirg moir.[7]

The hero to whom the marrow was due was told of this occurrence, and he arose up in great anger.

Despite the youth's righteous indignation he is slain by the stranger. It may be noted that syntactically the underlying construction here is *is dliged do*, reminiscent of the various syntagma discussed in the case of *dú, dúchas* and *dual* (where *diarba* and *diana* are forms that combine the copula *is* and the preposition *do:* 'to whom was' and 'to whom is', respectively). Thus we have a syntactic frame:

VERB **IS**	LEXICAL VARIABLE	PREPOSITION **DO**
'is'	*DLIGHEADH*	'to', 'for'

We shall return to the importance of the syntax of this construction presently, as examples based on further lexical variables accumulate.

Secondly, *dligheadh* also signifies the reverse side of 'right' or 'entitlement', in that it also denotes 'what is due *from* someone'; 'tax', 'tribute'. The following entry occurs in *Annála Ríoghachta Éireann* for 948 AD on the campaign of Ruaidhrí Ó Canannáin to subjugate Midhe and Breagha. The result of this campaign was that:

> do-riacht **dligheadha** righ Ereann as gach aird chuicce[8]
>
> the dues of the King of Ireland were sent him from every quarter

Here *dligheadh* in its particular context indexes the other aspect of entitlement: what is due *from* X. In the following passage from *Trí Bior-Ghaoithe an Bháis*, Céitinn draws on Anselm's analogy of the human condition as reflected in the parable of the talents: the miller is expected to reap profit from the mill for his lord and on failing to do so is thrown into prison for wasting the profits (*i ndíol shochair an mhuilinn do chor amudha*):

> gurab cosmhail an duine ré muilleóir do ghlacfadh muileann ó thighearna, ar choingheall go mbeith d'fhiachaibh air **dlighe** an mhuilinn do thabhairt don tighearna ┐ cíos cinnte do bheith dhó féin mar chothughudh óna thighearna; ┐ go measfadh an tighearna go bhfuighbheadh féin cruithneacht ┐ gach arbhar somholta oile ón muilleoir, **i ndlighe nó i ndualgus** an mhuilinn.[9]
>
> that man was like a miller who would take a mill from a lord on condition that he would be obliged to render to the lord the dues of the mill and who would have a fixed wage from his lord to maintain himself; and that the lord himself would expect to receive wheat and every other choice grain from the miller according to what was due or expected from the mill.

In this instance *dlighe* appears to be virtually conterminous with *dualgas*, as discussed in chapter 4. This brings us back into the pragmatic realm of what is *dual*, inevitable and therefore expected: both *dlighe* and *dualgas* here stand for what is due from and expected of the mill. It is worth recalling in this connection that sixteenth-century poem of protest to the O'Donnell examined in chapter 4, where a closely related sense of *dualgas* and *dligheadh* pervades the entire poem.

Bergin has published an amusing anecdote purporting to explain the nature of the English claim to Ireland. We are told that in the time of Domhnall Mór Ó Briain, king of Munster, a cardinal had come from Rome to instruct the Irish but had had his mules and asses stolen. In retribution, the Pope sold his right over Ireland to the English:

> Coni[d] de sin rorecustar comorbu Pedair **cis ⁊ dliged** Erenn fri Sax-anaib. Conidh he sin **cert ⁊ dliged** lenaid Saxain for Ghaoidhelaibh iniu. Ar ba cu comarbu Peaduir go Roimh teghedh **cis ⁊ dliged** Erenn cosin.[10]

> That is why the successor of Peter sold the tax and tribute of Ireland to the Saxons. And this is the right and claim that the Saxons follow today upon the Gaels. For until then the tax and tribute of Ireland used to go to the successor of Peter in Rome.

Here again we have both ends of what Binchy in relation to this etymon has called the *uinculum iuris* or 'legal chain': the same process is viewed from the point of view of claimant and debtor but denoted as one reflexive process, in a fashion reminiscent of *dualgas*.[11] Note how in this last extract the denotation (or connotation) of *dliged* seems to be coloured by the word with which it is coupled: with *cís* 'tax', 'rent', the natural reading is 'tribute' or 'due'; with *cert* 'right' it is the other side of the coin, 'entitlement'. Note that once again *dliged* appears as an argument of the verb *le(a)n-* 'follow', thus reinforcing the idea of custom or precedent.

We obtain further insights into this idea of a two-way process if we consider the uses of the finite verb *dlighidh* that goes with the form *dligheadh*. This form *dlighe(adh)* (Old Irish *dliged*) is the verbal noun of the verb *dlighidh* (Old Irish *dligid*), which is construed in two ways according to whether it is (*a*) active or (*b*) passive:

(*a*)   **Dligim** ní duit   I have a claim on you

(*b*)   **Dlegtir** féich dúib   You owe debts'; lit. 'Debts are claimed on you
        (pl.)[12]

The active sense (*a*) gives rise to a secondary sense, (*c*) 'deserves', 'merits', while the passive sense (*b*) develops a general sense of necessity or obligation to act (*d*). These developments have already occurred in the Irish of the eighth century:

(*c*)   ní **dlig** digail   he does not deserve punishment

(*d*)   **dlegair** dom-sa precept do cách   I am bound to preach to everyone[13]

In Middle and Early Modern Irish this generalized sense of necessity extends to the active, as shown by (*e*), where it develops a sense close to the English modal 'should':

(*e*)   ní **dlig** comraind curadmír   the champion's portion should not be divided (lit. is not entitled to division)

   ós ann **dhlighim** biad dod réir   since it is my duty I will obey you

   gurab eadh do **dhlighfidís** smuaineadh   so that it is that they should think[14]

The semantics and syntax of 'right' and 'natural'   143

It is also used of natural necessity, where it is close to the semantic range of *dual*, in the sense of something that cannot be otherwise, as already discussed in chapter 4 (and see the remarks on the relation with *dualgas* above):

> ca dobheir gach uili allus ar bíth co **ndlighenn** sé blais sailti do bheth air[15]

> why must all perspiration have a salty taste?

In fact the passive construction (*b* above) comes to mean the opposite of its original meaning, so that *dlegar x do y* = 'x is due *from* y' comes to mean 'x is due *to* y':

dleaghair do shluagh shíol Luighdeach	it is the right of the host of the race of Lughaidh
sreathnughadh cath sluagh Muimhneach.[16]	to lead in battle the Munster hosts.

This further emphasizes the element of reciprocity in the entire process of *dligheadh*. What emphasizes it even more is a parallel Middle Irish development whereby the active form comes to denote both ends of the spectrum, both right and obligation. There are plenty of examples of this in *Lebor na Cert* which deals with the rights and obligations of provincial kings and their subjects. The following excerpts elaborate on the relationship between Cashel on the one hand and Leinster, Connacht and the Dublin Norse on the other:

> **Dleagaid** Laigin ar báig aenlaithi teacht la báig ríg Caisil i cend Chuind nó allmarach. **Dliged** didiu ó Gallaib Átha Cliath ⁊ ó deoradaib Érind dula lais i cend catha . . . ⁊ **dligid** aiscid ar coicrích ó Chondachtaib.[17]

> The Laigin *are obliged* upon one day's summons to go at the summons of the king of Cashel against Leth Cuinn or against the foreigners. *It is due from* the Norse of Dublin and from the unfranchised of all Ireland that they go with him into battle . . . *he is entitled to* a gift on the frontier from the Connachta.

Note the shift in the final sentence from obligation to entitlement—a shift that is *pragmatic* rather than morphosyntactic in nature; that is, a function of the context and the relations of power projected within that context. These same relations are emphasized again in the poetry that follows the prose just quoted, where the active form has the sense of both (*a*) 'is entitled to' and (*b*) 'is obliged to':

(*a*) **Dligid** féin rí Caisil chain / trí cét n-édach ar Samain

The king of fair Cashel is entitled to three hundred suits of cloth at Samain

(*b*) **Dleagaid** Laigin dula leó[18]

The Laigin are bound to go with them

Otherwise the passive sense is still rendered by the morphological passive:

Dleagair a crích Corcamruad / cét caerach[19]

The territory of Corcamruad owes a hundred sheep

The passive form has the expected sense 'owes', 'is due (from)'. However, the examples under (*a*) above are notable in showing once again the importance of pragmatics in an explication of semantics: either end of the *uinculum iuris* can be implicated (that of right or obligation) depending on the relation between the participants as established by the context. A few further examples will serve to reinforce the point. The pragmatic nature of the interpretation of *dligid* is seen most clearly where the two intended senses are juxtaposed in the same context. A number of these occur in a poem appended to the main text in Dillon's edition, a poem that he interprets as in effect a reply on behalf of the northern half of Ireland against the claims of Cashel. Whoever is king of Tara, we are told, has the following entitlements:

(*a*)	**Dligid** beith i Temraig thréin	*He is entitled* to be in mighty Tara
	⁊ cách ica óigréir:	with everyone subject to him;
	mene fergna féin re goil	when he is not himself prepared for battle,
	ad riaraig dó a chúicedaig.	his provincial kings are at his command.
(*b*)	**Dligid** rí Ulad amra	The worthy king of the Ulaid
	flead dó cach sheachtmad Samna	*owes him* a feast each seventh Samain.
	is a cur dó cen gaindi	and to send it to him without stint,
	ós brú Lindi Luathgainni.[20]	on the border of Lind Luathgainne.

Similarly, we are told of the king of Cooley and the stipends due both (*a*) to and (*b*) from him:

(*a*)	**Dligid**, ce iarfaigid sin,	*He is entitled,* if you ask it,
	minba hé bus rí ar Ultaib	to eight coloured cloaks
	ocht mbruit datha ⁊ dá luing	two ships and a gleaming shield for each shoulder;
	co sciath ngel ar gach ngualaind.	if he not be king of the Ulaid.
(*b*)	Do ríg Rátha Móir Muigi	To the king of Ráith Mór Maige
	dligid ro-chrud rígraidi	*he owes* more than a royal fee
	dáig is é is uaisle astar	for his is the noblest service (?)
	is as túsca tuaristol.[21]	and he is the first to receive a stipend.

Here *dligid* denotes the opposite ends of the spectrum in each case, the particular interpretation being a function of context. In each case of (*a*) above, the active form *dligid* has the original 'active' interpretation 'has a claim on' or 'is entitled to from' while in (*b*) the active form has ousted the passive form in its original sense of 'is subject to claim' or 'owes', 'is bound to'.

Dír and *díre*

The term *díre* is an important one in early Irish law. It means literally 'off-payment' (verbal noun of *dí* 'off' and *-ren* 'pay'). Binchy discusses the two meanings that it has in the eighth-century law tract *Críth Gablach,* those of (i) honour price and (ii) penalty.[22] As he points out, there is a historical connection between the two senses: in the earliest period of Irish law every penalty was calculated on the basis of the injured party's honour-price. Thus we have again a word that encompasses both ends of the one spectrum. *DIL* gives a further, more generalized sense: 'one's due or right.' In the following excerpt from a fourteenth-century (non-legal) text, the king is being assured of general support among the men of Ireland because he has treated each according to their status. Here *dúchas* very much has the sense of heredity as a principle of social ordering, of getting what is one's due or birthright; and the significance of the passage is that it is here coupled with *díre* in the same general sense. We return here to an excerpt quoted in briefer form in chapter 2:

> Dóig do-géba tú colamhain Temrach dod chosnam . . . ┐ cletha cosanta Cuind Chédchathaigh ┐ do-ghébha-sa sluag Connacht dod chosnam. Uair gach nech is sine inaí-siu acu, is oidedha duit iat, ┐ gach comhaís is comalta, ┐ a macáimh i n-a ndaltaib dílsi duit; ┐ nár léigis uasal a n-inadhaibh ísil, ná daor a flaithes flatha, ná cam do chaithem re cóir, acht gach nech for a **díre** ┐ for a **dúthchas**.[23]

> Because you will get Tara's champions to protect you . . . and the defenders of Conn Cédchathach and you will get the hosts of the Connachta guarding you; since every one of them who is older than you is a foster-father to you; every one of the same age is a foster-brother and their young ones are your dear foster-children because you have not allowed the high-born to descend to lowly places, nor base elements to aspire to kingship, nor injustice to be used against what is right, but (have treated) every one according to his due and his *dúchas*.

Consider the following segment from a section of a text analysed above in some detail (*Lebor na Cert*) outlining the reasons for the supremacy of the king of Cashel, in particular over the Laigin and the Connachta. The text asserts the nature of Cashel's supremacy: when its king is not king of all Ireland he is overlord of the southern half:

> Is iad so beos tecusca Benén . . . corab ceand coitchenn cáich comarba Caisil feib is ed comarba Pádraic, ┐ in tan nába rí for Érind rí Caisil is ed as **dír** dó forlámus for leith Érind.[24]

> These are the teachings of Benén . . . that the heir to Cashel is the common head of all, as is the heir of Patrick; and when the king of

Cashel is not king of Ireland, he is entitled to the overlordship of half of Ireland.

As with a number of the lexical items already discussed, we will consider the ramifications of the syntax of this last example—*as dír do*—below. For the purposes of our syntactic frame what we have here is:

VERB **IS**	LEXICAL VARIABLE	PREPOSITION **DO**
'is'	*DÍR*	'to', 'for'

We will return to this syntactic frame below, and in fact we shall see that *dír* and the item we considered previously, *dligheadh,* are particularly closely associated within this frame.

Díleas/ruidhleas and *toich*

Díleas (Old Irish *díles*) is another legal term that covers both sides of a particular process in a reflexive sense. Binchy gives the literal meaning as 'excluded from remedy' (*dí* + *les*) and discusses the two-sided nature of its pragmatics as follows.[25] The meaning of *díles* as applied to any given situation depends on whether it works to the advantage or the detriment of the person concerned. In the former case the meaning is 'indefeasibly entitled', 'held in absolute ownership', and not subject to claim. In the latter case, where the person concerned is excluded from legal redress, the meaning is 'forfeit'. From the adjective *díles* is derived the abstract noun *dílse*, and there is a further formation from both adjective and noun by means of an intensifying prefix *ro*: an adjective *ruidhleas* and a corresponding noun *ruidhilse*. This adjective occurs jointly with *dúchas*, as in the following:

> Ros-fuairsett araill dona húaislibh **diarbho toich** an baile ⁊ na feroinn robtar comhfhoiccsi dhó baoghal an bhaile gurro ghabhsat ar éiccin é forsna Gallaibh. Do Chloinn nDonnchaid an Chorainn na hí lásro gabadh . . . ⁊ **ba dóib roba ruidhlius ar aoi ndúthchusa** an dúnadh.[26]

> Some of the nobles to whom the town and the lands near to it belonged by right took the town by surprise and captured it from the English. Those by whom it was captured were of the Clann Donncha of Corann . . . and the castle was theirs by hereditary right.

In other words, the castle was inalienably theirs, or *ruidhleas* to them, by reason of their *dúchas* or right of inheritance. Here *dúchas* stands in a relation to *ruidhleas* that is reminiscent of its association with *dual* discussed in chapter 4, as the particular instrument by which the idea of an inalienable right is achieved. Again we will defer detailed comment on the syntax in which the term *ruidhleas* is embedded here. For the moment, note how this passage also contains the word *toich*, which is another term worthy of comment in the present context. *DIL* gives the meanings 'inheritance', or 'patrimony', when used as a substantive, and we find the following gloss in O'Clery:

toich .i. dúthaig ('native, belonging to')[27]

However, this word is most frequently used predicatively in the syntagm *is toich (do)*, as in the following examples:[28]

(a)   Tighearna ná ro shanntaigh forbann ná fairbrígh neich oile do beith occa, acht in ro badh **toich** dia shinnseraibh ó chéin mhair.

A lord who had not coveted to possess himself of the illegal or excessive property of any other, except such as had been hereditary in his ancestors from a remote period.

(b)   **Toich** dó righi nEirenn iar ngenelach.

The kingship of Ireland was his by hereditary right.

The preposition *do* can be omitted, making the construction completely impersonal:

(c)   **Is toich** cia do-rattid-si ní dia muintir.

It is right that ye should give somewhat to his [Christ's] household.

Here we see the same concept of hereditary right embodied in the *dú—dúthaigh—dúchas* series. Another notable instance of this word *toich* was given in chapter 2 in reference to the tenure of the MacWilliam Burkes in north-west Connacht, where they were represented by some as interlopers who had deprived the original inhabitants (*na tuatha diarbho toich*) of their land:

Ba sain ceinél ro aitreibh í an ionbáidh sin ⁊ na tuatha **diarbho toich** ó chéin mháir. Búrcaigh slondadh an cheneoil rotus-n-aitreb an tan sin.[29]

The people who lived in it at that time were distinct from the people to whom it had rightfully belonged in antiquity. Burke was the name of the family who inhabited it at that time.

As a close equivalent of the concept of *dominium* 'natural hereditary right', as expounded in Suárezian natural law, Carroll cites this word *toich* 'inherently right'.[30] As we can see, it takes its place among more commonly attested words of the same kind. We shall return to the question of 'natural law' in its European context in chapter 6.

A second example of a correlation between *ruidhleas* and *dúchas* is taken from the *Leabhar Muimhneach*, probably compiled some time in the eighteenth century from earlier materials relating to the history of the Dál gCais in particular. In the following passage, which was quoted in chapter 3, Lorcán, son of Lachtna, arrives at the seat of the Munster high-kingship, Cashel, to make good his hereditary claim to the joint sovereignty (*cert comhdhúthchasa*) of Munster. When he approaches Cashel the high king, Cormac Cais, is asked by his followers what the stranger's mission might be, to which the king replies that he is seeking his inheritance in the house of Cashel (*Ag iarraidh a dhúthchasa féin i dtigh Chaisil atá*). He is questioned further, and answers as follows:

> 'Cia **dúthchas** dhlighes?' ol cách. 'Atá,' ol Cormac, 'leth an tighe ón dorus go roile. Is *dleacht* a thabhairt dó.[31]

> 'To what *dúchas* is he entitled?' asked everyone. 'He is entitled to half the house from one door to another,' said Cormac. 'It is legitimate to give it to him.'

In passing, it should be remarked that this word *dleacht* is a further derivative of the stem *dligh*, which of course underlies various forms that we have considered. Cormac then greets Lorcán with the following acknowledgment of the rights of the Dál gCais, and we may note how they are characterized here in terms of both *ruidhleas* and, once again, *dligheadh*:

> is annsin do chan Cormac do **dhlighedh** Dáil gCais .i. a **ruidhles díles** an tan nach biadh ríghe Caisil aca:

> It was then that Cormac spoke of the entitlement of the Dál gCais, that is, their inalienable right whenever they did not hold the kingship of Cashel:

. . . **Ruidhleas [do]** Dháil gCais na gcuradh	It is the entitlement of the Dál gCais of the heroes
i dtigh ríogh Caisil na gcliar	in the house of Cashel of the clerics
in leath thuaidh don tigh gan díchleith	the northern side of the house without deception
dlighid do gach ríghthigh riamh	they are entitled to every royal house before it.
Tosach ag dul i dtír námhad	(To be) in the vanguard into enemy territory
is deiredh leó ag techt tar ais	in the rearguard when returning
le méd a n-áigh fria gach ndoilgheas	for the sake of their valour in time of strife
is ní do **ruidhleas** Dáil gCais.[32]	is part of the entitlement of the Dál gCais.

There is a certain equivalence in this context, therefore, between *dligheadh*, *ruidhleas* and *dúchas* as forms of entitlement. Note that the first stanza above expressly relates what is *ruidhleas* to what had already been described as *dúchas* in the prose: an inalienable right of possession through heredity to half the house of Cashel. We saw in an earlier chapter how the lands of the Dál gCais were characterized as *fearann cloidhimh* 'sword land', which contrasts with terms such as *fearann cathaoire* on the one hand and *dúthaigh* or *dúchas* on the other. They had therefore refused to yield hostages to the high king of Munster, Feidhlimidh Mac Criomhthainn, since their land, being 'sword land' and having been conquered from Connacht in the sixth century, did not properly belong to Munster at all. Furthermore, the Dál gCais had also been denied their right of joint inheritance (*cert comhdhúthchasa*) to Cashel, which they had always claimed on the grounds of a claimed common genealogy with the ruling Eoghanachta:

> gach dlighe do bhiadh (bhíodh) ag rígh Caisil i dTuadhmhumhain . . . a **dílse** sin uile idir bhiadh agus coimhidecht, cíos, géill agus eidirecht, cáin agus cura do thabhairt do rígh Dál gCais go bráth in tan nach budh leó ríghe Caisil budhéin; agus **dílse forgabhála** Conaill Eachluaith in gach dúthaigh fón Mumhain.[33]

> Every entitlement which the king of Cashel had in Thomond . . . that entitlement between food and lodging, rent, hostages and sureties, tribute and verbal agreements to be given to the Dál gCais forever whenever they did not possess the kingship of Cashel itself; as well as the entitlements of conquest of Conall Eachluath in every region of Munster.

In addition, certain other of their indefeasible possessions (*a ruidhlesa dílse*), including those obtained by conquest (*forgabhála*), had been alienated from them:

> Agus bhádar a **ruidhleasa dílse**, agus **forgabhála** Conaill Eachluaith friú amuigh . . . agus in géin do bheidís sin 'na n-éagmais, agus nach aontóchaoi sealuighecht Chaisil do thabhairt dóibh nach tiubhraidís géill ná eidiredha ná sochruide dóibhsiomh.[34]

> And their inalienable rights and the rights of conquest of Conall Eachluath were being withheld . . . and as long as they were deprived of those and as long as there should be no agreement to give them the joint sovereignty of Cashel, they would not give hostages or sureties or retinue to them.

What is *dílse* or *díleas* can also be the result of conquest or force. In this connection we may note the following from O'Curry's law transcripts in the Royal Irish Academy on the subject of *ferann gaiscid* 'land acquired by prowess':

> Ferann gaiscid is **diles don** ti nos-cosna sech cach n-aen isin taith.[35]

> Land acquired by prowess is *díleas* to (held indefeasibly by) the one who wins it over everyone else in the tribe.

It may also be noted, however, that, as Ó Corráin points out, land held as *dílse* could be given away or sold, as in the following entry in *Annála Ríoghachta Éireann*:

> Iseall Ciarain do chendach ar **dhilsi** do Corbmac mac Cuinn . . . ó rígh Midhe.[36]

> The *dílse* of Iseall Chiaráin was bought by Corbmac mac Cuinn . . . from the king of Midhe (Meath).

Clonmacnoise already owned this land, but it was subject to rents and cess; its purchase *ar dhílsi* involved the acquisition of absolute ownership in a fashion somewhat reminiscent of the later 'commercialization' of *dúthaigh* referred to in chapter 3.

The concept of *ruidilse* in the sense of 'complete immunity' is found in the seventh-century law tract on judgements relating to bees, *Bechbretha* ('Bee Judgements'):

> Is di **ruidilsib** i mbechbrethaib la Féniu cip é forsa ruirset occa collud occa cumscuchad occa ngabáil occa ndécsin dara sostu ind aimsir i tochumlat.[37]

> Among the complete immunities in bee-judgements according to Irish law is the man on whom they have rushed when robbing them, moving them, seizing them, [or] looking at them over their hives at the time when they are swarming.

In other words, their owner is free from any liability with respect to any damage or injury the bees might inflict under the circumstances described. In addition, the adjectival form of the simplex (*díleas*) occurs in *Bechbretha* in the same passage with *ruid(i)les*:

> Fer fo-gaib fríth mbech hi ruud no dírainn no écmacht: is **díles do** uidiu ar is **óenruidles** la Féniu acht cuit n-ági fhine ⁊ cuit n-ecailse frisa mbí audacht.[38]

> The man who finds a stray swarm in a forest or unshared land or inaccessible country: it is immune for him, for it is one of the complete immunities in Irish law except for the share of the chief of the kindred and the share of the church to which he makes a bequest.

In other words, 'finders keepers': possession of the bees is absolute and beyond claim, except for the provisos stated. The phrase *is díles do* is another example of a type of construction that will feature in our discussion in the following section. From this section, therefore, we can add to our list of examples of the kind of syntax we are considering:

IS	DÍLEAS/RUIDHLEAS/TOICH	DO

In view of the accumulating evidence for this construction, it is time to turn our attention to a closer examination of its syntax.

The syntax of what is right and proper: *is . . . do*

We have already considered various words as they appear in association with *dúchas*. It remains to consider further aspects of the relationships of these items according to the syntactic structures in which they occur. As we have seen at various points, all members of the *dú—dúthaigh—dúchas* family occur in a construction preceded by the verb 'to be' and followed by the semantic subject governed by the preposition *do*, in more traditional terms, the indirect object. I present here some edited versions of examples already considered for summary purposes:

(a) léig díot, a bhráthair, na bearta **as dúthchus duit**

give up, brother, the tricks that come naturally to you

ba **dó** buddéin **ba dú** cendus ⁊ tighernus an tire

it was to himself that the leadership and lordship of the country was due

ba dúthaigh doibh cia no thiestais[39]

it was right that they should come

As we saw in chapter 4, the word *dual* (b) rarely occurs outside this type of syntactic structure[40] and can in fact be collocated with *dú* or *dúchas* in this way (c):

(b) **budh dual do** laogh an fhiaidh rith a bheith aige

it's natural for the fawn of a deer to have fleetness

(c) is é **is dú** agus **is dual/dúchas dó**[41]

it's in his very nature

The other items we have been considering all occur in the same type of construction: *dligheadh* (d); *dír* (e) and *díleas/ruidhleas* (f):

(d) atá a teglach in rig oglach **diana dligeadh** cech cnáim im a téit smir

there was a youth in the king's household to whom every marrow bone was due[42]

innister don laech ucud **diarba dlighed** an smior a ní sin

the hero to whom the marrow was due was told of this occurrence

(e) temair **nocho dír do-son**[43]

Tara does not belong to him

(f) fer fo-gaib fríth mbech hi ruud no dírainn no écmacht: **is díles do shuidiu**

the man who finds a stray swarm in a forest or unshared land or inaccessible country: it is immune for him

bá doiligh mór lais mídhiach na mainstre, ⁊ Goill do beith accá h-ionattacht, ⁊ agá h-aitreabhadh inon na mac m-bethadh ⁊ na c-céiledh n-Dé **diarbhó ruidhles** í có sin[44]

he was saddened by the monastery's ill fortune, with foreigners occupying it instead of the 'sons of life' and the *céili Dé,* by whom it had been rightfully owned till then

Furthermore, *dír* and *dligheadh* can be found juxtaposed in the same clause:[45]

(g)   **is dír ⅂ is dlighedh duinn** . . . bríathra fíri do chantain

it is right and proper for us to speak true words

laidh . . . **is dir ⅂ is dligeadh d'éicsib** d'aisnéis

a poem . . . which it is right and proper for poets to recite

as dior ⅂ as dligid do

it is right and proper for him

It turns out that in medieval Irish this syntax is very productive. We can present it in the following outline:

(i) VERB **IS**	(ii) LEXICAL VARIABLE	(iii) PREPOSITION **DO**
'is'	**DÚ/DÚTHAIGH/DÚCHAS /DUAL/DLIGHEADH/DÍR /TOICH/DÍLEAS/RUIDHLEAS**	'to', 'for'

The second column (ii) provides the specific semantic content of the expression; but it is the iconic relation between the parts in the formation of the whole that is of chief interest here. The most significant feature is the way in which the semantic or 'logical' subject is expressed as a 'dative' or prepositional subject, rather than a nominative or 'agentive' subject. So the construction says something like 'It is (X) to/for (you) (to do Y)'; that is, the general existence of the idea of what is right or natural or indefeasible is presented *iconically* (by means of the preposition *do*) as being external to the subject and therefore not originating within the subject. This point is crucial and will be developed more fully in the next section.

The important point here is the *pervasiveness* of such structures in Irish. The expressions above are only part of a more extensive patterning in the language that conforms to this type of structure. Two sub-types are of principal interest here: (i) general expressions of obligation or propriety and (ii) the so-called verbal of necessity. I present some examples of each type in turn before proceeding to a more general discussion.

(i) General expressions of obligation and appropriateness: One of the commonest and most prolific classes of predicates taking a verbal complement in Medieval and Early Modern Irish are those expressing terms of what we might call weakened necessity or obligation. The lexical items concerned are many and diverse and include the following (see opposite):

According to *DIL*, these encompass the following aggregate of meanings:

VERB **IS**	LEXICAL VARIABLE	PREPOSITION **DO**
'is'	e.g. **ADAS/CÓIR/COMADAS /CUBAID/DEITHBIR /CERT/IMMAIRCIDE/TACAIR**	'to', 'for'

'(it is) suitable, fitting, proper, right, correct, just, reasonable, natural, becoming, advisable'. These can be said to represent a generalized attitude to the appropriateness of an event and therefore convey a sense of an event or situation that is somehow meant to be: there is an important sense here of describing and prescribing what is *destined* to be. Predicates of weaker obligation thus shade into an evaluation of appropriateness or reasonableness. A few examples are presented here:

> **is tacir deit** ni táirle lat
>
> it is best for thee that he come not with thee!

> **ba deithbir do** dúilib Dé / ce imro-chloítis a ngné[46]
>
> it would have been fitting for God's elements . . . that they should change their aspect

The stronger term of obligation, 'necessary', also occurs in this construction:

> **is ecen dam** són nonda-ges dait-siu[47]
>
> it is necessary to me that I pray for them to thee

Note that the subject can also be expressed as part of the subordinate clause in Early Irish or omitted altogether, in which case the construction is further impersonalized:

> **is uisse** a molad[48]
>
> it is just to praise him

Consider further the relationship between the various terms for 'right' in the following passage, which we have previously considered with regard to *dúthaigh* and *dual*. The further items to consider here are *cóir* and *deithbir* (*degbir*) which receive the same syntactic treatment:

> Atbert imorro Brian **nirbo coir do-som** in ní sin [do radha] uair ba *dúthaig* do éc ocus ba *dúthaig* do Dail Cais uli . . . ocus nirbo *dual* imorro ocus nirbo *duthaig* doib tárna tarcaisin do gabail . . . Asbert Mathgamain imorro ba hi comarli **ba coir doib** do denaib .i. teacht i Casiul na rig . . . primtheglach clainni Aelella; **degbir** on ar ba he Aeleach Mumhan ocus Temair Lethi Moga.[49]

> Brian said then that he had no right to (say) that since it was right for him to die and it was right for the whole of the Dál gCais . . . and it was

not right/expected or right/natural for them to take that insult of theirs
. . . Then Mathgamhain said that what they should do was go to Cashel
of the Kings . . . the principal hosting of the Clann Ailella; that was fitting since it [Cashel] was the Aileach of Munster and the Tara of southern Ireland.

This construction is not confined to 'modal' predicates expressing attitudes to
rightness, fitness and propriety but has a rather wider evaluative remit, as the
following examples show. A mere selection is given here: *burbe* 'foolishness',
ferr 'better' and *col* 'crime':

is burbe dom cia do-gnéo móidim[50]

it is foolishness for me that I make boast

ba ferr dó do-gneth co grind/aithrigi n-etail n-érthind[51]

it would have been better for him had he diligently made a pious and
severe repentance

ní col dó cid less ar mbéo et ar mmarb[52]

it is no crime of his that we are his dead and alive

(ii) Perhaps most significantly in the present discussion, Irish has a verbal category called the 'verbal of necessity', which indicates that the action or state
signified by the verb must, or at least should, be realized. Thus from the verb
déan we derive the necessitative *déanta* (corresponding roughly to the Latin
gerundive), as in the following seventeenth-century example where the
notional subject is contained in the form *dhúinn* 'for/to us':

uime sin **is déanta dhúinn** comhairle Phóil[53]

for that reason we must/should carry out Paul's advice

In the following example from a mid-seventeenth-century poem, the nobles of
Ireland are castigated for their lack of loyalty to the Irish language (*ag tréigin
a gceirt san nGaeidhilg*), while the poet goes on to spell out the necessary prohibition, which is intended to have the force of general prohibition:

Innsigh dhósan gur léur liom	Tell him that I know well
go bfuilid úaisle Éiriond	that Ireland's nobles
monuar *ag tréigin* a gceirt	alas! Give up their rightful practice
san nGaeidhlig na n-uam n-oirrdheirc.	of the melodious Irish.
Níor thréigthe dhóibh í ile	It should never be laid aside [they should never] .
air bhéurla chríoch gcoigríchthe.[54]	for the speech of foreign lands.

More literally, 'it is to/for us to do'; that is, the obligation or imperative exists
for us; in the second case, 'it is not to/for them to abandon'. The syntax of the

Irish construction therefore relegates the role of human agency: the 'subject' is in fact an indirect object or 'patient' of the construction. This differs significantly from the corresponding English gloss 'we must/should', where the nominative subject stresses the idea of the subject's agency. Where the English construction is agentive ('we . . .'), the Irish is non-agentive ('there is . . . for us'), suggesting a viewpoint whereby the idea of obligation or appropriateness of action *happens to* the subject rather than originating with him or her. It is in this type of non-agentive construction, therefore, that the syntax of *dúthaigh* and *dúchas* is implicated, as well as the conceptually related *dual* and the other lexical items considered thus far. The relationship between the verbal of necessity and the type of more lexically based expressions of obligation considered in (i) above can be seen in the following excerpt from Céitinn. In this passage he compares the punishment and suffering inflicted by God on the Israelites in ancient times and on the Irish in his own day. Urging the Irish to repent and turn to God, he concludes using the verbal of necessity (*beitte*). A couple of lines later, however, he expresses the same sentiments using the lexical equivalent *cóir*:

> Uime sin **is beitte d'**Éireannchaibh Dia do ghuidhe . . . Mar an gcéadna **is cóir d'**Éireannchaibh a rádh. . .[55]

> The Irish must/should pray to God . . . In the same way, the Irish must/should say it.

As was observed with regard to type (i) above, the semantic subject governed by *do* can be omitted from the construction altogether, which nonetheless remains perfectly grammatical. Further examples of this deletion of the subject include:

(*a*)   **Ní séanta** go dtugthar saor-dháil d'anmaibh na marbh

  It should not be denied that release is given to the souls of the dead

(*b*)   Is **dénta** áil **d'**égin[56]

  Good should be made of necessity (Necessity is the mother of invention)

This omission of the subject gives the construction a greater sense of the general or impersonal. We shall defer a more detailed discussion of this construction in context until later; the important point here is that the structure *is . . . do* can be generalized over every verb in Irish. The syntax therefore conforms to the pattern we have been describing:

VERB	VARIABLE	PREPOSITION **DO**
IS	**ANY VERB**	'to'/various/'for'
'is'	+ (ENDING) *TA*	

We have thus far seen instances of the marking of necessity in Irish by means of an impersonal predicative construction with a prepositional subject governed by *do*. A very similar construction exists that involves marking the prepositional subject by means of the preposition *le* (Old Irish *la* and *fri,* later *re*) rather than by means of *do*. Thus we have the syntactic structure:

VERB **IS**	(LEXICAL VARIABLE)	PREPOSITION **LE** 'to' 'with'

In contrast to the *do-* type covering the range of obligation, necessity and appropriateness, the typical ranges of this construction are (i) desiderative, denoting the desire or disposition of the subject; (ii) emotive evaluation, including those of surprise and shame; and (iii) a subjective epistemic judgement of the type in English 'it seems/occurs to me':

(i)   **is ferr limm** ra-fesid cid calléic

      I prefer that ye should know it even now

(ii) **ní mebul lemm** cia fa-dam

      I am not ashamed that I suffer it

(iii) **is derb lium** attá lat-su[57]

      I am sure that thou hast it

An exception here is the use of the preposition *do* with the predicate *follus* 'manifest,' 'obvious', which gives it a saliently 'objective' quality when compared with the likes of *derb* 'sure' immediately above:

is follus dunni . . . as firdia[58]

      it is manifest to us that he is the true God

The choice of preposition between *do* and *le* is of some relevance here, as semantic contrasts are often possible based on that choice. Some pertinent examples are given here from the Christian Brothers' Modern Irish grammar (*Graiméar Gaeilge na mBráithre Críostaí*):

(*a*) Ní beag **duit** é   It's enough for you (You have enough)

(*b*) Ní beag **liom** é   *I think* it's enough

(*a*) Is cuma **duit** (é)   It doesn't affect you (Don't worry about it)

(*b*) Is cuma **liom**   It's all the same to me (*I don't think* it matters)

(*a*) Ní foláir **di** dul abhaile She has to go home

(*b*) Ní foláir **leis** imeacht   *He thinks* he has to leave (He insists on leaving)[59]

In each instance, the change of preposition alters the relationship of the semantic subject to the predicate nominal: the change from (*a*) *do* to (*b*) *le* introduces a further, more subjective component to the construction. As Genee notes, both prepositions *le* (Old Irish *la*) and *do* play an important role in Irish syntax in general.[60] The former can be categorized as *source*, or the person from whose viewpoint the semantic content of the predicate applies, the latter as *beneficiary*, or the person to or for whom the semantic content applies. In other words, where the preposition *le* indicates the source of the modality, the preposition *do* generally denotes the target.[61] With this comparison in mind we can shed further light on the similarities and differences between the words *dual* and *gnáth*, which we considered in chapter 4. *Dual* invariably appears with the 'objective' preposition *do*, as in the following passage:

> dísle do choimhéad do Ruaidhrí **amhail fá dual do** gach rígh dá mbíodh ar Laighnibh do dhéanamh do ríoghaibh Éireann.[62]

> [Diarmaid] was obliged to submit to and remain loyal to Ruaidhrí, as had [always] been *dual* to every king of Leinster to submit to the kings of Ireland.

On the other hand, *gnáth* generally takes the more 'subjective' preposition *le*, or Old Irish *la* 'with'. Note in the following example, however, that the form is that of the preposition *re* 'to' (Old Irish *fri*), with which it is often conflated:

> Agus an tan do shuidheadh Brian n-a shuidhe ríogh is é rí Mumhan do shuidheadh ar a dheasláimh; **amhail fá ghnáth ris** gach rígh d'fhuil Éireamhóin ríogha Uladh do chur ar a ndeasláimh.[63]

> And when Brian sat in his king's seat it was the king of Munster that used to sit by his right hand, as was the accustomed practice with all the kings of the descendants of Éireamhón to put the kings of Ulster on their right-hand side.

Because of the similarity of the syntax in which both expressions are embedded here—the syntax of precedence and custom—we can make a direct comparison between *dual* and *gnáth*, with the latter conceived as more likely to originate within the subject governed by *le/la/re* and the former construed as being more outside the subject's control governed by *do*.

The agentive and non-agentive in linguistic structure

In the previous section we were concerned with the question of the meaning of linguistic structure. One of the external motivations for linguistic structure is *iconicity*. The particular type of iconicity that we are concerned with here is *diagrammatic* or *syntagmatic* iconicity; in other words, an arrangement of signs 'whose relationship to each other mirrors the relationship of their referents'.[64] A simple example is sequentiality in narrative structure, where the narrated sequence of events typically follows the temporal sequence: *veni, vidi, vici*, for example. Linguistic structure can therefore be iconic with respect to the linear ordering of experience. As Croft points out, the great problem here is in identifying what constitutes the structure of 'experience' outside the mediation of that experience through language itself.[65] Are we comparing linguistic structure to the structure of external reality or our *conceptualization* of that structure? How can external reality be conceptualized except through language? Croft's elegant and persuasive solution is to turn the question on its head: the hypothesis of linguistic iconicity can be used to put forward further hypotheses concerning the cognitive and psychological structuring of the external world, which can then be tested by the disciplines of cognitive science and psychology, respectively. As Croft further points out, this procedure is eminently reasonable, as cognition is most explicitly made manifest through language to begin with, so that *hypotheses* regarding experiential structure may legitimately originate with considerations of linguistic structure. Another term used for the type of iconicity we are describing here is *structural isomorphism*, in which the structure of the utterance mirrors that of the concept, in particular where the linguistic distance between constituents of the sentence implies the same conceptual distance between the signified.[66]

In a comparison of English and Russian syntax, Wierzbicka discusses the issue of agentivity and non-agentivity that occupied our attention in the previous section.[67] She sets the scene for this comparison by making the general point that syntactic typology in general indicates that this is a basic distinction between

> 'two different ways of viewing one's life' . . . one can tend to view people's lives in terms of 'what I do' (an agentive orientation), and one can tend to view it in terms of 'what happens to me' (a patientive orientation).[68]

Syntactically, agentive constructions are usually given nominative marking, while non-agentive constructions receive dative marking. What is at issue here is the relative attention that languages give to these two poles of expression. Modern English emphasizes agentivity, although there are still more marginal dative-type constructions in the language (e.g. 'it seems/occurs to me'). Wierzbicka contrasts Russian, which is pervaded by the latter, non-agentive syntactic pattern and where, conversely, the agentive mode is not extended to other semantic domains. For example, there is a whole class of impersonal modal predicates of necessity requiring a dative subject that are very similar to those that have been discussed for Irish above.

Wagner makes a basic twofold classification of the verb in Irish into what he calls *Aktionsverben* (active verbs), which comprise the vast majority of finite verbs, and *Zustandsverben* or 'stative' verbs, which are divided into three subtypes:

(i) Finite verbs which are either modals (e.g. *féadaim* 'I can'); sensory verbs (*chím* 'I see', *measaim* 'I think') or genuine statives (e.g. *tá, is* both 'is')

(ii) Verbal-noun type statives which denote stative or iterative meaning, e.g. *tá sé ina shuí* 'He is sitting', lit. 'He is in his sitting'

(iii)   Impersonal nominal sensory/modal expressions; these are further sub-
        divided according to whether the stative verb is the substantive verb: *tá*
        e.g. *tá eagla orm* 'I'm afraid', lit. 'fear is on me'; or the copula *is: is dóigh*
        liom/is féidir liom/ba cheart dom.[69]

Sub-type (iii) is the type we have been considering, specifically the copula *is*,
and it contains many expressions that in other languages are expressed ver-
bally: compare, for example, Irish *tá eagla orm* 'I am afraid' with its German
equivalent *ich fürchte (mich)*. I give some some examples here from Wagner
with a view to comparing them with their conventional English equivalents:

is maith liom	I like
is iontach liom	I'm surprised
is toil liom	I like/choose
an léar duit?	Do/Can you see?
ní heagal duit é	Don't be afraid of it
is fíor duit	You're right
ba cheart duit	You should[70]

We can straightaway compare the Irish examples and their English glosses
according to subject marking: in Irish the subject is governed by a preposition
(either *le* or *do*), while in English the subject receives nominative marking (*I* or
you). Thus English gives the subject the same grammatical expression that it
receives in *agentive* constructions (where the subject is the real agent of the
action), whereas Irish does not. This ties in with Wagner's conclusion that Irish
makes a general grammatical distinction between agentivity and non-agentivity:
the finite verb is primarily agentive in orientation, leaving the expression of
what are essentially 'states' to non-verbal and 'impersonal' constructions.[71]

As in the discussion of habituality in the previous chapter, I now wish to
tease out some of the implications of this analysis of the syntax of non-
agentivity for the reading and interpretation of texts in their particular historical and cultural environment. In effect we return to Slobin's idea, discussed
in the previous chapter, of 'thinking for speaking', which in turn shapes the
'rhetorical style' of a language.[72]

A cultural and historical dimension for non-agentivity

We now consider two early seventeenth-century texts, both of which lament
the downfall of the hereditary bardic order. The general thematic content of
both poems is similar and yet the rhetorical style is entirely different, and I
will investigate the contribution of linguistic structure to that rhetorical contrast. The first poem, by Fear Flatha Ó Gnímh, has already been considered
briefly in the context of other discussions, where the issue is very much the
demise of what was part of hereditary right for the poets:

Mairg do-chuaidh re ceird ndúthchais:	Alas for him who has followed his family profession

rug ar Bhanbha mbarrúrthais	it has befallen Banbha of the fresh soft surface
nach **dualghas** athar is fhearr	that in Ireland's cool green field
i n-achadh fhuarghlas Éireann.[73]	one's father's natural calling is not the best.

Note again how the stage is set by the invocation of what is the poet's craft or hereditary calling, which is in turn depicted as the *dualghas athar*—that which is due or *dual* to the poet, in this instance as a result of heredity (*dúchas*). This of course recalls the common expression in Modern Irish *is dual athar dó é* 'like father like son', which was considered in the previous chapter:

Tá ceol maith ag Donnchadh agus ba **dual** athar dó sin[74]

Donnchadh plays music well, as you'd expect from his father

The poet continues that in such circumstances, where the hereditary bardic calling is being undermined and the poets' hereditary right is being denied, a change of occupation might be desirable. It is in this context that the verbal of necessity appears: what was previously the *dualghas athar* or the *ceard dhúthchais* has been set aside, and this process is depicted by means of a series of negated non-agentive constructions of the type analysed above. Note that the absence of a dative subject governed by *do,* the possibility of which was discussed above, here enhances the feeling of a generalized impersonal prohibition in each case (*Ní . . .*):

Ní **sníthe** snátha an fheasa,	One must not spin the threads of lore
ní **leanta** craobh choibhneasa	one must not follow up the branches of kinship
gréas duan ní **déanta** d'fhighe	one must not weave artistry of lyrics
luadh dréachta ní dlighfidhe.[75]	poetry should not be spoken of.

In the light of our discussion above, it is significant that the verb *dlighidh* (here in its passive conditional form *dlighfidhe*) appears as a more lexicalized version of the verbal of necessity (*luadh dréachta ní dlighfidhe*, literally 'the mention of poetry would not be legitimate'), remembering that this verb signifies precisely that same semantic range of right and entitlement we saw in various connections earlier in this chapter. In the following quatrain the phrase *fine Irial* 'the race of Irial' denotes the Magennises, to whom the needy poets should now have recourse. Again the required course of action is coded by the verbal of necessity, with the prepositional subject governed by *do* (**déanta don** droing fhoghlamtha . . . i gcoinne fhine Irial):

. . . Ó rug éigeantas ortha,	Since need has overtaken them
déanta don droing fhoghlamtha	the learned company must take the path
an tslighe do-roinne riamh	they took of old
i gcoinne fhine Irial.[76]	towards the race of Irial.

What is particularly noteworthy, however, is the way in which this objective, non-agentive syntax with the preposition *do* pervades the entire structure of the poem and not just with reference to expressions of general obligation. I give here some examples with their equivalent English glosses:

(*a*)	**Mairg d**'ollamh **da narbh aithnidh** ceard nábudh cúis iomaithbhir	Woe to the scholar *who knows not* some craft that would be no cause of censure
(*b*)	Do dhul a-mudha **don mhaoin**	Because all the riches *have gone astray*
(*c*)	Cia **dán cóir** a coimhéidse?	Who *ought to* defend her?
(*d*)	**Éigean dóibh**	(They) *were constrained*
	. . . teacht go rochloinn Rudhraighe	. . . to come to the great Children of Rudhraighe
(*e*)	**Triall** isan dturus gcéadna	The schools of the land of fair Séadna *are bound*
	do sgolaibh fhóid fhin Shéadna[77]	to travel in the same path

In all instances here the poet employs a non-agentive syntax, which generally corresponds in the English translation to an agentive one. With regard to his metalinguistic awareness we might say that what engages him at the more conscious level, the idea of the *dualgas* and *dúchas* that have been eroded, finds a more subconscious or unconscious expression at the more automated grammatical level, as coded by the pervasive use of the preposition *do* throughout the poem.

In same way Ó Gnímh's contemporary, Mathghamhain Ó hIfearnáin, laments the change in artistic fashion. In a poem addressed to his son in an effort to dissuade him from following the craft of his ancestors, the poet argues that poetry no longer has what is *dual* to it—*tús anóra* 'pride of place':

A mhic **ná mebhraig** éigsi	Son, don't even think about poetry
cerd do shen rót **ro-thréig-si**	abandon the craft of your ancestors before you
tús anóra gér dual di	though it really should have pride of place
fa tuar ansógha in éigsi.[78]	poetry has been a cause of misery.

Note the equivalence here of *cerd do shen* 'the craft of your ancestors' in this poem and Ó Gnímh's *re ceird nduthchais* 'hereditary profession' and the equivalence of both to *dualgas athar* 'a father's natural calling' in the poem just discussed above. However, if both poems deal with a loss of what is *dual* or *dualgas*, Ó hIfearnáin's rhetoric is markedly different, eschewing the non-agentive syntax of Ó Gnímh in favour of a more direct and personalized form of injunction: the imperative mood. The use of this mood dominates the poem: eleven of the twelve stanzas contain at least one such form. The first quatrain, quoted above, already contains two (*ná mebhraigh* and *ró-thréig-si*). Further examples include:

Ná **len** do dhiogha ceirde	Don't follow your dregs of a craft,
ná **cum** do ghres Gaoidheilge	don't spin your Gaelic web of words;
dán snasta as fuamfhoirfe fáth	a polished poem, perfect in sound and subject
gasta nuadhoirche nemghnáth.[79]	ingenious the strange new-fangled obscurity.

This quatrain offers a further clue to the poet's purpose: what was once *cerd do shen*, the ancestral profession to which the place of honour was *dual*, is now *do dhíogha ceirde* 'your dregs of a craft' and should accordingly be abandoned. It is this sense of urgency, of immediate compliance, of a new break, the adoption of what is *neamhghnáth* or unaccustomed, that triggers the use of the imperative. This urgent sense of the need to leave the past behind continues, the poet first urging his son to compose in the newfangled, easier, non-syllabic metres. Furthermore, the poet-to-be should in fact turn his back on the entire rationale of the hereditary poetic order. In particular, Irish patrons should be shunned and foreigners courted (imperative forms are emphasized in bold):

Sgar riu, ná **ríomh** a n-aithecht	Leave them, don't tell of their keen valour
ná **cuimhnig** a cronaicecht;	don't recall their chronicles;
iul molta Gaoidel **ná gab**,	don't recount history in praise of the Irish,
gach aoinfhear rompa **ríomhtar**.[80]	Let everyone else be recalled ahead of them.

Quite unlike Ó Gnímh's poem, Ó hIfearnáin's fairly seethes with resentment and a sense of betrayal. Where the former mourns the passing of a traditional, 'natural' order as conceived of through the prism of what is inherent in *dual-gas*, *dúchas* and *dligheadh*, the latter in a sense embraces the *neamhghnáth* 'the unknown', 'the unfamilar', that which was not habitually the case. In each case the poet 'finds' a linguistic structure to match his message. In view of the occurrence of the word *neamhghnáth* in Ó hIfearnáin's poem, it is worth returning to a poem already considered in relation to the expression of the habitual in the previous chapter: Tadhg Dall Ó hUiginn's poem to one of the MacWilliam Burkes ('T'aire Riot, a Riocaird Óig') on the inadvisability of assuming an English title in preference to his familiar native one.[81] Here the familiar 'habitual' Irish name is *ainm gnáth*, and the impossibility of separating from it is conceived of by means of the negated 'non-agentive' verbal of necessity (*dealoighthe*), here accompanied by the preposition *do* (in its 2nd singular form):

Mar sin **nár dhealoighthe dhoit**	Ever thus it were not for thee to part
ret ainm ngnáth, red ghníomh n-ordhruic,	from thy wonted title, thy well-known deeds

ris gach mbuaidh dá mbíoth oraibh,	with every triumph that thou hadst of old
ós uaidh fríoth a bhfuarabhair	since from it was got all that thou didst win
Dá bhfaghthá ceannus Chláir Fhloinn	Didst thou get the headship of Flann's plain
níorbh fhiú dhuit, a dhreach shéaghoinn	it would be of no advantage to thee, gallant form,
ainm allmhardha dá rádh ruibh	to reign over Banbha by a foreign title
fa chlár ndagh Bhanbha id dhúthaigh.[82]	in thy native land.

The familiar Irish name is otherwise referred to as the abiding or eternal name (*ainm síor*) and is contrasted with the title that is both borrowed and foreign (*ainm iasachta*). Note the occurrence of further non-agentive syntax (*dob aimhghlic dhuit; dob fhiú*) before the verbal of necessity reappears (*déanta*), again denoting the 'impossibility' of abandoning the native title, such a choice essentially being not for the subject (as coded again by *dhuit*) to make:

Do dháilis, a chruth corcra,	Thou gavest, ruddy-faced form
ainm síor ar ainm n-iasachta,	an abiding name for a temporary one
a námha chnuic bhaillbhric Bhreagh	O fighter of Brega's gaily-tinged hill
dob aimhghlic dhuit a dhéineamh	that was an imprudent deed of thine
Dob fhiú a dtárrais ó thosaigh	All that thou didest obtained from the start
don mhionn oirdhreic anmasoin	from that renowned jewel of a name was worth enough
a chlaochládh *nár* **dhéanta dhuit**,	that thou shouldst not displace it
a réalta ó chaomh Chlár Chormuic[83]	star from Cormac's noble plain

However, it should not be inferred from the examples already considered that the more impersonal verbal of necessity and the more direct imperative are incompatible to the extent that they cannot occur in the same situations. This same poem by Tadhg Dall in fact opens with an injunction to the same Riocard Óg, (coded imperative):

T'aire riot, a Riocaird Óig,	Give heed to thyself, Richard Óg
ná tabhair cúl red chéadmhóid,	do not forsake thine early disposition
San riocht i rabhabhair riamh	Be, even as thou hast ever been,
bí id Riocard mhac Mheic Uilliam.[84]	Richard, son of Mac William.

Here again we can ascribe a different rhetorical force to the two categories. The imperative is used to open the poem with a flourish: the poet expresses himself with immediacy and directness in order to grab the addressee's attention and appeal to his better instincts. At a certain point, however, more impersonal forces and prescriptions are invoked. The verbal of necessity is used after the poet has warmed to his theme of how the familiarity of the Irish title has ensured fame, prosperity and good health to the bearer: as everything that the bearer of the name possesses is due to the familiar title, it cannot be abandoned if the dedicatee is to retain any legitimacy in his land.

Conclusion and postscript:
Miller's *Exiles and Emigrants* (1985)

We have identified a construction that appears to be a productive one in Early Modern Irish. We can present it in the following outline:

(I) COPULA 'TO BE'	(II) NOUN/ADJECTIVE/ VERBAL ADJECTIVE	(III) PREPOSITION **DO**

The important point here is the *pervasiveness* of such structures in Irish, and for our present purposes we have isolated two related semantic domains: general lexical expressions of obligation and appropriateness and the verbal category known as the 'verbal of necessity', which indicates that the action or state signified by the verb must, or at least should, be realized, often with no regard for the semantic subject of the clause. These structures suggest a viewpoint whereby the idea of obligation or appropriateness of action *happens to* the subject rather than originating with him or her. It is in this type of non-agentive construction, therefore, that the syntax of *dúthaigh* and *dúchas* is embedded. Wagner points out that Irish makes a general grammatical distinction between agentivity and non-agentivity: the finite verb is primarily agentive in orientation, leaving the expression of what are essentially 'states' to non-verbal and 'impersonal' constructions.[85] The concepts *dúthaigh* and *dúchas* (as well as *dual*) are thus part of what Whorf might call 'a fashion of speaking', which gives syntactic expression to aspects of experience that are, strictly speaking, beyond the control of human agency.

It is within this syntactic framework that we can return briefly to the idea of the pragmatic in language. If it is accepted that pragmatics provides a functional perspective on language use in general, then the speaker's consciousness of such usage can be expressed in terms of a cline of what Silverstein has called *metapragmatic awareness*.[86] As was discussed in chapters 1 and 4, this involves the level of awareness on the part of the speaker of the linguistic act that he or she is performing and the means by which it is being performed.[87] There is a descending cline of consciousness from lexical items to grammatical markers, as we saw in chapter 4 for the expression of what is 'habitual'. For the purposes of the present discussion we can recall Nuinseań's expression of his own high level of awareness of the context-bound and pragmatic nature of *dúchas* presented above:

's labhra dhiamhuir ar ndúthchus[88] it's a mysterious saying: 'our dúchas'

In the case of *dúchas* as employed in the context of an overall syntax of non-agentivity that involves many other terms, however, we may argue that consciousness is correspondingly lower: here *dúchas* merely has its place within a much broader syntactic and semantic framework. This broader framework accords very well with the more 'conscious' semantics of *dúchas*—something that one derives from birth and from ancestry, beyond the control of one's own agency. But the more automated, syntacticized use can be a powerful reinforcer of a particular linguistic ideology, and I would argue that this is so here. Following the terms of Wierzbicka's discussion, we might say that the non-agentive nature of what is right and natural, hereditary and inalienable, of necessity the case, receives extensive *cultural elaboration* in Irish.[89]

In his study of Irish emigration to North America, Kerby Miller devotes a chapter to what he calls the 'culture of exile', a culture that in his view in its various aspects placed great value on the qualities of 'stasis', 'collective dependence' and 'passivity'.[90] This has already been referred to briefly in chapter 1 in the context of linguistic relativity. One dimension of this Irish 'world view' adduced by Miller is linguistic: he makes essentially the same comparison between Irish and English that I have above, following Wagner, in terms of the more pervasive formal marking of 'agency' or 'agentivity' in the latter, as against the predilection of Irish for non-agentive structures.[91] However, I find the conclusions drawn from this comparison, not to mention the methodology invoked, highly questionable.

Miller invokes the theories of Whorf in an attempt to show a correlation between language and cognition.[92] Whorf's views are immensely complex, and so there can be no question of a detailed discussion of them here.[93] However, Miller's attempt to use Whorf's ideas to substantiate his case is fatally undermined in two ways. The first has already been mentioned in chapter 1: Whorf was not seeking to establish relations of cause and effect between surface or *overt* grammatical structure and ways of thinking; rather, he was trying to establish the possible long-term effects of hidden or *covert* categories (semantic categories that do not receive formal marking as such in the grammar of the language) on entire conceptual domains.[94] In this he differs crucially from Boas, for whom surface categories channel speakers' attention to particular aspects of reality, as we saw in chapter 4. Whorf's argument is that overt morphology and structure is not sufficient for a full semantic definition of categories. As an example, consider his famous analysis of the conceptualization of time in English. He is concerned here first and foremost with the way in which this concept is arrived at by structural analogy. On the basis of everyday English expressions such as *a stick of wood* or *a cup of coffee* he reaches the conclusion that there is a general structure 'form X of formless Y' on the conceptual level. As the phrase *a moment of time* has the same structural analysis, we can speak of a certain objectification of time that leads further to its characterization as a forward linear progression of more or less discrete units. This leads to the evolution of a particular idea of 'historicity', which has its cultural effects in the production of chronicles, annals and what we regard as 'history' in general terms.[95]

This leads us to the second flaw in Miller's argument. Whorf crucially eschews any *direct* cause and effect between grammatical structure and cultural practice: his main concern was the possible relation between this kind of pervasive linguistic structure and *habitual* thought and behaviour, whereby the habitual mode of the individual is shaped by *analogous* 'fashions of speaking'. Whorf is concerned here with the notion of what Lucy terms 'cognitive appropriation' between the structural relations that obtain in various linguistic and, by extension, non-linguistic domains. In other words, large-scale linguistic patterns produce linguistically conditioned habitual thought and thence linguistically conditioned features of culture over a long period of co-existence. As Duranti puts it, 'Whorf was focusing on how a way of thinking may arise *by analogy* with 'fashions of speaking', rather than reflecting a direct mapping of lexical and grammatical structure on to everyday thought and practice.[96] This emphasis on habitual thought is important, because, despite its obligatory character, there is nothing to suggest that grammatical structure acts as a kind of mental straitjacket for speakers of any given language; in other words, that they are prisoners of their grammatical systems. This point was made by Boas and I quote Jakobson here, as he makes the essential point more eloquently and succinctly than I can (emphasis added):

> As Boas repeatedly noted, the grammatical concepts of a given language direct the attention of the speech community in a definite direction and through their compelling, obtrusive character exert an influence upon poetry, belief and even speculative thought *without, however, invalidating the ability of any language to adapt itself to the needs of advanced cognition*.[97]

Similarly, Lucy is at pains to stress that the remit of the linguistic relativity theory is 'habitual' rather than 'potential' thought, the latter being defined as 'what a given speaker or group of speakers *could conceivably think like* or think about in some circumstances' (emphasis added).[98] If the needs of 'advanced cognition' result in an Irish-speaker describing the *external* necessity to emigrate precisely in such terms of a necessity beyond his or her immediate control, this cannot be adduced as evidence of a linguistically determined, passive or fatalistic world view.

The question then shifts to consideration of the possible cultural and historical ramifications of such 'fashions of speaking', although it must be admitted that the thrust of the discussion here is somewhat 'negative', in that it attempts to show first and foremost how Whorf's views should *not* be used.[99]

However, in a more positive vein, the evidence surveyed in this and previous chapters shows that it is legitimate to think in terms of a cryptotypic category of what is right, natural and involuntary in Irish, a category that does not receive a single unitary expression but that seems to pervade linguistic struc-ture at many levels: vocabulary, morphology and syntax. In a case such as this we may follow Wierzbicka and characterize this domain of 'right' and 'natural' as one that is subject to considerable 'cultural elaboration' in Irish.[100]

Miller's discussion also founders on the rock of its own incoherence. Within the context of a linguistic culture that he alleges induces a feeling of 'passive necessity' rather than 'independent volition' in the world view of its speakers, which then conditions a particular cognitive view of the act of emi-gration, he makes the following claim:

> The Irish-speaker *can* employ a phrase *d'imthigh sé go Meirice* [sic] which conveys the sense of purposeful action. However, in terms of the central thesis of this work, it is very significant that by far the most common way for an Irish-speaker to describe his emigration has been *dob éigean dom imeacht go Meirice: 'I had to go to America'* . . . Thus Irish-speakers chose a patient over an active way of expressing their emigration.[101]

Two objections can be made. Firstly, Miller adduces no evidence in support of this claim. Secondly, even if this claim were true, Miller still depicts Irish-speakers as 'choosing' the patient over the active mode. *If* Irish-speakers choose mode X over mode Y, however, they are simply making a choice based on their cognitive appropriation of a given situation, and therefore there can be no question of a passively or fatalistically induced world view. In any case, this is not the kind of level at which Whorf's structural analysis works: as we have seen, he was more concerned with the conceptual than with the merely perceptual, with modes of conception that arise analogically or metaphorically between different cognitive domains and are thus so habituated that they are used more or less unreflectingly by speakers of the language in question. We thus re-approach the obligatory or automated end of the linguistic spectrum, as has been discussed in much of this and the previous chapter.

In fact, it may well be possible to argue for precisely such an analogical extension of the syntax of the preposition *do* in Irish. I am thinking of situa-tions where it is used in *backgrounding* the content of certain subordinate clauses, the purpose of which is to enhance narrative coherence by marginal-izing those segments of the text that are somehow secondary to the main flow of information. Such secondary segments are typically embedded in subordi-nate clauses.[102] The preposition *do* can mark the semantic subject of many adverbial clauses of time, making it a dative or prepositional subject, while the verb of the clause is the non-finite verbal noun governed by a variety of prepo-sitions. Once again, contrast the generally agentive equivalents in English (uppercase is the prepositional subject):

Beidh Pádraig anseo **ag imeacht DOMH**

Pádraig will be here when I go off (lit. 'going to me')

Ar chloisint na cainte DO DHIARMAID, cuireann sé a cheann . . .

When Diarmaid hears the talk, he puts his head . . . (lit. 'On hearing the talk to Diarmaid')

Sa lorgaireacht DI, is mála a thug sí léi

While she was searching, she took a bag (lit. 'In the searching to her')

Le linn casadh síos DI chun na farraige . . .

When she was turning down to the sea . . . (lit. 'On turning down to the sea to her . . .')

Th'éis DONA PUBANNA dúnadh, d'imigh muid abhaile

After the pubs closed, we went off home (lit. 'after to the pubs closing')

Bhí sé anseo **i ndéidh DOMHSA imeacht**

He was here after I went (lit. 'after to me leaving')

Druid an fhuinneog **roimh imeacht DUIT**[103]

Close the window before you go off (lit. 'before going to you')

Here are some further historical examples ranging from the seventeenth to the nineteenth centuries:

(*a*)   **Cenib do Ghoidelaibh DHÓ**

And though he was not of the Irish (lit. 'though not of the Irish *to him*')

(*b*)   **Mar sin DÓIBH** diaidh i ndiaidh

Thus they went on in succession (lit. 'Thus *to them* in succession')

(*c*)   No mas fíor, mar **is clos DOM**

Or if it is true, as I hear (lit. 'as is heard *to me*')

(*d*)   **Iar dteacht DO SPIRID NA SAOIRSE**[104]

After the spirit of freedom had come (lit. 'after coming *to the spirit of freedom*')

Here it is not the role of human agency as such but rather the role of the entire clause in the discourse structure that is demoted. It is interesting, however, that it is precisely the preposition *do* that marks the semantic subject in such clauses, even though the situation expressed is normally rendered in an agentive fashion in Irish as much as in English. Yet it is important to remember that this is precisely what we are talking about here: a discourse strategy, an aspect of rhetorical style that it used in the structuring and organizing of texts. It would be rash in the extreme to attempt to extrapolate an 'Irish world view' from such evidence, and I wish to stress, in this chapter as in the previous one, that this is expressly what I am *not* trying to do. What has been discussed in both chapters are examples of what Slobin calls 'thinking for speaking', whereby linguistic structure directs attention to certain aspects of human experience without, however, imposing constraints on the expression of other facets of that experience.[105]

6. AFTERWORD TO *DÚCHAS*: A VOCABULARY AND SYNTAX OF NATURAL LAW?

In chapters 2 and 3 we considered the evidence for *dúchas* the 'shifter' (or, in Daniel's phrase, 'fluid sign') in terms of its *indexicality*, the way in which it both presupposes certain contexts and creates others. In Nuinsean's phrase 's labhra dhiamhuir ár ndúthchas 'our dúchas is a mysterious saying' the poet attempts to engage metalinguistically with the content of the expression 'our *dúchas*'. This kind of act we have referred to in terms of the speaker's metapragmatic awareness.[1] In chapters 4 and 5 in particular we looked at possible ways in which features that reside on the lower end of the spectrum of awareness (grammar and syntax) interact with and tend to reinforce the aspects of linguistic usage of which speakers are more conscious (the lexicon). This process of the *habituation* of grammatical categories was noted by Boas, as we have seen, and extended by Whorf to encompass entire 'ways of speaking', or of thinking by analogy. In contrast to the relative automaticity of grammatical and syntactic usage, such as the habitual past or the syntax of non-agency, the use of words like *dual* or *dúchas* tends to be foregrounded in discourse as an object of conscious deliberation.[2] This chapter attempts to place these issues in a certain cultural and historical context.

Another exposition of the term *dúchas* that we considered in detail in chapter 3 and that, like Nuinsean's above, is high on the scale of awareness is that of Domhnall Ó Súilleabháin Béirre during the opening of his letter to Philip III. Let us return briefly to this text, sent from Kinsale in December 1601, two weeks before the Spanish surrender, appealing for further help against the English enemy. Here I concentrate on the articulation of what *dúchas* means as *gnáthúghadh* or 'practice'. On this occasion I give Ó Cuív's translation, leaving, however, the Irish word *dúchas* intact, for the reasons discussed in chapter 2:

> Atá riamh . . . ó aimsir go haimsir maille re **gnáthúghadh laoithamhail** go follas da hshíordhearbhadh eadrainne na hÉireannaigh nách fuil aonní amháin as neartmhuire oibrigheas inar ccroidhthibh do thuar ┐ do bhreith ar ngrádha ┐ ar n-inmhuine ina báidh nádúrtha an dúthchais ┐ cuimhniughadh an charadraidh **bhíos do g[h]náth ar ar n-aire** . . .[3]

> It has always been manifestly and continually asserted from one age to another, as well as in daily practice among us Irish, that there is no single thing which operates more powerfully in our hearts to merit and

obtain our love and affection than the natural fondness of *dúchas* and the recollection of the relationship of which we are constantly aware.

Here *dúchas*, and the 'natural love' thereof, is presented as the embodiment of history, which operates 'from age to age' (*ó aimsir go haimsir*) and which both formulates and regulates everyday practice and custom (*gnáthúghadh laoithamhail*). The nature of this regulation is made clear as the passage continues:

> . . . Ar mbheith dúinne, príomhGhaoighuil na hÉireann, cían ó hshoin ar ttarr[a]ng ar bphréimhe ⁊ ar mbunadhuis ó threibh ord[h]ruic fhíorúasal na nEasbáinneach .i. ó Mhíleadh mac Bile mhic B[h]reóghuin ⁊ ó Luighdeach mac Íotha mic B[h]reóghuin do réir fhiadhnuise ar sein-leabhur seanchuis, ar ngég ngeinealuigh, ar starthuidh ⁊ ar ccroiniceadh.

> Since we the chief Gaelic people of Ireland long ago took our root and foundation from the renowned and truly noble race of the Spaniards, that is from Míleadh, son of Bile son of Breóghan and from Luighdeach son of Íoth son of Breóghan according to the testimony of our ancient books of historical learning, our genealogical branches, our histories, our chronicles.

Here *dúchas* is expressly and literally 'rooted' (*ttarr[a]ng ar bphréimhe*) in the historical and genealogical lore that is *seanchas*: in the tradition and history of the Milesian Spanish connection, which is of course highly pertinent in this context. Echoing further the conclusions of Gumperz in a different connection, I would make the following points concerning this passage in particular.[4] Firstly, *dúchas* both indexes a relationship here (with Spain) and evokes the idea of activities specific to that relationship, in this case the whole synchronized, synthetic history of Ireland as elaborated from the seventh century onwards in the form of historical, legal and genealogical lore.[5] Secondly, the relation between *dúchas* and *gnáthughadh* is reflexive, in that a linguistic form has a communicative effect only to the extent that there is already a shared set of cultural dispositions in place, what the sociologist-anthropologist Pierre Bourdieu has called a 'habitus'.[6] This *habitus* is in turn partly a creation of linguistic practice. Cultural practices are thus both presupposed and reproduced, and the dispositions of the habitus are generative. Hanks draws attention to the fact that social actors interact in habitual ways, which in themselves stabilize practice and are thus formative of custom.[7] Crucially, as he points out, this applies equally to aspects of communication that speakers are relatively unaware of, as well as those that are high in linguistic consciousness. Thus a sense of *dúchas*, identity and origin, is both created and presupposed by *gnáthughadh*, daily practice or experience.

There is more to be said here on the nature of what is 'customary' if we note further the mechanics of verbal aspect in the above passage. Here both the verbal noun *gnáthughadh* 'practice', 'custom', 'usage', and the adverbial *do ghnáth* are used, the latter with the present habitual (relative) *bhíos* 'which is (usually)'. I give the passage here accompanied by Ó Cuív's translation:

> báidh nádúrtha an dúthchais ⁊ cuimhniughadh an charadraidh BHÍOS do g[h]náth ar ar n-aire . . .[8]

> the natural fondness of our patrimony and the recollection of the relationship *of which we are constantly aware.*

We can see a close correlation here between Bourdieu's *habitus* and the way in which we have had occasion to talk about the 'habituation' involved in linguistic structure, or in grammar.[9] Here, the idea of custom and practise (*gnáthughadh*) is reinforced by the related adverb *do ghnáth* 'constantly', or 'usually'. In a passage in a second letter sent by Ó Súilleabháin Béirre to the king of Spain he speaks in glowing terms of the loyalty of *ar ccara tairise* 'our trusty friend', Diarmaid Ó Drisceoil, whom he has sent as ambassador to Spain. This Diarmaid he commends:

> ar a' ndíothcheall DO-CHÍMUID **do ghnáth** aige sa chogadh c[h]atolica-sa

> because of the diligence we are accustomed to seeing him display in this Catholic war

There appears to be a certain vacillation in the case of the phrase *do ghnáth* between what is usually, habitually, ordinarily the case on the one hand and what is constantly the case on the other. Ó Dónaill's presentation of this item and various derivatives in his dictionary shows the historical development in a sense, in that meanings associated with habituality are predominant in the contemporary language while those associated with constancy survive more vestigially.[10] First of all, consider (i) modern *gnách*, which is historically the adjective built on the noun *gnáth* (*gnáth* + *ach*) and examples of which we had in chapter 4, then (ii) the noun *gnáth* itself, which is also used adjectively as (iii) a prefix:

(i)

> 1. *a.* Customary, usual; common, ordinary
>
> 2. (With copula) *is . . . (le)* it is customary (for)
>
> 3. *Go ~* ordinarily

(ii)

> 1. *m.* Custom, usage; customary thing
> (note *de ghnáth* 'as a rule')
>
> 2. Frequentation
>
> 3. Haunt, resort

> 4. *Lit. (pl)* intimates, associates
>
> 5. (Gs. as attrib. adj.) constant

(iii)

> 1. Usual, customary, ordinary; common, vulgar, standard
>
> 2. Constant, unremittent

For the earlier period, *DIL* glosses the phrase *do ghnáth* (or *co gnáth*) as both 'usually', 'habitually' and 'always', and other members of this semantic family seem to vacillate between the idea of habituality and continuousness[11]:

> gola **gnátha** constant weepings
>
> filliud glúine **gnáth** constant bending of the knees
>
> in béo é **do gnáth** sit vivus **semper**

The sense of *gnáth* as meaning 'continuous' is now marginal in Irish but in earlier sources it is very difficult to keep this meaning separate from the habitual one. Sometimes the interpretation may be a function of the verb form used, as in the following from Ó Súilleabháin Béirre's second letter, in which he explains to the king that he had proceeded to Castlehaven to render his submission to the Spanish fleet that had just landed there:

> do réir an rúin agus na toile do bhí **do ghnáth** ar am intinn[12]
>
> in accordance with the intention and desire which was ever in my mind

The use of the simple past here emphasizes continuousness, as we saw in chapter 4. In fact the use of *do ghnáth* with the simple past would now be very unusual in Irish, this adverb being regarded as a concomitant of the habitual aspect of the verb. Significantly, the lexical expression of habituality *gnáth* is often a concomitant of the grammatical form 'habitual', as in the following passage (and see chapter 4 for a discussion of this point):

> Mac Uilliam Búrc Seain . . . NÓ CHONCCNADH **do gnáth** lásan b-príonnsa do écc[13]
>
> Mac William Burke . . . who **always (usually)** assisted the sovereign, died

For the same kind of 'tension' between what is habitual and what is constant, consider the evidence of a poem already examined in chapters 4 and 5, Tadhg Dall's 'T'aire riot a Riocaird Óig'. In this case the distinction is between (*a*) *gnáth* and (*b*) *síor*, both of which, however, are contrasted with *iasachta*, which is both 'borrowed' and 'foreign':

(a)   Mar sin nár dhealoighthe dhoit

ret ainm ngnáth, red ghníomh
   n-ordhruic
an t-ainm iasachta uarais
níor thárraidh tú dá tharbha

nár sháraigh clú an chéadanma

Ever thus it were not for thee to
   part
from thy wonted title, thy well-
   known deeds
as for the foreign title thou hast got
never didst thou gain any
   advantage
that the fame of the former title
   did not outdo

(b)   Do dháilis, a chruth corcra,
ainm síor ar *ainm n-iasachta*[14]

Thou gavest, ruddy-faced form,
an abiding name for a temporary
   one

It should be noted here that both 'usually' and 'always' are compatible with the semantics of habituality in Irish. However, the use of *atá* in the passage from Ó Súilleabháin Béirre's first letter gives an effect analogous to the category of the perfect, as used in English and other languages, especially when coupled with the adverb *riamh* 'before', 'ever'—*Atá riamh* 'It **hath ever beene**' or 'It **has always been**'. Take the following modern example:

Táim ag éisteacht leis sin / á chloisteáil sin riamh[15]

I've been listening to / hearing that for ever

This usage is a concomitant of the use of the non-habitual forms to express unbroken continuity, as discussed above, to render what Comrie calls the 'perfect of persistent situation', describing an event that originates in the past but continues or persists into the present.[16]

In our discussion of both *dual* and *dúchas* we have been made aware of a certain 'tension' between what is 'natural' in the strict sense and what is more humanly contingent or 'customary' but yet conceived of as inevitable or preordained in the same way. In analogous fashion there is a certain ambiguity or ambivalence here in the case of *gnáth* between what is 'customary' and what is 'constant'.

The noun *gnáthughadh* is none other than a derivation of *gnáth*, the semantics of which were discussed in chapter 4, with some additional remarks in chapter 5. The Royal Irish Academy dictionary (*DIL*) glosses *gnáthughadh* as 'using', 'practising', 'frequenting'; 'use', 'custom'. The form is continued as Modern Irish *gnáthamh* and occurs in the following proverb:

Gnáthamh na hoibre an t-eólas[17]

Knowledge comes through practice (Practice makes perfect)

In fact Ó Cuív translates the phrase *gnáthúghadh laoithamhail* as 'daily practice'. In the sixteenth and seventeenth centuries the word often appears collocated with the genitive plural *Gaoidheal* 'the custom(s) of the Irish':

(a) Remann a Burc . . . do beith ina dhuine uasal, oirdeirc, iomráiteach **do reir gnathaighte Gaoídhel** an tan so.

Redmond Burke . . . was at this time a noble and renowned gentleman, according to the custom of the Irish.

(b) Do chraebhscailedh Cloinne Dalaigh o Domhnall Mor mac Eccnechain anuas. Ri Ceneil Conuill an Domhnall sin. As e do chum **gnathaighthi** ⁊ sochra Conullach ⁊ as e do islicch a ndochra ⁊ a n-anghnathaighthi.[18]

Of the genealogy of Clann Dálaigh from Domhnall Mór mac Eigneacháin down. That Domhnall was king of the race of Conall. It was he who established the customs and rights of the Conallaigh and it was he who lessened their disabilities and their malpractices.

Annála Ríoghachta Éireann records the death of Owny O'More as the result of a battle with English soldiers in August 1600 and gives his eulogy in the following terms—a man who had seized the governance of his own territory from foreigners and restored it to 'the Irish usage':

Duine ei-sidhe baí ina aén oidhre o chert ar a duthaigh, & do-bhen urlamhas a atharda . . . a dornaibh Danar, & deóradh . . . go t-tard-somh í fó a smacht, & fo a chumachtoibh budein . . . **do reir gnathaithghe Gaoidheal**.[19]

He was the only rightful heir to his territory and had seized control of his patrimony . . . from the hands of foreigners and adventurers . . . until he brought it under his own dominion . . . according to the Irish custom.

In this last passage particularly we are reminded again of the contrast between the natural right of possession of O'More, who was the *oidhre o chert ar a duthaigh* ('heir by right to his native land'), and the imposition of foreigners into whose possession the land had previously passed (*a dornaibh Danar, & deóradh* 'from the hands of foreigners and adventurers'). This recalls the contrast we have seen expressed between *dúchas* and *deóraidheacht* 'exile' in several sources. Both this opposition and its reconciliation are to be found in a line by Ó Bruadair that contains the phrase *deoradh dúthchais* 'an exile (*deoradh*) who comes home (his *dúchas*)':

a riar mar **dheoradh dúthchais**[20]

to treat him as an exile who comes home

Another term to consider here is the form *gnás* (*gnáth-as*), 'usage', 'custom', 'practice', and in particular its use in the compound *domnas* or *domgnas*, which occurs a number of times in *Annála Ríoghachta Éireann*. The second element is *gnás* as defined above, while the first is Old Irish *dom* (*domh*) 'house', 'home'. As a compound it therefore means 'place of habitation', 'habitat', with the wider sense of 'patrimony', 'native territory', and this connection is made clear by the lexicographers:

domhghnas .i. athardha no dúthaidh[21]

'patrimony, inheritance'

Usually either *dúthaigh* or *dúchas* follows *domhgnas* as an attributive genitive meaning 'native'. The following passage from *Annála Ríoghachta Éireann* resumes the account of the fate of the principality of Owny O'More after his own demise: Laois was taken by the English, who repaired their limestone houses and proceeded:

> acc suidhe h-i senáitibh Slechta Conuill Chernaigh **diar bó domhgnas duthaighe** Laoighis[22]

> to settle in the old places of the race of Conall Cearnach, to whom Laois was the hereditary homeland

This excerpt also replicates the non-agentive syntax discussed at length in chapter 5:

IS	DOMHGNAS DUTHAIGHE	DO

where the form *diarbó* again represents a coalescence of the verb *is* and the preposition *do* 'to whom was . . .' The following example refers to the hanging of Donough, the son of Murrough O'Brien, in 1582 in Limerick by Captain Mortant and by the Sheriff, Sir George Cusack. In 1581 O'Brien had formed a league with the sons of the Earl of Clanrickard, but, having repented, he returned under protection, which was, however, subsequently revoked, leading to his eventual demise:

> Ruccadh a chorp có **a domhgnas duthchasa** go ro h-adhnaicedh é i n-Inis.[23]

> His body was brought to his native land and buried in Ennis.

This word *domhgnas* can also appear conjoined with *dúthaigh* in *Annála Ríoghachta Éireann*, as in the following passage, where it is explained what befell the native land of Ulster in the aftermath of the Flight of the Earls in 1607:

> Bá de eiccin, & do imtheacht na n-Iarladh att-rubhramar, tainicc **a n-domhnus & a n-dúthaigh** . . . do bhein do Gaoidhelaibh Chóiccidh Uladh.[24]

> It was indeed from it, and from the Flight of the Earls we have referred to, it came to pass that their principalities and their native lands . . . were taken from the Irish of the province of Ulster.

In the form *domhghnas* we find a direct indexing of the relationship between place and habit, or that which is known, intimate and familiar. (For the etymology of *gnáth* and its derivatives see chapter 4.) The native place is thus the customary place, the 'habitat' in fact.

This compound raises in a particularly iconic and indexical fashion the putative relationship between the questions of 'right', natural or hereditary, and 'custom'. Clare Carroll has investigated early modern Irish critiques of English rule in Ireland, in particular those of Pilib Ó Súilleabháin Béirre writing in Latin on the Continent on the one hand and those of Mícheál Ó Cléirigh and Seathrún Céitinn writing in Irish in Ireland, but with an eye to the wider European context on the other.[25] In particular she looks at the influence of Spanish natural law theory on such writing, especially the concepts of *dominium* 'the natural right to property', *consuetudo* 'custom', and *indiginae* 'native or natural inhabitants'. As we saw in chapter 5, one Irish equivalent adduced by Carroll is the word *toich* 'inherently right' or 'natural hereditary right', 'propriety', which, as she says, 'comes very close to the natural law concept of *dominium*'.[26] Carroll furthermore points to the importance of the idea of *seanchas*, the 'traditional lore of Irish culture' in F. J. Byrne's definition, encompassing topographical, legal and genealogical material, wherein Pilib Ó Súilleabháin Béirre's 'defense of the Irish nation', as Carroll puts it, finds its source.[27] We may note here that Domhnall Ó Súilleabháin Béirre in his first letter to Philip III refers as his authority on the Milesian connection to 'the evidence of our old books of *seanchas*, our genealogies, our histories and chronicles' (*do réir fhiadhnuise ar seinleabhur seanchuis, ar ngég ngeinealuigh, ar starhuidh ⁊ ar ccroiniceadh*).[28] Custom or *consuetudo* establishes the justice of the law, the *ius gentium* or 'law of nations', which is both human in origin, as a form of civil law, and divinely ordained. It is the latter quality that gives it its universal application. Carroll shows that two of Ó Súilleabháin Béirre's contemporaries writing in Irish, Seathrún Céitinn and Mícheál Ó Cléirigh, 'whether they were readers of natural law theory or not'[29] express a number of similar concepts in their expositions of Irish political practice in the sixteenth and seventeenth centuries. I will concentrate here on two such concepts: the idea of *dominium* as the natural right to property (*bona*) and the role of *consuetudo* or custom in establishing the justice of the law. For Suárez, *consuetudo*, the nation's laws of custom and habit, was constitutive of the laws of nations (*ius gentium*) and had the power to set other types of law aside.[30] Again, for Irish, more than one term can be adduced as an equivalent. Carroll mentions Céitinn's use of *seanchas* 'tradition', 'history', 'genealogy', 'traditional law', in his *Foras Feasa ar Éirinn*,[31] and we will consider other aspects of his concern with customary or traditional practice below. Based on our discussion thus far we can safely say that *dúchas* expresses at least one of the bases for an Irish equivalent of *dominium*, specifically 'birthright'. We have already seen some very direct linguistic evidence of the connection between natural right on the one hand and inheritance, native place, on the other.

A further concept that Ó Súilleabháin Béirre associates with *dominium* is also worth mentioning briefly: those who exercise *dominium* are the natives or natural inhabitants. As Carroll puts it, 'O'Sullivan Beare relies on such concepts from the natural law tradition as *dominium* (the natural right of

ownership or property) and *indiginae* (indigenous natives or natural inhabitants).'[32] From our foregoing discussion we would advance the Irish concepts of *dúchas, dual, dligheadh* and *díleas/ruidhleas* as reflecting the native
ideology or mentality on *dominium* on the question of property and propriety of ownership; one notable example to recall here is Céitinn's treatment
of Fitzstephen's position as a foreigner in Ireland, discussed previously in
chapter 3. However, Irish also reflects the relationship between *dominium*
and *indigenae* very directly: if *dúchas* is, at least in part, *dominium* then the
indigenae are *dúchasaigh,* as in the following example from a poem by Ó Bruadair in reference to the exploits of Brian Bóromha:

> Tug éirle eachtrann airgthe is ionnradh a gcroidh
>
> . . . is tug réidh sealbh gach lesa dá **dhúthchaisioch**[33]

> He raided the lands of foreign earls and pillaged all their property
>
> . . . and gave each rightful owner back his mansion to possess in peace

As the editor of the poem points out,[34] Ó Bruadair is drawing here on Céitinn's
account in *Foras Feasa ar Éirinn*, which expresses the same ideas in terms of
that which is *dual* or 'natural':

> agus gach fearann dár bhean Brian amach do Lochlonnaibh lé neart a
> láimhe, ní d'aon dá chine féin tug é, acht tug gach críoch da gach cine
> **dar dhual** í i nÉirinn.[35]

> and every territory that Brian extracted from the Vikings by force of
> arms, he did not bestow it on one of his own race but he gave every
> land to every race whose natural right it was.

Dúchasaigh can also mean (*a*) one's followers, loyal subjects or blood relations
or more generally (*b*) 'inhabitants'[36]:

(a)   Ro cuireadh lais a **duthchasaigh** féin.

   His loyal followers were buried with him

(b)   duine ecin de **duthcasachaibh** an baile sin.

   one of the natives of that place

Noteworthy here, although from a later date, is the evidence of an English-
Irish vocabulary published in the United Irish anthology *Bolg an tSoláir* in
1795:

native country	*duthchus*
inhabitants	*duthchosach* [sic][37]

Historians have referred at various points to social aspects of the use of the word
dúchas and its derivatives in the medieval period. Ó Corráin refers to the transition from a tribal to a more feudal society in terms of the transition in the status of the ruler from king of a tribe or *túath* (*rí tuaithe*) to lord of a patrimony,

which is rendered by either *tigherna* or *toísech*, sometimes accompanied by the genitive *dúthchais* or *dúthchasa*.[38] Mac Niocaill refers to the function of the *óglach dúthchasa*, a kind of hereditary functionary, often a soldier, while Simms talks about the *dúthchasaigh* as 'hereditary proprietors' or 'native inhabitants'.[39]

We now revisit some of the relevant points made with respect to the role of natural and customary right in Irish ideology in chapters 2 to 5. As an example we saw Céitinn's treatment of the concept of *dúchas* in a wider, over-arching sense of *ceart* 'right', 'entitlement' (chapter 3), *dual* 'natural', 'inevitable', and *dualgas,* used of a 'right sanctioned by custom' (chapter 4). In the case of *ceart* we can add the following example, in which *dúchas* is presented as a specific type of *ceart* or 'right'. This example was already quoted in chapter 2:

Ó dearor gur dhealbhuis chraoibh	Since it is said that you have formed the branches
ríshliocht Gaoidhiol do gach taoibh	of descent of the Gaelic kings from every side
's go n-abra acht amháin Dál gCais	and you say that everyone, save the Dál gCais,
gur chaillsiod **ceart an dúthchois**.[40]	has lost the right of *dúchas* (birthright).

In addition, *dúchas* appears as subordinated to a sense of what was *dual* in Céitinn's treatment of Diarmaid Mac Murchadha's position in the passage discussed in chapters 2 and 3: his hereditary claim (*dúchas*) was to Leinster, but that birthright was in its turn subject to what was *dual* or sanctioned by custom as appearing to be predestined or pre-ordained, his submission to the high king of Ireland. In other instances *dúchas* appeared as the instrument of *dual*, where, for example, we were told of Colm Cille's right to the high-king-ship of Ireland being *dual* decause of his birthright and blood line (*o duthcas ⁊ o folaidheacht*). Similarly, *dúchas* is an instrument of what is *díleas* or *ruidhleas* in that sense of indefeasible or inalienable right, where a possession is *ruidhleas* to someone, or inalienable from them, on account of their hereditary right (but see chapter 5 for some qualifications). In chapter 5 we also noted the importance and pervasiveness of patientive or non-agentive syntax in reinforcing these concepts, which are thus conceptualized as existing in a general sense outside the sphere of ordinary human activity and yet being instrumental in shaping that activity.

Anthony Pagden discusses the relationship between *consuetudo* and *dominium* in seventeenth-century natural law theory.[41] In the legitimating of *dominium* from a *de facto* right to property to a *de jure* one of jurisdiction, the idea of custom (*consuetudo*) is the prescription (*praescriptio longi temporis*) that confers rights that can then be retrospective: the continuing successful existence of a claim constitutes its own legitimacy. I have contended in chapter 3 that this is precisely what Tadhg Dall Ó hUiginn was arguing in his poem for

Mac William Burke. This argument was clinched by ceding the Burkes the *dúthaigh*, which in this context stood for the symbolic centre of the Irish cultural world: Tara and the Boyne. When the various abstract and concrete ranges of meaning of *dúchas* on the one hand and *dual/dualgas* on the other are considered, we may say that the more abstract domain is representative of *consuetudo* (Irish *gnáthughadh*), while the more concrete domain conveys the realization of *dominium* (Irish *domhgnas*). In this connection it is interesting to look once again at the two uses of *dúchas* in Ó Súilleabháin Béirre's first letter to Philip III. In the first instance the phrase that describes English designs on Ireland is that they are 'coveting our patrimony' (*ag sanntughadh ár ndúthchuis*), with its connotations of greed and avarice on the part of the conqueror. Here we took *dúchas* as standing for a more material realization of its own pragmatic essence, as discussed in chapter 3, and this interpretation is supported by the contemporary English and Spanish translations. As we saw in virtually all our examples, supported by the evidence of linguistic structure, *dúchas* rarely appears devoid of all reference to its symbolic side, and reading 'hereditary right' certainly would do no violence to the text here. In any event *dúchas* seems to have much in common with the natural law idea of *dominium* in this case: the Irish are to be deprived of their natural hereditary right, of their patrimony, in effect. I rehearse this passage here in order to draw attention in this instance to the word *aindlightheach* 'unlawful', given the frequency with which *dligheadh* is associated with *dú* and *dúchas* (see chapters 4 and 5):

> a n-aghuidh ar n-eascarad atá ag múchadh an chreideimh Chatoilica go diabhluidhe, ag básughadh ar n-uaisle go díbhfheargach, ⁊ ag sanntughadh ar ndúthchais **go haindlightheach**.[42]

> against our Enemies that seek to overwhelme and extinguish the Catholike faith diabolically, put to death our Chieftaines tyrannously, coveting our Lands and Livings **unlawfully**.

Our second instance of *dúchas* in this letter proved somewhat more elusive in its pragmatics, and this was reflected in its erratic treatment at the hands of the translators. This we have reconsidered above with regard to its relationship to custom or *consuetudo* or, in Irish, *gnáthughadh*. The phrase *báidh nádúrtha an dúthchais* is also noteworthy for its inclusion of the word *nádúrtha* 'natural', and a few lines later, as Ó Súilleabháin Béirre elaborates on the Milesian connection, he describes the Irish and Spanish in the following terms, as 'natural branches' on the one genealogical tree:

> ní fhédmuid (mar ghéguibh **nádúrdha** don chran[n] ord[h]ruic óar fhásamar) gan roghrádh a[r] ccroidhe . . . do dhortadh go hiomshlán ar ar seanghaoltaibh tairise ⁊ ar an ccinél bhfíoruasal óa ttángamar.[43]

> we cannot (as natural branches of the renowned tree from which we have grown) but pour out fully all our heart's love . . . on our beloved kinsmen and on the truly noble people from whom we have come.

In contradistinction, his second letter to the Spanish king describes the Spanish capitulation to English ambitions and activities in Ireland in the aftermath of the battle of Kinsale in terms of its *mínádúrthacht* 'unnaturalness'. This betrayal of the bond between Ireland and Spain, Ó Súilleabháin Béirre fears, will only make the Irish more reticent to trust their natural allies:

> ní as baoghal liom, ara m[h]éid do ghráineamhlacht, do neamhaondacht agus do **m[h]í-nádúrthacht** . . . do-b[h]éra cúis do d[h]aoinibh eile gan ionntaoíbh a gcoda iná a bpearsann do thabhairt re Sbáineach dá éis.[44]

> an event which, because it is so odious, so 'disuniting', and so unnatural, will, I fear . . . give to others henceforth reason for not entrusting their property or their persons to a Spaniard.

This course of action is thus a direct affront to the naturalness of the Irish genealogical affinity with Spain expressed in Ó Súilleabháin Béirre's first letter.

Conclusion

One important fact about the occurrence of the term *dúchas* in medieval and early modern Ireland has already been briefly referred to in chapter 2: it appears to be a term that has primarily social and cultural resonance rather than being associated with the law in any codified form. Thus *dúchas* tends to occur in later medieval glosses to the main texts of the laws, which are generally of Old Irish origin, many of them being from the seventh and eighth centuries.[45] In this respect *dúchas* is significantly unlike many of the terms with which it is associated—*dligheadh, ceart, díre* and *díleas* for example—which are important *legal* terms in their own right. On the other hand the basic etymon *dú* does occur in the sense of entitlement in a passage in the eighth-century *Bretha Nemed Toísech*, where it appears to be synonymous with *coir* 'right':

> cingid coir airech déso deich séotu;   the due of the *aire déso* extends to
> ten *séts*
> . . . dligthius **dú** do airig ard fichit   . . . the *aire ard* is entitled to,
> sét sernar[46]   as his due, twenty *séts* which
> are ordained

This aspect of *dúchas*, and indeed *dual*, is of especial interest when one considers it in relation to Bourdieu's idea of *habitus*, alluded to above. The *habitus* is the mechanism that integrates social structure and everyday practice through the inculcation of shared norms and dispositions by which individuals in turn orientate themselves in their society. Social practice is therefore lent a certain consistency which is not necessarily the result of conscious intention on the part of individuals in society.[47] The dispositions of the *habitus* are thus pre-conscious or pre-reflective rather than arising from obedience to laws. Individuals in a given society or culture tend to share this inculcated system, and this is what leads to social cohesion. The non-appearance of *dúchas* and *dual* as specifically legal terms finds further resonance in this idea of the *habitus*, and we have already considered Ó Súilleabháin Béirre's testimony on the role of *dúchas* as the moving force of daily practice or *gnáthughadh*. For Bourdieu, human actors are not entirely created by either external (social, economic and political) factors or internal (mentalist) factors but rather arise through a history of structural couplings, whereby the actors interact both with one another and with their environment.[48] The most salient type of structural coupling is linguistic communication, and it is the accumulated history of such couplings that establishes conventional meanings and gives them their public character. This means that present meanings are inextricably linked to past ones: culture thus becomes a historically contingent network of signs. I follow Gumperz here in regarding 'culture' as referring to 'locally specific, taken-for-granted, knowledge of background information and verbal forms acquired through communicative collaboration'.[49] As Bourdieu himself puts it, the *habitus* is the 'product of history' which 'produces individual and collective practices'; it is 'embodied history, internalized as nature and so forgotten as history'.[50] This may in fact turn out to be as good a summing up of the history of the word *dúchas* itself as we will find. The interpretation of an indexical sign such as *dúchas* is intimately connected to culture-specific practices and dispositions, was argued particularly in chapter 3, and as we have seen further in the present chapter.

To paraphrase Bourdieu, we might say that *dúchas* is embodied, internalized history, both individual and collective, which is therefore forgotten as history, until activated by the appropriate context. So *dúchas* here forms a *habitus* in which it embodies and enacts history (*ó aimsir go haimsir*), is thereby naturalized and recursively activated through genealogy, chronicles and traditional lore (*seanchas*). Where *dúchas* occurs in a particular context, speakers apply their understanding of its pragmatics, an understanding that presupposes older contexts of use and potentially entails the creation of new contexts.

7. THE IRISH IDEA OF 'FREEDOM'

In chapter 1, I anticipated the nature of the following discussion: that important syntactic differences between English *freedom* and its Irish equivalent *saoirse* reflect the greater significance that attaches to individual freedom in the English case and to national freedom in the Irish one, a difference that is culturally and historically contingent. In fact it would be more accurate to describe Irish *saoirse* as *one* of the equivalents of English *freedom*, and this chapter will have more to say on that point as well.

Berlin's 'two concepts of liberty'

In an effort to correlate linguistic, specifically syntactic, considerations with a more general intellectual framework, I discuss briefly two conceptions of 'freedom', classically elaborated on by Isaiah Berlin in his essay 'Two concepts of liberty'. Reduced to syntactic terms the two concepts are as follows:

(1) 'Freedom *from*': the idea of 'negative freedom', which concerns the area of action that is open to the individual without interference from others. This idea is crucial to the classic English liberal idea of 'freedom': there is a certain minimal area of personal freedom that must be left inviolate.[1]

(2) 'Freedom *to*': the idea of 'positive freedom', which consists of the idea that I as a rational being am my own master; the crucial question here is 'who governs?' Berlin concentrates on the metaphor that is inherent in this position of 'self-mastery' when it is generalized to cover society as a whole. A classic statement of this position is Rousseau's 'The Social Contract' (1762), with its doctrine of the subservience of the individual to the 'general will' of society. Civil freedom may well entail the individual being 'forced to be free', in Rousseau's famous paradox.[2]

For Berlin this type of paradox makes 'negative freedom' the 'truer and more humane ideal'. If freedom is therefore to be defined as 'non-interference', then (for Berlin at least) it does not follow that 'freedom' has any necessary connection to social or political independence, as the question is not one of who exercises control but rather of how much control they exercise. Thus negative freedom is in principle compatible with autocracy. Quentin Skinner, however, criticizes Berlin's espousal of the ideal of negative freedom by questioning—much as the English republicans of the seventeenth century had done—the premise that negative freedom is jeopardized only by interference or coercion.[3] Skinner rehearses the idea that the mere fact of dependence on another's will and whimsy makes one unfree: the mere *possibility* of coercion or interference is an infringement of freedom. Historically, in the eighteenth and nineteenth centuries in Anglophone culture the classical liberal view wins out: the crucial question is no longer 'who governs?' but 'how do they govern'?

It is in relation to Berlin's positive evaluation of 'negative freedom' and his negative evaluation of 'positive freedom' that his unenthusiastic, indeed patronizing, discussion of the idea of collective social and ultimately national freedom must be considered. This he sees as, in a sense, not 'freedom' at all but rather the need for identification with a peer group, whether social or racial, and the desire for recognition within that wider network—what he calls 'the search for status and understanding'. Berlin's condescension here seems to have to do with his general critique of 'positive freedom': that it often appears to result in worse tyranny or dictatorship. The following passage is fairly representative of Berlin's attitude here:

> It is this desire for reciprocal recognition that leads . . . a member of some newly liberated Asian or African state to complain less today, when he is rudely treated by members of his own race or nation, than when he was governed by some cautious, just, gentle, well-meaning administrator from outside.[4]

In a similar vein, note Roberts:

> It is hard to see why unjust or bad government by people of your own nation should be thought to be morally better than just and good government by outsiders.[5]

As Skinner points out, Berlin is essentially an apologist for the idea of negative freedom and there is more than a hint of Mill's paternalism towards 'uncivilized' peoples here. We shall have reason below to consider the relation between ideas of individual and collective or national freedom in accordance with the linguistic evidence from various languages. I believe that Berlin's characterization of national freedom is totally inadequate and indeed something of a travesty when viewed against the linguistic evidence of Irish and Polish in particular.

Before proceeding, however, it is important to observe that in syntactic terms there is a third possibility:

(3)   'Freedom *of*': this indicates a particular domain within which freedom applies, for example 'freedom of speech'.

This is less ambiguously marked as either 'positive' or 'negative', although it could perhaps be argued that it belongs primarily to the latter: that is, the essential element of 'freedom of speech' is that no one can stop me from saying what I want to say. The linguistic evidence for these three syntagma ('freedom from/to/of') is considered below, especially in the light of Irish, English and Polish.

The idea of 'free' and 'freedom' in older Indo-European languages

Before going on to a historical survey of the range of *saoirse* in Irish it might be helpful to look at the attempt of Benveniste to explicate the rise of the very idea of 'free' and 'freedom' in early Indo-European societies.[6] Item (i) is the root *(H)leudh*, the basic meaning of which is 'growing or increasing together', which in (a) Greek and Latin is socialized to mean 'free' as opposed to being a slave or a foreigner, while in (b) Germanic and Slavic the meaning is the collective one '(the) people':

(i)   *(H)leudh-* 'grow,' 'increase.'

   (a) Greek: *eleutheros* (v. *doulos*)   Latin *liber* (v. *servus*)
   (b) German *Leute*   Russian *l'udi*

On the other hand, (ii) is the root *prí-* meaning 'to love', but again the idea is the socialization of the terminology of affection and closeness: those you feel close to as your 'family' you identify with as (a) 'free,' again as opposed to outsiders, or (b) as 'friend':

(ii)   *prí-* 'to love'   —*priyos* 'beloved'

   (a)   *priyā* 'wife'

   English *free* (OE. *frēo*)   Welsh *rhydd* 'free'

   (b) English *friend*   Russian *prijatel'* 'friend'

   Sanskrit *priya*

Item (i) is of course the basis of English *liberty*, while (ii) gives us *freedom*.

   Interestingly in view of the Welsh *rhydd* above, Irish shows no trace of this root; instead we have an innovation that is apparently paralleled only in Indo-Iranian, on the other extreme of the Indo-European world, as represented below by Vedic Sanskrit (b). This seems to consist of the prefix *so-* 'good' plus the word for 'man' (Old Irish *fer*, cf. Latin *vir*), from which an abstract noun is also formed:

(a)   *so-wir-os*   >   OI. *sóer* 'free'

      so-wir-(i)yá   >   OI. *soíre* 'freedom'

(b)   Sanskrit: *su-vír-ah* 'heroic' *su-vír-yam* 'heroic power'

In view of the meaning of the Sanskrit items we could hazard that 'free' in Irish is the socialization of a warrior bond, but that would be speculation. There is, however, some indication in Old Irish sources that the adjective *sóer* originally had a racial basis, as in the following examples:

> tri cenela **saera** randsat in indsi so
> Three free/noble races who have divided this island

> itir na **saer**chlannaib .i. Ulaidh ⁊ Feni Temrach ⁊ Erna Dedaid; no Ulaidh ⁊ Gaileoin ⁊ Erna[7]

> between the free/noble races, that is, the *Ulaidh* and the *Feni Temrach* and the *Erna Dedaid;* or the *Ulaidh* and the *Gaileoin* and the *Erna*

Following this summary treatment of early ideas of 'freedom' in Indo-European, we turn now to the treatment of the word *saoirse* in the lexicography of Modern Irish.

Saoirse in the lexicon of Modern Irish

We start once again, with an overview of examples presented in the two important Irish-English dictionaries of the twentieth century, those of Dinneen and Ó Dónaill.[8] Ó Dónaill gives the following meanings for *saoirse*, and again I have highlighted those ranges that I feel are historically of greatest importance:

1. *Lit.* Status of freeman, nobility

2.	**Liberty, independence**	
	saoirse na tíre	the freedom of the country
	~ cainte	freedom of speech
	~ coinsiasa	freedom of conscience
	~ an duine	human freedom, personal liberty
3.	**Immunity, exemption**	
	saoirse ó chánacha	exemption from taxes
	~ ar dhualgas	freedom from an obligation
	~ fónaimh	exemption from service
4.	*Lit.* **Privilege**	
	cinseal agus saoirse	power and privilege

5. Honorary privilege

6. Cheapness, inexpensiveness

As can be seen from the presentation, both 1 and 4 are acknowledged by Ó Dónaill to be 'literary' uses, while 5 is also an older, more specialized sense that has been carried over to the modern period. Item 6 is now obsolete, although the adjective *saor* continues to have this sense today. The core area therefore consists of 2 to 4 above, and more especially 2 and 3: 'freedom of' and 'freedom from' respectively. We will look briefly first at the syntax, as this is crucial to the argument that differences in the syntactic configuration of words like *saoirse* and *freedom* between languages can index conceptual differences between the cultures that those languages represent. In 2 in each case we have *saoirse* followed by a noun in the genitive case (i.e. the relation *saoirse of X*) that signifies the particular domain to which *saoirse* applies: country; speech; conscience; the individual or humanity in general. On the other hand in 3, in two of the three cases *saoirse* is followed by a preposition, either *ar* or *ó*, which in this instance mean the same thing: 'from'. In the third case in 3, the genitive has the same function as *saoirse* followed by the preposition: '*saoirse* with respect to service'. As stated above, this is a concept of 'freedom' referred to by Isaiah Berlin and others as 'negative freedom', and it is central historically to the concept of *saoirse* in Irish. However, I shall be making the argument that it is 2 that better represents the core idea of *saoirse* in Modern Irish and that 3 has become less salient over time. It is important to note that the syntactic and semantic history of *saoirse* is largely one of contraction of usage, both semantically in meaning and syntactically in structure, but this will become clear as we go through the linguistic evidence, especially in a more comparative framework.

For comparative purposes and further examples we can now consider Dinneen, who glosses *saoirse* as 'freedom', 'liberty', 'independence', 'franchise', 'immunity', 'freedom from restriction', 'rights'; 'free lands', 'freehold'; 'deliverance', 'release', 'exculpation'; 'cheapness'. This is indeed a fair aggregate of the historical range of *saoirse*. I give here his illustrative examples, which almost exclusively render the older senses of the word rather than those more current in the twentieth century:

(a) gan talamh gan **saoirse**   without land or privilege

  beidh **saoirse** aca ar thalamh   they will become owners of
                                              land

  beidh cinnseal agus **saoirse** ag éigsibh poets will have power and
                                              privilege

  saoirse a sinnsir   their ancestral rights

(b) **saoirse** choitcheann   general immunity

(c) **saoirse** do bheith ag a bpearsanaibh agus ag a spréidh
  their persons and cattle to enjoy immunity

(d) sirimid **saoirse** ó Chríost dá anam ar phéin
  we pray Christ to deliver his soul from suffering

(e) is do na bochtaibh ceapadh na flaithis mar **shaoirse**
  heaven was designed to be the poor man's inheritance

We see here that (a) designates rights and privileges to land, among other things: to be without land is to be without *saoirse*. The idea of traditional right also features in (b), which refers to the power and privilege of the poet class. Again (c) makes reference to tradition or ancestry as a basis for the enjoyment of *saoirse*. Senses (*d*) and (*e*), on the other hand, seem to be more of 'relief' or 'release' *from* something, and this 'negative' sense will be important below.

An important point to note is that, at all periods of Irish, *saor* 'free' and *saoirse* 'freedom' have their direct antitheses in *daor* 'unfree', 'captive', and *daoirse* 'slavery', 'captivity', and that these formal oppositions are in turn part of a wider family of moral values in which the *s*- word is the positive term and the *d*- word is a negative member of the opposition:

'good'			'bad'		
	sochar	*profit*		dochar	*loss*
	sonas	*happiness*		donas	*evil*
	suáilce	*virtue*		duáilce	*vice*
	sólás	*consolation*		dólás	*desolation*
	suairceas	*cheerfulness*		duairceas	*moroseness*

The examination of this semantic structure will be further developed elsewhere, but now we need to look at the semantic range of the abstract noun *saoirse* (and its early form *sóire* or *saíre*) over time. This is a necessary preliminary to taking a closer look at the syntax of *saoirse* and in so doing expanding the remit of the discussion to include other languages in an effort to suggest (as does Wierzbicka) how linguistic evidence could eventually provide us with a typology of 'freedom'.

Before proceeding to that task, however, let us consider the comments of Ó Ruairc on the similarities, but particularly on the differences, between the Irish and English instantiations of the concepts 'free' and 'freedom'.[9] In fact his brief discussion concerns exclusively the differing ranges of the adjective 'free' rather than the abstract noun. However, I give a couple of his examples to show how English *free* has in many cases nothing to do with Irish *saor*:

(*a*)	he is free with his promises	tá sé **maith** faoina ghealltanas (lit. 'good regarding his promise')
(*b*)	to make free with someone	bheith **dána** le duine ('to be bold with someone')

So what is given a unitary semantic realization in English as *free* involves two entirely different semantic domains in Irish. On the relation between the two abstractions 'freedom' in Irish and English, Ó Ruairc has the following to say (author's translation):

> Maidir le *saoirse* mar cháilíocht pholaitiúil, aigne, cainte nó eile, nó mar riocht eacnamaíoch, is ionann é sa dá theanga bíodh is nach ionann an chiall theibí a thug an Gaeilgeoir don nóisean *saoirse* agus a thug an Béarlóir, agus ní áirím an Sasanach.[10]

> With respect to *saoirse* as a political quality, as a quality of the mind, of speech and so on, or as an economic state, it is the same in both languages [i.e. as *freedom* in English] even though the abstract sense that the Irish-speaker associates with *saoirse* is not that which the English-speaker associates with *freedom,* never mind the Englishman.

Although the latter part of this observation is somewhat enigmatically phrased, it is precisely this line of thought that I will pursue in an effort to refine Ó Ruairc's formulation. To do so we must first take a look at the development of the word *saoirse* in Irish itself from the early period.

'Saoirse' before the late eighteenth century

Before turning to a consideration of the semantic range of *saoirse* in the earlier period, a word about some of the forms and usages that will be marginal to the present discussion. The earliest form of the abstract noun is either *soíre* or *saíre*. During the late Middle and early Modern Irish periods (eleventh to twelfth centuries) a new form, *saírse* or *soírse*, emerged, with the meaning 'freedom', 'exemption', 'immunity'. However, the older form was retained as the Modern Irish *saoire* in the sense of 'holy day' or 'holiday':

Old and Middle Irish	>	Modern Irish
saíre/soíre/saírse		(i) *saoirse*
		(ii) *saoire*

Thus in Modern Irish we have a formal and functional split between *saoire* and *saoirse*. However, it should be borne in mind in what follows that in many earlier examples the forms *saíre* and *soíre* stand for what later becomes *saoirse*. The modern *saoire* 'holiday' derives from the idea of an exemption or privileged status that applies to particular periods (as opposed to *saoirse* as a general concept):

Soíre Domnuig[11]   The sanctity of Sunday

Another of the earlier senses of both *soíre* and *saírse* is that of 'nobility of character':

(a)   i **sóiri** ceneóil

in nobility of race

(b)   Do dhearsgnaidh sidhsin ar mnáibh na cruinne . . . ar dheilbh, ar **shaoire**, ar shoibhéasaibh.

She surpassed the women of the whole world . . . in form, in nobility, in good manners.

(c)   Robadh lán Éire agus Alba d'iomráidhtibh na deise sin—Cearbhall dano ar **shaoire** ⁊ ar shoibhéasaibh.[12]

Ireland and Scotland were full of the fame of those two—Cearbhall moreover for nobility and good manners.

Noteworthy here is the association in both (b) and (c) of *saoire* with good manners. This semantic range is also found in 'freedom'-related words in Greek, Latin and medieval English and is discussed by C. S. Lewis as a process of the *moralization* of status words, whereby words denotative of rank, on the basis of social, economic or hereditary factors, have a tendency to become internalized in the individual as descriptive of traits of character.[13] Terms of superior status become positive character terms, while those of inferior status have a negative value. For our purposes a more centrally important sense of *saoirse* is that of an exemption of immunity *from* something, and this will form the basis of the next section.

The idea of *saoirse* in a Middle Irish text

The medieval *Betha Caoimhgin* ('Life of St Kevin') gives an insight into the application of the concept of *saoirse* in the earlier period. I will quote from this text at some length, as it gives a good idea of *saoirse* functioning as part of a kind of moral economy. First we are told that Kevin practises the unusual devotional exercise of repairing to a pen (*cró*) every Lent in order to ask favours of God, and then we are given the reason why:

Do ráidh Caoimhgin risan aingeal:	Kevin said to the angel
'As mo broid ni rach rém ré	'From my captivity I will not emerge
Go ffaghar do lucht mo chíosa	until I obtain for my tributaries
Saoirsi o Ísa mac Dé'.[14]	immunity from Jesus son of God'.

This immunity is duly granted, and we are later assured of this fact:

Do fág 'ga sgoil manach béil-binn,	He left with his school of melodious monks
Ocus ag cleircibh a mhionn	and with the clerks of his relics
A cíos do thionól gan **daoirsí**,	the collection of its tribute without enslavement
Ó thucc Dia **sáoirsi** da chionn.[15]	since God granted immunity for his sake.

In other words, the *saoirse* that once belonged to Kevin to collect his own *cíos* ('tribute') is secured for his own flock free of *daoirse*. This anticipates the various associations of *saoirse* with the idea of protection and sanctuary to be considered from later texts below. This theme recurs later when St Kevin vows to take vengeance on those who violate his people's *saoirse* and replace it with *daoirse*:

Caoimgin do-rinne an rand-sa,	Kevin made this verse
Ní mar fhallsacht do-rinne,	and it was not from idleness
D'fagail **saoirsi** dá bhochtaibh	to secure immunity for his poor
Ar olcaibh gacha linde.	from the evils of every age
Cádhas do fháccsat Gaoidil	The Gaels left honour
Do Chaoimhgin gan cain, gan cíos;	to Kevin without tax or tribute;
Ata an chill da t-tuccsat **saoirsi**	the church to which they gave freedom
'Ga cur fa **daoirsi** arís.[16]	is being enslaved again.

Note again here the collocation *saoirsi ar* to mean 'freedom from'. Here *saoirse* is closely associated with *cíos* 'tribute' and *cáin* 'tax' and not only involves being free from the imposition of these obligations but also seems to involve the freedom to impose them on others. In the next section we shall see a further example of the association of the word *cádhas* 'honour' with *saoirse* from an early seventeenth-century text (note in the quotation above, *Cádhus do fhácc-sat Gaoidil/Do Chaoimhgin gan cain, gan cíos* 'The Gaels left honour to Kevin without tax or tribute'). Furthermore, the collocation *do-bheir* (or *tucaid*) X *soírse do* Y 'X gives freedom to Y' (above in the form *an chill da t-tuccsat saoirsi* 'the church to which they gave freedom') is common in the medieval period, as in the following passage from a Life of St Brendan of Clonfert. A poor man asks Brendan to free him and his family from slavery to the king. The saint gives him a piece of sacred gold and says:

> 'Tabhair sin don righ, & sáerfaidh tú on dáersi ina bfuil tu aicce; & na hinnis dó cia tucc hé.' Gabhais an bocht an t-ór, & beiris leis dochum an righ é; & innisis dó amhail fuair h-é . . . 'Ór Chriost sin,' or se, 'Ocus ní meisi dlighes é, acht serbhfogantaidhe Dé féin. Ocus do-bheirim **sáersi** duit-si & dot chloinn i n-onóir do Dhia & do Brenainn'.[17]

> 'Give that to the king and it will free you from the enslavement that you are in and don't tell who gave it to you.' The poor man took the gold to the king and told him how he had obtained it . . . 'That is Christ's gold,' said the king, 'and it is not me who is entitled to it from the servant of God himself. And I give you and your children freedom in honour of God and of Brendan.'

As we shall see, this is a recurring, indeed enduring, piece of syntax: 'X **gives** *saoirse* to Y'. For now, however, I wish to consider two focal uses of this word *saoirse* in the medieval and early modern period that the above passages have brought up—firstly, as signifying a certain right or privilege to exemption or immunity from imposition and secondly, contrasted explicitly (or indeed implicitly) with its opposite, *daoirse*. We shall also see that these focal uses have important syntactic repercussions for the subsequent discussion.

Saoirse as exemption or immunity

Saoirse (usually in the forms *saíre* or *soíre*) is used in Early Irish legal material to indicate a type of privilege, in the form of an exemption or immunity from certain legal obligations that was enjoyed by people of a particular social status. This, however, was often contingent on the fulfilment of one's responsibilities and could be forfeited in cases of dereliction, as an Old Irish ecclesiastical rule tells us of the priest who is not in a fit state to meet the duties of his office (*a*); on the other hand, freedom of this kind could also be 'bought', according to one's merit (*b*):

(*a*) nach fer gráid didiu oc ná bí dlighed . . . ni dlig **sáire** ná eneclainn fhir gráid

any ordained man who is not mindful of the rule . . . is not entitled to
the exemption or honour-price of one ordained

(b)   is **saer** cid cach creanus a **suiri** dia dan[18]

he is free even the one who buys his freedom with his craft

This sense of 'exemption' or 'immunity' under the law is still the meaning that
saoirse usually has for Céitinn in the early seventeenth century. In this use,
saoirse is often associated with the word *tearmann*, meaning in general terms
'refuge', 'protection', as in (a) below, and this latter word is further associated
with *comairce*, also meaning 'protection', 'refuge', as in (b). Note too that this
saoirse can be applied to both persons and property. In (c) the association of
saoirse (here the older form *saoire*) is again linked with the idea of 'protection,'
represented in this case by *snádudh*.[19] In (a) Céitinn reports the testimony of
Camden that the Irish nobility kept poets, musicians, lawyers and historians
and granted them legal immunities (*saoirse*) with respect to their persons and
property. The following is their custom:

(a)   tearmainn do bhronnadh dóibh, agus fós **saoirse** do bheith ag a
       bpearsannaibh, ag a bhfearann, agus ag a spréidh

for sanctuary to be granted to them and also immunity to their persons,
land and property

(b)   do orduigheadar uaisle Éireann tearmann agus comairce do bheith ag
       fearann, ag pearsannaibh, agus ag spréidh na n-ollamhan

the nobles of Ireland had ordered that the land, the persons and the
property of the chief poets should have sanctuary and protection

(c)   ro thingheall beos da threalam décc marcaigh do Ua Domhnaill ar
       shaoire ⁊ shnadudh don chách do deachatar fora ionchaib don chur sin

he pledged, moeover, twelve horse trappings to Ó Domhnaill for the
security and protection of all

The phrase *saoirse choitcheann* 'general immunity' was given above in an example from Dinneen's dictionary and the following passage gives its wider socio-
cultural and historical context. The historical context, as given in the following
passage by Céitinn, is the convention of Druim Cett in 575 AD, when the privileges of chief poets (granted *fearann saor* 'free land' by their lords) were established by Colm Cille, who thus rescued them from banishment by the Church.
Part of the settlement is the guaranteeing of *saoirse choitcheann* 'a general
exemption' to the chief poets:

saoirse choitcheann is tearmann ó fhearaibh Éireann ag fearann is ag
maoin tsaoghalta gach ollamhan díobh[20]

general immunity and sanctuary from the men of Ireland for the land
and wealth of every one of these chief poets

Note again the occurrence of the word *tearmann* 'sanctuary'. One other thing that should again be noted here is the importance of the syntax *saoirse ó* 'immunity/freedom **from**'. In the passage above from the life of St Kevin we saw the word *cádhas* 'honour' associated with *saoirse*. This association is repeated by Céitinn along with *tearmann*; we see again the occurrence of the syntax *saoirse ó* 'freedom from' in the following passage, where he describes how the druids of Gaul attained their rights and privileges:

> **tearmann is saoirse is cádhas** ó uaislibh na Fraingce[21]
>
> sanctuary and immunity and respect from the nobility of France

It is clear that the concepts of *saoirse, tearmann, coimairce* and *cádhus* represent something of a socio-cultural semantic cluster in medieval and early modern Ireland revolving around the idea of exemption, immunity and protection *from* outside imposition. The importance of these ideas in a coherent social order is demonstrated in a notable poem of the 1570s, entitled 'Mairg rug ar an aim-sirsi' ('Unfortunate anyone overtaken by this time') dealing with the effects of English conquest and attempts to impose the Elizabethan Reformation in Munster at that time. While the word *saoirse* is not used, the closely associated *tearmann* and *comairce* are, and it is precisely their absence that is symbolic of the anarchy that has overtaken the traditional order:

Crúaidh an cás a ttarlamair	Harsh is our plight indeed
ar tteacht deiridh an domhain,	with the end of the world upon us
acht gurab iad allmhuraigh	(But) that the foreigners are
is dócha dúinn dár ccobhair	the most likely source for our help
As mór an cás comhairle,	It is a great matter for deliberation
dá mbía gábhadh ar dhuine,	if danger should befall anyone
cia gheabhus a **chomairce**	who will assume his protection
a dhíon cá háit a bhfuighe	where will he find sanctuary?
Ní díon múr ná mainistir	Sanctuary is not to be found in
	castle or monastery
ná t[e]armonn aosa dána,	or in the refuge of poets
dúinn is iom(sh)lán aithristear	fully it is rehearsed to us
nach fiú pinginn an pápa.[22]	that the Pope is not worth a penny.

Set in such a context, *saoirse* emerges as a bulwark of a system of rights and privileges in the early modern period, particularly as applied to the poetic order.

Saoirse as sovereignty and independence

This association of *saoirse* with the idea of 'protection' can be extended to apply to a particular (sacred) place that has to be defended (*cosnamh*) against outside imposition. The background to the next passage is that the High King of Ireland Máel Sechnaill's Irish rival, Brian Bóromha, has demanded that he give him either hostages or battle. In the course of a month's respite Máel Sechnaill appeals to the Uí Néill by sending them his chief poet as emissary, requesting that they join forces to engage Brian in battle for the defence of Tara. Otherwise, he would submit to Brian:

> muna dtigdís sin uile do chosnamh **shaoirse** Teamhrach da gcine féin atá, n-a seilbh lé cian d'aimsir go dtiubhradh féin braighde do Bhrian fá bheith umhal dó.[23]

> unless all of those came to defend the freedom of Tara for their own people, in whose possession it had been for a long time, he himself would give hostages to Brian with respect to his submission to him.

The Uí Néill, however, are not impressed, and they tell Máel Sechnaill to fight his own battles, just as they did when they possessed the high-kingship of Tara:

> An tan do bhí Teamhair ag Cinéal Eoghain . . . do chosnadar féin í, agus an té ag a bhfuil sí anois seasuigheadh a **saoirse**.

> When the Cinéal Eoghain had Tara . . . they defended it themselves, and he who has it now, let him defend its freedom.

This usage already occurs in the twelfth-century text *Cogadh Gaedhel re Gallaibh* 'The War of the Irish with the Foreigners', the foreigners in this case being the Vikings:

> ba fearr leo bas ocus éc ocus aeded . . . do agbail ic cosnum **sairi a n-athardha ocus a ceneoil** . . . ocus cid duad no docair fo-gabdaois ic cosnum **sairi** primtheghllaig Muman ocus im da uatni congbala follamnais ocus flathamnais Erend; ise ba coru **sairsi** do chosnamh ocus iarraid and.[24]

> they preferred to die defending the freedom of their fatherland and their people . . . and even if they found it difficult and strenuous defending the freedom of the chief family of Munster around the two sustaining pillars of the rule and sovereignty of Ireland; it was more just to defend and to look for freedom there.

Note that in this text the forms *saíre* and *saírse* occur side by side, with no apparent difference in meaning .

The idea of *saoirse* is again seen as embodying the 'negative' concept of 'freedom **from**', characterized as exemption from paying tax and tribute for land. The context as discussed by Céitinn is that after the battle of Tara in 980, when Máel Sechnaill, High King of Ireland, defeated the Dublin Norsemen under Olaf, the Irish forces besieged Dublin and won concessions from the Norsemen. Here *saoirse* is translated by the editor as 'allow them have their lands':

> Do bheanadar do Lochlonnaibh gan oighréir do bheith orra, is **saoirse** do bheith aca ó Shionainn go muir gan cíos ná cáin uatha do Lochlonnaibh.[25]

> They made the Vikings recognize their independence and liberty from the Shannon to the sea, without tribute or tax due from them to the Vikings.

Saoirse as opposed to *daoirse*

Another important sense of *saoirse* historically is that of physical freedom from a specific instance of captivity or enslavement (*dóire* or *daírse*), as in the following eighth-century gloss on the emergence of the Israelites from Egypt:

> tuidecht **asin doiri hi soiri** ⁊ taidchur dia críg[26]

> coming out of captivity into freedom and returning to their country

For a treatment of the idea of being free from a specific instance of oppression in a more national and political context I will concentrate on a poem by Seán Ó Gadhra, entitled 'Staid Nua na hÉireann', written in 1697, after the Williamite war and the flight of the Wild Geese. The first stanza (*a*) immediately brings up the theme of the *daoirse* ('captivity') of the Children of Israel, a pervasive analogy and rationalization for the plight of the Irish from the medieval period onwards, and the poem concludes with (*b*) an appeal to Mary and the able monarchs of this world to aid the Irish:

(*a*)   Is fada atá an ainnise ar Ghae dhluibh   Misery has long afflicted the Irish

faoi mhasla ag gach aicme dhá thréine;   and insults from everyone weak and strong

ní bhfuair a dhaoine ag Maoise ar aenchor   Moses' people never experienced

leath a **ndaoirse** thríd an Tréan-Mhuir.   the half of their oppression through the Red Sea.

(*b*)   Mar' dtugaid **saorse ón daorse** do Ghaedhlaibh   Unless they give the Irish freedom from slavery

go bhfaghaid bás gan spás i n-éinfheacht.[27]   may they die without delay together.

Once again we find the syntax of negative freedom: 'freedom from slavery' or *saorse ón daorse*. The theme of *daoirse* occurs throughout this poem, together with various reflexes of its polar opposite *saor,* for example the verb form *saer/saor* 'to free' (*a*). A further verb to appear in this context is *fuascail* 'free', 'liberate', as in (*b*) below. Note also that further words indicative of enslavement and oppression are used: in (*a*) *bruid* 'captivity', 'bondage' and in (*b*) *smacht* 'rule', 'subjection':

(*a*)   Minic **do saoradh ó dhaoirse** Éire,   Ireland has often been freed from slavery

Tuatha Dé Danann do scaipeadh le hÉibhear;   the Tuatha dé Danann were scattered by Éibhear

. . . ba mhóir **bruid** Mhic Con is Mhic Céachta.   great was the oppression of Mac Con and Mac Céachta.

(*b*)   Is é Tuathal **d'fhuascail** na céadtha   It was Tuathal who freed hundreds

> . . . is ní fada mhair smacht   not long did the tyranny of Oliver
> Oilibhérus.[28]   endure.

In fact the poetry of the eighteenth century is replete with the vocabulary of oppression and enslavement; *daoirse* is found repeatedly but significantly without, in many cases, evoking its antithesis *saoirse* as an abstraction. The verbs used in the following excerpts are (a) *tóg ó* 'take from,' 'lift from'; (b) *saor* 'free,' 'liberate'; (c) *fuascail* 'free,' 'liberate'. We can note also the prevalence of the preposition *ó* 'from,' where again the emphasis is on negative freedom:

(*a*)   Tógfaidh Gaeil ó **dhaoirse** Gall   He will rescue the Irish from
                                                   foreign oppression
        ag aiseag foinn is fearainn[29]   restoring land and territory

(*b*)   **saor** Éire ón daoscarshluagh[30]   Free Ireland from the rabble

(*c*)   Trí coróna do ghaibh Séamas . . . an leomhan cróga cascarthach gníomhéachtach cathbhuach le **bhfuascailtear** an Gael **ó dhaoirse agus ó dhaorpheannaid eachtrann** mar a deir an fáidh fíornaofa Ultán gurab é an flaith fíre se a chríochnamhas **ár ndaoirse** . . .[31]

James took the three crowns . . . the brave-hearted, triumphant, valiant lion victorious in battle by whom the Gael will be liberated from the slavery and oppressive purgatory of foreigners as the most holy prophet Ultán says that it is this true sovereign who will put an end to our enslavement . . .

In other words, an antidote to *daoirse* is presented, but more often than not it is in the form of a verb denoting an *act of freeing from* a particular instance of oppression rather than the sense of there being a universal idea of *saoirse* as an abstraction.

Before considering how this more abstract sense develops in Irish, there is an interesting sixteenth- or early seventeenth-century occurrence of the word juxtaposed with its equivalent, 'liberty', as borrowed (presumably) from English. The context is a letter written by one Fínghin Mac Carthaigh, who on two separate occasions was incarcerated in the Tower of London (1589–91 and 1601–2). In the course of writing he refers to the effect he hopes that delivery of the letter will have:

da mbeith gu bfuilim deimhnitach gú bfaedha mé fábhur mór ⁊ fairsingudha **libertao** *nó* **sháoirsi** air ason[32]

although I do assure myself that I shall haue great favour and som libertie whensoeuer I deliver it

The juxtaposition of the neologism *libertao* with the well-established, native *saoirse* is interesting here, and we shall have further cause to consider more attestations of 'liberty' in this period in Irish, a word that is very sparsely attested in the Irish of any period.

Saoirse in the eighteenth century (1)

A common collocation in the eighteenth century is to describe Ireland, or individuals pertaining to its former Gaelic aristocracy, as being *gan saoirse* 'without *saoirse*'. A variation on this takes the form *gan X saoirse* 'without X of *saoirse*', where X governs *saoirse* in the genitive case. Some excellent examples of this usage occur in a poem by Proinsias Ó Súilleabháin, dated 1746, lamenting the demise of his old patrons, the McCarthys and the O'Sullivans, who are without cattle, without land and without status (*gan tréad gan talamh gan gradam*), and the poet bemoans the absence of redemption in the form of the Stuarts:[33]

(*a*)   Réx ceart Chaisil is dragan is leóghan Laoi thoir
is an t-aon so mhaireas d'fhuil Eachadh **gan lór saoirse**,
scéal is measa gan mac aige i gcómhair sloinnte
ná aon ar a ainm le gairm san treó dhírigh . . .

The rightful king of Cashel, dragon and lion of the Lee in the east
and the only one who remains of the blood of Eochu without sufficiency
of *saoirse*
worst of all he has no son to perpetuate his surname
nor any of his name to maintain the true lineage . . .

(*b*)   Caesar gaisce an Ghleanna so is mó chaoinim,
an té aca cailleadh in Eachdhruim fós roímhe seo,
an té aca cailleadh 'san ngaisce is brón scís liom
tug mé i mbaitheas an tailimh **gan scóip saoirse** . . .

It is valorous Caesar of the Glen that I weep for most
the one moreover who died at Aughrim before this
the one who died in battle causes me grief
and leaves me on the face of the earth without scope of *saoirse* . . .

(*c*)   . . . Séarlas airgthe a Sacsaibh gan dóigh fillte
is dá réir, sin Banba i nglasaibh **gan cóir saoirse**

. . . Charles has been driven from England without hope of return
and accordingly, that's Ireland in chains without her share of *saoirse*

In translating these excerpts I am deliberately leaving open for now the issue of how best to gloss *saoirse* in English until further evidence has been considered. In particular I want to concentrate on the first stanza, where the Irish are described as being *gan tréad gan talamh gan gradam* 'without cattle without land without status' and to see how this perhaps relates to being *gan saoirse*. We can in fact adduce various further syntactic structures of the type *gan X gan saoirse* 'without X without *saoirse*', where the absence of *saoirse* is associated with the absence of the value of X. Examples are *réim* 'power,' 'sway', 'dominion', and *sealbh* 'occupancy', 'possession' or 'property'. The following is from Eoghan Rua Ó Súilleabháin's (1748–84) *aisling* poem *Ar Maidin Indé Cois Céidh na Slimbharc* ('Yesterday morning by the quay of the slender ships'):

acht ainnir gan bhréag do thaisteal i gcéin,	but a true maiden who travelled far
le teachtaireacht scéil ó Laoiseach:	with a message from Louis
gur gairid go ndéanfaidh díoghaltas	that it will not be long before he wreaks revenge
do ghlanfaidh le faobhar na faolchoin	that will clear at swordpoint the foreign wolves
ó fhearanntas Gaoidheal gan reachtmas, **gan réim**,	from Irish land without wealth without dominion
gan talamh, gan tréid, gan saoirse.[34]	without land without cattle without *saoirse*.

Note again the further association between lack of land (*talamh*) and cattle (*tréad*, pl. *tréid*) and lack of *saoirse* that we saw in Proinsias Ó Súilleabháin's poem above. The further perspective offered here on *saoirse* is that, when the English are banished, *they* will be without *saoirse*—clearly the issue is not (or not yet) one of political independence as such but rather of economic autonomy and social prestige:

(a)	Mar d'imigh gach díth ar chríochaibh Fáil	How every loss has been incurred by the land of Fál
	Gan sealbh gan saoirse ag síolrach seanda	the ancestral race with neither possession nor *saoirse*
	Ceannas i ndlí ná cíos ná ceannphoirt	authority in the law, rent nor leadership
(b)	Is lúbaidh go hurlainn bhur lanna go léir	And bend all your blades to the hilt
	i gcoinne gach dream d'fhág sibhse go fann	against everyone who has left you feeble
	le fada **gan sealbh gan saoirse**.[35]	a long time without possession or *saoirse*.

To be without wealth, land and prestige is therefore to be without *saoirse* in such cases. The following entry in *Annála Ríoghachta Éireann* for the year 1601 sheds further light on this idea of *saoirse* in the early seventeenth century:

Asseadh airecc ro thionchoiscc a ainshén do Dhiarmait, Iarla Desmumhan do thairbert don Presidens, & d'Iarla Tuadhmumhan dar cenn ionnmais, & edala, & **ar shaoirsi, & ar shochar dúthaighe**.[36]

The solution which his ill fortune indicated to Diarmaid was to hand over the earl of Desmond to the president and the earl of Thomond in return for wealth and property, and the liberty and profits of an estate.

Here we see the association of *saoirse* with wealth and the profits or privileges of owning an estate. It is also interesting to see *saoirse* collocated with the word *sochar* 'profit', 'advantage', 'privilege', 'due', as if perhaps they are the opposite sides of the same coin—*saoirse* as discussed above standing for the negative concept of exemption or immunity from outside imposition, with *sochar* as one of its positive correlates.

As we saw above in the Life of St Kevin, the collocation *do-bheir X sairse do Y* 'X gives freedom to Y' is common in the medieval period. A further instance of this construction with the verb 'to give' is from a poem by Aodh Buí Mac Cruitín 'A Shaoi Is a Shagairt tá ag Seasamh go Síorchróga' ('Wise Man and Priest Standing Externally Valiantl'), where the talk is again of freedom being 'given' to those who support a particular cause, in this case the Jacobite cause:

> Atá Laoiseach leadarthach lannartha líonmhórga
> 's an Prionsa paidreach ag preabadh go prímhbheoga
> chum **saoirse a thabhairt dá** leanfadh an fíorchóimhdhe
> 's biaidh bríste salach ag meathach na míomhóide.[37]

> The smiting, sword-wielding Louis of the great hosts
> and the prayerful Prince are rising up expectantly
> to give *saoirse* to those who would follow the true lord
> and the coward of the dastardly oath will have soiled breeches.

The word *réim* also occurs with *saoirse* after the verb 'to give' in a type of collocation familiar from the preceding discussion. The following is from Eoghan Rua's 'Tráth Indé Is Mé Tnáidhte i Bpéin' ('Yesterday While I Was Smitten in Pain'):

. . . bláth na ríoghan óg,	. . . the flower of the young queens
thug saoirse is réim do shaoithibh dréacht,	who gave *saoirse* and power to wise men
is míor don chléir re hurraim chuibhe,	and its share to the clergy with proper deference
ba dhíon-bhrat éigse, buime ríghthe,	protector of poets, foster-mother to kings
is caomhnaidhe treón.[38]	and keeper of heroes.

In fact what we see here is *saoirse* being used in a way that is not very different from its use in medieval sources, as evidenced from its syntactic behaviour: it is still something that can be conferred by someone on someone as a kind of favour or privilege.

In a poem from the 1750s by Liam Inglis, 'Atá an fhuireann so thall gan amhras díleas' ('This band yonder is without doubt true') the phrase *mar shaoirse* 'as saoirse' occurs in connection with the prospect of amortization money being bestowed on the Catholic clergy by the Stuart Pretender, again as a specific right or privilege. Note the use of Jacobite codes for the Pretender: *ár leanbh* 'the Child' and *an Craoibhín* 'the Branch':

Dá dtigeadh ár leanbh cé fada tá ar slighe chughainn
is deimhin go gcaithfidís Sasanaigh stríocadh
bheadh an t-airgead marbh ag ár sagairt mar **shaoirse**
leis an gCraoibhín aoibhinn áluinn óg.[39]

If our Child came even though he has been long on his way
it is certain that the English would have to clear out
our priests would have 'the dead's money' as *saoirse*
with the young, beautiful delightful Branch.

Summary

The important points to note about the word *saoirse* up to the end of the eighteenth century are as follows. Firstly, it embodies an essentially negative sense
of 'freedom'. This is indicated syntactically by the existence of the collocation
saoirse ó/ar 'freedom **from**' and the corresponding non-existence of expressions
like **saoirse fri/re/le/chun* 'freedom **to**' (the question of how 'positive freedom'
is expressed in Irish will be taken up in a later section). Secondly, within this
domain of negative 'freedom' there are two further points worth noting about
the use of *saoirse*:

(1)   Its status as a legal immunity or exemption from various types of impo-
        sition (*cáin* 'tax' and *cíos* 'rent') and its association with the idea of 'pro-
        tection', 'refuge' and 'sanctuary', as embodied in words like *tearmann*,
        comairc and *snádadh*. In addition there is the idea that this is something
        that is conferred or 'given' (i.e. *do-bheir X saoirse do Y*) as a favour or
        privilege but that can then be construed as a traditional or ancestral
        right by persons of a particular legal or social standing. It is primarily
        in these terms that *saoirse* is characterized in Jacobite poetry as some-
        thing that the Irish, or least a particular class thereof, are 'without', since
        they are also 'without' (*gan*) their lands, cattle and status.

(2)   Its status as the antithesis of *daoirse* 'enslavement', 'slavery', 'captivity',
        both on the personal and the collective level.

The following sections examine the development of these semantic domains
in the late eighteenth and early nineteenth centuries.

Saoirse in the eighteenth century (2): *'So chugainn ár saoirse'*

As Ó Buachalla points out in a number of publications,[40] the emphasis on terms
like *ceart* 'right' in seventeenth- and eighteenth-century poetry stems from the
Irish belief in the rightful Stuart king as the source of the common good. The
malign corollary of this is the usurper Hanoverian king who brings about the
ruin of the country by his very illegitimacy. It was, for the most part, less a message of revolution than of restoration, return and renewal, although the return
of the *status quo ante* was increasingly questioned during the eighteenth century.

As he also points out, Irish political rhetoric of the seventeenth and eighteenth centuries is characterized by its underlying belief in the providential and prophetic modes; this is the rhetoric of redemption in Irish Jacobite literature. As Ó Buachalla puts it, this pervasive rhetoric bears 'the universal characteristic of all millennial thought, wherever encountered. a strong sense of collective calamity and a demand for collective salvation'.[41] Ó Buachalla also argues that the most significant development in Irish literature in the early modern period is the emergence of the 'communal voice'. The numerous drinking songs of the period toasting the Pretender attest to this communal dimension. Into this context we may place what Ó Buachalla counts as the first attestation of *saoirse* as an abstract concept in Irish (as opposed to 'freedom from' something), a Jacobite drinking song of the 1740s composed by Tadhg Ó Neachtain:

A Thaidhg, a Sheáin, Diarmaid thráth,	Tadhg, Seán, Diarmaid also
bígí grámhar dílis;	be amiable and faithful
so an lá bhá dhíbh i dtár	this is the day that was prophesied for you
a aicme bhreá Míle;	you fine sons of Míl;
. . . óir so chugainn **ár saoirse**.[42]	. . . because here comes our freedom.

Note the use of the collective voice here, '*our* freedom', in association with the common Irish names Tadhg, Seán and Diarmaid. This song is full of the rhetoric of Jacobitism, and it is interesting to note the use of *saoirse* in this context. In general this word is not central to the ideology of Jacobitism in the way that *ceart* 'right', *dualgas* 'due' and *dílis* 'right', 'proper', are; however, Ó Neachtain's poem is the harbinger of things to come. Furthermore, as Ó Buachalla points out, Ó Neachtain's work is of particular interest in that it operates outside the traditional poet–patron nexus and is written in an urban intellectual milieu.[43] This could account for a certain innovation here.

The personification of 'freedom': 'Is ainm domh Saoirse'

In a macaronic song of the 1790s, 'Is Ainm Damh Saoirse' ('My name is Freedom'), *Saoirse* is personified as coming from France to Ireland. A longer, all-English version of this song appears in *Paddy's Resource,* while the Irish version was collected in Co. Donegal and was published by Ó Muirgheasa. I give both the Irish and English texts as they occur there where they are not necesssarily close translatons of each other:[44]

Is ainm damh **Saoirse** nó lánríoghacht,	My name is Freedom, I sailed o'er
ag agrad carad dílis	Privately to this nation

'Saoirse' then walks the length and breadth of Ireland to find her friends and allies but discovers a certain reticence among the inhabitants:

Tá'n chomhursa liom go carthan-
    nach saor
	The neighbours are all kind and
	    free

le lóisdín a thabhairt do stráinséir,	to entertain a stranger,
acht is eagal leobh aidmheáil gur leobh féin mé,	yet dare not own me as their own,
mar bhíomsa 'gcomhnuidhe i ndáinséir.	so I'm exposed to danger.

It will be noted that the first two lines differ considerably in the two versions, in particular the collocation *Saoirse nó lánríoghacht* in the Irish version. This is an intriguing collocation and one I shall return to below. Note too that in both versions there is a play on *saor* 'free', here used in the sense of 'liberal', 'generous'. The second verse presents *saoirse* as originating in France, where it became the light of many nations, while the third stanza presents a new metaphor for *saoirse,* the tree of liberty, which is directly opposed to the malodorous 'Orange' tree; the former will continue to thrive while the latter wilts:

beidh an **tSaoirse** 'gcomhnuidhe a méadughadh	then liberty's sure to flourish

Here *saoirse* is to be identified with the 'tree of liberty', as in the United Irishman catechism printed in Cork in December 1797:

> 'What is that in your hand?' 'It is a branch.' 'Of what'? 'Of the Tree of Liberty.' 'Where did it first grow?' 'In America.' 'Where does it bloom?' 'In France.' 'Where did the seeds fall?' 'In Ireland.'[45]

The song under discussion is also noteworthy for containing the first reference that I have found to *saoirse* preceded by the definite article *an* (lit. 'the freedom'). This in itself is indicative of a greater level of abstraction and universality than previously: in other words *saoirse* is now one and indivisible. It should be noted also that the United Irishman journal *Bolg an tSoláir,* of which one issue appeared in Belfast in the 1790s, mentions the words *saoirseacht* 'liberty' and *codramacht* 'equality' in an Irish–English vocabulary, while the same two words are reported to have been used as passwords by the United Irish Society of Philadelphia in 1797.[46]

On the question of the significance of the word *lánríoghacht*, its most literal translation would be 'full kingship', but a possible, and more apposite, translation might be 'full sovereignty'.[47] In this regard it is worth considering a poem by the Cork scribe and United Irishman Mícheál Óg Ó Longáin (1766–1837), who has the idea of *saoirse* as something that can be seized or appropriated for oneself in his poem of 1819 'Is Díth Liom na Gaeil-se a Bheith Tláith Lag Fann'.[48] It begins by lamenting the abject state of the Irish people as witnessed by the persecution of their religion and the occupation of their land by a foreign power. The poet finds an exemplar in the mythological kings of Ireland's prehistory, the Milesian forebears of the Gaels, who took 'freedom' by force:

> ghaibh **saoirse** san tír-se le barr a lann
>
> they seized freedom in this land with the points of their weapons

Both *flaithius* and *ríge* (later *ríghe*) in the sense of 'sovereignty' are frequently preceded by the verb *gaibid* (*gaibhidh*) 'takes', 'seizes', in earlier Irish, although this is not the case for *saoirse* and its earlier forms. In this context one could easily read the passage as 'they seized the sovereignty'. This in turn could have a bearing on the form *lánríoghacht* encountered earlier, particularly in view of its association with *saoirse*: *is ainm domh Saoirse nó lánríoghacht* 'my name is Freedom or full sovereignty'. This can be further referred to a tendency in Irish for words that mean primarily 'rule', 'sovereignty', to also mean 'kingdom', 'realm'; compare *flaithius, flaithemnas* and *ríge* (and later *ríoghacht*).

Saoirse in the nineteenth century (1): '*Ag ardughadh meirge na saoirse*'

The idea of *saoirse* as being of foreign provenance and 'coming' from overseas to Ireland becomes common at this time, for example in Mícheál Óg Ó Longáin's poem 'Tig Fuacht i nGaoth Gheimhridh' ('Cold comes in winter's wind', 1811), where the impression is given that everything under the sun comes around, except the advent of *saoirse* to Ireland:

> tig gual ar loing taoibh liom tar farraigí anall
> 's mo bhuairt **nach dtíd saoirse** do chlannaibh Gaíol ndonn[49]
>
> coal comes close by me on ships from over the sea
> but alas that freedom does not come to the families of the fine Irish

In his discussion of the transition of Irish political thought from 'Jacobite to Jacobin' towards the beginning of the nineteenth century, Ó Buachalla ascribes a central role to Ó Longáin and his poetry.[50] Furthermore, Ó Buachalla points to the centrality of the term *saoirse* to Ó Longáin's political rhetoric, contextualizing it within the mainstream of contemporary Irish and international developments.[51]

In fact developments in the use of the word *saoirse* at this period may be taken as symbolic of a wider process of evolution, itself encapsulated in Ó Longáin's work in general. This is what Ó Buachalla calls 'the confluence . . . of the "residual" with the "emergent"' in Irish ideology in the late eighteenth and early nineteenth centuries.[52] In this vein we have a story in the tradition of the early modern Irish romantic tale[53] entitled *Tóruigheacht Chalmair* 'The pursuit of Calmar' (1826), composed by the scribe, schoolmaster and political activist Amhlaoibh Ó Súilleabháin (1780–1838). 'Calmar' is a pseudonym for the leader of the O'Tooles, who is being pursued by the authorities in the aftermath of 1798. While fleeing the authorities he meets the O'Neill and, as they discuss the defeats of 1798, O'Neill enquires of O'Toole where he is now headed. There occurs the following passage, in which the word *saoirse* is given some emphasis:

> Is e a dubhairt Calmfear: 'Ba mhian liom dul don domhan nua, agus gleanntan uaigneach eigin d'faill amach cois na h-Ohio no na Misisipi no [na] Miosourai, agus deireadh mo bheatha do chathaim ag caoine Clanna Gaodal faoi gearsgrios Gall. No mas fior, mar is clos dom, go bhfuill fuasgalthoir ag eirge san Ameiricia Theas, is doith go rachfuinn ag comhrughadh leis ag ardughadh **meirge na saoirse** air Sliabh Cordileras.' 'Is cosamhail go bhfuil **saoirse ag triall** chum cinighe an domhain,' ar Ua Neill, 'ata leighion na leathnughadh; ceart an chine daona da mhiniughadh; siorcheart De da saoibhscealadh . . . Dar ndoith is cuimhin leat, iar dteacht do **spirid na saoirse** o hAmeiricea gus an bhFrainc, tar eis tuiltighe fola Sasanaigh do dhorta[dh] faoi taoiseach Frederic, an t-easbog malaighte, go bhfuair Clanna Gaoidil fionnfuaradh beag eile.'[54]

> This is what Calmar said: 'I'd like to go to the New World and find some lonely valley out by the Ohio, the Mississippi or Missouri and spend the rest of my life weeping for the Irish under English oppression. Or if it is true, as I hear, that a liberator is arising in South America, I'd probably go and help him raise the standard of freedom on the Sierra Condileras.' 'It seems that freedom is coming to the people of the earth,' said O'Neill, 'education is becoming more widespread, the rights of man are being explained and the eternal right of God is being disseminated . . . Of course you remember that after the spirit of freedom had come from America to France, and after floods of English blood had been shed under the renegade bishop Frederick, that the Irish gained another small respite.'

This passage contains a number of interesting references to contemporary and recent events. In the first place the *fuasgalthoir* or 'liberator' referred to is Simón Bolívar, who in 1819 defeated the Spanish and who subsequently became the first president of the republic of Colombia, incorporating present-day Colombia, Ecuador, Venezuela and Panama. Secondly, the reference to 'Frederic' is to Frederick Augustus, Duke of York and Albany, second son of King George III, who led the British army on two disastrous campaigns against republican France in the Low Countries in 1799. On the more general level again the idea is that *saoirse* is coming (*ag triall*) not just to Ireland but to the peoples of the world, and the 'tree of liberty' idea is rehearsed in terms of freedom's progression (*iar dteacht do **spirid na saoirse** o hAmeiricea gus an bhFrainc*).[55]

The idea of freedom as a universal right is found elsewhere in Ó Súilleabháin's writings, as in the following extract from his diary *Cín Lae Amhlaoibh* for 1830 on the war in the Low Countries. Note in particular the identification of *saoirse* with O'Connell:

> 5.x.1830: Tá muintir Hanóbhar, Bhrunsuic agus Shasana Shean ag éileamh a gcirt .i. **saoirse**. Is iomdha fear ag ardú a ghutha le Dónall Ó Conaill anois trés an Eoraip, thoir, thiar, thuas agus theas.[56]

5.x.1830: The people of Hanover, Brunswick and Saxony are demanding their right, i.e. freedom. There is many a man raising his voice now
with Daniel O'Connell throughout Europe, east, west, north and
south.

This conceptualization of *saoirse* in the late eighteenth and early nineteenth centuries shows a new sense of universalism: *saoirse* is for everyone but especially
for *us* as a collective entity; it is personified as being 'over there' in America or
France but it is coming 'here' as part of this same universal progress and it is
something that can be 'seized' or 'taken'. These ideas are completely new in Irish
and would have been inconceivable at an earlier period. However, these developments do not necessarily mean that *saoirse* is conterminous with *freedom* as
that concept is instantiated in English, and I shall return to this question shortly.
This concept of *saoirse* as an individual and therefore universal ideal is found in
Ó Súilleabháin's remark (writing in his diary for 27 August 1827 about a thrush
that has made its nest secure with one egg in it and then abandons it):

is ionúin le gach dúil faoi neimh **saoirse**[57]

every creature under heaven loves freedom

Ó Súilleabháin's diary contains a number of references to *saoirse* with regard
to Catholic Emancipation, which he calls *saoirse Chaitliceach* or *saoirse do
Chaitlicibh*:

8.i.1828: Atáid muintir Challainn chum achainí do chur chum Feise na
Breataine ag iarraidh **saoirse** Chaitliceach gan fuíoll ar bith, gan con-
radh i dtaobh creidimh ná ag tabhairt suas aon chumhachta noch atá
againn cheana, agus ag iarraidh an acht i gcoinne na dtiarnaí tacair do
chur ar gcúl . . . agus ag iarraidh **saoirse** do thabhairt do Phrotestanta-
igh na Sasana.

13.i.1828: Bhá comhthionól againn inniu i séipéal an pharóiste chum
achainí do chur chum Feise na dTrí Rí ag iarraidh **saoirse** do
Chaitlicíbh.

11.x.1828: Chuas féin . . . go Butler Clerke . . . ag iarraidh air a ainm
do chur le Rá na Sasanach chum **saoirse** do thabhairt do na
Caitliceachaibh . . . Nach mór an trua clanna Gael ag iarraidh **saoirse**
mar dhéirc ina dtalamh dílis féin. Ach is iad féin do thuill an **daoirse**
dhochraideach se bheith orthu ag eachtrainn Ghallda tré a n-easaontas
féin ó aimsir Bhriain Bhóraimhe go Síocháin Uí Chonaill an lá eile.[58]

8.i.1828: The people of Callann are to send a petition to the British Parliament asking for complete Catholic Emancipation, without any bar-
gaining over matters of religion or the concession of any powers that we
have already and asking for the act against the landlords' agents to be
deferred . . . and asking for the emancipation of the Protestants (i.e.
Presbyterians) of England.

13.i.1828: We had a meeting today in the parish church to send a petition to the British Parliament asking for Catholic Emancipation.

11.x.1828: I went myself to Butler Clerke . . . asking him to sign the Protestant Declaration to give freedom to Catholics . . . Isn't it a great shame that the Irish are asking for freedom as if it were charity in their own country? But it is they themselves who have deserved this distressing enslavement at the hands of the English on account of their own lack of unity from the time of Brian Bórú to O'Connell's peace the other day.

In the third extract we note again the play of *saoirse* against *daoirse:* a contrast that continues to be exploited in the nineteenth century for rhetorical purposes.

Of further note in this same context of the 1820s is the Irish translation of an address by Daniel O'Connell to the people of Ireland on the dangers of joining secret societies. In the translation, the English 'Catholic Emancipation' of the original is referred to simply as *bhur saoirse* 'your freedom':

Gur b'iad na hiaragair riachtanach do leannas a samhail si, do thoirmeasgan an ditchiol dlisdineach do dheanaidhmid chum ar namhaid, na cealgbuidheachain d[o] chlaoidh, chum ur n-anacra do leasughadh—**bhur saoirse** do saothrughadh.[59]

That the necessary consequences of such disturbances and Whiteboy Societies is to impede our legal and constitutional exertions in our progress to put down the Orange faction, to obtain redress for many of the oppressions and grievances under which you labour, and, in fine, to achieve Catholic Emancipation.

Saoirse in the nineteenth century (2): 'The Spirit of the Nation'

The following poem by Mícheál Mac Carrtha from the 1840s appears to be an echo or a response to a poem published in 1844 entitled 'What Are Repealers?' by Edward Walsh with the subtitle 'Papa! What are Repealers?—MY SON'.[60] Mac Carrtha echoes this with his own title, 'Mamma, Am I a Repealer?' in a letter to Seán Ó Dálaigh (John O'Daly) dated 23 May 1846.

The use of capital letters is as in the manuscript.

Ag sinnim duit ranna na **saoirse**, a mhic,	Singing you the verses of freedom, my boy,
. . . Chun catha i n-aghaidh curtha na **daoirse**, a mhic	to do battle with the champions of slavery, my boy
Och! Péarla na mara má bhíonn, a mhic,	Och! If the Irish have the Pearl of the Sea, my boy,
Ag Gaedhlaibh mar bhaile 'n **saoirse**, a mhic,	as a home as their freedom, my boy,
'Na brollach gan ghruaim	In her breast without gloom
Nach séanmhar a suan	How peaceful their swoon

Is **SAOIRSE** agus tusa chun dín di, a mhic.[61]	and FREEDOM and you to protect her, my boy.

The word *saoirse* appears frequently in Mac Carrtha's poetry, as in the following excerpt from his lament for Thomas Davis ('Ar bhás Thomáis Dáibhis') which is composed in the finest bardic encomiastic tradition. Davis is described as the 'sage of sages' who would have won Ireland's 'freedom', a 'freedom' that will, however, never cease to be demanded (*a*) while his death is 'freedom's' loss (*b*)[62]:

(*a*)	'Saoi na suadh' a rug buadh na dréachta	Wisest of the wise who mastered the Muse
	saoi gan locht, is bocht liom traochta;	sage without fault I grieve he is laid low
	saoi do-gheóbhadh **saoirse** do Ghaedhlaibh,	the sage who would have achieved freedom for the Irish
	saoirse a bheidh choidhche **dá héileamh**.	freedom that will ever be demanded.

Note that this same verb *éileamh* 'demanding', 'to demand', was also used by Amhlaoibh Ó Súilleabháin in connection with the Catholics of the Low Countries 'demanding' their right to freedom. Again this is not a verb that could readily have combined with *saoirse* or *soíre* in the Early Irish period but represents a new and more democratic conceptualization of 'freedom'. A piece of syntax that becomes increasingly prevalent at this period is the use of *saoirse* in the genitive preceded by the definite article (here *na*):

(*b*)	Mo chreach gan tógaint, i gcomh rainn go tréith thú!	My grief without respite, in a coffin all spent
	mo chreach gan leigheas, ag leaghadh faoi chré thú!	My grief without remedy, you rotting in the ground!
	A chreach na saoithe, na **saoirse** is gach sean-nós	Loss of wise men, of freedom and every traditional practice
	is creach na dtáinte nár tháinig 'on tsaoghal fós.[63]	the loss of the many as yet unborn.

From the same period we have a lament for Daniel O'Connell by the poet Séamus Mac Cruitín in a letter sent by Domhnall Mac Connsaidín to Standish Hayes O'Grady. The poem is dated 1847 and is entitled 'Marbhna Dhomhnaill Uí Chonaill, Ceann-Tíorthach na hÉireann' ('Lament for Daniel O'Connell, the leader of Ireland'). Interestingly, the poem is written in a loose imitation of the classical *deibhí* metre, which passed out of general usage two centuries previously. Again O'Connell is eulogized in traditional terms and described as the 'protector of freedom and prosperity' for the Irish and the 'spirit of freedom, flower of the Irish':

Mairg do Ghaoidhil a ccómhlach catha	Alas for the Irish their mainstay of battle

a ccómhna **saoirse** 'gus deagh-ratha	their guardian of freedom and prosperity
aniúgh go tláth gan réim gan rian	laid low today without power or sway
fá chluithche-caointe a ccríoch imchian	lamented copiously in a foreign land
. . . Go bhfoillsigheadh an chruinne cian ré chéile . . .	Until the people of the earth might proclaim their sorrow together
méid a méala 'a ttruaighmhéile;	the extent of their grief and lamentation
'ndiaigh **spioraid na saoirse**, Bláth na nGaodhal	after the spirit of freedom, the Flower of the Irish
suan síorruídhe le saoghal na saoghal.[64]	eternal rest to him for ever and ever.

There are references to *saoirse* also in the writings of Irish emigrants in the nineteenth century. From a manuscript in Queen's University, Belfast, we have the following anonymous poem of exile written by an Irish emigrant in Dumfries in Scotland bearing the date 1848, 'Taoim Cásmhar a' Machtnamh am Aonar' ('I'm sorrowful, meditating alone'). In it the poet complains of the baleful effects of English rule in Ireland, particularly on the practice of poetry, which has declined:

> . . . mar neadaigh go buídheanmhar na Seóin do chéas sínn le rachtaibh na **daoirse** 'sle teaxana bíodhbhadh dár mbreó; is go mairiom le hamharc **ár saoirse**, agus gallaphuic claoidhte go deó.[65]

> . . . because the English have settled in force, who tormented us with the writ of slavery and crushed us with the taxes of criminals, so that we live for the sight of our freedom and eternal defeat of the foreign bucks.

We find here again the collective voice noted above in the case of Ó Neachtain. The following example is found in the Irish-American paper *An Gaodhal*, first issued in Brooklyn in 1881 by Mícheál Ó Lócháin from Co. Galway. The context is a poem written by one Seán Ó Ceallaigh from Co. Mayo on a place called Dalystown, in Irish Baile Bhós Dálaigh or Baile Mhuráid. The poet is praising the eponymous local leader Donncha Bhós Dálaigh, of whom he says:

> Fear fíor a thóig a ghuth le h-Onraoi Gratan
> A bh-feis dheighionach Ath-Chliath n-aghaidh díol air ór ann
> **Saoirse na hÉireann** do mhuintir na Sacsan.[66]

> A true man who raised his voice with Henry Grattan
> In the last Dublin parliament against the sale for gold
> Of Ireland's freedom to the people of England.

One further instance of *saoirse* from *An Gaodhal* will be discussed in the next section.

The new conception of 'saoirse'

I now consider further evidence that *saoirse* was being considered or reconsidered as something new in the eighteenth and nineteenth centuries. Item (i) is an example of how *saoirse* is used as a critique of earlier ideas within the tradition, while (ii) concerns other lexical items and formations that surface as alternatives to *saoirse*.

(i) From 'Táid cléir ag guí 's ag agall' ('The clerics are praying and preaching'), in a Maynooth manuscript:

(a)	Sin gártha ag Gaoil re haiteas	Thus shout the Irish for joy
	fághaid **saoirse** feasta	they'll get freedom from now on
	's a námhaid cloíte i dtreasaibh	their enemies defeated in the throes of death
	báis insa scléip;	in the fight;
	'S is fearr a maíomh sin measaim	And that's a lot more to shout about I reckon
	ná ráite baois an raiste	than the silly rantings of that waster
	Seán Ó Duibhir an Ghleanna	Seán Ó Duibhir an Ghleanna
	ag áireamh a ghéim.[67]	counting his game.

Note the derision expressed towards the traditional seventeenth-century song 'Seán Ó Duibhir an Ghleanna', part of which follows:

(b)	míle liú ag marcaighin	A thousand shouts from horsemen
	is bean go dúch sa mbealach	and a woman standing sadly in the way
	ag áireamh a cuid gé	counting her geese
	Anois tá an choill á gearradh	Now the wood is being felled
	triallfaimíd tar caladh	we'll go across the sea
	is a Sheáin Uí Dhuibhir an Ghleanna	and Seán Ó Duibhir an Ghleanna
	tá tú gan géim.	you are without your game.

The final part of the poem is put in the mouth of Seán Ó Duibhir himself:

	Anois táim ruaigthe óm fhearann . . .	Now I'm banished from my land . . .
	is mura bhfaigheadsa suaimhneas feasta	and if I don't get peace from now on
	is cead fuireach aige baile	and liberty to stay at home

| tréigfidh mé mo shealbh | I'll abandon my possessions |
| mo dhúthaigh is mo **réim**.[68] | my patrimony and my dominion. |

There is a sense in which 'Seán Ó Duibhir an Ghleanna' is about *saoirse* in its older, 'aristocratic' meaning, as discussed above, and its subsequent loss. The poem concerns one of the O'Dwyer's of Coill na Manach in Co. Tipperary who lost his lands as part of the Cromwellian settlement of the 1650s. Note how the words *réim* and *sealbh* are used in this context of dispossession, remembering their association with *saoirse* as discussed above. Particularly significant here is the way in which the later song turns the tables on 'Seán Ó Duibhir': in 'counting (the loss of) his game' he now assumes the pathetic pose of the woman in the original poem lamenting the loss of her geese to the depredations of Ó Duibhir's huntsmen. This hunting, with its attendant misery for others, was part of the landed notion of *saoirse*, especially as collocated with *réim*, but this has been superseded by a new idea, that the Irish people will get their own freedom, and will be indebted to no one else for it.

(ii) Another type of evidence that suggests a new concept of freedom is the existence of other forms alongside *saoirse* in the late eighteenth and early nineteenth centuries, notably *saorgacht* and *libeartaigh*:

> Is é fáth ár dtionóil anseo le fonn agus fíormhian ár dteanga mhilis mháthardha .i. an Ghaeilge ghéarfhoclach d'athnua agus do leasú; óir san am seo ina bhfuil príomhcheannaibh prionsúil agus fostaibh fíoruaisle ár dtíre **ag saothrú ár saorgacht** go fíordhíleas i mórdháil na hÉireann i mBaile Átha Cliath, is cuí agus is dlitheach dhúinne . . . cúnamh re chéile.[69]

> The reason that we are assembled here is the earnest desire to regenerate and reform our sweet mother tongue i.e. the keen-worded Irish; for at this time when our princely potentiaries and the noble representatives of our country are striving most faithfully for our freedom in the parliament of Ireland in Dublin it is right and fitting for us . . . to help each other.

We shall consider a further example of *saorgacht* below. More striking is Art Mac Bionaid's nativization of the English *liberty* in his historical tract *Comhrac na nGael agus na nGall le Chéile* (1850), already mentioned in chapter 2. In the text the word *libeartaigh* occurs thirteen times, as against once for *saoirse*. This preponderance is striking and indeed somewhat idiosyncratic, as far as I can tell, although, as we have seen before and will see again below, a form corresponding to English *liberty* is not unknown in Irish. I can only speculate that it is perhaps an indication that for some Irish-speakers in the eighteenth and nineteenth centuries *saoirse* still had too many of the older connotations of aristocratic privilege:

(*a*) An tse a thuitfidhis, tuitfidh se go glormhur a' trod air son an cheart, air son **libeartaigh** agus air son a thir dhuchas.

Whoever falls will fall gloriously fighting for right, for liberty and for his native land.

(b)   **libeartaigh a gcreidigh** agus seilbh siothchantach a dtalta[70]

freedom of religion and peaceful possession of their lands

However, alongside *libeartaigh a gcreidigh* Mac Bionaid also has the more conventional *saoirse*:

reim agus saoirse a gcreidigh, a dtalta 'fhaighil air ais a risd.[71]

the practice and freedom of their religion and their lands to be restored.

This last quotation from Mac Bionaid brings into relief a common collocation in the eighteenth century that again brings the old aristocratic connotations to the fore and perhaps provides a clue to why he preferred *libeartaigh*. The fuller quotations in each case have been given above:

reachtmas **gan réim** / gan talamh gan tréid **gan saoirse**

thug **saoirse is réim** do shaoithibh dréacht

Later we will consider some other alternatives to the word *saoirse* that were available in the late eighteenth and nineteenth centuries. It is worth noting at this point, however, that a form of the English 'liberty' seems to have enjoyed some currency in Irish in the sixteenth and seventeenth centuries. We have already seen the example of Fínghin Mac Carthaigh from this period, written in the Tower of London, to which the following pair of examples can be appended. Example (a) is from a poem of welcome composed by Eochaidh Ó hEodhasa in honour of the accession of King James I in 1603 'Mór theasda dh'obair Óivid' ('Much is wanting from Ovid's work). Among the benefits accruing from this development is the restoration of freedom or liberty of speech to the weak and timid:

(a)   Atá **libeirte a labhra**   The man who is timid of utterance
      'gun anbhfainne agallmha;   has freedom of speech;
      a bruth as éadána ar fhear,   its fury is gentle towards one
      guth na héagcára as íseal.[72]   the voice of injustice is subdued.

Example (b) is from a document entitled 'Cín Lae Ó Mealláin', or Ó Mealláin's Diary, a diary relating to the events of the war of the 1640s. The writer describes the arrival of Cardinal Rinuccini to Ireland in 1645 and the advice he gave to the Confederates in the following terms:

(b)   Tánic Ardesbog Parma .i. Nunntius Apostolicus go hÉirinn ó Phápa Innocentius X, mailli re hór, re hairgiod, agus re harmáil. A chomhuirle dhóibh gan síth do dhénamh re feruibh Sasan acht re **liberti coinnséis**, agus a nd[uthaidhe] féin don Egluis Catoilici.[73]

      The Archbishop of Parma, that is, the Apostolic Nuncio, came to Ireland from Pope Innocent X with gold, silver and munitions. His advice to

them was not to make peace with the English except in return for freedom of conscience and [the restoration of] its own lands to the Catholic
Church.

The various syntactic complements of 'liberty' here are of great interest, as they
show a 'modern' range that does not come to the fore with *saoirse* until later:
'freedom *of speech* or *of conscience*'. The importance of such complements will
be discussed below. For the moment, however, they make a fascinating comparison with the range of usage of *saoirse* itself in the early modern period.

Summary of eighteenth- and early nineteenth-century developments

What we see in the late eighteenth and early nineteenth centuries is a growing 'collectivization' or 'nationalization' of the word *saoirse:* the collocations
ár/bhur saoirse 'our/your (pl) freedom' appear for the first time. *Saoirse* is something that must be demanded and seized as the occasion arises. However,
saoirse also has a growing universal or international significance: as we have
seen, it is continuously related to contemporary events in other countries. In
addition, it is to come to Ireland from France and America. In the course of
the nineteenth century *saoirse* establishes itself conclusively as the word for
'national freedom' in Irish. The following are some examples from the period
1914–22, the period when Ireland's fight for independence reached a peak of
intensity:

(*a*)   gurab as an uaigh so agus as na huaghannaibh atá inar dtimcheall éire-
ochas **saoirse Ghaedheal**.

that it is from this grave and the graves around us that the freedom of
the Irish will rise.

(*b*)   agus an fhaid a théidheann mo thuiscint-se i stair na hÉireann, thuigeas
riamh go mbeadh **saoirse** againn nuair imeodh arm Shasana as an dtír.[74]

and as far as I understand Irish history, I have always thought that we
would have freedom when the English army left the country.

The following example is from the official correspondence between politicians
Eamon de Valera and David Lloyd George concerning the Treaty negotiations
of 1921. Note in the Irish how *saoirse* alternates with a new word, *neamhspleadhchas* 'independence', and how in turn 'independence', 'liberty' and 'freedom' are all used in the official translation to gloss *saoirse*:

Má théigheann ceart **saoirse an náisiúin bhig** [*a small nation's right to
independence*] ar cheal chomh luath is chuireann comhursa neartmhar
dúil 'san tír i gcomhair airm no pé buntáiste eile bheadh le baint as, sin
deireadh le **saoirse** [*an end to liberty*]. Ní fhéadfadh náisiún beag súil do
beith aici le **neamhspleadhchas** iomshlán [*a separate sovereign existence*]

feasta. D'fhéadfaidhe Tír fo Thuinn is Danmharc do chur fé smacht na Gearmáine, Flondras fé smacht na Gearmáine no na Frainnce, an Portainéal fé smacht na Spáinne. Náisiúin dár ceangladh d'impireachtaibh le neart fóiréigin, má chaillid a **neamhspleadhchas** dá dheascaibh, níl **aithbreith na saoirse** i ndán dóibh feasta [*no rebirth of freedom*] [75]

If a small nation's right to independence is forfeit when a more powerful neighbour covets its territory for the military or other advantages it is supposed to confer, there is an end to liberty. No longer can any small nation claim a right to a separate sovereign existence. Holland and Denmark can be made subservient to Germany, Belgium to Germany or to France, Portugal to Spain. If nations that have been forcibly annexed to empires lose thereby their title to independence, there can be for them no rebirth of freedom.

As will emerge in the following section, this sense of the 'nationalization' of *saoirse* is crucial to an analysis of its linguistic behaviour, which contrasts markedly with that of *freedom* in English.

Negative freedom in English and Irish

The foregoing sections on the semantics of *saoirse* have been a necessary preliminary to a thoroughgoing examination of more purely syntactic evidence and it is here that cross-linguistic considerations come into their own. Here we will concentrate on the English words *liberty* and *freedom* and the Polish word *wolność* 'freedom'. First we can look at 'negative' freedom in English ('freedom from') and the way in which the type of complement that this governs has changed in the history of English from (*a*) to (*b*):

(*a*)   Freedom from folly/childishness/losses/evils/cant

(*b*)   Freedom from tyranny/harassment/oppression/interruption

As Wierzbicka points out, this is in accordance with the development of individualism and liberalism in the nineteenth and twentieth centuries, whereby 'freedom from' denotes primarily the area where each individual should be free from interference or coercion on the part of another wilful agent.[76] This is why the collocations in (*a*) appear somewhat strange today. With the Polish word *wolność,* however, this type of expression is impossible in ordinary usage, and indeed the equivalent positive collocation 'freedom to' does not exist either:

*wolność do	freedom to
*wolność od	freedom from[77]

Where *wolność* is used productively, however, is in collocations where it is followed by a genitive of domain (as we saw with *saoirse* above):

wolność słowa	freedom of speech
wolność sumienia	freedom of conscience
wolność wyznania	freedom of religion[78]

For now, we establish the fact that the Polish *wolność* is syntactically much more restricted in range than its English 'counterpart' *freedom*. I will return to the significance of this, but first I want to revisit *saoirse* with regard to its historical syntax. As noted above, *saoirse* occurs with the prepositions *ar* and *ó* to signify 'freedom from'. Some examples:

(a) saoirse ar **bhuannacht**   freedom/exemption from billeting

(b) saoirsi . . . ar **oboir ┐** ar **shluaighedh ┐** ar gach **dáil ghábhuidh** ar cheana

   exemption from work, from mobilization and from other dangerous situations besides

(c) saoirsi . . . ar **olcaibh**   freedom from evils

(d) sairi o **na Dessib**   freedom from the Déise (a people of early Ireland)

(e) saorse ón **daorse**   freedom from slavery

(f) saoirse ar **phéin**[79]   freedom/relief from pain

Of course in some instances cultural change will have rendered the relevant complement naturally obsolete. It is interesting to consider these examples in relation to those given by Ó Dónaill above. The complements in the latter case all smack of legal exemption or immunity (from duty, taxation, service) and I would argue that *saoirse* in Irish today is not really equivalent to the Modern English notion of 'negative' freedom as freedom from interference, imposition and coercion on the part of another. This argument is somewhat speculative for want of a wider range of data, but my strong sense is that *saoirse ar/ó* is nowadays very much confined to legal language. In any case it is significant that in the texts of the period crucial to the present discussion (the eighteenth and nineteenth centuries) the word *saoirse* is either simply *saoirse* without any prepositional complement governed by *ó* or *ar* ('from') or, alternatively, takes a genitive complement (for example *saoirse na hÉireann*) or an adjectival one (*saoirse Chaitliceach*). It is particularly noteworthy that phrases like *saoirse ó dhaoirse* 'freedom from slavery' no longer occur (our example above was from the seventeenth century), even though the equivalent adjective *saor* continues to occur in this way in the late eighteenth and nineteenth centuries:

> Biaidh an fearann so Éireann **saor ó shraithibh**[80]

> This land of Ireland will be free of taxes.

As with the syntactic restrictions on Polish *wolność*, this fact speaks to the growing elevation and abstractness of *saoirse* as a concept in this period.

Positive freedom in Irish: *'cead'* and *'saorchead'*

As regards 'positive' freedom ('freedom to'), *saoirse,* from a historical viewpoint at least, has no part of it in Irish. Nevertheless, the phrase *saoirse chun* occurs in the Constitution of Ireland:

> Ní theorannóidh an fo-alt seo **saoirse chun taisteal** [*freedom to travel*] idir an Stát agus stát eile.[81]

> This sub-paragraph will not restrict the freedom to travel between the State and another state.

This usage, however, is not in keeping with historical practice. Note further that article 44 has both *saoirse* and the compound *saorchead,* a compound of *saor* 'free' and *cead* 'permission':

> Ráthaítear do gach saoránach **saoirse** choinsiasa is **saorchead** admhála is cleachta creidimh [*freedom of conscience and the free profession and practice of religion*], ach gan san a dhul chun dochair don ord phoiblí ná don mhoráltacht phoiblí.[82]

> Every citizen is guaranteed freedom of conscience and the free profession and practice of religion as long as these do not damage the public order or public morality.

We can say here that *saoirse* indicates a more abstract *domain* of freedom, whereas *saorchead* denotes a specific *target* of freedom, even though syntactically it takes the genitive as well. Otherwise *saorchead* takes the preposition *chun* 'to', as in the following eighteenth-century example (*a*) from the Co. Clare poet Tomás Ó Míocháin, and in two instances from the nineteenth century, (*b*) Amhlaoibh Ó Súilleabháin addressing an anti-tithe demonstration in Bally-hale, Co. Kilkenny in 1832 and (*c*) the Armagh scribe Art Mac Bionaid:

(*a*) Ag seo **saorchead** sona le síothoilteacht **do** Phádraig uasal Ó Conaill **chum** siúil is síorimtheachta ar feadh poibleacha prionsabálta príomhchreidimh in Éirinn.

This is full liberty with good grace for noble Patrick O'Connell to walk and traverse forever the principal communities of the primary religion in Ireland.

(*b*) Do seasadar na Caitilıcıghe amach a Luimneach go laidir an aghaidh na h-Orange go bhfuaradar geallamhain o Rig Uilliam **saorchead** tradála, **cead** léas fada eastait do cheannach, agus os cionn gach uile nidh, **cead** ar cCreidimh.

The Catholics held out strongly in Limerick against the Orangemen until they received from King William a pledge of freedom of trade, freedom to purchase long leases of estates and, above all else, the freedom of our religion.

(c)   D'iarr an Seursalach **cead saoir** oca um a gcreideamh a leanmhun.[83]

Sarsfield requested that they should have full liberty to follow their religion.

Note the variation here: (i) the lexical choice between *cead, saorchead* and *cead saor* and (ii) the choice between a genitive noun and a verbal noun clause complement. *Cead* ('permission', 'leave' or 'licence') is the basic lexeme, with *saor* (the adjective 'free') functioning as an intensifier to produce *saorchead*. The compound *saorchead,* as opposed to the simplex *cead,* is now obsolete in Irish, but in fact both words correspond very closely to a use of *liberty* in English in the eighteenth and nineteenth centuries, in particular the phrase 'full liberty'.[84] Note again the variation in syntax between complements governed by *to* and *of*:

You have my **full liberty** [*saorchead*] *to* publish them (1749)

Bid him come in and wait for **liberty** [*cead*] *to* talk (1833)

You have the **liberty** *of* doing so (1796)

The basic notion here is clearly that of *cead,* which the dictionaries gloss as 'permission', 'leave', 'licence'. The word is found in the text of the sixteenth-century treaty between O'Donnell and Argyll which we considered briefly in chapter 2. Here *cead trialla* signifies the 'freedom to leave':

costus na luinge ꞂＺ na marinell agus a tuarusdil do bheth ar On Domhnaill o do fhágfas cala no port an Albainn no go bhfaghann **cead trialla** o Erinn.[85]

on O'Donnell who shall also bear the cost of the ship, the mariners and their pay from the time it shall leave harbour or port in Scotland till it is free to leave Ireland.

For contemporary Irish, here are some dictionary examples from Ó Dónaill:

(a)	**saorchead** a bheith agat le rud a dhéanamh	to be quite at liberty to do something
(b)	**saorchead** isteach[86]	free admission/freedom of access

Note the way Irish handles the idea of individual (physical) 'freedom to' by using a body metaphor in the genitive preceded by *cead*:

(c)	**cead a chinn** a thabhairt do dhuine	to let someone go free, have his own way
	ligeadh **cead a chinn** leis	he was set free
	cead a choise a thabhairt dó	to let him move about, go where he pleases
	ó tá **cead ár gcos** againn	since we are foot-loose
	bíodh **cead a shróine** aige	let him follow his nose
	tá **cead a rith is a léim** aige[87]	he is free to disport himself as he pleases

Here we have *cead a chinn* (genitive of *ceann* 'head') meaning 'freedom (to follow) his head'. Similarly *cead a choise* (genitive of *cos* 'foot') means 'freedom (to follow) his foot', or *cead ár gcos* (genitive plural of *cos*) 'freedom (to follow) our feet' or go wherever our feet take us; *cead a shróine* (genitive of *srón*) 'freedom (to follow) his nose'. It is interesting and revealing in particular to compare (*d*) and (*e*) below, where *cead* is followed by a genitive, with the equivalent syntactic configuration featuring *saoirse*, such as was given above:

(*d*)   **cead** imeartha/taistil/staidéir   permission to play/travel/study

(*e*)   **cead** cainte   leave to speak

Again we see that *cead* refers to a particular or specific target of freedom, whereas *saoirse* consistently denotes a more abstract, idealized or universal domain of freedom. Compare in particular *cead cainte* 'leave/permission/freedom **to speak**', i.e. in a specific case or on a particular occasion, with *saoirse cainte* 'freedom **of speech**', which is conceived of in less specific, more universal terms.

Although the locus of *cead* and *saoirse* is positive and negative freedom, respectively, there is some indication that in certain collocations at least there is some historical overlap. In the following eighteenth-century example, compare Ó Míocháin's use of (*a*) *cead féir is uisce* and (*b*) *saoirse féir is fearainn* in very similar contexts.[88] In (*a*) the poet speaks of the reign of plenty that Ireland will experience under its lawful, faithful spouse, the Stuart Pretender, while in (*b*) he looks forward to the day when poets and bards will be free from imposition:

(*a*)   Beidh **réim** ag filí, is go saol an   Poets will hold sway and till
            iolair   doomsday
          Cead féir is uisce ag Gaelaibh,   the Irish will have the freedom of
                                                                               land and water,
          Is na géaga ag filleadh re héigean   the branches will bend low with
            duille   the weight of their foliage
          Is na héisc ag lingeadh as a líon-   the fish leaping from their pools.
            taibh.

(*b*)   Cé docht bhur gcéim ag plé le cíos,   Though difficult your situation
                                                                               concerning rent,
          gan **réim** ag ríomh le maoraibh   without power in dealing with
            measta,   bailiffs,
          Is feas i ngaobhar dhaoibh séan is   you know that prosperity and
            síth,   peace are close at hand,
          Saorgacht, saoirse féir is fearainn. Freedom, liberty of land and
                                                                               territory.

It is difficult to establish any functional distinction between *saoirse* and *cead* in these contexts: from a historical viewpoint one could perhaps argue that *saoirse féir is fearainn* emphasizes the 'negative' aspect of a freedom from outside imposition, whereas *cead* represents the 'positive' aspect of a freedom to dispose of the land as we ourselves wish, to be our own masters, in other words. However, from a semantic-referential viewpoint the two uses are so close as to be, in this context, virtually indistinguishable. Once again, the close association of *réim* with words denoting ideas of 'freedom' should be noted in these passages.

That is, however, emphatically not the case in a poem published almost exactly a century later, entitled 'A mbeidh ar dtír mhocht [*sic*] áluinn saor *go deo?*' ('Will our poor beautiful country ever be free?'), which appeared in *An Gaodhal* in November 1885. The author, who styles himself 'Gall Gaodhal', criticizes precisely this narrow, economically based idea of what *saoirse* entails. Specifically he attacks

> Daoinibh nach bh-feiceann insa bh-focal '**Saoirse**'
> acht cead a n-ainmhianta féin do dheunamh:—
> 'Talamh gan cíos' a's gach nidh bun os cionn.[89]

> People who see nothing in the word 'Freedom'
> but leave to exercise their own passions:
> 'Land without rent' and everything upside down.

It is particularly interesting to see the word *cead* used here where, qualified by the noun *ainmhianta* 'immoderate desires', 'passions', it emerges as somehow the antithesis of what the writer feels that *saoirse* should consist of:

> Clann len-a g-croidhthibh lán de **spioraid fíor
> na saoirse**:—clann ag nach m-béidh mímheas
> air neithibh bhaineas lena sliocht 'sa d-tír,—
> Clann mar na daoinibh rinne saor an Ghréig,
> nár chleachd aon teanga acht a d-teanga féin
> nár chrom a nglún roimh neart a m-buaidhtheoir,
> nár fhiafruigh a **saoirse** acht le claidheamh a's lainn
> 's nár fhóghluim caint na námhad a sgrios iad![90]

> Children with their hearts full of the true spirit
> of freedom—children who will not despise
> what pertains to their ancestry and their country—
> Children like those who liberated Greece
> who spoke no language but their own
> who refused to bend the knee to the strength of their conqueror
> who sought freedom only by means of a sword and sharp blade
> who did not learn the language of the enemy that destroyed them!

Essentially it is a question of the right national values: Ireland will not have freedom until it has children worthy of their heritage, most especially their linguistic heritage.

'Toil shaor' and *'saorthoil'*

Another usage worthy of comment in relation to 'positive freedom' in Irish centres on the word *toil* 'will' used in conjunction with the adjective *saor* 'free'. This appears either compounded as *saorthoil* or as *toil shaor* with the normal order of Irish, where adjective follows noun. Literally therefore this means 'free will', but in context it sometimes translates more naturally as 'freedom', for example 'freedom to procreate', as in the eighteenth-century *Cúirt an Mheán Oíche*:

> D'óg is d'aosta **saorthoil** síolraigh.   Of sexual freedom for young and
> for old.
> Cuirfidh an dlí seo gaois   This new law will make the Irish
>   í nGaelaibh.[91]   proud.

On 1 April 1798 the Bishop of Elphin, Dr Edmund French, sent a pastoral letter to the clergy of his diocese to be read in every church as a caution to the general Catholic population on the dangers of sedition and rebellion. This letter appears in a manuscript now in the Royal Irish Academy (23 B 27), Dublin, with an Irish translation appended. The scribe in both instances is Mícheál Ó Braonáin, who may well have been the translator. In any case the translation can be taken as more or less contemporary with the English original. In one part of the letter *saorthoil* is used to gloss *liberty*:

> Cuirídh i gcéill da bhuir dtréada, ma ta meas no uráim dha laíghead acu ar **sháorthoil**, ar mháoin, no air inmhe shaogalta . . . ar choínnsías no air chreidiodh . . . íad féin d'íomchur go ceart cneasda céannsaidh ceatúil, is íad féin a chuiméad go róighríonalach ar gan i bheog no mhór do dh'áisíamplairidhe miosguiseacha no do chealgaireacht thrúaillidh lucht easáird.[92]

> Signifie to them that if the least regard for **liberty**, property . . . or conscience lies centred in their breast . . . the least spark of religion . . . let their conduct carry with it a marked guard against seditious men.

It is interesting to note that the word *saoirse* is also used in this letter but in its most traditional, conservative sense of a favour, privilege or immunity conferred, in this case by King George III, as a reward to his subjects for the allegiance due to him:

> do thug dhúinn moran **sáorsadh** agus muínteardhuis agus soin go léir mar chúitiúghadh i n-éiric íonracuis agus dísleadh bhuir sinnsir da ríghthe. Ata se cinntidh gur **sáorsa** agus cumáoineacha íad so nach raibh suil agáinn fhághail.[93]

> a principle of gratitude to the best of kings and benign legislature which have extended to us **immunities** and conferred on us favours in reward for the fidelity of our ancestors which they in the height even of their allegiance did not . . . expect.

This theme of the allegiance due to the king by divine right is very much the tenor of the letter and it is in that context that the use of *saorsa* (*saoirse*) and indeed *saorthoil* is to be understood here. A contrasting example is a contemporary poem of uncertain authorship on the French Revolution and its aftermath which appears in a manuscript compiled in Dundalk in the 1820s: 'Tá na Franncaigh san am so 'cur céim ar gcúl' ('The French at this time are setting privilege aside'). The poem begins by proclaiming the spread of French egalitarianism into the neighbouring regions of Flanders and the Rhineland. This presages the downfall of kings and tyrants everywhere:

> Ní bhíonn Laoighseach nó rí eile ó'n aimsir so suas
> Ins na críochaibh 'cur **daoirse** ar gach deaghmhac go buan;
> Béidh na daoine lán críonacht gan ghéibheann, gan ghuais,
> 'S **toil shaor** ag Chlanna Mhílidh le séan go Lá an Luain.[94]

> Neither Louis nor any other king in any country from this time on
> will ever oppress each good citizen;
> the people will be wise without enslavement, without peril,
> and the Irish will have freedom and prosperity till the end of time.

Literally 'the Irish will have *free will* and prosperity till the end of time'. This could perhaps be accommodated within the discussion above of the use of words like *libeartaigh* and *saorgacht* as alternatives to *saoirse* in the late eighteenth and early nineteenth centuries; perhaps the poet here was consciously looking for an expression of 'positive freedom' that he felt was absent from *saoirse*, particularly in view of the very traditional way in which that word could still be used, on the evidence of French's pastoral letter. However, it must be pointed out that *saoirse* in the late eighteenth and early nineteenth centuries can indeed translate *liberty*, as in (*a*) a sermon by Bishop William Gahan on habitual sin from 1799 and (*b*) in the text of O'Connell's address of 1824 already referred to:

(*a*)   aisig orainn **saoirse** mhilis do chlainne ionus go bhforálfamaois iodhbairt altaighthe duit

   restore us to the sweet liberty of Thy children that we may sacrifice to Thee a host of Thanksgiving

(*b*)   Ta fear ionaid an Riogh fein aguinn, flath uasal oirdhearc d'ar ttir fein, agus do ghradhas a thir dhuthchais . . . agus mar b'e a mhian duthrachtach síth, sonus agus **saoirse** d'achtugadh dhi.[95]

   We have, for Lord Lieutenant, an Irish Nobleman who loves the land of his birth . . . and who is sincerely solicitous to give her peace, quiet, liberty and happiness.

In general, however, collocations with *toil* are not as central to the idea of 'positive freedom' in everyday Irish usage as those containing *cead*.

On the syntax of 'freedom' in various languages

Having looked at both the Irish *saoirse* and the Polish *wolność* from a syntactic viewpoint, we now take a brief look at the somewhat complex position of *liberty* and *freedom* in English, complex from the historical point of view at least. First let us consider a comparison of the historical ranges of (*a*) *liberty* and (*b*) *freedom*:

(i) Exemption or release from captivity, bondage or slavery (the personal sphere):

(*a*)   that vnto **libertie Fro** thraidam han vs gwit (1410)

This libertie which Christians have, is a spirituall **libertie** . . . a **liberty of the soul** . . . which setteth the soul **at liberty from** destruction (1604)

(*b*)   the other **uridom** is the ilke thet habbeth the guodemen . . . thet god heth yuryd . . . uram the threldome of the dyeule (1340)[96]

In this sense 'freedom' is glossed as 'personal liberty', just as *saoirse* is in relation to *daoirse*.

(ii) Exemption from arbitrary despotic or autocratic rule or control (the civil sphere):

(*a*)   **Libertie** of conscience (1572)

The **Liberty of Man**, in Society, is to be under no other Legislative Power, but that established by Consent in the Commonwealth (1690)

(*b*)   **Freedom** consists in a people's being governed by laws made with their own consent (1725)[97]

In respect of (a) above, recall the Irish collocation *liberti coinnséis* from the early seventeenth century, discussed above.

(iii) The state of being able to act without hindrance or restraint; the faculty or power to do as one likes; free opportunity, range or scope to do (obsolete *of doing*) something; hence 'leave', 'permission' (i.e. 'freedom/liberty *to*'):

(*a*)   He kept his **libertie** to do justice and equite (1390)

I enjoy Large **liberty** to round this Globe of the Earth (1671)

(*b*)   Fissches that han **fredom** to enviroun all the Costes of the Sea, at here owne liste (1400)

As we have seen, this domain of the concept 'freedom' is not covered by Irish *saoirse* at any period but is rather the province of *cead* and *toil*.

(iv) The state of not being affected by (a defect, disadvantage, etc.); exemption *from* a specific burden, charge or service; an immunity, privilege (older Irish *soíre/sairse*). This is exclusively the domain of *freedom* in English, as opposed to *liberty*, and we have seen that this is also the *locus classicus* historically of *saoirse* in Irish:

> Though age **from folly** could not give me **freedom**
> It does **from childishnesse** (1606)

> promising to the doers long life, health . . . **freedome** from losses, and the like (1614)

> the contemplation of our own **freedom** from the evils which we see represented (1756)

> there is a **freedom** from cant about the authoress (1823)

> **freedom** from arrest, a privilege at that time necessary for the cause of liberty (1839)

> the **freedom** from interruption he thought essential for his work (1991)

There is also the area of contact between *franchise, liberty* and Irish *saoirse* in the medieval period referring to the domain or district over which the privilege of a corporation, individual or clan extends.

Wierzbicka argues that English *freedom* is essentially the freedom from imposition or interference and is therefore unlike Latin *libertas* (and indeed unlike English *liberty*, generally speaking). There are two aspects of the concept of 'negative' freedom as analysed by Wierzbicka:

(*a*)   'if I don't want to do something then I don't have to'

(*b*)   'if I want to do something, I can: you can't say: "you can't do it"'[98]

This is reflected in syntax: *freedom from* as well as *to* or *of*; the range of complements permitted to *freedom from* has changed since the seventeenth or eighteenth centuries to where they now must refer to interference for which others can be held responsible. The important point is that this freedom from interference is a universal that therefore rules out the concept of 'doing anything I want'.

The essential syntactic property of the word *freedom* is that it takes the preposition *from*, which *liberty* in its ordinary usage does not. Though *freedom from* has been possible in English for centuries, the range of complements has shifted. Thus earlier English has phrases like:

> freedom from folly/childishnesse/losses/evils/cant

whereas in Modern English the prepositional phrase should include an expression that indicates outside interference or coercion:

> freedom from tyranny/harassment/oppression/interruption

In Wierzbicka's view, the negative semantics of *freedom* thus express the ideal of non-imposition in Anglophone culture.

On the other hand, as Wierzbicka argues, the English word *liberty* in the eighteenth century denoted primarily the opposite of slavery and oppression (like French *liberté*). It is the rise of democracy in the Anglophone world (Britain and America) and the growth of individualism and the concept of individual rights that has led to its being superseded by *freedom* in the sense of opposition to interference and imposition. The semantic range of *liberty* has consequently contracted and is now specialized as 'public rights' within given structures as 'a word for an abstract ideal'. So *freedom* in Modern English essentially concerns the private domain, *liberty* the public. Nouns of this 'public' kind tend to be very limited in the types of syntactic complements or prepositional phrases they can govern: they refer to an 'unquestionable (moral) value judgement', and this is a concomitant of a narrowing in meaning. In general the collocation *liberty **from*** does not occur, although Wierzbicka notes the following from a treatise on legal philosophy (given in the *Oxford English Dictionary*) that does not necessarily correspond, therefore, to normal usage:

> Political or civil **liberty** is the **liberty from** legal obligation which is left or granted by a sovereign government to any of its subjects (1832)[99]

In earlier usage *liberty* at times approaches the force of 'permission'. In the first example especially we are in the realm of Irish *saorchead,* as we have seen:

> You have my **full liberty** to publish them (1749)
>
> You have the **liberty** of doing so (1796)
>
> Bid him come in and wait for **liberty** to talk (1833)

The earlier range of English *freedom* is closer to *liberty* without the 'negative' concept associated with *freedom* later: the older concept of *freedom* makes no reference to things one doesn't want to do. Note the following examples and especially the conjoining of *freedom* and *liberty* in the earlier period:

> They died for the **Libertie and Freedom** of their Cittie (1606)
>
> **Fredome and lyberte** is better than ony gold or syluer (1484)

The following examples are reminiscent of earlier uses of *saoirse* as a privilege and recall the Irish *saoirse dúthaighe* discussed above:

> Hee would not permit Merchants and Sea-men to enjoy a **freedom of that Sea** . . . but at an extraordinairie rate (1652)
>
> All Foreigners might freely come and reside in any part of the Kingdom with the like **Privileges and Freedoms** as ourselves (1719)

This last example in particular recalls early Modern Irish collocations such as *cinseal agus saoirse* or *réim agus saoirse* 'power and privilege'. In general, therefore, the meaning of *freedom* has changed in the 'negative' direction: the older meaning does not refer to things we don't want to do or to the attempts of others to stop us doing what we want to.

We can now summarize the syntactic formulas that pertain to the various words under consideration (the asterisk signifies that the particular usage does not occur or is less likely to occur):[100]

	liberty	**freedom**
(a)	*liberty from	freedom from
(b)	liberty to	freedom to
(c)	liberty of	freedom of

	wolność	**saoirse**
(a)	*wolność od	*saoirse ó/ar
(b)	*wolność do	*saoirse chun/le (cead chun/le)
(c)	wolność (+ gen.)	saoirse (+ gen.)

Bearing in mind the salience of *freedom from* in English, it is worth noting that other languages do not allow this combination, such as (a) Latin and (b) Russian:

(a)   *libertas a/ab

(b)   *volja ot

Note also the impossibility of the following collocations in Irish using *saoirse* against their acceptability with English *freedom*:

*saoirse rogha   freedom of choice

*mothú/braistint saoirse a feeling of (personal) freedom

A few concluding remarks are in order on the shifting historical range of *saoirse*. In (a) below, *saoirse* has the sense of 'relief' from illness or fever or 'respite' from something; in (b) the meaning is that of 'costing nothing', which sense Irish still has but only with the adjective *saor*:[101]

(a)   gibe fiabrus bhios ar neach ⁊ gan **saoirsi** d'fhaghail . . . an treas la

whatever fever a person has, if they do not get relief the third day

níor chorruigh a chroidhe chum **saoirse** dhéanamh

his heart was not moved to grant respite

(b)   ní ar iasacht . . . ná ar **sóirse** . . . fuair an tsaoi úd fíriúil fóirfe

It was neither by borrowing . . . nor was it for nothing that that eminent true perfect sage acquired his skill . . .

Saoirse could not be used in either of these senses today. Sense (b) arises from the 'negative' idea of freedom, specifically the sense of exemption, in this case exemption from cost. Although this use of the adjective exists in English and Irish, it does not exist in a number of languages.[102]

To return to the question of genitive noun complements governed by *saoirse* (i.e. 'freedom **of**'), the following are some historical examples of such complements:

(*a*) na saoirse **cóigidh**

the provincial liberties

(*b*) ar shaoirsi & ar shochar **dúthaighe** do fein

the freedom and profits of an estate for himself

(*c*) saoirse **féir is fearainn**

freedom of territory (i.e. to have it free of rent)

(*d*) soirsi **priomh-locha, & priomh-aibhne** Ereann do thraighthechaibh & mharcachaibh

the freedom of the chief lakes and the chief rivers of Ireland to footmen and horsemen (i.e. the chief lakes and the chief rivers of Ireland were passable to travellers on foot and horsemen)

(*e*) saoirse a **gcreidigh**[103]

the freedom of their religion

Item (*a*) is unusual in that it seems to involve a plural that is otherwise unattested for *saoirse*. A plural is quite apposite in translation: 'the provincial liberties'. Items (*b*) to (*d*) involve aspects of the physical landscape to quite different effect. Both (*b*) and (*c*) concern, once again, the largely aristocratic right to dispose of land as one's own property without interference from outside, whereas (*d*) merely refers to the fact that in the year 854 a hard freeze had made the rivers and lakes of Ireland passable by foot and on horseback—*saoirse* here means something like 'passage'. On the other hand (*e*), from the nineteenth century, is recognizably modern and would be accepted usage today: 'freedom of religion'. This fits in with the types of complements given above from Ó Dónaill's dictionary, which I rehearse here:

Saoirse		
	(*a*) **na tíre**	freedom of the country (political independence)
	(*b*) **an duine**	of the individual
	(*c*) **cainte**	of speech
	(*d*) **coinsiasa**	of conscience

There is a superficial similarity here between twentieth-century *saoirse na tíre* and seventeenth-century *saoirse dúthaighe*: the former indicates political independence for a country from foreign domination, the latter denotes the freedom of a particular individual to enjoy the country free from imposition. Note that the range of complements is morally and ethically more 'elevated' in Modern Irish, as it is in Polish, and in conclusion I now want to tease out the implications of this.

As was indicated above, Polish *wolność* has a much narrower syntactic range of uses than English *freedom,* being inextricably and irrevocably linked to the struggle for national independence in Poland after the partitions of 1773–95. This lofty and morally exalted connotation seriously limits the syntactic freedom of this particular word in Polish: in other words, it is felt to refer to an idealized state more acutely than English *freedom*, which can also encompass more 'everyday' types of 'freedom'. Thus the collocations associated with both positive ('to') and negative ('from') freedom in English are at best rare and at worst non-existent in Polish, as we have seen.

These types of freedom as expressed in Polish all apply to the individual, but Wierzbicka's crucial point is that the salient meaning of *wolność* fuses the individual and the public or national: the very mention of the word is resonant above all of a fight for national freedom in a way that English *freedom* in Anglophone culture is not. In this way what Wierzbicka terms the vital personal 'freedoms'—religion, speech and conscience—are inseparably linked to public and national 'freedom'. It is a striking fact—and not, I think, a coincidence—that these three vital 'freedoms' are precisely those given by Ó Dónaill in his dictionary.

Wierzbicka's analysis of the Polish evidence, therefore, is what I am proposing for Irish *saoirse*. It seems to me that the crucial point in the comparison between *saoirse* and *freedom* is arrived at precisely at that moment when in the English-speaking world *freedom* and *liberty* begin to diverge—where, under the influence of the 'negative' concept of non-imposition associated with *freedom*, the word *liberty* takes on more abstract, less 'individual' connotations than *freedom*.[104] In earlier English, *liberty* and *freedom* are much closer concepts, as can be seen from their syntactic behaviour, which was summarized briefly above. In its turn, Irish *saoirse* before 1798 is close to this unified idea of *liberty–freedom*, whereas in the nineteenth century it goes in the opposite direction to *freedom* and becomes more of an abstract term for an ideal state that has less individual and more national connotations.

Thus *saoirse* in Irish has nothing to do with the English idea of *freedom* as representing options, nor with relatively 'trivial' freedoms such as 'the freedom to roam around'. It also has little to do with 'feeling free' or at ease, as noted above. Historically, the timing of this divergence is provocative as has been suggested: the growth of individualism and individual rights in Britain, as against the growth of mass political awareness in Ireland. We can see here the operation of the culturally specific within a more universal dimension. The general development of Irish *saoirse* has obvious analogues in the development of English *freedom* and Polish *wolność*. This is part of the general process of what Hughes calls the 'democratization' of the language of legal privilege (feudalism).[105] What we have seen, however, is that within this general paradigm of change the range, denotation and connotation of 'freedom' in different languages reflect directly the historical experience of the speakers of those languages.

Summary of the syntactic evidence

The essential linguistic facts about *saoirse* as an expression of 'national freedom' as opposed to 'individual freedom' in Irish are:

(i)   The virtually complete absence of the possibility of saying 'freedom to' using *saoirse* (Irish historically uses *cead* or *saorchead*). This apparently extends even to the adjective *saor*. Thus *saoirse* is excluded from relatively 'everyday' types of 'freedom' (of movement, access, etc.).

(ii)   The marginalization of the collocation *saoirse ar/ó* 'freedom from' in the modern period: note that all Ó Dónaill's examples relate to externally imposed 'legal' obligations (taxes, duty, service). This relates both to the historical practice in Irish and to the typical range of arguments governed by *freedom from* in Modern English, which has also changed and become limited to the idea of non-imposition or interference from others (oppression, persecution, tyranny, coercion). This, however, is more marginal in Irish today, compared both with English and with earlier usage in Irish itself.

(iii)   The change in the types of domain words governed by *saoirse* to a higher moral level compared both with earlier Irish and with Modern English (so, for example, 'freedom of action/trade' are impossible with *saoirse* in Modern Irish).

In these respects, Irish *saoirse* is linguistically closer to the range of another 'national freedom' word, *wolność* in Polish, than to *freedom* in English.

Appendix: towards a typology of 'freedom'

Based on our discussion of Irish *saoirse* and Wierzbicka's discussion of 'freedom' words in various languages, the following notes are a first attempt to incorporate Irish within a cross-linguistic 'typology of 'freedom'. We should keep the following characterizations in mind as representing culturally salient rather than exclusive meanings.

(1)   a. English *freedom*: the individual's right to be left alone (opposed to 'interference')
        b. Russian *volja*: the individual's right to be physically free (opposed to *tjurma* 'prison')

(2)   a. Irish *saoirse* and
        b. Polish *wolność*: the collective right to independence

(3)   Japanese *jiyū*: 'freedom' viewed critically or with puzzlement (opposed to *amae* 'loving dependence')

Both Russian *volja* and the Polish *wolność* are reflexes of the Indo-European root *wel-* 'will', 'wish', which gives English *will*, Latin *volo* 'I want' and *voluptas* 'pleasure'. So originally this is 'freedom' as 'will', i.e. 'positive freedom'. In addition, both Russian and Polish have a further word for 'freedom', *svoboda* and *swoboda*, respectively, which seems to embody a more neutral, less charged type of 'freedom'. Russian *svoboda* in particular characterizes an ease or absence of restraint. Japanese *jiyū* traditionally embodies a concept that is alien to the central Japanese values of *amae* 'loving dependence', *enryo* 'non-assertiveness', *on* 'infinite indebtedness to others', and *giri* 'obligation to others'.

One particularly interesting feature of the Irish–Polish comparison is the fact that the items in question have converged in response to comparable historical circumstances: *saoirse* is a form of negative freedom, *wolność* originally a positive notion of the will. This is evidenced by the fact that in sixteenth-century Polish the expression

   wolność k temu   the freedom to do so

was perfectly idiomatic. In addition, it is in relation to this period that the expression

   Zlota Wolność   'Golden Freedom'

came to characterize a period of unparalleled freedom, and the abuse thereof by the Polish nobility. There is an obvious parallel here with the earlier senses of *saoirse* discussed above, but the salient idea in Irish culture is one of negative freedom, or 'exemption/immunity from'. This convergence from two 'opposite' semantic directions is in itself good evidence for the influence of historical experience on linguistic communities. We could summarize an initial typology as follows (non-Irish evidence again from Wierzbicka).

In conclusion, I turn to a further recent critique by Skinner of Berlin's two concepts of freedom.[106] Skinner draws attention to a particular difficulty with Berlin's treatment of positive freedom, in that he fails to isolate it as a concept separate from negative freedom; i.e. one that is completely independent of the absence of constraint. It turns out that this latter type of freedom is tantamount to something like complete self-realization (and Skinner discusses the immediate intellectual tradition that underlies Berlin's analysis). More importantly, however, he resuscitates an alternative view of the nature of negative freedom, one that was current among the seventeenth-century English Parliamentarians, whereby the mere awareness of one's dependence on the (arbitrary) good will of others constitutes a restraint on freedom. This is precisely the argument to be used against the remarks of Berlin and Roberts cited above. This theory of freedom, as Skinner points out, is ultimately derived from the Roman distinction between slavery and freedom, the idea of being entirely in one's own power. Therein lies the crucial difference between freedom as a right and freedom as licences or privileges that can be revoked at the discretion of another. The only viable political solution in this view is the self-governing republic that reflects the wishes of all its citizenry. This is, in effect, a third concept of liberty, and it is this concept which has greatest relevance to national independence movements, as Skinner expressly points out

NATIONAL/COLLECTIVE	INDIVIDUAL
IRISH **saoirse**	ENGLISH **freedom**. Has the greatest semantic and syntactic freedom. Both 'positive' and 'negative' freedom.
	RUSSIAN **volja**. Specifically opposed to **tjurma** 'prison'.
POLISH **wolność**	RUSSIAN **svoboda**. Opposed to **stesnenie** 'constriction', 'tightness'. Idea of 'boundless space' in which to operate.
Characterized by significant syntactic constrictions on everyday usage.	
Also restricted to individual freedom of the more 'elevated' or 'morally charged' type.	POLISH **swoboda**. More 'everyday' types of 'freedom' than '**wolność**'.
	IRISH **cead/saorchead**. 'Positive freedom' ('to'). Again more 'everyday' types of 'freedom' than **saoirse**.
	JAPANESE **jiyū**. Regarded as antisocial. Opposed especially to **amae** (loving dependence).

and Berlin seeks essentially to deny. I believe that a close, comparative linguistic analysis of Irish and Polish on the one hand, and English on the other, bears out Skinner's conclusions as well.

NOTES

Introduction

1. For the relationship between linguistics and anthropology see Duranti, *Linguistic Anthropology*, Foley, *Anthropological Linguistics: An Introduction*, Palmer, *Towards a Theory of Cultural Linguistics*. For a discussion of the relevant terminology (i.e. 'anthropological linguistics' v. 'linguistic anthropology') see Duranti, 'Linguistic anthropology: history, ideas and issues', in Duranti (ed.), *Linguistic Anthropology: A Reader*, pp. 1–38.
2. Ibid., pp .1–2.
3. Watkins, 'New parameters in historical linguistics, philology, and culture history', p. 785.
4. See Sapir, 'The status of linguistics as a science'. See also *Selected Writings of Edward Sapir in Language, Culture and Personality*. Edward Sapir (1884–1939) was born in Germany and moved to the United States when he was five years old. It was while studying at Columbia University that he met Franz Boas, founder of modern linguistic anthropology.
5. Wierzbicka, *Understanding Cultures through Their Key Words*, p. 5.
6. Duranti, *Linguistic Anthropology*, pp. 17–20.
7. Koselleck, Conze and Brunner, *Geschichtliche Grundbegriffe*, vol. 1, p. xxiii.
8. Silverstein, 'The limits of awareness'. On p. 386 Silverstein defines 'unavoidable referentiality' as follows: 'In isolating the aspect of the signal that enters into the pragmatic opposition in question, we have thereby identified a constituent that enters into referential oppositions.'
9. See Labov, 'On the adequacy of natural languages'. This is discussed further in chapter 4.
10. Franz Boas, 'Introduction to *A Handbook of American Indian Languages*'; Sapir, *Selected Writings and Language*. Franz Boas (1848–1942) was born in Germany, settled in the United States in 1887 and taught anthropology at Columbia University between 1896 and 1936. He pioneered the study of the grammatical structure of Native American languages. He also advocated the use of the native language of the people being studied as an integral part of the anthropologist's methodology.
11. Boas, 'Language', in *General Anthropology*, p. 127.
12. Sapir, 'Language', p. 36.
13. Slobin, 'From "thought and language" to "thinking for speaking"'.
14. Ibid., p. 71.
15. Williams, *Keywords*, pp. 9–24.
16. Ibid., p. 11.
17. Wierzbicka, *Understanding Cultures through Their Key Words,* pp. 156–97.
18. Ibid., p. 16.
19. Although less central to an analysis of the lexical items *per se,* worthy of mention here also are analyses of cognitive linguists such as those of Lakoff and Johnson. They suggest that metaphors, rather than being simply decorative or

rhetorical, are conceptual structures that pervade and channel everyday thought and language. See, for example, their analysis of the UP–DOWN metaphor that permeates our conceptualizations of happiness v. sadness, health v. sickness or consciousness v. unconsciousness. See Lakoff and Johnson, *Metaphors We Live By*, pp. 14–21. Crucial to this is the systematic nature of metaphor. Thus Lakoff and Turner identify a pervasive metaphor LIFE IS A JOURNEY which informs an entire mode of speaking about the daily experience of living in the world, e.g. *I got a good start in life, I'm over the hill, my life is at a standstill,* etc. See Lakoff and Turner, *More than Cool Reason*, pp. 3–4. Our primary physical experience of the world forms the existentialist basis for the use of such metaphors. Johnson argues that the basic conceptual structures formed in this way are generalized between higher cognitive functions called *image schemas*. He refers to these as 'gestalt structures', the internal organization and logic of which produce patterns that can be repeated and thus generalized between a number of cognitive domains. Thus the LIFE IS A JOURNEY metaphor already alluded to is a development of what Johnson terms a 'path schema', which reflects and develops our everyday experience of physical movement in time and space. See Johnson, *The Body in the Mind*, p. 21ff.

20. Wierzbicka, *Understanding Cultures through Their Key Words,* p. 125.
21. Berlin, 'Two concepts of liberty', pp. 122–31; Skinner, *Liberty before Liberalism*, pp. 113–17, and 'A third concept of liberty'.
22. Hughes, *Words in Time*, p. 60.
23. Ní Thiarnaigh, 'An diagacht agus an dúchas', p. 155.
24. Ó Cearúil, *Bunreacht na hÉireann*, p. 55.
25. O'Donnell and de Fréine, *Ciste Cúrsaí Reatha*, p. 243.
26. Williams, *Keywords*, p. 12.
27. See Silverstein, 'Shifters, linguistic categories and cultural description', 'Language structure and linguistic ideology', 'The limits of awareness' and 'The three faces of "function" '.
28. See, for example, Silverstein, 'The limits of awareness', p. 400.
29. R. M. W. Dixon, 'A method of semantic description'; Silverstein, 'The limits of awareness', pp. 383–5.
30. Rumsey, 'Wording, meaning and linguistic ideology'.
31. Sapir, 'The status of linguistics', p. 396.
32. Voloshinov, 'Multiaccentuality and the sign', p. 45. See also Voloshinov, *Marxism and the Philosophy of Language*. Valentin Nikolaevich Voloshinov (1895–1936) was a poet and music critic, with interests in the philosophy of language, psychology and literary criticism. His book *Marxism and the Philosophy of Language,* published in 1929, offers a critique of what he calls the 'abstract objectivism' of Saussure and argues that the key to language is its social and ideological context, in which signs are free-floating and indeterminate.
33. Ferdinand de Saussure (1857–1913), born in Switzerland, was one of the major influences on twentieth-century linguistics. His aim was to study linguistics as a science, which for him meant an abstract, closed system or structure (*langue*), rather than the study of individual speech acts in their context (*parole*). *Langue* consists of signs whose ultimate value is differential. It is not that Saussure considered the study of language and culture or language and history uninteresting, simply that such facets of language were thought irrelevant to the *scientific* study

of language. Saussure's theories were published posthumously by his students in 1916 as *Cours de Linguistique Générale*. For an English translation see *Course in General Linguistics*, translated with an introduction and notes by Wade Baskin. For a discussion of Saussure's views see Hodge and Kress, *Social Semiotics*, pp. 18–36, Matthews, *A Short History of Structural Linguistics*, Culler, *Ferdinand de Saussure*, and Crowley, *Language in History*, pp. 6–29.

34. Hodge and Kress, *Social Semiotics*, p. 17.
35. Peirce, *Collected Papers*, §5.484. See also Hodge and Kress, ibid., pp. 20–1. Peirce (1839–1914) was, along with Saussure, the founder of modern semiotics.
36. Daniel, *Fluid Signs*, p. 21.
37. Jakobson, 'Shifters, verbal categories and the Russian verb'.
38. Ibid., p. 131.
39. Duranti, *Linguistic Anthropology*, p. 37.
40. Jakobson, 'Quest for the essence of language' and 'A few remarks on Peirce'.
41. Duranti, *Linguistic Anthropology*, p. 2.
42. Palmer, *Towards a Theory of Cultural Linguistics*.
43. Duranti, *Linguistic Anthropology*, p. 12.
44. Watkins, 'New parameters in historical linguistics, philosophy, and culture history', p. 785.
45. Koselleck et al., *Grundbegriffe*, vol. 1, p. xxiii.
46. Ibid., p. xxii.
47. Hodge and Kress, *Social Semiotics*, pp. 186–92.
48. Haiman, *Iconicity in Syntax*.
49. Jakobson, 'Metalanguage as a linguistic problem'.
50. See in particular the various essays in Lucy, *Reflexive Language*.
51. Silverstein, 'Metapragmatic discourse and metapragmatic function'.
52. Silverstein, 'The limits of awareness', p. 386: 'a specific, effective instance of a pragmatic signal is linked to, and requires, for its effect, some independently verifiable contextual factor or factors'.
53. Boas, 'Introduction to *A Handbook of American Indian Languages*', pp. 60–4.
54. There has been a considerable literature on this topic over the past ten years or so. For a comprehensive overview, including a discussion of various developments in both the linguistic-anthropological and comparative psycholinguistic strands of research into this question since the time of Boas, Sapir and Whorf, see Lucy, *Language Diversity and Thought*; see also the various essays in Gumperz and Levinson, *Rethinking Linguistic Relativity*. For summary accounts see Duranti, *Linguistic Anthropology*, pp. 51–83, Duranti, *Linguistic Anthropology: A Reader*, pp. 11–17, Foley, *Anthropological Linguistics*, pp. 192–214, and Palmer, *Towards a Theory of Cultural Linguistics*, pp. 10–26.
55. Miller, *Emigrants and Exiles*, pp. 102–30.
56. Benjamin Lee Whorf (1897–1941) is the most famous proponent of the principle of linguistic relativity. He was an avocational linguist whose work reflects on the one hand his training in the natural sciences and on the other hand his growing interest in the human sciences following his acquaintance from 1931 with Sapir, under whom he subsequently studied linguistics. Whorf was very much taken by the radical differences that he discovered between Native American languages such as Hopi and what he termed 'standard average European' languages, such as English.

57. See, for example, von Humboldt, *Linguistic Variability and Intellectual Development,* and in particular the citation given in Duranti, *Linguistic Anthropology,* p. 11.
58. Foley, *Anthropological Linguistics,* pp. 193–4.
59. Duranti, *Linguistic Anthropology,* p. 11.
60. Foley, *Anthropological Linguistics,* pp. 194–6.
61. Lucy, *Language Diversity and Thought,* pp. 11–17
62. Ibid., pp. 17–24.
63. Whorf, 'Discussion of Hopi linguistics'; 'The relation of habitual thought and behavior to language'.
64. See here Lucy, *Language Diversity and Thought,* p. 46, and Foley, *Anthropological Linguistics,* pp. 203–8.
65. Whorf, 'The relation of habitual thought and behavior to language', p. 158.
66. Duranti, *Linguistic Anthropology,* p. 14.
67. Silverstein, 'Language structure and linguistic ideology'.
68. For this assessment of the importance of Silverstein's research for the theory of linguistic relativity see Duranti, *Linguistic Anthropology,* pp. 15–6, and Foley, *Anthropological Linguistics,* pp. 211–13.
69. Ibid., pp. 211–13.
70. Silverstein, 'The limits of awareness', p. 386ff.
71. See Lucy, 'Reflexive language and the human disciplines', in *Reflexive Language,* pp. 1–32.
72. Hanks, 'Notes on semantics in linguistic practice'.
73. Bourdieu, *Outline of a Theory of Practice* and *The Logic of Practice.*
74. Hanks, 'Notes on semantics in linguistic practice', p. 140.
75. Verschueren, 'Pragmatics', p. 242.
76. Breatnach, 'The chief's poet'.

The internal and external dimensions of *dúchas*

1. Ó Dónaill, *Foclóir Gaeilge-Béarla*; Dinneen, *Foclóir Gaedhilge agus Béarla.* My purpose in presenting a synoptic view of the definitions of *dúchas* given by Dinneen and Ó Dónaill is simply to give the reader a quick and convenient overview of the types of semantic ranges, some of which will be considered in the following chapters. The evidence of both dictionaries is conflated for precisely this reason.
2. O'Reilly, *An Irish–English Dictionary.*
3. See Matthews, *A Short History of Structural Linguistics,* p. 126.
4. Saeed, *Semantics,* p. 63.
5. Hughes, *Words in Time,* pp. 18–19.
6. Lehrer, 'The influence of semantic fields on semantic change', p. 286. Such interrelationships are, for example, *synonymy* (*big* and *large*), *antonymy* (*big* and *small*), *hyponymy* (*rose* and *flower*), *converseness* (*buy* and *sell*) and *incompatibility* (*dog* and *cat*). For classic examples of the application of this method see Lyons, *Structural Semantics.* Lyons analyses the various words for 'knowledge' in Plato's dialogues according to the type of syntactic relations and collocations into which they enter; see also Anttila's analysis of structural shifts in Latin legal terminology in his *Historical and Comparative Linguistics,* pp. 146–7.
7. Lyons, *Semantics,* vol. 1, 270ff.

8. Wierzbicka, *Semantics: Primes*, p. 171.
9. Ó Doibhlin, *Gaoth an Fhocail.*
10. Todd, *Cogadh Gaedhel re Gallaibh*, p. 68.
11. Watkins, *The American Heritage Dictionary of Indo-European Roots.*
12. (*a*) Atkinson, *The Passions and Homilies from Leabhar Breac*, line 1568; (*b*) Todd, *Leabhar Breathnach*, p. 250; (*c*) Alfred Nutt, *The Voyage of Bran*, vol. 1, p. 53.
13. Miller, 'O'Clery's Irish glossary', *Revue Celtique* 4, p. 405.
14. Ó Ruairc, *Díolaim d'Abairtí Dúchasacha*, under *nature;* Mac Clúin, *Caint an Chláir*, p. 369.
15. Mackechnie, 'Treaty between Argyll and O'Donnell', p. 98.
16. Mac Domhnaill, *Dánta is Amhráin Sheáin Uí Ghadhra*, p. 31, lines 41–2.
17. Sapir, 'The status of linguistics as a science', p. 397.
18. Knott, *The Bardic Poems of Tadhg Dall Ó hUiginn*, no. 24, p. 174, §11, lines 41–4.
19. Ibid., no. 1, p. 5, §33, lines 129–32.
20. *Dictionary of the Irish Language.*
21. See further chapter 3.
22. (*a*) Dinneen, *Foras Feasa ar Éirinn*, iii, line 5102; (*b*) Ó Grianna, *Le Clap-sholus*, p. 118.
23. Mag Craith, *Dán na mBráthar Mionúr*, i, p. 187, §57.
24. Dinneen, *Foras Feasa ar Éirinn*, iii, line 5113.
25. Ó Tuama and Kinsella, p. 150, line 10. Dinneen, *The Poems of Egan O'Rahilly*, iv, p. 18, line 10.
26. O'Kelleher and Schopperle, *Betha Colaim Chille*, p. 60, line 25.
27. Todd, *Cogadh Gaedhel re Gallaibh*, p. 216.
28. The stanza is quoted from Ní Cheallacháin, *Filíocht Phádraigín Haicéad*, p. 21, lines 13–16.
29. Dinneen, *Foras Feasa ar Éirinn*, iii, line 2768.
30. Jackson, *Cath Maige Léna*, line 1367.
31. O'Kelleher and Schopperle, *Betha Colaim Chille*, p. 124, line 25.
32. Meyer, *Trecheng Breth Féne*, §205.
33. The word *dúchas* is not mentioned in Kelly's *A Guide to Early Irish Law.*
34. Williams, *Pairlement Chloinne Tomáis*, line 848.
35. Ó Maonaigh, *Scáthán Shacramuinte na hAithridhe*, p. 160, line 13.
36. Williams, *Pairlement Chloinne Tomáis*, line 917.
37. McErlean, *Duanaire Dháibhidh Uí Bhruadair*, iii, p. 126, §I, and p. 128, §II.
38. Ibid., p. 40, §III.
39. Ó Cuív, *Párliament na mBan*, line 795.
40. Dinneen, *The Poems of Egan O'Rahilly*, xviii, p. 106, lines 77–80.
41. Ó Dochartaigh and Ó Baoill, *Trí Rainn agus Amhrán*, p. 101, lines 9–10; see also Ó Fiaich and Ó Caithnia, *Art Mac Bionaid: Dánta*, p. 62, lines 9–10.
42. See also McMahon, *Understanding Language Change*, p. 186.
43. Hughes, *Words in Time*, p. 18.
44. Ibid., p. 60.
45. Lewis, *Studies in Words*, p. 22.
46. McKenna, *Aithdioghlaim Dána*, no. 38, p. 157, §43.
47. Bergin, *Irish Bardic Poetry*, no. 24, p. 108, §1.
48. Walsh, *Beatha Aodha Ruaidh Uí Dhomhnaill*, ii, p. 154, §10.
49. Greene, *Duanaire Mheig Uidhir*, p. 184, lines 2340–3.

50. McKenna, *Iomarbhágh na bhFileadh*, no. vi, p. 70, §121 and no. xviii, p. 182, §32.
51. As Calhoun puts it in 'Habitus', p. 79.
52. O'Rahilly, *Eachtra Uilliam*, p. 115, line 4188.
53. McKenna, *Iomarbhágh na bhFileadh*, no. xv, p. 138, §20.
54. Nic Pháidín, *Cnuasach Focal ó Uíbh Ráthach*, under *dúchas*.
55. Murphy, 'Poems of exile by Uilliam Nuinsean mac Barúin Dealbhna'.
56. Ibid., p. 12, §5.
57. Mac Giolla Léith, *Oidheadh Chloinne hUisneach*, (a) line 169; (b) line 147.
58. 'Dia libh a laochruidh Ghaoidheal', in Mac Airt, *An Leabhar Branach,* pp. 142–3.
59. Ó Donnchadha, *Mícheál Óg Ó Longáin*, (a) p. 101, lines 1–2; 15–16 (b) p. 91, line 30.
60. For a discussion of this text in the context of the European 'baroque' of the seventeenth century see Ó Dúshláine, *An Eoraip agus Litríocht na Gaeilge,* pp. 19–81.
61. Bergin, *Trí Bior-Ghaoithe an Bháis*, line 6013.
62. O'Kelleher and Schopperle, *Betha Colaim Chille*, p. 52, line 24.
63. Bergin, *Trí Bior-Ghaoithe an Bhais,* line 6355.
64. Ó Muirí, *Lámhscríbhinn Staire an Bhionadaigh*, line 4557.
65. Beckett, *Aodh Mac Domhnaill: Dánta*, §1, line 1.
66. Ó Coigligh, *Filíocht Ghaeilge Phádraig Mhic Phiarais*, p. 14, lines 7–8.
67. Miller, *Emigrants and Exiles,* p. 105.
68. (a) Ní Chléirigh, *Eolas ar an Domhan*, p. 13, n. 14; (b) Ó Neachtain, *Stair Éamoinn Uí Chléire*, line 2555; (c) Ua Duinnín, *Amhráin Eoghain Ruaidh Uí Shúilleabháin*, line 603; (d) Ó hÓgáin, *Duanaire Thiobraid Árainn*, p. 61, lines 53–6; (e) de Brún, 'Forógra do Ghaelaibh', p. 156.
69. Bakhtin, *The Dialogic Imagination.*
70. Walsh, *Beatha Aodha Ruaidh,* i, p. 114, line 12.
71. Breatnach, 'The first third of *Bretha Nemed Tóisech',* p. 14.
72. Stokes and Windisch, *Acallam na Senórach*, line 5311.
73. (a) Hyde, *Gabháltas Serluis Mhóir*, p. 96; (b) Mulchrone, *Caithréim Cellaig*, line 659.
74. See, for example, Heine, 'Grammaticalization as an explanatory parameter', ; Sweetser, *From Etymology to Pragmatics*, and Traugott, 'On the rise of epistemic meaning'.
75. Ibid., pp. 33–5.
76. Ibid., p. 34.
77. (a) Mac Clúin, *Caint an Chláir*, p. 369; (b) Ó Grianna, *An Clár*, p. 178.
78. (c) McErlean, *Duanaire Dháibhidh Uí Bhruadair,* iii, p. 106, §XXIX; (d) Ó Muirithe (ed.), *Tomás Ó Míocháin: Filíocht*, p. 50, line 29.
79. Haiman, *Iconicity in Syntax*; Newmeyer, *Language Form and Language Function*, p. 114ff.
80. Harman, *Iconicity*, p. 1.
81. Meyer, 'Mitteilungen aus Irischen handschriften', p. 110.
82. Meyer, *The Instructions of King Cormac Mac Airt*, p. 12, §5.
83. Jackson, *Aislinge*, lines 370; 414, §31.
84. O'Rahilly, *A Miscellany of Irish Proverbs*, p. 5, §14.
85. Ibid., p. 5, §15.
86. (a) McErlean, *Duanaire Dháibhidh Uí Bhruadair,* i, p. 110, lines 23–4; (b) Ibid., ii, p. 74, line 6.

87.   Mac Grianna, 'Ár ndúchas—ár gcinniúint', (a) p. 103, (b) p. 117.

88.   Ó Doibhlinn, 'Téama an dúchais i nualitríocht na Gaeilge', in *Aistí Critice agus Cultúir*, (c) p. 227, (d) p. 229.

89.   Ó Ruairc, *Dúchas na Gaeilge*, p. xi.

The pragmatics of *dúthaigh* and *dúchas*

1.   Silverstein, 'Shifters, linguistic categories and cultural description' and 'The limits of awareness'.

2.   Ó Donaill, *Foclóir Gaeilge-Béarla*.

3.   Duranti, *Linguistic Anthropology*, p. 37.

4.   For the idea of a linguistic sign as a 'shifter' see Jakobson, 'Shifters, verbal categories and the Russian verb'.

5.   Dinneen, *Foclóir Gaedhilge agus Béarla*.

6.   Mac Giolla Léith, *Oidheadh Chloinne hUisneach*, line 169.

7.   Ó Cuív, 'An appeal to Philip III of Spain'.

8.   Stafford, *Pacata Hibernia*, pp. 228–9.

9.   Ó Cuív, 'An appeal to Philip III of Spain', p. 24.

10.   Ibid., p. 22.

11.   Ó Corráin, 'Nationality and kingship in pre-Norman Ireland', p. 5; Carney, 'Three Old Irish accentual poems', p. 73. For a discussion of the origin of the connection between Ireland and Spain see Baumgarten, 'The geographical orientation of Ireland in the time of Isidore and Orosius'. Baumgarten argues that this connection arose from the doctrine of Isidore of Seville and Orosius that Ireland lay opposite Spain and was visible from it and was further enhanced by the similarities between the Latin names for the two countries (*Hibernia* and *Hiberia*). For a synoptic discussion of the position of the origin legend of the Gaels in the general evolution of *Lebor Gabála Érenn*, see Carey, *A New Introduction to Lebor Gabála Érenn*, pp. 1–20. For an edition of the text itself, see Macalister, *Lebor Gabála Érenn*.

12.   *Annals of the Four Masters*, M1602.1.

13.   Lambert McKenna, *Iomarbhágh na bhFileadh*, no. V, p. 42, §115.

14.   For the historical background of the Dál gCais and their relationship with the high-kingship of Munster see Ó Corráin, 'Dál gCais: church and dynasty' and 'Caithréim Chellacháin Chaisil', especially p. 56, and Ó hÁinle, 'Cogadh Gaedhel re Gallaibh'.

15.   Todd, *Cogadh Gaedhel re Gallaibh*, p. 70.

16.   Duranti, *Linguistic Anthropology*, p. 37.

17.   Gumperz, 'The linguistic and cultural relativity of conversational inference'.

18.   Walsh, *The Flight of the Earls*, p. 12, §IV.

19.   Todd, *Cogadh Gaedhel re Gallaibh*, p. 68.

20.   Interestingly, in view of the twelfth-century origin of the text and of its Eoghanacht counterpart, 'Caithréim Chellacháin Chaisil', Ó Corráin, in placing the latter within the general context of the themes prevalent in European literature of the same period, makes the following comment: 'The themes of the great and just king, of the sainted royal ancestor and patriotism, (for which the Irish used the long-peaceful Norse as a whipping-boy), all well developed in Irish historical writing, are also present in the European literature of the age.', pp. 68–9.

21. Todd, *Cogadh Gaedhel re Gallaibh*, pp. 68; 70.
22. Rees and Rees, *Celtic Heritage*, p. 118.
23. Literally 'The Book of the Taking of Ireland'. This text, essentially the Irish origin legend, was compiled in the eleventh century but was the culmination of the work of several centuries, beginning in the seventh century, the purpose of which was to synchronize Irish tradition with the chronology of the wider Judaeo-Christian world. See note 11 above and Scowcroft, 'Miotas na gabhála i *Leabhar Gabhála*' and '*Leabhar Gabhála*: part I' and '*Leabhar Gabhála*: part II'.
24. Dinneen, *Foras Feasa ar Éirinn*, ii, 247ff.
25. Rees and Rees, *Celtic Heritage*, p. 148.
26. Best, 'The Settling of the Manor of Tara', p. 121.
27. Mac Cana, 'Early Irish ideology and the concept of unity'.
28. Knott, *The Bardic Poems of Tadhg Dall Ó hUiginn*, p. 108–19.
29. Caball, *Poetry and Politics*, p. 48.
30. Knott, *The Bardic Poems of Tadhg Dall Ó hUiginn*, no. 16, p. 109, §6, lines 21–2.
31. Mac Cana, 'Early Irish ideology and the concept of unity', p. 76.
32. Knott, *The Bardic Poems of Tadhg Dall Ó hUiginn*, (a) no. 16, p. 111, §23, lines 89–92; (b) no. 16, p. 117, §60, lines 237–40; (c) no. 16, p. 118, §§67–8, lines 265–72.
33. Mac Airt, *An Leabhar Branach*, pp. 142–3.
34. Brendan Bradshaw, 'Native reaction to the westward enterprise'.
35. Mac Airt, *An Leabhar Branach*, p. 142, line 3737.
36. Ibid., lines 3743–4.
37. Ibid., lines 3750–1.
38. Ibid., lines 3753–60.
39. Ibid., lines 3769–72.
40. Black, 'A manuscript of Cathal Mac Muireadhaigh', p. 199, §22.
41. O'Rahilly, *Measgra Dánta II*, p. 144–7.
42. Ibid., p.145, lines 33–40.
43. Ibid., p. 146, lines 45–8.
44. Ibid., p. 146, lines 61–8.
45. Gillies, 'A poem on the downfall of the Gael', §§ 9, 11, 12, 14.
46. Dunne, 'The Gaelic response to conquest and colonization'. For a more recent discussion that similarly emphasizes the failure of the native literati to formulate a positive and dynamic response to conquest and colonization see O Riordan, *The Gaelic Mind and the Collapse of the Gaelic World*. For the opposing view, which stresses the flexibility and dynamism of the Irish reaction, see two reviews of O Riordan's book: Ó Buachalla, 'Poetry and politics in early modern Ireland', and Caball, 'The Gaelic Mind and the Collapse of the Gaelic World: an appraisal'.
47. Gibbons, 'Identity without a centre', pp. 137–9.
48. Cohn, 'Regions, subjective and objective'.
49. Rees and Rees, *Celtic Heritage*, p. 148; Best, 'The settling of the manor of Tara', p. 121.
50. Ó Corráin, 'Nationality and kingship in pre-Norman Ireland', p. 8.
51. Ibid., p. 4.
52. Ibid., pp. 6–7.
53. Cited in Mac Cana, 'Early Irish ideology and the concept of unity', p. 72.
54. Ibid., p. 74.

55.   Ó Cuív, 'An appeal to Philip III of Spain', p. 22.

56.   Ó Buachalla, 'Cúlra is tábhacht an dáin "A leabhráin ainmnighthear d'Aodh"', p. 410.

57.   Caball, *Poetry and Politics,* pp. 45–8, and '*The Gaelic Mind and the Collapse of the Gaelic World:* an appraisal'.

58.   Todd, *Cogadh Gaedhel re Gallaibh,* p. 70.

59.   O'Donovan, 'The Irish correspondence of James Fitzmaurice Fitzgerald of Desmond', pp. 362–4.

60.   Mac Craith, 'Creideamh agus athartha', p. 7.

61.   Ó Donnchadha, *An Leabhar Muimhneach,* p. 95.

62.   Ibid., p. 96.

63.   Ibid., p. 97.

64.   McKenna, *Aithdioghluim Dána,* vol. 1, pp. 118–23.

65.   Leerssen, *Mere Irish and Fíor-Ghael,* pp. 165–7.

66.   McKenna, *Aithdioghluim Dána,* vol. 1: p. 121, (a) §20–1; (b) §23.

67.   Ibid.: p. 122 (c) §29; (d) §33–4; (e) p. 123, §36.

68.   Ibid.: (f) p. 120, §14–5; (g) p. 121, §17.

69.   Knott, *The Bardic Poems of Tadhg Dall Ó hUiginn,* no. 17, pp. 120–31. For a discussion see Caball, *Poetry and Politics,* p. 46.

70.   Ibid., no. 17, §1–2, lines 1–8, and p. 120, §3, lines 13–16.

71.   Rees and Rees, *Celtic Heritage,* p. 118.

72.   Caball, *Poetry and Politics,* p. 46.

73.   Knott, *The Bardic Poems of Tadhg Dall Ó hUiginn,* no. 17, p. 122–3, §17–19, lines 65–76.

74.   Leerssen, *Mere Irish and Fíor-Ghael,* p. 177.

75.   Dunne, 'The Gaelic response to conquest and colonization', pp. 13–15.

76.   Caball, *Poetry and Politics,* p. 45

77.   Knott, *The Bardic Poems of Tadhg Dall Ó hUiginn,* no. 17, p. 123, §§20–2, lines 77–89.

78.   Caball, *Poetry and Politics,* p. 47

79.   Knott, *The Bardic Poems of Tadhg Dall Ó hUiginn,* no. 17, p. 131, §69, lines 273–6.

80.   Caball, *Poetry and Politics,* p. 47.

81.   See, for example, Morgan, 'Faith and fatherland ideology in sixteenth-century Ireland', p. 20.

82.   Walsh, *Beatha Aodha Ruaidh Uí Dhomhnaill,* 1, p. 114, line 3. For the semantics and syntax of *toich* see chapter 5.

83.   Ibid., p. 252, line 7.

84.   *Annals of the Four Masters,* M1580.3

85.   Cohn, 'Regions, subjective and objective'.

86.   For a discussion of the historical context in which Céitinn's history was written see Ó Buachalla, 'Annála Ríoghachta Éireann agus *Foras Feasa ar Éirinn'*, and Bradshaw, 'Geoffrey Keating: apologist of Gaelic Ireland'.

87.   Dinneen, *Foras Feasa ar Éirinn,* iii, line 5099.

88.   Ibid., line 5588.

89.   Ibid., line 5765.

90.   Comyn, Ibid., i, p. 34.

91.   Bradshaw, 'Geoffrey Keating', p. 189.

92. Skinner, *The Foundations of Modern Political Thought,* vol. 2, pp. 168–72.
93. Ó Súilleabháin Béirre, *Historiae Catolicae Hiberniae Compendium.* See Carroll, *Circe's Cup,* pp. 124–34. See also Pagden, 'Dispossessing the barbarian,' pp. 80–1.
94. Pagden, *Lords of All the World,* p. 89.
95. Ó Dónaill, *Foclóir Gaeilge-Béarla,* under *dúiche.*
96. Murphy, 'Poems of exile by Uilliam Nuinseann mac barúin Dealbhna'.
97. Bradshaw, 'The Elizabethans and the Irish', p. 241.
98. Elliott, 'Revolution and continuity in early modern europe', p. 47.
99. Caball, *Poetry and Politics,* p. 77.
100. Simms, 'Bards and barons', p. 197.
101. Mac Craith, 'Ireland and the Renaissance', p. 68; Caball, *Poetry and Politics,* p. 130.
102. O'Rahilly, *Measgra Dánta II,* p. 139, lines 1–4.
103. Ibid., p. 141, lines 53–6.
104. Caball, *Poetry and Politics,* p. 79.
105. Morgan, 'Faith and fatherland ideology in sixteenth-century Ireland', pp. 11–14.
106. Bradshaw, 'The Elizabethans and the Irish', p. 241. See Ó Buachalla, 'Annála Ríoghachta Éirinn agus Foras Feasa ar Éirinn', pp. 75–6, on the joint flowering of the notions of *patria* and the idea of 'national' history in the sixteenth century within its general European, Renaissance–humanist context.
107. Bradshaw, 'Geoffrey Keating', p. 174.
108. O'Rahilly, *Measgra Dánta II,* p. 141, lines 57–60.
109. Walsh, *Beatha Aodha Ruaidh Uí Dhomhnaill,* 1: (*a*) p. 116, line 33; (*b*) p. 118, line 25.
110. O'Kelleher and Schopperle, *Betha Colaim Chille,* p. 64, line 25.
111. *Annals of the Four Masters,* M1591.1.
112. McKenna, *The Book of O'Hara,* p. 1.
113. Walsh, *Beatha Aodha Ruaidh Uí Dhomhnaill,* 1, p. 34, line 15.
114. (*a*) Dinneen, *Foras Feasa ar Éirinn,* iii, line 5042; (*b*) 'Cín Lae Ó Mealláin', p. 33.
115. Stapleton, *Catechismus,* p. 41.
116. Bergin, *Trí Bior-Ghaoithe an Bháis:* (*a*) line 6013; (*b*) line 6355.
117. Mac Craith, 'Creideamh agus athartha', p. 10.
118. *Annals of the Four Masters:* (*a*) M1608.4; (*b*) M1616.1.
119. O'Donovan, 'The Irish correspondence of James Fitzmaurice Fitzgerald', p. 364.
120. Mac Craith, 'Creideamh agus athartha', p. 7.
121. Morgan, 'Faith and fatherland ideology in sixteenth-century Ireland', pp. 13–15.
122. Bradshaw, *The Irish Constitutional Revolution of the Sixteenth Century,* pp. 276–82.
123. Mac Craith, 'Creideamh agus athartha', p. 10.
124. Daniel, *Fluid Signs,* pp. 61–104.
125. Silverstein, 'Shifters, linguistic categories and cultural description'.
126. For Arabic, Bassam Tibi discusses the term *watan,* which in Classical Arabic has the sense of the country of one's origin, or the country in which one lives. In the writings of the nineteenth-century Egyptian nationalist al-Tahtawi the word can have both a local sense, in referring to his home village, Tahta, and a national sense, in referring to Egypt as his *patrie.* In this dual or shifting usage *watan* is comparable to the Irish use of *dúthaigh* and *dúchas* and the Tamil use of *ūr.* See Bassam Tibi, *Arab Nationalism: A Critical Enquiry,* p. 61.

127. Todd, *Cogadh Gaedhel re Gallaibh,* p. 68.

128. Ó Dónaill, *Foclóir Gaeilge-Béarla.*

129. O'Rahilly, *A Miscellany of Irish Proverbs,* p. 120.

130. Stapleton, *Catechismus, Oraid don Leaghthoir,* p. 26.

131. Breatnach, 'The Second Earl of Tyrconnell', p. 171.

132. Power, *The Life of St. Declan,* p. 32.

133. Elliot, 'Revolution and continuity in early modern Europe,' p. 50.

134. *Annals of the Four Masters,* M1601.1.

135. Mac Cuarta, 'Conchubhar Mac Bruaidheadha and Sir Matthew de Renzy', p. 124.

136. *Annals of the Four Masters,* M1600.1.

137. For a brief discussion of the history of the term *nation* in various European languages see Hobsbawm, *Nations and Nationalism since 1780,* p. 14.

138. Walsh, *The Flight of the Earls,* p. 42, §XXXI.

139. Ó Maonaigh, *Scáthán Shacramuinte na hAithridhe:* (*a*) line 67; (*b*) line 6286; (*c*) line 6273. For a discussion of this text in the context of the European 'baroque' of the seventeenth century see Ó Dúshláine, *An Eoraip agus Litríocht na Gaeilge,* pp. 82–115.

140. Both Bradshaw and Ó Buachalla draw attention to important developments in the political lexicon of Irish in the early seventeenth century. Bradshaw focuses on Céitinn's development of a mode of Renaissance humanist discourse in Irish based on terms such as *tír athardha* or *patria* as the 'object of ultimate political loyalty'. See Bradshaw, 'Geoffrey Keating', p. 168. Ó Buachalla's discussion centres on terms concerning the sovereign (*prionsa*), the Crown (*an choróin*) and commonweal (*maitheas poiblighe*). He adds two more central and pervasive elements: *ríoghacht* 'kingdom' and *náision* 'nation'. See Ó Buachalla, 'James', p. 14. As both scholars point out, such concepts were part of the burgeoning ideology of the emergent nation-states in early modern Europe.

141. Williams, *Pairlement Chloinne Tomáis.*

142. Caball, 'Pairlement Chloinne Tomáis': a reassessment'.

143. Williams, *Pairlement Chloinne Tomáis,* line 707.

144. Ibid., line 110.

145. Ibid., line 725.

146. Ibid., lines 45, 1165.

147. Ibid., line 713.

148. Ibid., line 713.

149. Ibid., line 373

150. Ibid., line 848.

151. Ibid., line 914.

152. Bergin, *Irish Bardic Poetry,* no. 28, p. 120, §§1–2.

153. O'Grady and Flower, *Catalogue of Irish Manuscripts in the British Museum,* i, p. 392.

154. Hughes, *Words in Time,* p. 6.

155. Silverstein, 'The indeterminacy of contextualization, p. 55. See also Duranti, *Linguistic Anthropology,* pp. 17–19.

156. Verschueren, 'Pragmatics', p. 242.

157. Voloshinov, *Marxism and the Philosophy of Language,* pp. 23 and 81.

158. Wierzbicka, *Understanding Cultures through Their Key Words,* pp. 156–97.

159. Anderson, *Imagined Communities,* p. 143.

The pragmatics of *dual* and the habitual

1. Ó Dónaill, *Foclóir Gaeilge-Béarla.*
2. Ó Ruairc, *Díolaim d'Abairtí Dúchasacha*, under *nature.*
3. Hughes, *Robert Shipboy MacAdam.* The examples cited are (*a*) §412, (*b*) §413, (*c*) §397, (*d*) §393.
4. Mac Maoláin, *Cora Cainte as Tír Chonaill*, p. 62.
5. Hughes, *Robert Shipboy MacAdam*, §291.
6. Ibid., §286.
7. O'Rahilly, *A Miscellany of Irish Proverbs*, p. 10.
8. Hughes, *Robert Shipboy MacAdam*, §285.
9. Mac Maoláin, *Cora Cainte as Tír Chonaill*, p. 61.
10. (*a*) Calder, *Togail na Tebe*, line 2432; (*b*) McKenna, *Aithdioghluim Dána*, p. 247, §29.
11. O'Grady, *Silva Gadelica*, ii, p. 286.
12. O'Rahilly, *Dánfhocail*, p. 21.
13. Cecile O'Rahilly, *Eachtra Uilliam*, line 4184.
14. O'Donovan, *The Banquet of Dún na nGedh and the Battle of Mag Rath*, p. 116.
15. Dinneen, *Foras Feasa ar Éirinn*, iii, line 5114.
16. O'Kelleher and Schopperle, *Betha Colaim Chille*, p. 60, line 24.
17. Ní Chléirigh, *Eachtra na gCuradh*, p. 19.
18. (*a*) Stokes and Windisch, 'Acallam na Senórach', line 476; (*b*) Calder, *Togail na Tebe*, line 1821; (*c*) Ní Shéaghdha, *Agallamh na Seanórach*, I, p. 40.
19. Benveniste, *Indo-European Language and Society*, p. 53.
20. Watkins, 'New parameters in historical linguistics, philology, and culture history', pp. 786–7.
21. Watkins, 'The etymology of Irish *dúan*'.
22. (*a*) O'Grady, *Silva Gadelica*, p. 203; (*b*) Stokes and Windisch, 'Acallam na Senórach', line 5311; (c) Stokes, 'The Gaelic abridgement of the book of *Ser Marco Polo*', 1, p. 372, §78.
23. (*a*) McErlean, *Duanaire Dháibhidh Uí Bhruadair*, ii, p. 244, §VIII; (*b*) Donlevy, *Teagasg Críostuidhe do réir Ceasda agus Freagartha*, p. 70.
24. De Brún, 'Forógra do Ghaelaibh, 1824', p. 158.
25. Dinneen, *Foras Feasa ar Éirinn*, iii, line 5151.
26. Breatnach, 'A poem of protest', pp. 91–100. For a discussion of the relationship between poet and patron in the medieval and early modern periods see Breatnach, 'The chief's poet'.
27. Breatnach, 'A poem of protest', p. 96, §4.
28. Ibid., §§8–9. For a discussion of this verb and its lexical family see chapter 5.
29. Ibid., §§13 and 16.
30. Ibid., p. 93.
31. Breatnach, 'An address to Aodh Ruadh Ó Domhnaill in captivity', p. 211, §39.
32. Mac Cionnaith, *Dioghluim Dána*, p. 422, §33.
33. (*a*) Bergin, *Irish Bardic Poetry*, p. 120, §1–2; (*b*) O'Grady and Flower, *Catalogue of Irish Manuscripts in the British Museum*, i, p. 392. For a discussion and references see Caball, *Poetry and Politics*, pp. 94 and 97, and Leerssen, *Mere Irish and Fíor-Ghael*, pp. 199–200.
34. Williams, *Pairlement Chloinne Tomáis*, lines 641–4.

35. Ibid., line 421.
36. Gwynn, *The Metrical Dindshenchus*, iii, p. 276, lines 1–2.
37. Ibid., p. 278, lines 31–6.
38. Ibid., p. 278, lines 36–40.
39. Ibid., p. 284, lines 96–100.
40. McKenna, *Aithdioghluim Dána*, pp. 247–8, §29 and 38.
41. Ibid., p. 244, §4.
42. Ó Donnchadha, *Dánta Sheáin na Ráithíneach*, p. 105, line 54.
43. McKenna, i, no. 44, pp. 177–80, §23. For a discussion and further references see Caball, *Poetry and Politics*, pp. 85–9.
44. Ó Muirithe, *Tomás Ó Míocháin*: (*a*) p. 39, lines 47–8; (*b*) p. 50, lines 29–32.
45. (*a*) Cited in Ó Buachalla, *Aisling Ghéar*, p. 238; (*b*) Ó Tuama and Kinsella, p. 150, lines 9–12. See also Dinneen, *The Poems of Egan O'Rahilly*, §iv, p. 18, line 10. See Ó Buachalla, 'Na Stiobhartaigh agus an tAos Léinn', pp. 88 and 127; *Aisling Ghéar*, p. 234ff. for the origins of the Jacobite view of 'right' (*ceart*) in the seventeenth century, especially the indefeasible nature of hereditary right. Ó Buachalla, *Aisling Ghéar*, p. 234, also points to the central position of the terms *dligheach* 'lawful' and *cóir* 'right' in Scottish poetry at this time.
46. Dwelly, *Illustrated Gaelic–English Dictionary*.
47. Ní Suaird, 'Jacobite rhetoric and terminology in the political poems of the Fernaigh manuscripts', p. 122.
48. Kelly and Edwards, *Bechbretha*, §18.
49. *Graiméar Gaeilge na mBráithre Críostaí*, p. 171, §334.
50. Ó Searcaigh, *Coimhréir*, pp. 216 and 219; Ó Cadhlaigh, *Gnás*, pp. 7 and 13.
51. Ó Siadhail, *Modern Irish*, pp. 177–8.
52. Ó Baoill and Ó Tuathail, *Úrchúrsa Gaeilge*, p. 105.
53. Ibid., p. 108.
54. O'Rahilly, *A Miscellany of Irish Proverbs*, pp. 17, 30, 37, 93 and 94.
55. Ibid., p. 17.
56. Ibid., p. 31.
57. Skerrett, 'On the meaning of "Habitual"'.
58. Ibid., p. 253.
59. Ibid., p. 254.
60. Comrie, *Aspect*, pp. 27–8.
61. Dinneen, *Foras Feasa ar Éirinn*, ii, line 2443.
62. Chung and Timberlake, 'Tense, mood and aspect', p. 221.
63. Ibid., p. 221.
64. Dinneen, *Foras Feasa ar Éirinn*, iii, line 4178.
65. Slobin, 'From "thought and language" to "thinking for speaking"', p. 84.
66. Bergin, *Irish Bardic Poetry*, no. 6, pp. 41–4.
67. Ibid., p. 141, §1–2, and p. 142, §7.
68. Ibid., p. 144, §20.
69. Caball, *Poetry and Politics*, p. 141.
70. Knott, *The Bardic Poems of Tadhg Dall Ó hUiginn*, no. 22a, pp. 160–8.
71. Caball, *Poetry and Politics*, pp. 47–8.
72. Knott, *The Bardic Poems of Tadhg Dall Ó hUiginn*, no. 22a, p. 161, §9, lines 33–6 and p. 162, §19, lines 73–6.
73. Caball, *Poetry and Politics*, p. 48.

74. Knott, *The Bardic Poems of Tadhg Dall Ó hUiginn,* no. 22a, p. 161, §7–8, lines 25–32.

75. Ibid.: (*a*) p. 62, §16, lines 61–4 and §18, lines 69–72; (*b*) p. 163, §22, lines 85–8.

76. Ibid., p. 167, §48–50, lines 189–200.

77. Ibid., p. 167, §52, lines 205–8.

78. Ibid., p. 167, §53, lines 209–12.

79. Bergin, *Irish Bardic Poetry,* no. 30, pp. 127–9. See Caball, *Poetry and Politics,* p. 94.

80. Bergin, *Irish Bardic Poetry,* p. 128, §3 and p. 129, §11.

81. McErlean, *Duanaire Dháibhidh Uí Bhruadair,* i, (*a*) p. 36, §xxv; (*b*) p. 38, §xxvii; (*c*) p. 38, §xxix. Translation from Hartnett, *Ó Bruadair,* pp. 33–4.

82. McErlean, ibid., p. 44, §xl.

83. Ibid., ii, (*a*) p. 26, §iv–v; (*b*) p. 28, §ix.

84. Walsh, *Beatha Aodha Ruaidh Uí Dhomhnaill,* ii, p. 138, §§1 and 5.

85. Gillies, 'A poem on the downfall of the Gael', §3 and 11.

86. Mac Giolla Eáin, *Dánta, Amhráin is Caointe Sheathrúin Céitinn,* p. 77, §i, and p. 78, §x.

87. Silverstein, 'The limits of awareness'.

88. Labov, 'On the adequacy of natural languages'.

89. Hopper and Traugott, *Grammaticalization,* p. 215.

90. Lehmann, 'Grammaticalization', especially p. 306.

91. Hopper and Traugott, *Grammaticalization,* p. 64.

92. Haiman, *Talk is Cheap,* p. 148.

93. 'Le caractère mécanique de l'obligation qui définit ce qu'on appelle "la grammaire"'. See Hagège, 'Du thème au thème en passant par le sujet', especially p. 22.

94. Sankoff, 'Variability and explanation in language and culture', p. 62.

95. Lehmann, 'Grammaticalization', p. 315.

96. Wagner, *Linguistic Atlas and Survey of Irish Dialects,* i, p. 296.

97. Bergin, 'Irish Grammatical Tracts', pp. 171–2.

98. Mac Curtin, *The Elements of the Irish Language,* p. 67.

99. Mac Aogáin, *Graiméir Ghaeilge na mBráthar Mionúr,* p. 58.

100. Fleischman, 'Imperfective and irrealis', p. 537.

101. Chung and Timberlake, 'Tense, mood and aspect', p. 221.

102. Givón, *Functionalism and Grammar,* p. 116.

103. Wagner, *Das Verbum in den Sprachen der Britischen Inseln,* p. 21.

104. Silverstein's research represents an important development of the idea of linguistic relativity, in the sense that his principle of *metapragmatic awareness,* or the extent to which speakers can consciously engage with the pragmatics of their own language use, expands on the discussions of Boas, Sapir and Whorf on the largely unconscious nature of grammatical usage.

105. Silverstein, 'The limits of awareness', p. 385.

106. Foley, *Anthropological Linguistics,* p. 212.

107. For a convenient overview see, for example, Duranti, *Linguistic Anthropology,* pp. 11–17.

108. Jakobson, *Selected Writings* II, pp. 489–96; Boas, 'Language', p. 127.

109. Slobin, 'From "thought and language" to "thinking for speaking"', p. 91.

110. Ibid., pp. 79–88. Basing his conclusions on an analysis of data received from English, Spanish, German and Hebrew-speaking children, Slobin finds that, while English and Spanish are closer together in making more elaborate *aspectual* distinctions, such as progressive–nonprogressive (English) and perfective–imperfective (Spanish), as opposed to German and Hebrew, they diverge sharply in their treatment of space, specifically verbs of *motion*, English in this case aligning more closely with German in requiring prepositional or adverbial elaboration, whereas Hebrew and Spanish favour bare motion verbs. Slobin formulates his conclusion as follows: 'It is clear that, for psycholinguistic purposes, typological differences must be considered separately for each semantic domain' (p. 86).

111. Lucy, *Language Diversity and Thought*, pp. 268–75; Palmer, *Towards a Theory of Cultural Linguistics*, pp. 16–18, 159–63.

112. Dahl, *Tense and Aspect Systems*, p. 97.

113. Ibid., p. 100.

114. Bybee, Perkins and Pagliuca, *The Evolution of Grammar*, p. 159.

115. Ibid., p. 151.

116. Ibid., p. 154.

117. Watkins, *The American Heritage Dictionary of Indo-European Roots*, p. 23.

118. Greene, 'Ir. *gnás*: W. *gnaws*; OHG. *kunst*'.

119. Boas, 'Language', p. 127.

120. Slobin, 'From "thought and language" to "thinking for speaking"', p. 71.

121. Boas, 'Introduction to *A Handbook of American Indian Languages*', pp. 38–9.

The semantics and syntax of 'right' and 'natural'

1. Ó Dónaill, *Foclóir Gaeilge-Béarla*.

2. Dineen, *Foras Feasa ar Éirinn*, iii, line 2752.

3. 'Cathréim Cellacháin Caisil', p. 2, §3.

4. Ní Mhuirgheasa, *Imtheacht an Dá Nónbar agus Tóraigheacht Taise Taoibhghile*, p. 27.

5. Dillon, *Lebor na Cert*, line 510.

6. *Dictionary of the Irish Language.*

7. O'Donovan, *The Banquet of Dún na nGedh and the Battle of Mag Rath*: (a) p. 70, line 1; (b) p. 70, line 10.

8. *Annals of the Four Masters*, M948.15.

9. Bergin, *Trí Bior-Ghaoithe an Bháis*, line 10073.

10. Bergin, 'What brought the Saxons to Ireland?', p. 244.

11. Binchy, *Críth Gablach*, p. 84.

12. Stokes and Strachan, 'Codex'. The passages cited here are (a) 32a20 and (b) 4a10.

13. Ibid.: (c) 4c23; (d) 1b8.

14. Henderson, *Bricriu's Feast*, p. 86, line 8, McKenna, *Iomarbhágh na bhFileadh*, § xiv, p. 126, §5, and Bergin, *Trí Bior-Ghaoithe an Bháis*, line 153, respectively.

15. From RIA ms. 24P3 173.24, cited in *Dictionary of the Irish Language* under *dligid*.

16. Dineen, *Foras Feasa ar Éirinn*, iii, line 3074.

17. Dillon, *Lebor na Cert*, line 212.

18. Ibid.: (a) line 255; (b) line 251.

19. Ibid., line 367.
20. Ibid., line 1842ff.
21. Ibid.: (*a*) line 1914; (*b*) line 1910.
22. Binchy, *Críth Gablach,* p. 84.
23. Jackson, *Cath Maige Léna,* line 1360.
24. Dillon, *Lebor na Cert,* line 206.
25. Binchy, *Críth Gablach,* p. 83.
26. Walsh, *Beatha Aodha Ruaidh Uí Dhomhnaill,* 1, p. 186, line 15.
27. Miller, 'O'Clery's Irish Glossary', *Revue Celtique,* 5, p. 157.
28. (*a*) John O'Donovan (ed.), *Annals of the Kingdom of Ireland by the Four Masters, 1616,* p. 2374; (*b*) Stokes, *Lives of Saints,* line 749; (*c*) Stokes and Strachan, 'Codex', 16c11.
29. Walsh, *Beatha Aodha Ruaidh Uí Dhomhnaill,* i, p. 114, line 3.
30. Carroll, *Circe's Cup,* p. 133.
31. Ó Donnchadha, *An Leabhar Muimhneach,* p. 115.
32. Ibid., p. 115.
33. Ibid., p. 92.
34. Ibid., p. 97.
35. O'Curry's law transcripts in the Royal Irish Academy, 2093, cited in *Dictionary of the Irish Language* under *ferann.*
36. Ó Corráin, 'Nationality and kingship in pre-Norman Ireland', p. 24; the passage is *Annals of the Four Masters,* M1089.11.
37. Kelly and Edwards, *Bechbretha,* §27.
38. Ibid., §49.
39. Williams, *Pairlement Chloinne Tomáis,* line 848; Walsh, *Beatha Aodha Ruaidh Uí Dhomhnaill,* i, p. 114, lines 12; 15.
40. Hughes, *Robert Shipboy MacAdam,* §291.
41. Ó Ruairc, *Díolaim d'abairtí dúchasacha,* under *nature.*
42. O'Donovan, *The Banquet of Dún na nGedh and the Battle of Mag Rath,* p. 70, lines 1; 10.
43. Dillon, *Lebor na Cert,* line 1830.
44. Kelly and Edwards, *Bechbretha,* §49; *Annals,* M1601.18.
45. Stokes and Windisch, 'In Cath Chatharda: the civil war of the Romans', lines 629–30; O'Donovan, *The Banquet of Dún na nGedh and the Battle of Mag Rath,* p. 92, line 4, and p. 264, line 11.
46. Stokes and Strachan, 'Codex', 30d20; Carney, *The Poems of Blathmac,* line 257.
47. Stokes and Strachan, 'The Milan Glosses on the Psalms', 21b9.
48. Stokes and Strachan, 'Codex', 28a16.
49. Todd, *Cogadh Gaedhel re Gallaibh,* p. 68.
50. Stokes and Strachan, 'Codex', 17c20.
51. Carney, *The Poems of Blathmac,* line 445.
52. Stokes and Strachan, 'Codex', 6b20.
53. Bergin, *Trí Bior-Ghaoithe an Bháis,* line 9565.
54. Walsh, *Gleanings from Irish Manuscripts,* p. 90, §§7–8. McKibben draws attention to the pervasive use of the verb *tréig* in seventeenth-century texts to describe cultural, linguistic and religious betrayal. See her essay 'Born to die . . . and to live on: terminal metaphors in the life of Irish', pp. 94–5.
55. Bergin, ibid., line 6110.

56.   Ibid., line 4508; O'Rahilly, *A Miscellany of Irish Proverbs*, p. 104.
57.   Stokes and Strachan, ibid., (i) 12a1; (ii) 29d27; (iii) 29d14.
58.   Ibid., 2d8.
59.   *Graiméar Gaeilge na mBráithre Críostaí*, pp. 240–1.
60.   Genee, *Sentential Complementation in a Functional Grammar of Irish*, p. 421.
61.   Chung and Timberlake, 'Tense, mood and aspect', p. 242.
62.   Dinneen, *Foras Feasa ar Éirinn*, iii, line 5118.
63.   Ibid., line 4178.
64.   Haiman, *Iconicity in Syntax*, p. 515.
65.   Croft, *Typology and Universals*, p. 171.
66.   Ibid., p. 174.
67.   Wierzbicka, *Semantics, Culture and Cognition*, p. 413. Wierzbicka refers to the opposite of agentivity as 'patientivity'. In the present context, I prefer the more neutral 'non-agentivity'.
68.   In keeping with the preceding footnote, I prefer 'non-agentive' to 'patientive' here.
69.   Wagner, *Das Verbum in den Sprachen der Britischen Inseln*, p. 31.
70.   Ibid., pp. 45–6.
71.   Ibid., pp. 47–8.
72.   Slobin, 'From "thought and language" to "thinking for speaking"', p. 84.
73.   Bergin, *Irish Bardic Poetry*, no. 28, pp. 102–3, §1.
74.   Mac Maoláin, *Cora Cainte as Tír Chonaill*, p. 61.
75.   Bergin, ibid., p. 120, §3.
76.   Ibid., p. 122, §15.
77.   Ibid.: (*a*) p. 120, §4; (*b*) p. 121, §6; (*c*) p. 121, §8; (*d*) p. 121, §11; (*e*) p. 122, §14; (*f*) p. 122, §17 and (*g*) p. 122, §18.
78.   O'Grady and Flower, *Catalogue of Irish Manuscripts in the British Museum*, i, p. 392, §1.
79.   Ibid., §2.
80.   Ibid., §5.
81.   Knott, *The Bardic Poems of Tadhg Dall Ó hUiginn*, no. 22a, pp. 160–8.
82.   Ibid., p. 161, §§7 and 9.
83.   Ibid., p. 167, §§48–9.
84.   Ibid., p. 160, §§1–2.
85.   Wagner, *Das Verbum in den Sprachen der Britischen Inseln*, pp. 47–8.
86.   Silverstein, 'The limits of awareness'.
87.   Verschueren, 'Pragmatics', p. 92.
88.   Murphy, 'Poems of exile by Uilliam Nuinseann mac barúin Dealbhna', p. 13, §1.
89.   Wierzbicka, *Understanding Cultures through Their Key Words*, p. 16.
90.   Miller, *Emigrants and Exiles*, pp. 102–30.
91.   Ibid., pp. 119.
92.   Ibid., p. 105.
93.   See Whorf, *Language, Thought and Reality*. For a discussion and criticism see the various essays in *Rethinking Linguistic Relativity*, edited by Gumperz and Levinson; Lucy, *Language Diversity and Thought*, pp. 25–68; Foley, *Anthropological Linguistics*, pp. 199–208; and Duranti, *Linguistic Anthropology*, pp. 57–60.
94.   Whorf, 'Discussion of Hopi linguistics', pp. 102–11.
95.   Whorf, 'The relation of habitual thought and behavior to language', pp. 134–59.

96. Duranti, *Linguistic Anthropology*, p. 14.
97. Jakobson, *Selected Writings* II, p. 492.
98. Lucy, *Linguistic Diversity*, p. 7.
99. See here Lucy, ibid., p. 46, and Foley, *Anthropological Linguistics*, pp. 203–8.
100. Wierzbicka, *Understanding Cultures through Their Key Words*, p. 16.
101. Miller, *Emigrants and Exiles*, p. 121.
102. For the close, though not absolute, correlation between narrative background-ing and subordination see Givón, 'Beyond foreground and background', and Thompson, '"Subordination" and narrative event structure'. Furthermore, Hopper and Thompson present evidence for a strong correlation between back-grounding and categories showing relatively low levels of *transitivity*. Transitivity is defined here as the effectiveness with which an action is transferred from agent to patient. Nominative-marked subjects, therefore, show at least an analogical extension of highly transitive agentive marking, while dative-marked subjects, as in the examples above, show the opposite. See Hopper and Thompson, 'Tran-sitivity in grammar and discourse'.
103. Ó Siadhail, *Modern Irish*, pp. 281–3. Ó Siadhail has the following comment on p. 283: 'It must be noted that these verbal noun complements which identify the subject with *do* 'to/for' belong for the most part in Munster and Connacht to a marked narrative style. The use of *théis/tar éis* etc. seems more colloquial. How-ever, in Donegal, the usages with *ar* and *roimh* as well as *i ndéidh* are features of ordinary colloquial speech.'
104. (*a*) Walsh, *Beatha Aodha Ruaidh Uí Dhomhnaill, i*, p. 252, line 5; (*b*) Dinneen, *Foras Feasa ar Éirinn*, ii, line 2443 (see chapter 4); (*c*) and (*d*) are from McGrath, *Cinn Lae Amhlaoibh Uí Shúileabháin*, iv, pp. 138 and 140 (see chapter 7).
105. Ailbhe Ó Corráin has presented a convincing argument that several of the gram-matical phenomena relating to voice and degrees of transitivity in Irish can be attributed to a hidden or cryptic semantics of the 'middle voice'. This is to be regarded as intermediate between active and passive voice and includes such phenomena as reflexivity (e.g. *I washed **myself***). Such phenomena also include the type of syntactic structures discussed in this chapter. In a future study I plan to investigate in more detail the extent to which the 'middle voice' represents a Whorfian covert or cyptotypic category in Irish. See Ó Corráin, 'Aspects of voice in the grammatical structure of Irish'.

Afterword to *dúchas*

1. Silverstein, 'The limits of awareness'.
2. Hanks, 'Notes on semantics in linguistic practice', p. 238.
3. Ó Cuív, 'An appeal to Philip III of Spain by Ó Súilleabháin Béirre', p. 22.
4. Gumperz, 'The linguistic and cultural relativity of conversational inference', pp. 402–3.
5. Ó Corráin, 'Nationality and kingship in pre-Norman Ireland', p. 5; Carney, 'Three Old Irish accentual poems', p. 73.
6. Bourdieu, *Outline of a Theory of Practice* and *The Logic of Practice*.
7. Hanks, 'Notes on semantics in linguistic practice,' p. 237.
8. Ó Cuív, 'An appeal to Philip III of Spain by Ó Súilleabháin Béirre', p. 23.
9. For the idea of grammar as 'habituation' see Haiman, *Talk Is Cheap*, p. 148.

10. Ó Dónaill, *Foclóir Gaeilge-Béarla*.
11. For references see *Dictionary of the Irish Language*, under *gnáth*.
12. Breatnach, 'Donal O'Sullivan Beare to King Philip III'.
13. *Annals of the Four Masters*, M1580.3.
14. Knott, *The Bardic Poems of Tadhg Dall Ó hUiginn*, no. 22a: (a) p. 161, §§7–8; (b) p. 167, §48.
15. *Graiméar Gaeilge na mBráithre Críostaí*, p. 281, §580.
16. Comrie, *Aspect*, p. 60.
17. O'Rahilly, *A Miscellany of Irish Proverbs*, p. 11.
18. (a) *Annals of the Four Masters*, M1600.36; (b) Walsh, *Beatha Aodha Ruaidh Uí Dhomhnaill*, ii, p. 158.
19. *Annals of the Four Masters*, M1600.28.
20. Mac Erlean, *Duanaire Dháibhidh Uí Bhruadair*, iii, p. 56, §xxxiii.
21. Miller, 'O'Clery's Irish glossary', *Revue Celtique*, 4, p. 404.
22. *Annals of the Four Masters*, M1600.37.
23. Ibid., M1582.4.
24. Ibid., M1608.2.
25. Carroll, *Circe's Cup*, pp. 124–34. For a further discussion of the position of both Céitinn and Ó Cléirigh's work in the wider post-Renaissance European context see Breandán Ó Buachalla, 'Annála Ríoghachta Éireann agus Foras Feasa ar Éirinn'.
26. Ibid., p. 133.
27. Ibid., p. 126; Byrne, 'Senchas', p. 38.
28. Ó Cuív, 'An appeal to Philip III of Spain by Ó Súilleabháin Béirre,' p. 22.
29. Carroll, ibid., p. 124.
30. Ibid., p. 127.
31. Ibid., p. 124.
32. Ibid., p. 124.
33. Mac Erlean, *Duanaire Dháibhidh Uí Bhruadair*, i, p. 204, §xviii.
34. Ibid., p. 206.
35. Dinneen, *Foras Feasa ar Éirinn*, iii, line 4109.
36. (a) *Annals of the Four Masters*, M1582.16; (b) O'Kelleher and Schopperle, *Beatha Colaim Chille*, p. 38, line 16.
37. *Bolg an tSoláir*, p. 51.
38. Ó Corráin, 'Nationality and kingship in pre-Norman Ireland,' pp. 9–10.
39. Mac Niocaill, 'A propos du vocabulaire social irlandais du bas moyen âge', p. 534; Simms, *From Kings to Warlords*, p. 86.
40. Mag Craith, *Dán na mBráthar Mionúr* i, p. 187, §57.
41. Pagden, *Lords of All the World*, pp. 89–90.
42. Ó Cuív, 'An appeal to Philip III of Spain by Ó Súilleabháin Béirre', p. 24.
43. Ibid., p. 22.
44. Breatnach, 'Donal O'Sullivan Beare to King Philip III', p. 320, line 36.
45. Kelly, *A Guide to Early Irish Law*.
46. Breatnach, 'The first third of *Bretha Nemed Tóisech*', p. 14.
47. Eagleton, *Ideology: An Introduction*, p. 156.
48. Foley, *Anthropological Linguistics*, p. 13.
49. Gumperz, 'The linguistic and cultural relativity of conversational inference', p. 402.
50. Bourdieu, *The Logic of Practice*, pp. 54 and 56.

The Irish idea of 'freedom'

1. Berlin, 'Two concepts of liberty', pp. 122–31. The classic statement of this position is that by John Stuart Mill in his essay 'On liberty' (1859). See *On Liberty*, edited by Edward Alexander.
2. Berlin, ibid., pp. 132–4. See *Rousseau: The Social Contract and Other Later Political Writings*, edited and translated by Victor Gourevitch.
3. Skinner, *Liberty before Liberalism*, pp. 113–17.
4. Berlin, 'Two concepts of liberty', p. 157.
5. Roberts, *Shorter Illustrated History of the World*, p. 375.
6. Benveniste, *Indo-European Language and Society*, p. 262.
7. O'Donovan and O'Curry, *The Ancient Laws of Ireland*: i, p. 78, line 12; i, p. 80, line 2 (commentary).
8. Ó Dónaill, *Foclóir Gaeilge-Béarla*; Dinneen, *Foclóir Gaedhilge agus Béarla*.
9. Ó Ruairc, *Dúchas na Gaeilge*, p. 31.
10. Ibid., p. 31.
11. Hull, 'Cáin Domnaig', p. 160, §1.
12. (a) Stokes and Strachan, 'Codex Paulinus Wirzburgiensis', 17c15; (b) Ní Laoire, *Bás Cearbhaill agus Farbhlaidhe*, line 4; (c) ibid., line 258.
13. Lewis, *Studies in Words*, p. 22.
14. Plummer, *Bethada*, p. 141, §8.
15. Ibid., p. 144, §11.
16. Ibid., p. 147, §§2–3.
17. Ibid., p. 79.
18. (a) O'Keeffe, 'The rule of Patrick', p. 218, §2; (b) O'Donovan, 'The ancient laws of Ireland', v, p. 14, line 28.
19. (a) Comyn, *Foras Feasa ar Éirinn*, i, p. 70, line 60; (b) ibid., i, p. 72, line 89; (c) Walsh, *Beatha Aodha Ruaidh Uí Dhomhnuill*, 1, p. 46, line 31.
20. Dinneen, *Foras Feasa ar Éirinn*, iii, line 1480.
21. Ibid., ii, line 959.
22. Breatnach, 'Anarchy in west Munster', p. 58, §§2–4.
23. Dinneen, *Foras Feasa ar Éirinn*, iii, lines 3924 and 3933.
24. Todd, *Cogadh Gaedhel re Gallaibh*, pp. 68–70.
25. Dinneen, *Foras Feasa ar Éirinn*, iii, line 3862.
26. Stokes and Strachan, 'The Milan glosses on the psalms', 131c10.
27. Mac Domhnaill, *Dánta is Amhráin Sheáin Uí Ghadhra*, pp. 19–21: (a) lines 1–4; (b) lines 49–52.
28. Ibid., lines 37–44.
29. Seán Ó Neachtain, quoted in Ó Buachalla, *Aisling Ghéar*, p. 270.
30. Tadhg Ó Neachtain, quoted in ibid., p. 375.
31. Raghnall Mac Domhnaill, quoted in ibid., p. 306.
32. De Brún, 'Litir ó Thor Londain', p. 52.
33. Ó Foghludha, *Cois na Ruachtaighe*, pp. 70–1: (a) lines 5–8; (b) lines 17–20; (c) lines 43–4.
34. Ua Duinnín, *Amhráin Eoghain Ruaidh Uí Shúilleabháin*, line 765.
35. Ó Murchú, (a) *Cúirt an Mheon-Oíche le Brian Merriman*, line 76–8; (b) Ó Muirithe, *Tomás Ó Míocháin*, p. 81, lines 6–8.
36. *Annals of the Four Masters*, M1600.16.

37. Aodh Buí Mac Cruitín, quoted in Ó Buachalla, *Aisling Ghéar*, p. 280.

38. Ua Duinnín, *Amhráin Eoghain Ruaidh Uí Shúilleabháin*, lines 817–22.

39. Ó Foghludha, *Cois na Bríde*, no. 22, p. 37, lines 29–32.

40. Ó Buachalla, 'An mheisiasacht agus an aisling'; 'Irish Jacobite poetry' pp. 40–9; 'Irish Jacobitism and Irish nationalism'.

41. Ó Buachalla, 'Irish Jacobite poetry,' p. 47.

42. Quoted in Ó Buachalla, 'Seaicibíteachas Thaidhg Uí Neachtain', pp. 57–8.

43. Ibid., p. 35.

44. For the English version see *Paddy's Resource*, pp. 70–1. For the Irish version see Ó Muirgheasa, *Dhá Chéad de Cheoltaibh Uladh*, pp. 39–41.

45. Quoted in Whelan, *The Tree of Liberty*, p. 57.

46. Dickson, 'Paine and Ireland', p. 148.

47. As suggested to me by two of my colleagues at the University of Notre Dame, Breandán Mac Suibhne and Kevin Whelan.

48. Ó Donnchadha, *Mícheál Óg Ó Longáin*, no. 29, p. 121, lines 1–8.

49. Ibid., no. 24, p. 113, lines 11–16.

50. Ó Buachalla, 'From Jacobite to Jacobin', pp. 85–95.

51. Ibid., p. 94. 'If the centrality of *saoirse* to his rhetoric, rather than other libertarian ideals, discommodes us, we should remember that it is no more central than freedom was to the American colonists or "Liberté" to the Lumières; and if his notion of *saoirse* seems to us to be somewhat ethnocentric, rather homespun, it was also congruent with other realizations of United Irishmen rhetoric.'

52. Ibid., p. 93.

53. De Bhaldraithe, *Cín Lae Amhlaoibh*, p. xl.

54. McGrath, *Cinn Lae Amhlaoibh Uí Shúileabháin,* iv, pp. 138–40.

55. For a discussion of the reception of foreign events in Irish-speaking Ireland at this time, particularly in America and France, see various essays by Buttimer: 'A Cork text on a Napoleonic campaign', 'Degrés de perception de la France dans l'Irlande gaélique de la pré-famine', and 'Cogadh Sagsana Nuadh sonn'.

56. De Bhaldraithe, *Cín Lae Amhlaoibh*, p. 77, lines 2480.

57. Ibid., p. 15, line 471.

58. Ibid., p. 26, lines 830–7; p. 27, lines 870–2; p. 48, lines 1521–32.

59. De Brún, 'Forógra do Ghaelaibh', p. 164.

60. Davis, *The Spirit of the Nation*, pp. 140–1.

61. Torna, 'Congantóirí Sheáin Uí Dhálaigh', p. 220.

62. Torna, 'Congantóirí Sheáin Uí Dhálaigh VII', p. 18.

63. Ibid., p. 19.

64. Torna, 'Séamus Mac Cruitín cct.', p. 224.

65. McKernan, 'Poems from manuscripts preserved in Queen's University, Belfast', p. 104, §4.

66. Mac Eoin, 'Mise Raifteirí: 1', p. 230.

67. From a Maynooth manuscript (MN 5: 281), quoted in Ó Buachalla, *Aisling Ghéar*, p. 618.

68. De Brún, Ó Buachalla and Ó Concheanainn, *Nua-Dhuanaire I*, pp. 66–7.

69. Ó Muirithe, *Tomás Ó Míocháin*, no. 1, p. 33.

70. Ó Muirí, *Lámhscríbhinn Staire an Bhionadaigh*: (a) line 4557; (b) line 5708.

71. Ibid., line 6252.

72. Breatnach, 'Metamorphosis 1603', p. 172, §5.
73. Ó Donnchadha, 'Cín Lae Ó Mealláin', p. 33.
74. (a) Patrick Pearse, graveside panegyric for O'Donovan Rossa, *Corpus of Electronic Texts*, p. 133; (b) Ald. Liam de Róiste, Treaty debates in Dáil Éireann, December 1921 to January 1922, session 5, ibid., p. 158.
75. Éamon de Valera, letter to David Lloyd George, 24 August 1921, *Corpus*.
76. Wierzbicka, *Understanding Cultures through Their Key Words*, pp. 131–2.
77. Ibid., p. 149.
78. Ibid., p. 149.
79. (a) Ó Donnchadha, *Leabhar Cloinne Aodha Buidhe*, p. 46, line 31; (b) Best, *Comhrag Fir Diadh ocus Chon cCulainn*, p. 277, line 12; (c) Plummer, *Bethada*, p. 147, §2; (d) Meyer, *Tucait indarba na nDéssi*, p. 23, line 7, note 7; (e) Mac Domhnaill, *Dánta is Amhráin Sheáin Uí Ghadhra*, p. 21, line 51; (f) Dinneen, *Foclóir Gaedhilge agus Béarla*, under *saoirse*.
80. Quoted in Ó Buachalla, 'From Jacobite to Jacobin', p. 88.
81. Ó Cearúil, *Bunreacht na hÉireann: A Study of the Irish Text*, article 40.3.3, p. 549.
82. Ibid., article 44.2.1, p. 630.
83. (a) Ó Muirithe, *Tomás Ó Míocháin*, p. 71; (b) McGrath, *Cinn Lae Amhlaoibh Uí Shúileabháin*, 4, p. 110; (c) Ó Muirí, *Lámhscríbhinn Staire an Bhionadaigh*, line 8666.
84. Examples are from the *Oxford English Dictionary*.
85. MacKechnie, 'Treaty between Argyll and O'Donnell', p. 98.
86. Ó Dónaill, *Foclóir Gaeilge-Béarla*, under *saocheadr.*
87. Ibid., under *cead.*
88. (a) Ó Muirithe, *Tomás Ó Míocháin*, p. 84, lines 21–24; (b) ibid., p. 86, lines 9–12.
89. From *An Gaodhal* (November 1885), reproduced in Uí Fhlannagáin, *Mícheál Ó Lócháin*, p. 10.
90. Ibid.
91. Ó Murchú, *Cúirt an Mheon-Oíche le Brian Merriman*, line 636.
92. Ó Cuív, 'Tréadlitir ó 1798', p. 62.
93. Ibid., p. 60.
94. Ó Mórdha, 'Dán faoi Mhuirthéacht na Frainnce', p. 203, §II.
95. (a) Ó Súilleabháin, 'Seanmóir ar ghnáithchleachtadh an pheacaidh', p. 287; (b) de Brún, 'Forógra', p. 164.
96. All examples and definitions are from the *Oxford English Dictionary*.
97. My impression from the *Oxford English Dictionary* is that *liberty* is used more often in the early period to cover this range than *freedom*.
98. Berlin, 'Two concepts of liberty', pp. 122–3; Wierzbicka, *Understanding Cultures through Their Key Words,* p. 131.
99. Ibid., p. 286, note 3.
100. For the Russian, Polish, English and Latin formulas see, ibid., p. 129.
101. (a) RIA ms. 23K42: 52.15, cited in *Dictionary of the Irish Language*, under **2. sairse**; (b) Ó Foghludha, *Amhráin Phiarais Mhic Gearailt*, p. 81, line 1427; (c) McErlean, *Duanaire Dháibhidh Uí Bhruadair*, ii, §v, p. 224.
102. In Latin, French or German, for example. See Wierzbicka, *Understanding Cultures through Their Key Words,* p. 288, note 11.
103. (a) McKenna, *Iomarbhágh na bhFileadh*, no. vi, p. 60, §51; (b) *Annals of the Four Masters*, M1600.16; (c) Ó Muirithe, *Tomás Ó Míocháin*, p. 86, line 12; (d) *Annals*

of the Four Masters, M854.8; (*e*) Ó Muirí, *Lámhscríbhinn Staire an Bhionadaigh*, line 6252.

104. The idea of liberty associated with the various forms of nineteenth- and twentieth-century liberalisms (in France, England and, to some degree, the United States) could be said to contain or include various ideas of freedom, centrally 'freedom of conscience'—meaning usually freedom from dogmatic religious beliefs but also a belief in a relationship between 'freedom' and 'law'. There is a liberal tradition in nineteenth-century France (de Staël, Constant, Montalembert, Guizot, Jouffroy, Bonald, Tocqueville, Rémusat, etc.) that is at the very least the equal of its English counterpart, despite the vast difference in historical experience, particularly of course that of the Revolution and Napoléon Bonaparte. So Wierzbicka's intimation that liberalism is an Anglophone phenomenon should be modified somewhat (Séamus Deane, personal communication).

105. Hughes, *Words in Time*, p. 60.

106. Skinner, 'A third concept of liberty'.

BIBLIOGRAPHY

Primary sources

Annála Ríoghachta Éireann: see *Annals of the Four Masters,* Corpus of Electronic Texts, National University of Ireland, Cork, 2000.

Atkinson, Robert (ed.), *The Passions and Homilies from Leabhar Breac* (Dublin: Royal Irish Academy, 1887).

Beckett, Colm (ed.), *Aodh Mac Domhnaill: Dánta* (Dublin: An Clóchomhar, 1987).

Bergin, Osborn (ed.), 'What brought the Saxons to Ireland', *Ériu,* 1 (1904), p. 244.

—— *Trí Bior-Ghaoithe an Bháis* (Dublin Institute for Advanced Studies, 1931).

—— 'Irish grammatical tracts: III irregular verbs', *Ériu,* 14 (1946), pp. 167–250.

—— *Irish Bardic Poetry* (Dublin Institute for Advanced Studies, 1970).

Best, R. I. (ed.), 'The settling of the manor of Tara,' *Ériu,* 4 (1908–10), pp. 121–72.

—— (ed.), 'Comhrag Fir Diadh ocus Chon cCulainn, Táin Bó Cúailnge', *Zeitschrift für Celtische Philologie,* 10 (1915), pp. 274–308.

Binchy, D. A. (ed.), *Críth Gablach* (Dublin Institute for Advanced Studies, 1944).

Black, Ronald (ed.), 'A manuscript of Cathal Mac Muireadhaigh', *Celtica,* 10 (1974), pp. 193–209.

Bolg an tSoláir, or Gaelic Magazine (Belfast: Athol Books, c. 1999).

Breatnach, Liam (ed.), 'The first third of *Bretha Nemed Tóisech,*' *Ériu,* 40, p. 1–40 (1989).

Breatnach, Pádraig A. (ed.), 'Metamorphosis 1603: dán le hEochaidh Ó hEodhasa', *Éigse,* 17 (1977–8), pp. 169–80.

—— 'A poem of protest,' *Celtica,* 17 (1985), pp. 91–100.

—— 'An address to Aodh Ruadh Ó Domhnaill in captivity, 1590', *Irish Historical Studies,* 25, no. 98, pp. 198–213.

—— 'The second Earl of Tyrconnell', *Éigse,* 28 (1994–5), pp. 169–71.

Breatnach, R. A. (ed.), 'Anarchy in west Munster,' *Éigse,* 22–3 (1987–9), pp. 57–66.

Breatnach, R. B. (ed.) 'Donal O'Sullivan Beare to King Philip III, 20th February, 1602,' *Éigse,* 6 (1948–52), p. 314–25.

Calder, George (ed.), *Togail na Tebe* (Cambridge University Press, 1922).

Carney, James (ed.), *The Poems of Blathmac* (Dublin: Irish Texts Society, 1967).

Cathréim Cellacháin Caisil, Corpus of Electronic Texts, National University of Ireland, Cork, 1996.

Corpus of Electronic Texts, National University of Ireland, Cork (www.ucc.ie/celt/irlpage.html).

Comyn, David, (ed.), *Foras Feasa ar Éirinn,* vol. i (London: Irish Texts Society, 1902).

Davis, Thomas (ed.), *The Spirit of the Nation, 1845* (reprinted Washington: Woodstock Books, 1998).

De Bhaldraithe, Tomás (ed.), *Cín Lae Amhlaoibh* (Dublin: An Clóchomhar, 1970).

De Brún, Pádraig (ed.), 'Forógra do Ghaelaibh, 1824', *Studia Hibernica,* 12 (1972), pp. 142–66.

——'Litir ó Thor Londain', *Éigse,* 22 (1987), pp. 49–53.

De Brún, Pádraig, Ó Buachalla, Breandán, and Ó Concheanainn, Tomás (eds.), *Nua-Dhuanaire I* (Dublin Institute for Advanced Studies, 1976).

Dillon, Myles (ed.), *Lebor na Cert: The Book of Rights* (Dublin: Irish Texts Society, 1962).

Dinneen, Patrick S (ed.), *The Poems of Egan O'Rahilly* (London: Irish Texts Society, 1900).

——*Foras Feasa ar Éirinn*, vols. ii–iv (London: Irish Texts Society, 1908–14).

Donlevy, Andrew (ed.), *Teagasg Críostuidhe do Réir Ceasda agus Freagartha* (Paris: James Guérin, 1742).

Dwelly, Edward (ed.), *The Illustrated Gaelic–English Dictionary* (Glasgow: Gairm Publications, 1977).

Gillies, W. (ed.), 'A poem on the downfall of the Gael', *Éigse*, 13 (1970), pp. 203–10.

Greene, David (ed.), *Duanaire Mheig Uidhir: The Poembook of Cú Chonnacht Mag Uidhir, Lord of Fermanagh, 1566–1589* (Dublin Institute for Advanced Studies, 1991).

Gwynn, Edward (ed.), *The Metrical Dindshenchus*, vol. 3 (Dublin Institute for Advanced Studies, 1991).

Hartnett, Michael, *O Bruadair* (Dublin: Gallery Press, 1985).

Henderson, George (ed.), *Bricriu's Feast* (London: Irish Texts Society, 1899).

Hughes, A. J. (ed.), *Robert Shipboy MacAdam: His Life and Gaelic Proverb Collection* (Belfast: Institute of Irish Studies, Queen's University, 1998).

Hull, Vernam (ed.), 'Cáin Domnaig', *Ériu*, 20 (1966), pp. 151–77.

Hyde, Douglas (ed.), *Gabháltas Serluis Mhóir* (London: Irish Texts Society, 1917).

Jackson, Kenneth (ed.), *Cath Maige Léna* (Dublin Institute for Advanced Studies, c. 1990).

——*Aislinge Meic Con Glinne* (Dublin Institute for Advanced Studies, 1990).

Kelly, Fergus, and Edwards, Thomas Charles (eds.), *Bechbretha* (Dublin Institute for Advanced Studies, 1976).

Knott, Eleanor (ed.), *The Bardic Poems of Tadhg Dall Ó hUiginn*, 2 vols. (London: Irish Texts Society, 1922).

Mac Airt, Seán (ed.), *An Leabhar Branach,* (Dublin Institute for Advanced Studies, 1944).

Macalister, R.A. Stewart, *Lebor Gabála Érenn: The Book of the Taking of Ireland* 5 vols. (Dublin: Irish Texts Society, 1938).

Mac Cionnaith Láimhbheartach, (ed.), *Dioghluim Dána* (Dublin: Oifig an tSoláthair, 1938).

Mac Cuarta, Brian (ed.), 'Conchubhar Mac Bruaidheadha and Sir Matthew de Renzy', *Éigse*, 27 (1993), pp. 122–6.

Mac Domhnaill, an tAthair, (ed.). *Dánta is Amhráin Sheáin Uí Ghadhra* (Dublin: Oifig an tSoláthair, 1955).

Mac Eoin, Gearóid S. (ed.), 'Mise Raifteirí: 1', *Éigse*, 12. (1967–8), pp. 229–32.

Mac Erlean, John C. (ed.), *Duanaire Dháibhidh Uí Bhruadair,* 3 vols. (London: Irish Texts Society, 1910–17).

Mac Giolla Eáin, E. C. (ed.), *Dánta, Amhrain is Caointe Sheathrúin Céitinn* (Dublin: Connradh na Gaeilge, 1900).

Mac Giolla Léith Caoimhín (ed.), *Oidheadh Chloinne hUisneach* (London: Irish Texts Society, 1993).

McGrath, Michael (ed.), *Cinn Lae Amhlaoibh Uí Shúileabháin,* 4 vols. (Dublin: Irish Texts Society, 1937).

MacKechnie, John (ed.), 'Treaty between Argyll and O'Donnell', *Scottish Gaelic Studies,* 7 (1951), pp. 94–102.

McKenna, Lambert (ed.), *Iomarbhágh na bhFileadh,* 2 vols. (London: Irish Texts Society, 1918).

——*Aithdioghlaim Dána*, 2 vols. (Dublin: Irish Texts Society, 1939–40).

——*The Book of O'Hara* (Dublin Institute for Advanced Studies, 1951).

McKernan, Owen (ed.), 'Poems from manuscripts preserved in Queen's University, Belfast', *Éigse*, 3, (1940) pp. 103–7.

Mac Maoláin, Seán (ed.), *Cora Cainte as Tír Chonaill* (Dublin: An Gúm, 1992).

Mag Craith, Cuthbert, *Dán na mBráthar Mionúr*, 2 vols. (Dublin Institute for Advanced Studies, 1967).

Meyer, Kuno (ed.), *Trecheng Breth Féne: The Triads of Ireland* (Dublin: Hodges, Figgis, 1909).

——*The Instructions of King Cormac Mac Airt* (Dublin: Hodges, Figgis, 1909).

——'Tucait indarba na nDéssi', in O. J. Bergin, R. I. Best, K. Meyer, and J. G. O'Keefe, (eds), *Anecdota from Irish Manuscripts* (Dublin: Hodges, Figgis, 1907–12), vol. 1, pp. 15–24.

——'Mitteilungen aus Irischen Handschriften', *Zeitschrift für Celtische Philologie*, 8 (1912), pp. 102–20.

Mulchrone, Kathleen (ed.), *Caithréim Cellaig* (Dublin Institute for Advanced Studies, 1978).

Murphy, Gerard, 'Poems of exile by Uilliam Nuinsean mac Barúin Dealbhna', *Éigse*, 6 (1948), pp. 8–15.

Ní Cheallacháin, Máire (ed.), *Filíocht Phádraigín Haicéad* (Dublin: An Clóchomhar, 1962).

Ní Chléirigh, Meadhbh (ed.), *Eachtra na gCuradh* (Dublin: Oifig an tSoláthair, 1941).

——*Eolas ar an Domhan* (Dublin: Oifig an tSoláthair, 1944).

Ní Laoire, Siobhán (ed.), *Bás Cearbhaill agus Farbhlaidhe* (Dublin: An Clóchomhar, 1986).

Ní Mhuirgheasa, Máire (ed.), *Imtheacht an Dá Nónbhar agus Tóraigheacht Taise Taoibhghile* (Dublin: Oifig an tSoláthair, 1954).

Ní Shéaghdha, Nessa (ed.), *Agallamh na Seanórach* 1 (Dublin: Oifig an tSoláthair, 1942).

Nutt, Alfred, *The Voyage of Bran*, vol. 1 (London: David Nutt, 1895).

Ó Coigligh, Ciarán (ed.), *Filíocht Ghaeilge Phádraig Mhic Phiarais* (Dublin: An Clóchomhar, 1981).

Ó Cuív, Brian (ed.), 'Tréadlitir ó 1798,' *Éigse*, 12 (1964), pp. 57–64.

——*Párliament na mBan* (Dublin: Dublin Institute for Advanced Studies, 1977).

——'An appeal to Philip III of Spain by Ó Súilleabháin Béirre, December 1601', *Éigse*, 30 (1997), pp. 18–26.

Ó Dochartaigh, Cathair, and Ó Baoill, Colm (eds.), *Trí Rainn agus Amhrán* (Belfast: Lagan Press, 1996).

Ó Donnchadha, Rónán (ed.), *Mícheál Óg Ó Longáin* (Dublin: Coiscéim, 1994).

Ó Donnchadha, Tadhg (see also Torna).

Ó Donnchadha, Tadhg (ed.), 'Cín Lae Ó Mealláin', *Analecta Hibernica*, 3 (September 1931), pp. 1–61.

——*Leabhar Cloinne Aodha Buidhe* (Dublin: Oifig an tSoláthair, 1931).

——*An Leabhar Muimhneach, maraon le Suim Aguisíní* (Dublin: An Gúm, 1939).

——*Dánta Sheáin na Ráithíneach* (Dublin: Connradh na Gaedhilge, 1907).

O'Donovan, John (ed.), *The Banquet of Dún na nGedh and the Battle of Mag Rath: An Ancient Historical Tale* (Dublin: Irish Archaelogical Society, 1842).

O'Donovan, John, and O'Curry, Eugene (eds.), *The Ancient Laws of Ireland*, 6 vols. (Dublin: Alexander Thom, 1865–1919).

Ó Fiaich, Tomás, and Ó Caithnia, Liam (eds.), *Art Mac Bionaid: Dánta* (Dublin: An Cló-chomhar, 1979).

Ó Foghludha, Risteárd (ed.), *Amhráin Phiarais Mhic Gearailt* (Dublin: Connradh na Gaedhilge, 1905).

——*Cois na Bríde: Liam Inglis, 1709–78* (Dublin: Oifig an tSoláthair, 1937).

——*Cois na Ruachtaighe* (Dublin: Oifig an tSoláthair, 1938).

O'Grady, Standish Hayes, *Silva Gadelica* (London: Williams and Norgate, 1892).

O'Grady, Standish Hayes, and Flower, Robin (eds.), *Catalogue of Irish Manuscripts in the British Museum*, vol. 1 (London: Trustees of the British Museum, 1926).

Ó Grianna, Séamus ('Máire'), *Le Clap-sholus* (Dublin: Oifig an tSoláthair, 1967).

——*An Clár is an Fhoireann* (Dublin: Oifig an tSoláthair, 1955).

Ó hÓgáin, Dáithí (ed.), *Duanaire Thiobraid Árainn* (Dublin: An Clóchomhar, 1981).

O'Keeffe, J. G. (ed.), 'The Rule of Patrick,' *Ériu*, 1 (1904), pp. 216–24.

O'Kelleher, Andrew, and Schopperle, G., *Betha Colaim Chille. Life of Columcille* (reprinted Dublin Institute for Advanced Studies, 1994).

Ó Maonaigh, Cainneach (ed.), *Scáthán Shacramuinte na hAithridhe* (Dublin Institute for Advanced Studies, 1952).

Ó Mórdha, Séamus P (ed.), 'Dán faoi Mhuirthéacht na Frainnce', *Éigse*, 7 (1953), pp. 202–4.

Ó Muirgheasa, Énrí (ed.), *Dhá Chéad de Cheoltaibh Uladh* (Dublin: Oifig an tSoláthair, 1934).

Ó Muirí, Réamonn (ed.), *Lámhscríbhinn Staire an Bhionadaigh: Comhrac na nGael agus na nGall le Chéile* (Éigse Oirialla, 1994).

Ó Muirithe, Diarmaid (ed.), *Tomás Ó Míocháin: Filíocht* (Dublin: An Clóchomhar, 1988).

Ó Murchú, Liam P. (ed.), *Cúirt an Mheon-Oíche le Brian Merriman* (Dublin: An Cló-chomhar, 1982).

Ó Neachtain, Eoghan (ed.), *Stair Éamoinn Uí Chléire* (Dublin: M. H. Gill, 1918).

O'Rahilly, Cecile (ed.), *Eachtra Uilliam* (Dublin Institute for Advanced Studies, 1949).

O'Rahilly, Thomas F. (ed.), *Dánfhocail* (Dublin: Talbot Press, 1921).

——*Measgra Dánta II* (Cork University Press, 1977 [1927]).

Ó Súilleabháin, Pádraig (ed.), 'Seanmóir ar ghnáithchleachtadh an pheacaidh', *Éigse*, 13 (1970), pp. 279–90.

Ó Súilleabháin Béirre, Pilib, *Historiae Catolicae Hiberniae Compendium* (Lisbon, 1621), edited by Matthew Kelly (Dublin, 1850).

O'Tuama, Seán and Kinsella, Thomas, *An Duanaire 1600–1900: Poems of the Dispossessed* (Portlaoise: Dolmen Press, 1981).

Paddy's Resource, Being a Collection of Original and Modern Patriotic Songs, Toasts and Sentiments, Compiled for the Use of All Firm Patriots (Philadelphia, 1796).

Power, P. (ed.), *The Life of St. Declan of Ardmore and the Life of St. Mochuda of Lismore* (London: Irish Texts Society, 1914).

Plummer, Charles (ed.), *Bethada Náem nÉrenn: Lives of Irish Saints* (Oxford University Press, 1922).

Stafford, Thomas, *Pacata Hibernia* (London, 1633).

Stapleton, Theobald, *Catechismus, seu Doctrina Christiana, Latina-Hibernica, per Modum Dialogi, inter Magistrum et Discipulum* (Brussels, 1639; facsimile, Dublin: Irish Manuscripts Commission, 1945).

Stokes, Whitley (ed.), 'The Gaelic abridgement of the book of *Ser Marco Polo*', *Zeitschrift für Celtische Philologie*, 1, pp. 245–73, 362–438.

——*Lives of Saints from the Book of Lismore* (Oxford: Clarendon Press, 1890).

Stokes, Whitley, and Strachan, John (eds.), 'The Milan glosses on the psalms', in *Thesaurus Palaeohibernicus* (Dublin Institute for Advanced Studies, reprinted 1975), vol. 1, pp. 7–483.

——'Codex Paulinus Wirzburgiensis', in *Thesaurus Palaeohibernicus* (Dublin Institute for Advanced Studies, reprinted 1975), vol. 1, pp. 499–714.

Stokes, Whitley, and Windisch, Ernst, 'Acallam na Senórach', in *Irische Texte* IV, I (Leipzig: Hirzel, 1900).

——'In Cath Catharda', *Irische Texte*, IV.2 (Leipzig: Hirzel, 1909).

Todd, James H. (ed.), *Cogadh Gaedhel re Gallaibh* (London: Longmans, 1867).

——*Leabhar Breathnach annso sis* (Dublin: Irish Archaeological Society, 1848).

Torna [Tadhg Ó Donnchadha], 'Congantóirí Sheáin Uí Dhálaigh', *Éigse*, 2 (1940), pp. 213–33.

——'Congantóirí Sheáin Uí Dhálaigh VII', *Éigse*, 3 (1940), pp. 8–20.

——'Séamus Mac Cruitín cct.' ('Marbhna Dhomhnaill Uí Chonaill'), *Éigse*, 4, (1943–4) pp. 220–4.

Ua Duinnín, Pádraig (ed.), *Amhráin Eoghain Ruaidh Uí Shúilleabháin* (Dublin: Connradh na Gaedhilge, 1901).

Wagner, Heinrich (ed.), *Linguistic Atlas and Survey of Irish Dialects* (reprinted Dublin Institute for Advanced Studies, 1981–2).

Walsh, Paul (ed.), *The Flight of the Earls* (Dublin: Gill and Son, 1916).

——*Gleanings from Irish Manuscripts* (Dublin, 1933).

——*Beatha Aodha Ruaidh Uí Dhomhnaill*, 2 vols. (Dublin: Irish Texts Society, 1957).

Williams, N. J. A. (ed.), *Pairlement Chloinne Tomáis* (Dublin Institute for Advanced Studies, 1981).

Secondary sources

Alexander, Edward (ed.), *On Liberty* (Peterborough, Ontario: Broadview Press, 1999).

Anderson, Benedict, *Imagined Communities: Reflections on the Origins and Spread of Nationalism* (London and New York: Verso, 1983).

Anttila, Raimo, *Historical and Comparative Linguistics* (Amsterdam: John Benjamins, 1989).

Bakhtin, M. M., *The Dialogic Imagination: Four Essays* (Austin: University of Texas, 1981).

Baumgarten, Rolf, 'The geographical orientation of Ireland in the time of Isidore and Orosius', *Peritia*, 3 (1984), pp. 189–203.

Benveniste, Emile, *Indo-European Language and Society*, translated by Elizabeth Palmer (University of Miami Press, 1973).

Berlin, Isaiah, 'Two concepts of liberty', in *Four Essays on Liberty* (Oxford University Press, 1969), pp. 118–72.

Bloomfield, Leonard, *Language* (London: Allen and Unwin, 1933).

Boas, Franz (ed.), *General Anthropology* (Boston: D. C. Heath, 1938).

——'Introduction to *A Handbook of American Indian Languages*', edited by Preston Holder (University of Nebraska, 1966).

Bourdieu, Pierre, *Outline of a Theory of Practice*, translated by Richard Nice (Cambridge University Press, 1977).

——*The Logic of Practice*, translated by Richard Nice (Stanford University Press, 1990).

Bradshaw, Brendan, 'Native reaction to the westward enterprise: a case study in Gaelic ideology', in K. R. Andrews, N. P. Canny and P. E. H. Hair (eds.), *The Westward Enterprise: English Activities in Ireland, The Atlantic and America, 1480–1560* (Liverpool University Press, 1978), pp. 65–80.

—— 'The Elizabethans and the Irish: a muddled model', *Studies,* 70 (1981), pp. 233–44.

—— *The Irish Constitutional Revolution of the Sixteenth Century* (Cambridge University Press, 1979).

—— 'Geoffrey Keating: apologist of Gaelic Ireland', in Brendan Bradshaw, Andrew Hadfield and Willie Maley (eds.), *Representing Ireland: Literature and the Origins of Conflict, 1534–1660* (Cambridge University Press, 1994), pp. 166–90.

Breatnach, Pádraig A., 'The chief's poet', *Proceedings of the Royal Irish Academy,* vol. 83c (1983), pp. 37–79.

Buttimer, Cornelius G., '*Cogadh Sagsana Nuadh Sonn:* reporting the American Revolution', *Studia Hibernica,* 28, (1994), pp. 63–101.

——'A Cork text on a Napoleonic campaign', *Journal of the Cork Historical and Archaeological Society,* 95 (1990), pp. 107–19.

——'Degrés de perception de la France dans l'Irlande gaélique de la pré-famine', in C. Laurent and H. Davies (eds.), *Irlande et Bretagne: Vingt Siècles d'Histoire* (Rennes: Terre de Brume, 1994), pp. 178–89.

Bybee, Joan L., Perkins, Revere, and Pagliuca, William, *The Evolution of Grammar* (Chicago University Press, 1994).

Byrne, F. J., '*Senchas:* the nature of Gaelic historical tradition', in J. G. Barry (ed.), *Historical Studies 9* (Belfast: 1974), pp. 137–59.

Caball, Mark, '*Pairlement Chloinne Tomáis:* a reassessment', *Éigse,* 27 (1993), pp. 47–57.

——'*The Gaelic Mind and the Collapse of the Gaelic World:* an appraisal', *Cambridge Medieval Celtic Studies,* 25 (summer 1993), pp. 87–96.

——*Poetry and Politics: Reaction and Continuity in Irish Poetry, 1558–1625* (Cork University Press, 1998).

Calhoun, Craig, 'Habitus, Field and Capital', in Craig Calhoun, Edward LiPuma, and Moisha Postone (eds.) *Bourdieu: Critical Perspectives* (University of Chicago Press, 1993), pp. 62–88.

Carey, John, *A New Introduction to Lebor Gabála Érenn* (London: Irish Texts Society, 1993).

Carney, James, 'Three Old Irish accentual poems', *Ériu,* 22 (1971), pp. 23–80.

Carroll, Clare, *Circe's Cup: Cultural Transformations in Early Modern Writing about Ireland* (Cork University Press, 2001).

Chung, Sandra, and Timberlake, Alan, 'Tense, mood and aspect', in Tim Shopen (ed.), *Linguistic Typology and Grammatical Description,* 2 (Cambridge University Press, 1985), pp. 202–58.

Cohn, Bernard, 'Regions, subjective and objective: their relation to the study of modern Indian history and society', in Robert Crane (ed.), *Symposium on Regions and Regionalism in South Asian Studies: An Exploratory Study* (Duke University Press, 1966), pp. 5–37.

Comrie, Bernard, *Aspect* (Cambridge University Press, 1976).

Croft, William, *Typology and Universals* (Cambridge University Press, 1990).

Crowley, Tony, *Language in History: Theories and Texts* (London: Routledge, 1996).

Culler, Jonathan, *Ferdinand de Saussure* (Ithaca: Cornell University Press, 1986).

Dahl, Östen, *Tense and Aspect Systems* (Oxford: Blackwell, 1985).

Daniel, E. Valentine, *Fluid Signs: Being a Person the Tamil Way* (University of California Press, 1984).

De Saussure, Ferdinand, *Course in General Linguistics,* translated with an introduction and notes by Wade Baskin (New York and London: McGraw-Hill, 1959).

Dickson, David, 'Paine and Ireland', in David Dickson, Dáire Keogh and Kevin Whelan (eds) *The United Irishmen: Republicanism, Radicalism and Rebellion* (Dublin: The Lilliput Press, 1993), pp. 135–50.

Dictionary of the Irish Language (Dublin: Royal Irish Academy, 1983).

DIL, see *Dictionary of the Irish Language*

Dinneen, Patrick S., *Foclóir Gaedhilge agus Béarla* (Dublin: Irish Texts Society, 1927).

Dixon, R. M. W., 'A method of semantic description', in D. D. Steinberg and L. A. Jakobovits (eds), *Semantics: An Interdisciplinary Reader in Philosophy, Linguistics and Psychology* (Cambridge University Press, 1979), pp. 436–71.

Dunne, T. J., 'The Gaelic response to conquest and colonization: the evidence of the poetry', *Studia Hibernica,* 20 (1980), pp. 7–30.

Duranti, Alessandro (ed.), *Linguistic Anthropology: A Reader* (Oxford: Blackwell, 1997).

——, *Linguistic Anthropology* (Cambridge University Press, 1997).

Eagleton, Terry, *Ideology: An Introduction* (London: Verso, 1991).

Elliott, J. H., 'Revolution and continuity in early modern Europe', *Past and Present,* 42 (1969), pp. 35–56.

Fleischman, Suzanne, 'Imperfective and irrealis', in Joan L. Bybee and Suzanne Fleischman (eds.), *Modality in Grammar and Discourse* (Amsterdam: John Benjamins, 1995), pp. 519–51.

Foley, William A., *Anthropological Linguistics: An Introduction* (Oxford: Blackwell, 1997)

Genee, Inge, *Sentential Complementation in a Functional Grammar of Irish* (The Hague: Holland Academic Graphics, 1998).

Gibbons, Luke, 'Identity without a centre: allegory, history and Irish nationalism', in *Transformations in Irish Culture* (Cork University Press, 1996), pp. 134–47.

Givón, Talmy, *Functionalism and Grammar* (Amsterdam: John Benjamins, 1995).

—— 'Beyond foreground and background', in Russell Tomlin (ed.), *Coherence and Grounding in Discourse* (Amsterdam: John Benjamins, 1987), pp. 175–88.

Gourevitch, Victor (ed.), *Rousseau: The Social Contract and Other Later Political Writings* (Cambridge University Press, 1997).

Graiméar Gaeilge na mBráithre Críostaí (Dublin: Gill and Son, 1960).

Greene, David, 'Ir. *gnás: W. gnaws*; OHG. *kunst*,' *Celtica,* 6 (1963), pp. 62–3.

Gumperz, John J., 'The linguistic and cultural relativity of conversational inference', in John J. Gumperz and Stephen Levinson (eds.), *Rethinking Linguistic Relativity* (Cambridge University Press, 1996), pp. 374–406.

Gumperz, John J., and Levinson, Stephen (eds.), *Rethinking Linguistic Relativity* (Cambridge University Press, 1996).

Hagège, Claude, 'Du thème au thème en passant par le sujet: pour une théorie cyclique,' *La Linguistique* 14 (2) (1978), pp. 3–38.

Haiman, John (ed.), *Iconicity in Syntax* (Amsterdam: John Benjamins, 1985).

——*Talk Is Cheap: Sarcasm, Alienation and the Evolution of Language* (Oxford University Press, 1998).

Hall, R., *Leonard Bloomfield: Essays on His Life and Work* (Amsterdam: John Benjamins, 1987).

Hanks, William F., 'Notes on semantics in linguistic practice', in Craig Calhoun, Edward LiPuma and Moishe Postone (eds.), *Bourdieu: Critical Perspectives* (University of Chicago Press, 1993), pp. 139–55.

Heine, Bernd, 'Grammaticalization as an explanatory parameter', in William Pagliuca (ed.), *Perspectives on grammaticalization* (Amsterdam: John Benjamins, 1994), pp. 255–87.

Hobsbawm, Eric, *Nations and Nationalism since 1780: Programme, Myth, Reality* (Cambridge University Press, 1990).

Hodge, Robert, and Kress, Gunther, *Social Semiotics* (Ithaca: Cornell University Press, 1988).

Hopper, Paul, and Thompson, Sandra A., 'Transitivity in grammar and discourse', *Language*, 56 (1980), pp. 251–99.

Hopper, Paul, and Traugott, Elizabeth Closs, *Grammaticalization* (Cambridge University Press, 1993).

Hughes, Geoffrey, *Words in Time: A Social History of the English Vocabulary* (Oxford: Blackwell, 1988).

Hymes, Dell (ed.), *Language in Culture and Society: A General Reader in Linguistic Anthropology* (New York: Harper and Row, 1964).

Jakobson, Roman, 'Quest for the essence of language', in *Selected Writings* II, pp. 345–59.

—— 'A few remarks on Peirce, pathfinder in the science of language', in *The Framework of Language*, pp. 31–9.

—— 'Metalanguage as a linguistic problem', in *The Framework of Language*, pp. 81–92.

—— *The Framework of Language* (University of Michigan: Michigan Studies in the Humanities, 1980).

——'Shifters, verbal categories and the Russian verb', in *Selected Writings* II, pp. 130–47.

—— *Selected Writings* II (The Hague: Mouton, 1971).

Johnson, Mark, *The Body in the Mind: The Bodily Basis of Meaning, Imagination and Reason* (University of Chicago, 1987).

Kelly, Fergus, *A Guide to Early Irish Law* (Dublin Institute for Advanced Studies, 1988).

Koselleck, Reinhard, Conze, Werner, and Brunner, Otto, *Geschichtliche Grundbegriffe: Historisches Lexicon zur Politisch-Sozialen Sprache in Deutschland*, 8 vols. (Stuttgart: E. Kleit, 1972–97).

Labov, William, 'On the adequacy of natural languages, I. The development of tense', in John Victor Singler (ed.), *Pidgin and Creole Tense-Mood-Aspect Systems* (Amsterdam: John Benjamins, 1990), pp. 1–58.

Lakoff, George, and Johnson, Mark, *Metaphors We Live By* (University of Chicago Press, 1980).

Lakoff, George, and Turner, Mark, *More than Cool Reason: A Field Guide to Poetic Metaphor* (University of Chicago Press, 1989).

Leerssen, Joep, *Mere Irish and Fíor-Ghael: Studies in the Idea of Irish Nationality, Its Development and Literary Expression prior to the Nineteenth Century* (Cork University Press, 1996).

Lehmann, Christian, 'Grammaticalization: synchronic variation and diachronic change,' *Lingua e Stile*, 20 (1985), pp. 303–18.

Lehrer, Adrienne, 'The influence of semantic fields on semantic change', in J. Fisiak (ed.), *Historical Semantics, Historical Word Formation* (Amsterdam: John Benjamins, 1985), pp. 283–96.

Lewis, C. S., *Studies in Words* (Cambridge University Press, 1967).

Locke, John, *An Essay Concerning Human Understanding,* edited by A. C. Fraser (Oxford: Clarendon Press, 1959 [1690]).

Lucy, John, *Language Diversity and Thought* (Cambridge University Press, 1992).

—— (ed.), *Reflexive Language: Reported Speech and Metapragmatics* (Cambridge University Press, 1993).

Lyons, John, *Structural Semantics: An Analysis of Part of the Vocabulary of Plato* (Oxford: Blackwell, 1963).

—— *Semantics,* 2 vols. (Cambridge University Press, 1977).

Mac Aogáin, Parthalán (ed.), *Graiméir Ghaeilge na mBráthar Mionúr* (Dublin Institute for Advanced Studies, 1968).

Mac Cana, Proinsias, 'Early Irish ideology and the concept of unity', in Richard Kearney (ed.), *The Irish Mind: Exploring Intellectual Traditions* (Dublin: Wolfhound Press, 1985), pp. 56–78.

Mac Clúin, Seoirse, *Caint an Chláir* (Dublin: Oifig an tSoláthair, 1940).

Glanmor Williams and Robert Owen Jones (eds), Mac Craith, Mícheál, 'Ireland and the Renaissance', in Oifig an tSoláthair, *The Celts and the Renaissance: Tradition and Innovation.* Proceedings of the Eighth International Congress of Celtic Studies, 1987 (Cardiff: University of Wales Press, 1990), pp. 57–89.

—— 'Creideamh agus athartha: idé-eolaíocht pholaitíochta agus aos léinn na Gaeilge i dtús an seachtú haois déag', in Máirín Ní Dhonnchadha (ed.), *Nua-Léamha: Gnéithe de Chultúr, Stair agus Polaitíocht na hÉireann, c.1600–c.1900* (Dublin: An Clóchomhar, 1996), pp. 7–19.

Mac Curtin, Hugh, *The Elements of the Irish Language* (Louvain: van Overbeke, 1728 [facsimile reprint, Menston: Scholar Press, 1972]).

Mac Grianna, Seosamh, 'Ár ndúchas——ár gcinniúint', in *Pádraic Ó Conaire agus Aistí Eile* (Dublin: An Gúm, 1986 [1936]), pp. 103–17.

McKibben, Sarah E, 'Born to die . . . and to live on: terminal metaphors in the life of Irish', in *Irish Review,* 26 (2000), pp. 89–99.

McMahon, April S., *Understanding Language Change* (Cambridge University Press, 1994).

Mac Niocaill, Gearóid, 'A propos du vocabulaire social irlandais du bas moyen âge', *Études Celtiques* xii, 2 (1970–1), pp. 512–46.

Matthews, Peter, *A Short History of Structural Linguistics* (Cambridge University Press, 2001).

Miller, Arthur K. W., 'O'Clery's Irish Glossary', *Revue Celtique,* 4 (1879–80), pp. 349–428, and 5 (1881–3), pp. 1–69.

Miller, Kerby A., *Emigrants and Exiles: Ireland and the Irish Exodus to North America* (Oxford University Press, 1985).

Morgan, Hiram, 'Faith and fatherland ideology in sixteenth-century Ireland,' *History Ireland,* vol. 3, no. 2 (summer 1995), pp. 13–20.

Newmeyer, Frederick J., *Language Form and Language Function* (Cambridge, MA: MIT Press, 2000).

Nic Pháidín, Caoilfhionn, *Cnuasach Focal ó Uíbh Ráthach* (Dublin: Royal Irish Academy, 1987).

Ní Suaird, Damhnait, 'Jacobite rhetoric and terminology in the political poems of the Fernaigh manuscripts (1688–1693)', *Scottish Gaelic Studies,* 19 (1999), pp. 93–140.

Ní Thiarnaigh, Éilis, 'An diagacht agus an dúchas', *Irisleabhar Mhá Nuat* (1993), pp. 155–67.

Ó Buachalla, Breandán, '*Annála Ríoghachta Éireann* agus *Foras Feasa ar Éirinn*: an comhthéacs comhaimseartha', *Studia Hibernica*, 22–3 (1982–3), pp. 59–105.

—— 'An mheisiasacht agus an aisling', in Pádraig de Brún (ed.) *Folia Gadelica* (Cork University Press, 1983), pp. 72–87.

—— 'Na Stiobhartaigh agus an tAos Léinn: Cing Séamas', *Proceedings of the Royal Irish Academy*, vol. 83c (1983), pp. 81–134.

—— 'Cúlra is tábhacht an dáin "A leabhráin ainmnighthear d'Aodh"', *Celtica*, 21 (1990), pp. 402–16.

—— 'Poetry and politics in early modern Ireland', *Eighteenth Century Ireland: Iris an Dá Chultúr*, 7 (1992), pp. 149–75.

—— 'Irish Jacobite poetry', *Irish Review*, 12 (1993), pp. 40–9.

—— 'Irish Jacobitism and Irish nationalism: the literary evidence', in Michael O'Dea and Kevin Whelan (eds.), *Nations and Nationalisms: France, Britain and the Eighteenth-Century Context* (Oxford: Voltaire Foundation, 1995), pp. 103–116.

—— 'Seaicibíteachas Thaidhg Uí Neachtain', *Studia Hibernica*, 26 (1993), pp. 31–64.

—— *Aisling Ghéar: An tAos Léinn agus na Stiobhartaigh, 1603–1788* (Dublin: An Clóchomhar, 1996).

—— 'From Jacobite to Jacobin', in Thomas Bartlett, David Dickson, Dáire Keogh and Kevin Whelan (eds.), *1798: A Bicentenary Perspective* (Dublin: Four Courts Press, 2003), pp. 75–96.

—— 'James our true king: the ideology of Irish royalism', in D. George Boyce, Robert Eccleshall and Vincent Geoghegan (eds.), *Political Thought in Ireland since the Seventeenth Century* (London: Routledge, 1993), pp. 7–35.

Ó Cadhlaigh, Cormac, *Gnás na Gaedhilge* (Dublin: Oifig an tSoláthair, 1940).

Ó Cearúil, Micheál, *Bunreacht na hÉireann: A Study of the Irish Text* (Dublin: Oifig an tSoláthair, 1999).

Ó Corráin, Ailbhe, 'Aspects of voice in the grammatical structure of Irish', in Brian Ó Catháin and Ruairí Ó hUiginn (eds.), *Béalra: Aistí ar Theangeolaícht na Gaeilge* (Maynooth: An Sagart, 2001), pp. 98–122.

Ó Corráin, Donnchadh, 'Dál gCais: church and dynasty', *Ériu*, 24 (1973), pp. 52–63.

—— 'Caithréim Chellacháin Chaisil', *Ériu*, 25 (1974), pp. 1–70,

—— 'Nationality and kingship in pre-Norman Ireland,' in T. W. Moody (eds.), *Nationality and the Pursuit of National Independence*, Historical Studies, 11 (Belfast: Appletree Press, 1978), pp. 1–35.

Ó Doibhlin, Breandán, *Aistí Critice agus Cultúir* (Dublin: Foilseacháin Náisiúnta Teoranta, s.d.).

—— *Gaoth an Fhocail: Foclóir Analógach* (Dublin: Sáirséal-Ó Marcaigh agus Coiscéim, 1998.

Ó Donaill, Niall (ed.), *Foclóir Gaeilge–Béarla* (Dublin: Oifig an tSoláthair, 1978).

O'Donnell, Jim, and de Fréine, Seán, *Ciste Cúrsaí Reatha* (Dublin: An Foras Riaracháin, 1992).

O'Donovan, John (ed.), 'The Irish correspondence of James Fitzmaurice Fitzgerald of Desmond', *The Journal of the Kilkenny and South-East of Ireland Archaeological Society*, 2 (1858–9), pp. 354–68.

Ó Dúshláine, Tadhg, *An Eoraip agus Litríocht na Gaeilge 1600–1650: Gnéithe den Bharócachas i Litríocht na Gaeilge* (Dublin: An Clóchomhar, 1987).

Ó hÁinle, Cathal, 'Cogadh Gaedhel re Gallaibh', *Léachtaí Cholm Cille,* 13 (1982), pp. 41–98.

O'Rahilly, Thomas F., *A Miscellany of Irish Proverbs* (Dublin: Talbot Press, 1922).

O'Reilly, Edward, *An Irish–English Dictionary* (Dublin, 1821).

O Riordan, Michelle, *The Gaelic Mind and the Collapse of the Gaelic World* (Cork University Press, 1990).

Ó Ruairc, Maolmhaodhóg, *Dúchas na Gaeilge* (Dublin: Cois Life, 1996).

——*Díolaim d'Abairtí Dúchasacha* (Dublin: Coiscéim, 1996).

Ó Searcaigh, Séamus, *Coimhréir Ghaedhlig an Tuaiscirt* (Dublin: Oifig an tSoláthair, 1939).

Ó Siadhail, Mícheál, *Modern Irish: Grammatical Structure and Dialect Variation* (Cambridge University Press, 1989).

Oxford English Dictionary, 20 vols. (Oxford University Press, 1989).

Pagden, Anthony, 'Dispossessing the barbarian: the language of Spanish Thomism and the debate over the property rights of the American Indians', in *The Languages of Political Theory in Early-Modern Europe* (Cambridge University Press, 1987), pp. 79–98.

——*Lords of All the World: Ideologies of Empire in Spain, Britain and France, c.1500–c.1800* (Newhaven and London: Yale University Press: 1995).

Palmer, Gary B., *Towards a Theory of Cultural Linguistics* (Austin: University of Texas, 1996).

Peirce, C. S., *Collected Papers* (Cambridge, MA: Belknap Press, 1940–65).

Pinker, Steven, *The Language Instinct* (New York: William Morrow, 1994).

Rees, Alwyn, and Rees, Brinley, *Celtic Heritage: Ancient Tradition in Ireland and Wales* (London: Thames and Hudson, 1961).

Roberts, John, *Shorter Illustrated History of the World* (Boston: Houghton, 1993).

Rumsey, Alan, 'Wording, meaning and linguistic ideology', *American Anthropologist, 92* (1990), pp. 346–61.

Saeed, John, *Semantics* (Oxford: Blackwell, 1997).

Sankoff, Gillian, 'Variability and explanation in language and culture: cliticization in New Guinea Tok Pisin', in Muriel Saville-Troike (ed.), *Linguistics and Anthropology* (Washington: Georgetown University Press, 1977), pp. 59–73.

Sapir, Edward, 'The status of linguistics as a science', in Lucy Burke, Tony Crowley and Alan Girvin (eds.), *The Routledge Language and Cultural Theory Reader* (reprinted London: Routledge 2000), pp. 395–400.

—— *Language: An Introduction to the Study of Speech* (New York: Harcourt, Brace and World, 1921).

—— *Selected Writings of Edward Sapir in Language, Culture and Personality,* edited by David Mandelbaum (Berkeley: University of California Press, 1949).

—— 'Language', in *Culture, Language and Personality,* edited by David Mandelbaum (Berkeley: University of California Press, 1957).

Scowcroft, Mark, 'Miotas na gabhála i *Leabhar Gabhála*', *Léachtaí Cholm Cille*, 13 (1982), pp. 41–75.

—— '*Leabhar Gabhála*: part I: The growth of the text', *Ériu*, 38 (1987), pp. 81–140.

—— '*Leabhar Gabhála*: part II: The growth of the tradition', *Ériu*, 39 (1988), pp. 1–66.

Silverstein, Michael, 'Shifters, linguistic categories and cultural description', in K. Basso and H. Selby (eds.), *Meaning in Anthropology* (Albuquerque: University of New Mexico, 1976), pp. 11–56.

—— 'Language structure and linguistic ideology', in *The Elements: A Parasession on Linguistic Units and Levels* (Chicago Linguistic Society, 1979), pp. 193–247.

—— 'The three faces of "function": preliminaries to a psychology of language', in M. Hickman (ed.), *Social and Functional Approaches to Language and Thought* (New York: Academic Press, 1987), pp. 17–38.

—— 'The indeterminacy of contextualization: when is enough enough?', in P. Auer and A. diLuzio (eds.), *The Contextualization of Language* (Amsterdam: John Benjamins, 1992), pp. 55–76.

—— 'The limits of awareness' (1981), reprinted in Alessandro Duranti (ed.), *Linguistic Anthropology: A Reader* (Oxford: Blackwell, 1997), pp. 382–401.

—— 'Metapragmatic discourse and metapragmatic function', in John Lucy (ed.), *Reflexive language*, pp. 33–58.

Simms, Katharine, *From Kings to Warlords: The Changing Political Structure of Gaelic Ireland in the Later Middle Ages* (Woodbridge: Boydell Press, 1987).

——'Bards and barons: the Anglo-Irish aristocracy and the native culture', in Robert Bartlett and Angus Mackay (eds.), *Medieval Frontier Societies* (Oxford University Press, 1989), pp. 177–97.

Skerrett, R. A., 'On the meaning of "Habitual", *Celtica*, 11 (1976), pp. 251–54.

Skinner, Quentin, *The Foundations of Modern Political Thought*, vol. 2 (Cambridge University Press, 1978).

—— *Liberty before Liberalism* (Cambridge University Press, 1998).

—— 'A third concept of liberty,' *London Review of Books*, vol. 24, no. 7, 4 April 2002, pp. 16–18.

Slobin, Dan I., 'From "thought and language" to "thinking for speaking"', in John J. Gumperz and Stephen C. Levinson (eds.), *Rethinking Linguistic Relativity* (Cambridge University Press, 1996), pp. 70–96.

Sweetser, Eve, *From Etymology to Pragmatics* (Cambridge University Press, 1990).

Thompson, Sandra A., '"Subordination" and narrative event structure', in Russell Tomlin (ed.), *Coherence and Grounding in Discourse* (Amsterdam: John Benjamins, 1987), pp. 435–54.

Tibi, Bassam, *Arab Nationalism. A Critical Enquiry*, edited and translated by Marion Farouk-Sluglett and Peter Sluglett (New York: St. Martin's Press, 1981).

Traugott, Elizabeth Closs, 'On the rise of epistemic meaning: an example of subjectification in language change', *Language*, 65 (1989), pp. 31–55.

Uí Fhlannagáin, Fionnuala, *Mícheál Ó Lócháin agus An Gaodhal* (Dublin: An Clóchomhar, 1990).

Verschueren, Jeff, 'Pragmatics', in Paul Cobley (ed.), *The Routledge Companion to Semiotics and Linguistics* (London: Routledge, 2001), pp. 83–4; p. 242.

Voloshinov, V. N., *Marxism and the Philosophy of Language*, translated by Ladislav Matejka and I. R. Titunik (Cambridge, MA: Harvard University Press, 1973).

—— 'Multiaccentuality and the sign', reprinted in Lucy Burke, Tony Crowley and Alan Girvin (eds.), *The Routledge Language and Cultural Theory Reader* (London: Routledge, 2000), pp. 39–47.

von Humboldt, Wilhelm, *Linguistic Variability and Intellectual Development*, translated by George C. Buck and Frithjof A. Raven (University of Pennsylvania Press, [1836], 1971).

Wagner, Heinrich, *Das Verbum in den Sprachen der Britischen Inseln* (Tübingen: Max Niemeyer, 1959).

Watkins, Calvert, 'The etymology of Irish *dúan*', *Celtica*, 11 (1976), pp. 270–7.

—— *The American Heritage Dictionary of Indo-European Roots* (Boston: Houghton, 1985).

—— 'New parameters in historical linguistics, philology, and culture history', *Language*, 65 (1989), pp. 783–99.

Whelan, Kevin, *The Tree of Liberty: Radicalism, Catholicism and the Construction of Irish Identity, 1760–1830* (Cork University Press, 1996).

Whorf, Benjamin Lee, 'Discussion of Hopi linguistics', in John B. Carroll (ed.), *Language, Thought and Reality: Selected Writings*, pp. 102–11.

—— 'The relation of habitual thought and behavior to language', in *Language, Thought and Reality: Selected Writings*, pp. 134–59.

—— *Language, Thought and Reality: Selected Writings*, edited by John B. Carroll (Cambridge, MA: MIT Press, 1956).

Wierzbicka, Anna, *Semantics, Culture and Cognition: Universal Human Concepts in Culture-Specific Configurations* (Oxford University Press, 1992).

—— *Semantics: Primes and Universals* (Oxford University Press, 1996).

—— *Understanding Cultures through Their Key Words* (Oxford University Press, 1997).

Williams, Raymond, *Keywords: A Vocabulary of Culture and Society* (Oxford University Press, 1976).

INDEX

Acallam na Senórach: relationship between *dual* and *dúthaigh* 106–7

ainbhfine eachtrann 'foreign rabble': compared with *dúchas* 81, 83

aindlightheach 'unlawful': on the nature of English designs on Ireland 180. See also *dligheadh*.

Aisling Meic Con Glinne: parody of *dúchas* 50–1

allmhardha: collocated with *ainm* 'foreign title' 124

America: as the source of *saoirse* 'freedom' 212

An Gaodhal 208ff, 218

ancestry: and *dúchas* 35, 50–1

Anderson, Benedict: on the vocabulary of patriotism 98

andúthchas 'foreignness': opposite of *dúchas* 27–8

ANNÁLA RÍOGHACHTA ÉIREANN 58, 77, 81ff, 91–2, 141, 149, 175–6

Annála Ríoghachta Éireann: on the affinity (*báidh*) between Ireland and Spain 58–9

Annála Ríoghachta Éireann: evidence for the concepts of *dúthaigh* and *athartha* 81ff

Annála Ríoghachta Éireann: the phrase *saoirse agus sochar dúthaighe* 91–2

Annála Ríoghachta Éireann: on Mac William Burke 77

Annála Ríoghachta Éireann: on the buying and selling of *dílse* 119

Annála Ríoghachta Éireann: on the death of Owny O'More 175–6

Annála Ríoghachta Éireann: examples of *domhghnas* 176

'Ar bhás Thomáis Dáibhis' (poem) 207

Argyll, Earl of: sixteenth century treaty with O'Donnell 26–7, 216

athartha 'fatherland' 31–2, 42–3, 60, 81ff, 84–6, 124, 175–6

athartha: with attributive genitive *dúchais* 42–3

athartha: and *dúchas* 32, 81ff

athartha: and *bunadhus* 60

athartha: and *dúthaigh* 81ff, 124

athartha: and *dúthaigh*: syntax compared 81–3

athartha and *domhghnas* 175–6

athartha: collocated with *iris* ('faith and fatherland') 84–6

bádhach (re/le) 'fond (of)': as the feeling towards one's *dúchas* 58–9

BÁIDH 'affinity' 57ff

báidh: collocated with *nádúrtha* as the natural feeling for one's *dúchas* 57ff

báidh: on the affinity (*báidh*) between Ireland and Spain 58

Baile Bhós Dálaigh (Dalystown, Co. Mayo) 208

Baile Mhuráid (Dalystown) 208

BALLYHALE (CO. KILKENNY) 215

Ballyhale (Co. Kilkenny): anti-tithe rally in 1832 addressed by Amhlaoibh Ó Súilleabháin 215

Baltinglass, Viscount: revolt of 1580 63

BETHA COLAIM CHILLE 29–30, 42, 82, 105

Betha Colaim Chille: on *dúchas* and *folaigheacht* 'bloodline' 29–30, 105

Betha Colaim Chille: on *dúchas* and *dual* 29–30, 105

Betha Colaim Chille: on *dúchas* and *athartha* 'fatherland' 32, 82–3

Betha Colaim Chille: on the collocation *athartha dúchais* 'native land' 42–3

BEATHA AODHA RUAIDH UÍ DHOMH-NAILL 46–7, 76, 82, 84–5

Beatha Aodha Ruaidh Uí Dhomhnaill: on the predicative use of *dú* and *dúthaigh* 46–7

Beatha Aodha Ruaidh Uí Dhomhnaill: on the relationship between the Burkes and the O'Donnells 76–7

Beatha Aodha Ruaidh Uí Dhomhnaill: on the comparative syntax of *dúthaigh* and *athartha* 82

Beatha Aodha Ruaidh Uí Dhomhnaill: on the phrase 'faith and fatherland' (*iris agus athartha*) 84–5

Bechbretha (Old Irish law tract): on the concepts of *díleas* and *ruidhleas* 150

Belfast 202

BENVENISTE, EMILE 106, 185

Benveniste, Emile: on early ideas of 'freedom' 185

Benveniste, Emile: on the semantics and pragmatics of exchange and reciprocity 106

Bergin, Osborn 141–2

BERLIN, ISAIAH 8, 183–4, 187, 228–9

Berlin, Isaiah: on negative and positive freedom 8, 183–4

Berlin, Isaiah: condescension towards collective freedom 184

Berlin, Isaiah: critiqued by Skinner 228–9

Betha Caoimhgin: on *saoirse* and *daoirse* in Middle Irish 190–1

Bingham, Sir Richard 62

BOAS, FRANZ 3, 6, 14, 15, 16, 17, 134, 136, 137, 166, 170

Boas, Franz: on the obligatory nature of grammar 3, 6, 16, 17, 134, 136

Boas, Franz: on metalinguistic awareness 14

Boas, Franz: and linguistic relativity 15

Boas, Franz: on the partial nature of grammar 136–7

Bolg an tSoláir: Irish-English vocabulary of political terms 178, 202

Bolívar, Simón 204

Bourdieu, Pierre 18, 171–2, 181–2. See also 'habitus'.

BOYNE, RIVER 62–3, 66, 75–6

Boyne, River: as part of the symbolic centre of Ireland 62, 66, 75–6

BRADSHAW, BRENDAN 63–4, 78–79, 85

Bradshaw, Brendan: on the political poetry of the O'Byrnes 63–4

Bradshaw, Brendan: on Céitinn's views on conquest 78–79

Bradshaw, Brendan: on sixteenth-century patriotism 85–6

Bréifne 63, 71

Bretha Nemed Toísech (Old Irish law tract): *dú* in the sense of 'right', 'entitlement' 47, 181

Brooklyn, NY: home of *An Gaodhal* newspaper 208

bunadh: in compound *bunadhchenél* 'race of origin' 76

BUNADHUS 'origin', 'foundation' 58ff

bunadhus: and *athartha* 60

Búrc, Riocard Óg: as subject of Tadhg Dall Ó hUiginn's poem 124ff, 162ff

Burke, Tibbot 76–7, 82

Bybee, Joan: on habituality in language 135–6

Byrne, Francis John: definition of *seanchas* 177

CABALL, MARC 69, 75–6, 80–1, 93–4, 123–4

Caball, Marc: on Fearghal Óg Mac an Bhaird's poem to Flaithrí Ó Maolchonaire 123–4

Caball, Marc: on the rise of a seventeenth-century entrepreneurialism 93–4

Caball, Marc: on sixteenth-century patriotism 80–1

Caball, Marc: on Tadhg Dall Ó hUiginn's poem to Seán Mac Uilliam Búrc 69, 75–6

CÁIN 'tax', 'tribute' 190–1

cáin: in relation to *saoirse* and *daoirse* 190–1, 194–5. See also *cíos*.

CAIRT AINBHFINE 'foreign charter' 71–2

cairt ainbhfine: contrasted with the legitimacy of physical force 71

cairt ainbhfine: contrasted with the legitimacy of hereditary claim 71–2

Camden, William 192

CARROLL, CLARE 78–9, 147, 177–8

Carroll, Clare: on Spanish debates on indigenous rights 78–9, 147, 177–8

Carroll, Clare: on *toich* as an Irish equivalent to *dominium* 147, 177–8

Cashel 59ff, 64, 70–1

Cashel: claim of the Dál gCais as to their *dúchas* 59ff, 64, 70–1

Castlehaven 173

CATHOLIC CONFEDERATES 211–12

Catholic confederates: in the cause of native land (*dúthaigh*) 211–2

Catholic confederates: in the cause of liberty of conscience (*liberti coinnséis*) 211–2

CEAD 'leave', 'permission', 'liberty' 215–19, 221, 224

cead: as Irish expression of positive freedom 215–19

cead: overlap with *saoirse* 217–18, 221

cead: as Irish expression of physical freedoms 216–17

CEANTAR 'district' 9–10

ceantar: compared with *dúthaigh* 9–10

CEART (CERT) 'right' 71, 73ff, 79, 142, 200, 201

ceart: and *dúchas* 28–9, 77ff, 179

ceart: and *dualgas* 114ff

ceart: and *dliged* (*dligeadh*) 142

ceart: and joint sovereignty (*cert comhd-húthchasa*) 71, 147

CÉITINN, SEATHRÚN 19, 30, 41, 42, 74, 77–8, 84, 104, 105, 119ff, 141, 177, 178, 192–4

Céitinn, Seathrún: on the concepts of *saoirse*, *tearmann*, *comairce* and *cádhus* 192–3

Céitinn, Seathrún: on *saoirse* as sovereignty to be defended 192–3

Céitinn, Seathrún: on types of conquest 78

Céitinn, Seathrún: on the use of past habitual and its rhetorical effect 119–121

Céitinn, Seathrún: on indigenous rights 78

Céitinn, Seathrún: on *ceart*, *dúchas* and *dual* 28–9, 77–8, 104–5, 179

Céitinn, Seathrún: on *dúchas* and *dligheadh* 30–1, 139

Céitinn, Seathrún: on the establishment of *Midhe* as the symbolic fifth province 61

Céitinn, Seathrún: use of *seanchas* 177

Céitinn, Seathrún: *dúthaigh* and *dúchas* contrasted with exile 41, 42, 84

Céitinn, Seathrún: the relationship between *dlighe(adh)* and *dualgas* 141

Céitinn, Seathrún: poem on the prostitution of Ireland 129–30

CÍN LAE AMHLAOIBH 204–6

Cín Lae Amhlaoibh: *saoirse Chaitliceach* as Catholic Emancipation 204–6

Cín Lae Amhlaoibh: on the universal nature of *saoirse* 204–5

CÍOS 'rent', 'tribute' 142, 190–1

cí(o)s: in relation to *dliged* 142. See *dligheadh*.

cíos: in relation to *saoirse* and *daoirse* 190–1, 194. See also *cáin*.

Clann Tomáis 93ff

cnú / clú: as a reciprocal lexical pair in poetry 106

codramacht: used as password of the United Irish Society, Philadelphia 1797 202

COGADH GAEDHEL RE GALLAIBH 23ff, 27, 30, 31, 39, 59, 60, 61, 69, 70, 71, 76, 77, 194

Cogadh Gaedhel re Gallaibh: on the importance of symbolic sites 60–1

Cogadh Gaedhel re Gallaibh: on the relation-ship between *dúthaigh* and *fearann cloidhimh* 69–70, 76

Cogadh Gaedhel re Gallaibh: on the Dál gCais claim to Cashel 30, 60, 70–1

Cogadh Gaedhel re Gallaibh: on the relation-ship between *dúthaigh* and *dúchas* 23–5

Cogadh Gaedhel re Gallaibh: on the relation-ship between *dúthaigh*, *dúchas* and *bunadhus* 59–60

Cogadh Gaedhel re Gallaibh: on the relation-ship between *dúchas* and *fuil* 'blood' 30, 31

Cogadh Gaedhel re Gallaibh: on defending the freedom (*sairi*) of the fatherland 194

COHN, BERNARD 67, 87–8

Cohn, Bernard: on the cultural basis for regional identity in India 67–8, 87–8

COIGRÍOCH 'foreign land' 84

coigríoch: as opposed to the native land (*dúthaigh* and/or *dúchas*) 84

Coill na Manach (Co. Tipperary) 210

cóir 'right' 73–5, 77–8, 108–9, 155. See also *ceart*.

Colm Cille 82, 105, 192

Columbia, Republic of 204

COMHRAC NA nGAEL AGUS NA nGALL LE CHÉILE 43, 210

Comhrac na nGael agus na nGall le chéile: on the syntax of *tír dhúchais* 43

Comhrac na nGael agus na nGall le chéile: on the use of the loanword *libeartaigh* 210

Comrie, Bernard: on the semantics of habituality 119

CONSUETUDO 'custom' 78–9, 177, 179

consuetudo and *gnáthughadh* 179, 180–1

creideamh 'faith', 'belief': and *dúthaigh* ('faith and fatherland') in letters of James Fitzmaurice Fitzgerald 70, 85–6

críoch 'land', 'territory': syntax of, compared to *dúthaigh* and *dúchas* 87–90

Críth Gablach (Old Irish law tract): on the concept of *díre* in early Irish law 145

Croft, William: on comparing linguistic and extra-linguistic structure 157–8

Cruachain: as symbolic centre of Connacht 61–2, 64, 71–3

cúige (*cóiced*) 'fifth', 'province': as the basis for the political organization of Ireland and Irish cultural unity 61, 71

Cúirt an Mheán Oíche 219

custom: see *gnáth* and *gnáthughadh*

Dahl, Osten: on the typology of habitual aspect 135

Dál gCais 59, 70–1, 147. See also Cashel; Cogadh Gaedhel re Gallaibh.

DANIEL, E.VALENTINE 11, 12, 55, 86ff, 170

Daniel, E.Valentine: and Peirce's semiotic theory 11

Daniel, E.Valentine: and Jakobson's idea of a 'shifter' 12, 170

Daniel, E.Valentine: and Tamil words for locality and nation 86ff

DAOIRSE 'captivity', 'enslavement' 188ff

daoirse: and verbs of 'freeing' 195–6

daoirse: opposed to saoirse 188, 190, 195ff, 206

daor 'unfree' 188

Davis, Thomas 207

de las Casas, Bartholome 78

de las Casas, Bartholome: on indigenous rights in the Americas 78

de Renzy, Matthew 91

deimhnioghadh 'affirming': as a grammatical term for the non-habitual past 132

DEORADH 'exile', 'foreigner' 73, 74, 175

deoradh: contrasted with dúchas or dúthaigh 73, 74

deoradh: with attributive genitive dúchais 'returned exile' 175

DEORAIDHEACHT 'exile', 'domicile' 84, 175

deoraidheacht: contrasted with dúchas 84, 175

de Valera, Eamon 212–3

DÍLEAS 'personal property' 5, 138, 146ff, 150, 152ff, 164, 178

díleas: predicative syntax (with dúchas / dual etc.) 150–1, 152ff, 164

díleas: and ruidhleas 150–1

díleas: and natural law 178

DÍLIS 'own' 83, 138ff, 201

dílis: collocated with dúthaigh 'native land' and the reflexive féin 'own' 83

dílse 'proprietary right', 'ownership', 'property' 5, 138ff

Dinneen, Patrick S. 19, 20, 56, 186

DÍR 'due', 'proper' 5, 138, 145–6

dír: predicative use of, collocated with dligheadh 145–6

DÍRE 'due', 'right' 5, 31, 138, 145, 149

díre: concept of in early Irish law 145

díre: and dúchas 31, 145

dleacht 'rightful' 108

dleathach 'lawful' 113–4

DLIGHE(ADH) 'lawful right', 'tax', 'tribute' 5, 31, 108, 138, 139ff, 178

dligheadh: and dúchas 31, 139–40

dligheadh: and the verbal of necessity 160

dligheadh: pragmatics of 143–4

dligheadh: predicative use of 146

dligheadh: the concept of in Lebor na Cert 140, 143ff

dligheadh: and dualgas 140

dligheadh: and natural law 177–8

dlitheach 'lawful' 113–4

DOMHGHNAS 'place of habitation', 'native land' 175–6

domhghnas: and athartha 175–6

domhghnas: and dúthaigh 175–6

DOMINIUM 'natural right of ownership' 78–9, 177

dominium: and native ideology of 'right' 177–8

dominium: and domhghnas 179–80

dominium: de facto/de iure 79, 179

Donlevy, Andrew: use of dualgas in his Catechism 107

DÚ 'place', 'native place' 4, 46–7, 55–6, 88

dú: predicative syntax of (with dúthaigh and dúchas) 46–7, 88

dú: dictionary definitions of (with dúthaigh and dúchas) 4, 55–6

dú: attributive syntax (with dúthaigh and dúchas) 47

dú: in the sense of 'right', 'entitlement' 46

DUAL 'native', 'natural', 'fitting' 4, 6, 78, 99ff, 122, 178

dual: and dúchas 29, 100ff, 179

dual: and dualgas 99ff, 103

dual: and predicative syntax 99ff, 103

dual: in proverbs 100–1

dual: dictionary definitions of (with dualgas) 99

dual: and gnáth 117, 118, 134, 137, 157

dual: with the concepts of gnáth and iongnadh in Mac an Bhaird's poem 'Fúarus iongnadh a fhir chumainn' 122–3

dual: concept of in the poem 'Anocht is uaigneach Éire' 129

dual: with the concepts of gnáth and iongnadh in Céitinn's poem 'A Bhanbha bhogomh dhona dhuaibhseach' 129–30

dual: and natural law 177

dualas 108, 109, 112. See also dualgas.

DUALGAS 'natural right', 'due', 'duty' 5, 99ff, 106ff, 122, 201 *dualgas*: compared with Sc. *dualchas* 115

dualgas: and *dúchas* 115

dualgas: concept of in the poem 'Senchas cía lín non-iarfaig' 111–13

dualgas: concept of in the poem 'Créd fuarais oram, a Aoidh?' 108–10

dualgas: on relationship with the loanword *páigh* in *Pairlement Chloinne Tomáis* 110–11

dualgas: and *dligheadh* 141

dúan / dúas: as a reciprocal lexical pair in poetry 106

DÚCHAS 'hereditary right', 'native land', inherent characteristic' 4, 6, 9 20–98 and *passim*

dúchas: as native land, collocated with *athartha* 31–2, 81ff

dúchas: as native land, associated with *dúthaigh* and *dú* 23ff and *passim*

dúchas: and attributive genitive *fearann dúchais* 'native land' 40–1

dúchas: and attributive genitive *fód dúchais* 'native land' 41–2

dúchas: and attributive genitive *tír dhúchais* 'native land' 5, 42–4

dúchas: and attributive genitive *athartha dúchais* 'native land' 42

dúchas: and *díre* 'due', 'right' 31, 145

dúchas: and *dligheadh* 'natural right' 31, 139–40

dúchas: as hereditary right, collocated with *ceart* 'right' 28–9, 179

dúchas: and 'joint sovereignty' (*cert comhd-húthchasa*) 71, 147

dúchas: compared with *dual* 'what is native, natural, fitting' 29, 100ff, 179

dúchas: and *folaigecht* 'bloodline', 'descent' 29–30

dúchas and attributive genitive *cearda dúchais* 'hereditary professions/callings' 33, 95

dúchas: and its internalized meanings (character traits) 32ff, 48ff

dúchas: and *tallann* 'talent' 35

dúchas: and *dúil* 'desire' 33–4

dúchas: and *cinnteacht* 'stinginess' 34–5

dúchas: and *fuinneamh* 'energy' 34

dúchas: and proverbs 38, 52, 58–9, 101

dúchas: syntax of: used as attributive genitive 40ff

dúchas: syntax of: used in predicative constructions 30ff and *passim*

dúchas: syntax of: restricted use of with adjectival complements 88–9

dúchas: dictionary definitions 4, 20–1, 46, 55–6

dúchas: and *andúchas* 'foreignness' 27–8

dúchas: contrasted with *eachtruinn* 'foreign-ers' 65

dúchas: contrasted with *deoradh* 'foreigner', 'exile' 73, 74

dúchas: contrasted with *ainbhfine eachtrann* 'foreign rabble' 81, 83

dúchas: attributive genitive in phrase *deoradh dúchais* 'returned exile' 175

dúchas: contrasted with *deoraidheacht* 'exile', 'domicile' 83, 175

dúchas: use of in exile poetry 79–81

dúchas: and Renaissance patriotism 79ff

dúchas: and natural law 177

dúchasach: 'native', 'inhabitant' 21–2, 178

dúchasaigh: = *indiginae* of natural law theory 178

Dumfries (Scotland) 208

Dundalk (Co. Louth) 220

Dunne, T. J. 67, 75

DURANTI, ALESSANDRO 1, 12, 15, 17, 56, 59, 166

Duranti, Alessandro: definition of 'index' 12, 56, 59

Duranti, Alessandro: on language and culture 1

Duranti, Alessandro: on Whorf's 'fashions of speaking' 17, 166

Duranti, Alessandro: on linguistic relativity 15

DÚTHAIGH 'hereditary land', 'native land', 'estate' 4, 6, 23ff, 55–98 and *passim*. See also *dúchas*.

dúthaigh: as 'heaven' 84

dúthaigh: collocated with *nádúrtha* to mean 'Ireland' 90

dúthaigh: collocated with *creideamh* 'faith' in the letters of James Fitzmaurice Fitzgerald 85

dúthaigh: and *athartha* 81ff, 124

dúthaigh: and *athartha*, syntax compared 82

dúthaigh: collocated with *fírinneach* 'true' to mean 'heaven' 84

dúthaigh: collocated with the genitive *fíre* 'true' 73

dúthaigh: and the idea of being permanent in one's native place 79

dúthaigh: and *domhghnas* 176

dúthaigh: collocated with *dílis* and *féin* to mean 'one's own place' 83 *dúthaigh*: compared and contrasted with *fear-ann cloidhimh* 'sword land' 70ff, 148

dúthaigh: defence of associated with *fíor (g)catha* 'just cause' 69, 76

dúthaigh: restricted use of with adjectival complements 89

dúthaigh: predicative use 25ff and *passim*

Dwelly, Edward 115

Eachtra Uilliam: *dúchas* in proverbial usage 38, 103–4

eachtruinn 'foreigners': contrasted with *dúchas* 41, 65

éigean 'force': compared to and contrasted with *ceart* 'right' 73–4

ÉIREANNACH 'Irish' 63, 69

Éireannach: and the term *Gaedheal* (Gael) 69

eleutheros (Greek) 'free' 185

Elizabeth I 70

Elliott, J. H.: on sixteenth-century European patriotism 80

exile: theme of, contrasted with *dúchas* 42, 57, 73, 74, 79–81, 84, 175

faith and fatherland ideology (general). See under *creideamh*; *dúthaigh*; *iris*; *athartha*

FEARANN 69ff, 87, 88, 89–90, 148, 192

fearann: syntax of, compared to *dúthaigh* and *dúchas* 87–9

fearann forgabhála 'conquered land' 70ff

fearann cathaoire 'mensal land' 71, 148

fearann saor 'free land' 192

fearann cloidhimh 'sword land': compared and contrasted with *dúthaigh* 69ff, 148

fíor (g)catha 'just cause': associated with defending the *dúthaigh* 69

FITZMAURICE FITZGERALD, JAMES 70, 85–6

Fitzmaurice Fitzgerald, James: letters in Irish 70, 85–6

Fitzmaurice Fitzgerald, James: on Irish terms for faith (*creideamh*) and fatherland (*dúthaigh*) 70, 85–6

Fitzmaurice Fitzgerald, James: on just cause (*fíor gcatha*) 69

FITZSTEPHEN, ROBERT 28–9, 77–8, 104–5, 108, 178

Fitzstephen, Robert: foreign origin as precluding *dúchas* in Ireland 28–9, 77–8, 104–5, 178

Fitzstephen, Robert: plunders Dublin 108

Flanders 220

Fled Dúin na nGédh: on the idea of *dligheadh* 140–1

folaidecht 'bloodline', 'descent': and *dúchas* 29–30

FORAS FEASA AR ÉIRINN 28–9, 31, 61, 74, 77–8, 104–5, 120–1, 177, 179, 192–3, 194–5

Foras Feasa ar Éirinn: on the concepts of *saoirse*, *tearmann*, *comairce* and *cádhus* 192–3

Foras Feasa ar Éirinn: on *saoirse* as sovereignty to be defended 192–3

Foras Feasa ar Éirinn: on types of conquest 78

Foras Feasa ar Éirinn: on the use of past habitual and its rhetorical effect 120–1

Foras Feasa ar Éirinn: on indigenous rights 79

Foras Feasa ar Éirinn: on *ceart*, *dúchas* and *dual* 28–9, 77–8, 104–5, 179

Foras Feasa ar Éirinn: on *dúchas* and *dligheadh* 30–1, 139

Foras Feasa ar Éirinn: on the establishment of Midhe as the symbolic fifth province 61

Foras Feasa ar Éirinn: use of *seanchas* 177

foreignness: theme of, contrasted with *dúchas* 27–8, 65, 71–2, 81, 73–4, 78, 83, 104–5, 115 (Scottish *dualchas*), 178

France 202, 205, 212

Frederick Augustus, Duke of York and Albany 204

free (English) 185

FREEDOM (GENERAL) See under *cead*; *liberti*, *libheirte*, *libeartaigh*; *saoirse*, *saorthoil*, *saorgacht*, *saorchead*, *toil* (Irish); *freedom*; *liberty* (English); *wolność*; *swoboda* (Polish)

freedom (concept) domain 'of' 183

freedom (English) 183, 221ff

freedom, positive 183 and *passim*. See also Berlin, Isaiah and Skinner, Quentin. For Irish, see *cead*, *réim*, *saorchead*, *saorthoil*, *toil shaor*.

freedom, negative 183 and *passim*. See also Berlin, Isaiah and Skinner, Quentin. For Irish, see *saoirse*.

French, Edmund (Bishop of Elphin): 1798 sermon on sedition 219, 220

French Revolution: poem in Irish on 220

friend (English): as derived from an Indo-European root meaning 'free' 185

gabháltas Críostamhail 'Christian conquest':
Céitinn's discussion of 78
gabháltas pagánta 'pagan conquest': Céitinn's
discussion of 78
Gahan, Bishop William 220
'Gall Gaodhal' 210
Genee, Inge: comparison of the prepositions
le and *do* in Irish 156
George III 204, 219
Gibbons, Luke 67
GNÁCH (GNÁTHACH) 'usual', 'customary'
117, 132
gnách (gnáthach): in proverbs 117
gnách (gnáthach): as lexical equivalent of past
habitual category 132
GNÁTH 'usage, custom' 117–8, 123,
129–30, 134, 137, 157, 172–3
gnáth: in proverbs 117
gnáth: dictionary definitions of 172–3
gnáth: contrasted with *iongnadh* 123,
129–30
gnáth: discussion of Indo-European cognates
136
gnáth: compared with *dual* 117, 118, 134,
137, 157
gnáthaighthe Gaoidheal 174–5
GNÁTHUGHADH 'use', 'custom', 'practice'
170ff
gnáthughadh: and *consuetudo* 'custom' 180–1
gnáthughadh: and *dúchas* as daily practice
170ff
gnáthughadh: and the adverb *do ghnáth* 'usually', 'constantly' 171–2
gnáthughadh: modern form *gnáthamh*, in
proverb 174
Graiméar Gaeilge na mBráithre Críostaí 156
grammaticalization: as process of the evolution of grammatical structure 130ff
GUMPERZ, JOHN 171, 182
Gumperz, John: on culture and context 171,
182

HABITUALITY 115ff
habituality: and rhetorical style in Irish 121ff
habituality: lexical and grammatical 132
habituality: and linguistic typology 135
habituality: as a complex state 118
habituality: and concomitant adverbs 116
habituation: and grammar 170
'habitus' 171ff, 181–2. See also Bourdieu,
Pierre.
Hagège, Claude: on the mechanical nature of
grammar 131

Haicéad, Pádraigín 30
Haiman, John: on iconicity in syntax 49
Hanks, William: on integrating linguistic
structure and practice 18, 171
Hawaiian Creole: Labov's study of the evolu-
tion of 130
Heimat (German) 'homeland' 97–8
Herder, Johannes 15
hereditary right: and *dúchas* 35ff
HEREDITY 35, 46, 100ff
heredity: and *dúchas* 35, 46
heredity: and *dual* 100ff
Hodge, Robert 13
homeland. See native land.
HUGHES, GEOFFREY 22, 35, 51, 96, 226
Hughes, Geoffrey: on the democratization of
status words 22, 35, 51, 96, 226
Hughes, Geoffrey: on semantic fields 35–6,
51, 96, 226

iasacht: genitive *iasachta* collocated with *ainm*
'name' 125,–6, 163, 174
iconicity in syntax 49, 152, 157
imperative mood and verbal of necessity:
rhetorical effect compared 162–4
indiginae: Irish *dúchasaigh* as an equivalent of
178
Inglis, Liam 199
inmhe: in relation to *dualgas* and *dúchas* 109
internalization of meaning 36, 39, 49, 50,
51, 52, 94
iongnadh: opposite of *gnáth* 'what is usual'
122ff, 128. See also *gnáth* and *dual*.
iris 'faith': with *athartha* 'fatherland' 85
Iomarbháigh na bhFileadh: on the phrase
dúchas re 37
IRISH CONSTITUTION 215FF
Irish Constitution: use of *saorchead* 215ff
Irish Constitution: use of *saoirse chun* 'freedom to' 215ff
Israelites: Irish compared to 44, 81

JAKOBSON, ROMAN 12, 13, 166
Jakobson, Roman: on Boas' theory of gram-
matical meaning 166
Jakobson, Roman: on linguistic signs as
'shifters' 12, 13
JAMES I 211
James I: Mac an Bhaird's poem of welcome in
1603 113
James I: Ó hEodhasa's poem of welcome in
1603 211

Kinsale 57, 170
kirāmamm(Tamil) 'village' 86
Koselleck, Reinhard: on interpreting concepts 13
Kress, Gunther 13

l'udi (Russian): as derived from an Indo-European root meaning 'grow', 'increase' 185
Labov, William: on the evolution of grammar 130–1
láindeimhnioghadh 'full affirming': as a grammatical term for the non-habitual past 133
LEABHAR MUIMHNEACH 70–1, 147–8
Leabhar Muimhneach: on relationship between *ruidhleas*, *dligheadh* and *dúchas* 147–8
Leabhar Muimhneach: on relationship between *fearann cathaoire* and *fearann cloidhimh* 70–1
Leabhar Muimhneach: on the Dál gCais claim of joint sovereignty (*cert comhdhúthchasa*) over Cashel 71, 147–8
LEBOR NA CERT 140ff
Lebor na Cert: on the reciprocal nature of duty and entitlement 140ff
Lebor na Cert: on *dligheadh* and *dúchas* 140
LEBOR GABÁLA ÉRENN 61ff, 68, 74
Lebor Gabála Érenn: Tadhg Dall Ó hUiginn's use of 74ff
Lebor Gabála Érenn: Seathrún Céitinn's use of 61
Lebor Gabála Érenn: on *Midhe* as the 'fifth fifth' 61
Leerssen, Joep: on Gaelic Irish and Old English 75
Lehmann, Christian: on the loss of specific semantic content in grammar 131
Lehrer, Adrienne: on semantic fields 22
leithdeimhnioghadh 'half-affirming': as a grammatical term for the habitual past 133–4
Leute (German): as derived from an Indo-European root meaning 'grow', 'increase' 185
Lewis, C. S.: on the moralization of status words 35 51, 189
libeartaigh: as loanword in the nineteenth century 210–1
libertao: and *saoirse* in Fínghin Mac Cárthaigh's letter 196–7
liberti: in seventeenth-century phrase *liberti*

coinnséis 'liberty of conscience' 211–12
liber (Latin) 'free' 185
liberty (English) 221ff
libheirte: in seventeenth-century phrase *libheirte labhra* 'liberty of speech' 211
LINGUISTIC ANTHROPOLOGY 1–18 and *passim*
Linguistic anthropology: semiotics 11ff
Linguistic anthropology: indexicality 2, 8ff, 56–7, 59 (and *passim*), 182
Linguistic anthropology: metapragmatics 2, 13ff, 130, 134, 164
Linguistic anthropology: pragmatics 6, 10, 14, 18
Linguistic anthropology: symbol 11
Linguistic anthropology: shifter 12
Linguistic anthropology: icon 11
Linguistic anthropology: index 10, 12
Lloyd George, David 212
LONDON, TOWER OF 196, 211
London, Tower of: Fínghin Mac Cárthaigh's letter from 196, 211
Louvain (St. Anthony's College) 92, 122
Low Countries, The 207
Lucy, John: relation between linguistic and extra-linguistic facets of cognition 16

Mac Adam, Robert: nineteenth-century collection of Ulster proverbs 38, 100, 101
MAC AINGIL, AODH 33, 92
Mac Aingil, Aodh: on Luther's inherent pride as his *dúchas* 33
Mac Aingil, Aodh: and early use of the word *náision* 92
MAC AN BHAIRD, FEARGHAL ÓG 110, 113, 122–3
Mac an Bhaird, Fearghal Óg: on the taking of their *dúchas* from poets 110
Mac an Bhaird, Fearghal Óg: poem of welcome for James I 113
Mac an Bhaird, Fearghal Óg: poem to Flaithrí Ó Maolchonaire 122–3
MAC BIONAID, ART 35, 43, 210–11, 215
Mac Bionaid, Art: on *dúchas* and *tallann* 'talent' 35
Mac Bionaid, Art: use of the collocation *tír dhúchais* 'native land' 43
Mac Bionaid, Art: use of the loanword *libeartaigh* 'liberty' 210–11, 215
Mac Criomhthainn, Feidhlimidh: high-king of Munster 70

Mac Cana, Proinsias: on early Irish concepts
of unity 62, 68–9
Mac Carrtha, Mícheál: poem on *saoirse*
206–7
Mac Cárthaigh, Fínghin: letter from the
lower of London 196, 211
Mac Colla, Raghnall: mercenary leader dur-
ing Desmond Rebellion 85
Mac Connsaidín, Domhnall 207
Mac Con Uladh Mhic an Bhaird,
Maolmhuire: poem of protest to
Aodh Ó Domhnaill 108, 122–3
MAC CRAITH, MÍCHEÁL 70, 80, 85
Mac Craith, Mícheál: on exile poetry and the
idea of patria 80
Mac Craith, Mícheál: on Irish terms for 'faith
and fatherland' 85
Mac Craith, Mícheál: on *dúthaigh* as local
rather than national 70, 85
Mac Cruitín, Séamus 207
Mac Domhnaill, Aisdunn: mercenary leader
during Desmond Rebellion, in letters
of Fitzmaurice Fitzgerald 70
Mac Domhnaill, Aodh 43
Mac Grianna, Seosamh: on the idea of *dúchas*
53–4
Mac Lonáin, Flann: tenth-century poet 50
Mac Maoláin, Seán: collection of Donegal
sayings 101–2
MAC MURCHADHA, DIARMAID: in
Céitinn's Foras Feasa 28–9, 77–8,
104–5, 108
Mac Murchadha, Diarmaid: hereditary
claims (*dúchas*) contrasted with
Fitzstephen's foreignness 28–9, 77–8,
104–5
Mac Murchadha, Diarmaid: subject to high-
king of Ireland as his *dual* 28–9,
77–8, 104–5
Mac Murchadha, Diarmaid: exacts tribute
from the citizens of Dublin as his
dualgas 108
Mac Niocaill, Gearóid: on the term *óglach*
dúthchasa 179
Mac William Burke 69, 75–7, 79, 81, 108,
147, 162, 180
Máel Sechnaill: high-king of Ireland 193–4
'Marbhna Dhómhnaill Uí Chonaill' (poem)
207–8
McCarthys: in poem by Proinnsias Ó Súil-
leabháin 197
MCCURTIN, HUGH / MAC CRUITÍN
AODH BUÍ 133, 199

McCurtin, Hugh / Mac Cruitín Aodh Buí:
Jacobite poem (*saoirse*) 199
McCurtin, Hugh / Mac Cruitín Aodh Buí: on
Irish grammar 133
metapragmatics. See linguistic anthropology.
Midhe, as symbolic centre of Ireland 61ff, 60,
73, 81, 96, 141, 149
Míl of Spain: ancestor of Gaelic Irish 58, 68
Milesian schema: Old English grafted on to
in Tadhg Dall Ó hUiginn's poem 75
Milesian connection: shared genealogy of the
Irish and Spanish in Ó Súilleabháin
Béirre's letter 66
Miller, Kerby 15, 16, 44, 164ff
Miller, Kerby: on static nature of *dúchas* 44
Miller, Kerby: on alleged influence of Irish
syntax on its speakers 164ff
mínádúrthacht: in relation to a possible treaty
between England and Spain 181. See
also *nádúrtha*.
Morgan, Hiram: on 'faith and fatherland' ide-
ology 85

NÁDÚRTHA 57ff, 180
nádúrtha: collocated with *báidh* 'affinity' 57ff
nádúrtha: the Irish connection with Spain
described as 180. See also
mínádúrthacht.
NÁISION 92–3
náision: first attestations of in Irish 92–3
náision: fixed denotation, as compared with
dúthaigh and *dúchas* 93
NATIVE LAND (GENERAL). See under
dúchas, *dúthaigh*, *athartha* (Irish);
ojczyzna (Polish); *Vaterland* (German); *patria* (Latin); *rodina* (Russian);
Heimat (German); *tanah air* (Indonesian); *úr*, *nátu* (Tamil)
native land: vocabulary of, as natural and
involuntary 98
natural. See *nádúrtha*. See also various words
listed under 'right'.
nátu (Tamil) 'nation' 86
neamhghnáth 162. See also *gnáth*.
neart: in relation of *ceart* 'right' in Tadhg Dall
Ó hUiginn's poem 73–4
Ní Thiarnaigh, Éilis: on the metapragmatics
of *dúchas* 50
Nine Years' War 94
NON-AGENTIVE SYNTAX 157ff
non-agentive syntax in Irish: cultural and
historical context for 159ff
Nugents (Nuinseanaigh) 79

NUINSEAN, UILLIAM (WILLIAM
NUGENT) 39–40, 80, 164–5, 170
Nuinsean, Uilliam (William Nugent): poems
of exile 39–40, 80, 164–5, 170
Nuinsean, Uilliam (William Nugent):
attributive syntax of *dúchas* 39–40
Nuinsean, Uilliam (William Nugent): on the
nature of *dúchas* 80, 164–5, 170

Ó Braonáin, Mícheál: nineteenth-century
scribe 219
Ó Broin, Fiach mac Aodha (Feagh McHugh
O'Byrne): rebellion of 1580 63
Ó BRUADAIR DÁIBHÍ 33, 34, 49, 52, 107,
127–8, 178
Ó Bruadair, Dáibhí: on *dúchas* and *dúil*
'desire' 33–4
Ó Bruadair, Dáibhí: on the *dúchas* of inani-
mate objects 52
Ó Bruadair, Dáibhí: lament for Séamus de
Barra 107
Ó Bruadair, Dáibhí: poems of the
Cromwellian aftermath in Ireland
127–8
Ó Bruadair, Dáibhí: rhetorical effect of the
past habitual 127–8
Ó Bruadair, Dáibhí: on the idea of a
returned exile as *deoradh dúchais* 178
Ó BUACHALLA, BREANDÁN 200–1, 203
Ó Buachalla, Breandán: on Tadhg Ó Neach-
tain's Jacobitism 200–1
Ó Buachalla, Breandán: on Mícheál Óg Ó
Longáin's rhetoric (*saoirse*) 203
Ó Neachtain, Tadhg: early use of *saoirse* as
an abstract idea 201, 208
Ó Ceallaigh, Seán 208
Ó Cianáin, Tadhg: and early use of the word
náision 92
Ó Cléirigh, Cú Coigríche 37
Ó Cléirigh, Lughaidh: author of the seven-
teenth-century life of Aodh Rua Ó
Domhnaill 76, 86
Ó Cléirigh, Micheál: redactor of *Annála
Ríoghachta Éireann* 177
Ó Cobhthaigh, Diarmaid: fifteenth-century
poem on Christ's *dualas* 112
Ó Conchobhair, Ruaidhrí: high-king of
Connacht, in Céitinn's *Foras Feasa*
77
Ó CORRÁIN, DONNCHADH 68, 178
Ó Corráin, Donnchadh: on the *toísech
dúthchasa* and feudalism in the
medieval period 178

Ó Corráin, Donnchadh: on early Irish ideas
of unity 68
Ó Cuív, Brian 57ff, 69, 170
Ó Dálaigh, Lochlainn: poem on the Planta-
tion of Ulster 67
Ó Dálaigh, Muireadhach Albanach: thir-
teenth-century poet 37
Ó Dálaigh, Seán (John Daly) 206
Ó Doibhlin, Breandán: on the idea of *dúchas*
53
Ó Domhnaill, Aodh mac Ruaidhrí 90
Ó DOMHNAILL, AODH RUA 58, 82–3, 84,
108–9
Ó Domhnaill, Aodh Rua: and the Spanish
connection 58
Ó Domhnaill, Aodh Rua: as defender of his
fatherland 82–3
Ó Domhnaill, Aodh Rua: relationship with
the McWilliam Burkes 82–3, 84
Ó Domhnaill, Aodh Rua: Mac Con Uladh's
poem of protest to 108–9
Ó Domhnaill, Conn: in Tadhg Dall Ó hUig-
inn's poem for Seán Mac Uilliam Búrc
76
Ó Domhnaill, Ruaidhrí 85
Ó Dónaill, Niall: Modern Irish dictionary 19,
20, 55, 89, 106, 138, 186, 214, 225,
227
Ó hEODHASA, EOCHAIDH 126, 211
Ó hEodhasa, Eochaidh: on the seventeenth-
century change in literary fashion
127
Ó hEodhasa, Eochaidh: on James I and 'liberty of conscience' 211
Ó hEodhasa, Giolla Bhríde: on Irish grammar 133
Ó GADHRA, SEÁN: seventeenth-century
Connacht poet 27, 195
Ó Gadhra, Seán: poem on the aftermath of
the Williamite wars 195
Ó GNÍMH, FEAR FLATHA 65, 73, 95, 110,
159–1
Ó Gnímh, Fear Flatha: poem on the Plantation of Ulster and loss of *dúchas* 65,
73
Ó Gnímh, Fear Flatha: poem on the demise
of the hereditary bardic order 95,
110, 159–60
Ó Gnímh, Fear Flatha: rhetorical use of non-
agentive syntax 159–1
Ó hIFEARNÁIN, MATHGHAMHAIN: 95,
110, 161–2

Ó hIfearnáin, Mathghamhain: poem of the
demise of the hereditary bardic order
95, 110, 161–2

Ó hIfearnáin, Mathghamhain: rhetorical use
of the imperative mood 161–2

Ó Lócháin, Mícheál: founder of the Irish
American newspaper *An Gaodhal* 208

Ó LONGÁIN, MÍCHEÁL ÓG 117, 203–4

Ó Longáin, Mícheál Óg: nineteenth-century
collection of Irish proverbs 117

Ó Longáin, Mícheál Óg: on the idea of
saoirse in the nineteenth century
203–4

Ó Maolchonaire, Flaithrí: Mac an Bhaird's
poem to 122

Ó MÍOCHÁIN, TOMÁS 49, 113–4, 215,
217

Ó Míocháin, Tomás: use of *dual* and *dúchas*
in relation to the Stuarts 113–4

Ó Míocháin, Tomás: poems on the American
Revolution 215, 217

Ó Neachtain, Seán 44, 114

Ó Néill, Aodh (Hugh O'Neill): as defender of
his faith and fatherland 85–6

Ó Raghallaigh, Eoghan: lord of Bréifne, subject of Tuathal Ó hUiginn's poem
71–2

Ó RATHAILLE, AOGÁN 35, 114

Ó Rathaille, Aogán: on *dúchas maith* as
opposed to *cinnteacht* 'stinginess' 35

Ó Rathaille, Aogán: on the right of the Stuarts as *rí-dhualgas* 114

Ó Ruairc, Brian na Múrtha: poem to by
Tadhg Dall Ó hUiginn 62–3

Ó RUAIRC, MAOLMHAODHÓG 54, 188–9

Ó Ruairc, Maolmhaodhóg: on 'natural' in
Irish 54

Ó Ruairc, Maolmhaodhóg: on 'free' and 'freedom' in Irish 188

Ó Siadhail, Mícheál: on use of the preposition *do* in Modern Irish 116

Ó Súilleabháin, Amhlaoibh 203–5, 207, 215

Ó SUILLEABHÁIN BÉIRRE, DOMHNALL:
letters to Philip III of Spain 57ff,
170–4, 180–1

Ó Súilleabháin Béirre, Domhnall: on *dúchas*
and daily practice (*gnáthughadh*)
170ff, 173–4, 180–1

Ó Súilleabháin Béirre, Domhnall: on *dúchas*
and Ireland's relationship with Spain
57ff, 171

Ó Súilleabháin Béirre, Domhnall: phrase
báidh nádúrtha an dúthchais 57ff

Ó Súilleabháin Béirre, Domhnall: on the
Catholic cause 172

Ó SÚILLEABHÁIN, EOGHAN RUA 44, 198,
199

Ó Súilleabháin, Eoghan Rua: use of *dúchas*
44

Ó Súilleabháin, Eoghan Rua: use of *saoirse*
198, 199

Ó Súilleabháin Béirre, Pilib: challenges legitimacy of English rule in Ireland 78–9,
177–8

Ó Súilleabháin, Proinsias: poem on the
McCarthys and their lack of *saoirse*
197–8

Ó hUiginn, Maolmhuire (archbishop of
Tuam 1586–90) 80–1

Ó hUIGINN, TADHG DALL 19, 27–8, 62ff,
69, 72ff, 79–81, 108–9, 123ff, 162–3

Ó hUiginn, Tadhg Dall: poem for Seán mac
Oilibhéir Búrc 62ff, 69, 72ff, 79–81,
179–80

Ó hUiginn, Tadhg Dall: on the concepts of
dúthaigh and *fearann cloidhimh* 62ff,
69, 72ff, 79–81

Ó hUiginn, Tadhg Dall: rhetorical style of
poem to Riocard Óg Búrc 123ff,
162–3

Ó hUiginn, Tuathal: poem for Eoghan Ó
Raghallaigh of Bréifne 71ff

O'Byrnes (Col Raghnaill): 63

O'CONNELL, DANIEL 44, 107, 205–6,
207–8, 220

O'Connell, Daniel: address to the Catholic
Association in 1824 44, 107, 220

O'Dwyers: of Coill na Manach, Co. Tipperary,
as in the seventeenth-century poem
'Seán Ó Duibhir an Ghleanna' 210

O'Grady, Standish Hayes 208

O'More, Owny 17

O'RAHILLY, T. F. 52, 101, 102–3

O'Rahilly, T. F.: collection of Irish proverbs
52

O'Rahilly, T. F.: collection of Irish epigrams
102–3, 118

O'Sullivans 196

óglach dúthchasa: hereditary follower of a
leader in the medieval period 179

Oidheadh Chloinne Uisnigh: on *dúchas* as the
native land 57

oireacht 'assembly', 'partimony' 65

Orange, William of: descendants of as foreigners in Scotland 115

ojczyzna (Polish) 'homeland' 97–8

Pagden, Anthony: on indigenous rights 179
Pagliuca W.: on habituality in language 135–6
PAIRLEMENT CHLOINNE TOMÁIS 32–3,
    93–5, 110–1
Pairlement Chloinne Tomáis: on the emergence
    of a new social and cultural dispensa-
    tion 93–5
Pairlement Chloinne Tomáis: on the internaliza-
    tion of dúchas 32–3
Pairlement Chloinne Tomáis: on the relation-
    ship between dualgas and the loan-
    word páigh 110–1
patria 'fatherland' (Latin) 79, 98
Pearse, Patrick 43
Peirce, Charles Sanders: triadic division of
    signs 11, 12
Perkins R.: on habituality in language 135–6
Philadelphia: United Irish Society 202
Philip III of Spain: letters to from Domhnall Ó
    Súilleabháin Béirre 58, 123, 170
positive freedom: See freedom, positive
PRAESCRIPTIO LONGI TEMPORIS: Roman
    law concept of length of tenure 79,
    81, 179
praescriptio longi temporis: use of similar ideas
    by Tadhg Dall Ó hUiginn and
    Seathrún Céitinn 79, 81, 179–80
pragmatics of past habitual 121ff
PREDICATIVE SYNTAX 150ff
predicative syntax and dúchas/dual/díleas etc.
    152ff, 164
predicative syntax and verbal of necessity
    154ff
predicative syntax and adas/cóir etc. 152ff
prepositions le and do contrasted 156–7
priya (Sanskrit) 'loved one' 185
priyatel (Russian) 'friend' 185

Rees brothers 61, 68
RÉIM 'sway', 'dominion', 'reign' 197–8, 199,
    210, 211
réim: collocated with dúthaigh 210
réim: as a kind of positive freedom collo-
    cated with and complementary to
    saoirse 197–8, 199, 210–11
Renaissance: sixteenth-century patriotism
    79–80, 91
Rhineland, The 220
rhydd (Welsh) 'free' 185
right (concept): See under ceart; dír; díre;
    díleas; dílse; dligheadh; dual; dualgas;
    dúchas; dúthaigh; ruidhleas; toich.
Rinnucini, Cardinal 211

ROBERTS, J. M. 184, 228
Roberts, J. M.: critiqued by Skinner 228–9
Roberts, J. M.: condescension towards col-
    lective freedom 184
rodina (Russian) 'native land' 98
Rousseau, Jean Jacques 183
RUIDHLEAS 'absolute rightful ownership'
    146ff, 178
ruidhleas: and dúchas 146, 148
ruidhleas: and dílse 149–50
ruidhleas: and natural law 178

Saeed, John 22
saíre / saoire 'holy day' 188, 189
Sankoff, Gillian: on the evolution of gram-
    mar 131
SAOIRSE 'freedom', 'liberty' 7–8, 183–230
    passim
saoirse: dictionary definitions 186–8
saoirse: and liberty (libeartaigh) in nineteenth
    century 210–11
saoirse: and liberty (libertao) in Fínghin Mac
    Cárthaigh's letter 196–7
saoirse: and liberty of speech (libheirte labhra)
    211
saoirse: and liberty of conscience (liberti
    coinnséis) 211–12
saoirse: and saorgacht 'freedom' 210, 217–18
saoirse: syntax of: preceded by the definite
    article 202
saoirse: syntax of: non-occurrence with
    prepositional complement 'to' (fri / re
    / chun) 186–8, 190, 192, 200
saoirse: syntax of: with prepositional comple-
    ment (ar / ó) 186–8, 190, 192, 200
saoirse: syntax of: in genitive preceded by the
    article 207
saoirse: syntax of: followed by genitive com-
    plements 186–7, 225–6
saoirse: syntax of: preceded by plural posses-
    sives 201–2, 206 (bhur); 208 (ár)
saoirse: syntax of: with the verb tabhair (do-
    beir) 'gives' 191 (Middle Irish), 199,
    205
saoirse (saírse), prior to eighteenth century
    189ff
saoirse (saírse): in a Middle Irish text 190
saoirse: opposed to daoirse 188, 190, 195ff,
    200, 206
saoirse: as sovereignty or independence (ear-
    lier periods) 193ff
saoirse: as exemption or immunity (from)
    191ff, 219–20 (saorsa(dh))

saoirse: and *snádudh* 'protection' 192–3, 200

saoirse: and *comairce* 'protection' 192–3, 200

saoirse: and *tearmann* 'protection' 192–3

saoirse choitcheann: privilege of the poet class 192

saoirse: and *cádhus* 'honour' 193

saoirse: in eighteenth century 197ff

saoirse: in collocations with *gan* 197ff

saoirse: collocated with *réim*, sometimes preceded by *gan*: *gan réim gan saoirse* 198

saoirse: collocated with *sealbh*, sometimes preceded by *gan*: *gan sealbh gan saoirse* 198

saoirse: new conception of in eighteenth century 209ff

saoirse: as personified 201ff

saoirse: idea of its coming (*ag triall*) to Ireland 204

saoirse: *spiorad na saoirse* 'the spirit of freedom' 204–5, 208

saoirse: *meirge na saoirse* 'the standard of freedom' 204

saoirse: equated with *neamhspleadhchas* 'independence' 213

saoirse: and *éileamh* 'demanding' 207

saoirse: in phrase *saoirse agus sochar dúthaighe* 'freedom and profit of an estate' 198

saoirse: historical uses now obsolete 224–6

saoirse: followed by the genitive 'of Ireland' *na hÉireann* 208

saoirse: negative freedom in Irish, English and Polish 213–4

saoirse: *Chaitliceach/do Chaitlicibh* 'Catholic Emancipation' 205

saoirse: overlap with *cead* 216–18. See *cead*.

saoirseacht: used as password of the United Irish Society, Philadelphia 1797 202

saorchead: as equivalent to English 'full liberty' 216

saorchead: positive freedom 215–19. See also *cead*; *saorthoil*; *toil shaor*.

saorgacht: as alternative to *saoirse* 210, 220

saorthoil: as expression of positive freedom 219–20

SAPIR, EDWARD 1, 3, 10, 12, 16, 17

Sapir, Edward: on the lexical and grammatical in language 3

Sapir, Edward: influence of the lexicon on thought 16–7

Sapir, Edward: language as a guide to culture 1, 10, 12

Sapir, Edward: on the unconscious nature of linguistic usage 17

Saussure, Ferdinand de: one of the founding figures of modern semiotics 11

sealbh 'possession': collocated with *saoirse* 198, 210. See *saoirse*.

'Seán Ó Duibhir an Ghleanna', critiqued in relation to *saoirse* 209–10

seanchas 'traditional learning': F. J. Byrne's definition of 177

Sepúlveda, Juan: on the conqueror's right to enslave 78

SILVERSTEIN, MICHAEL 2, 10, 12, 14, 17, 55, 87, 96, 99, 134, 164

Silverstein, Michael: on pragmatics vs. semantics 10, 87

Silverstein, Michael: on indexicality in language 2, 12, 55, 96

Silverstein, Michael: on the metapragmatics of language 2, 14, 99

Silverstein, Michael: on metapragmatic awareness 17, 134, 164

Simms, Katharine: on sixteenth-century patriotism 80

sinsir 'ancestors': 31, collocated with *dúchas* 45. See *dúchas*.

síor 'perpetual': collocated with *ainm* 'name' 173

Skerrett, R. A.: on the nature of habitual aspect in Irish 118–9

Skinner, Quentin: critique of Berlin's two concepts of liberty 8, 183–4, 228–9

Slige Dála: poem from the Metrical Dindshenchas 111–2

SLOBIN, DAN 3, 4, 6, 17, 121, 134–5, 136, 159

Slobin, Dan: grammar and rhetorical style of a language 121, 159

Slobin, Dan: influence of grammar on construing experience 17, 136–7

Slobin, Dan: linguistic relativity 134–5

Slobin, Dan: on the obligatory nature of grammar 3–4, 6

sochar: in phrase *saoirse agus sochar dúthaighe* 'freedom and profit of an estate' 198–9

sóer 'free' (Old Irish) 185

sóire 'freedom', 'holy day' (Old Irish) 185, 188, 189. See also *saoirse*.

Spain: historical connection with Ireland 57ff

Stapleton, Theobald: uses of the word *dúthaigh* 90

Suarezian natural law 78–9

suvírah (Sanscrit) 'hero' 185
suvíryam (Sanscrit) 'heroic power' 185
Sweetser, Eve: on the internalization of
    meaning 48–9

Tailte: see Tailtiu
Tailtiu (Tailte): as part of the symbolic centre
    of Ireland 61–2, 64, 66
Tamil (Southern India): the vocabulary of
    locality and nationhood 86ff
tanah air (Indonesian) 'homeland' 98
TARA (TEAMHAIR) 60ff, 64, 66, 68, 75–6,
    77, 96, 194
Tara (Teamhair): symbolic centre of Ireland
    60ff, 64, 66, 68, 75–6, 77, 96
Tara (Teamhair): sovereignty of (saoirse) 194
técam (Tamil < Sanscrit désh) 'country' 87
Thomond 59
tigerna / toísech dúthchasa 'lord of a patri-
    mony' 179
TÍR 5, 42–4, 87–90
tír: in phrase tír dhúchais 'native land' 5,
    42–4
tír: syntax of, compared to dúthaigh and
    dúchas 87–90
Tlachtga: as part of the symbolic centre of
    Ireland 61–2
TOICH 'rightful ownership' 76, 146ff, 177
toich: and ruidhleas 146
toich: compared to natural law dominium 146
toich: predicative syntax of 147, 150ff
toil shaor: as expression of positive freedom
    219–20. See saorthoil; saoirse.
TÓRUIGHEACHT CHALMAIR 204–5
Tóruigheacht Chalmair: association of saoirse
    with South American developments
    203–4
Tóruigheacht Chalmair: association of saoirse
    with America and France 203–4
Tóruigheacht Chalmair: on the universal
    nature of saoirse 203–4
TRÍ BIOR-GHAOITHE AN BHÁIS 41, 42,
    83–4, 141
Trí Bior-Ghaoithe an Bháis: dúthaigh and
    dúchas contrasted with exile 41–2,
    83–4
Trí Bior-Ghaoithe an Bháis: the relationship
    between dlighe and dualgas 141
Tuatha Dé Danann: in the Lebor Gabála
    Érenn 72
Tyrawley (Co. Mayo): home of the Mac
    William Burkes 27, 76
Tecosca Cormaic (ninth-century speculum

principis): on dúchas as a royal
    attribute 50–1
The Flight of the Earls: on the relationship
    between origin (bunadhus) and native
    land (athartha) 60
'The Settling of the Manor of Tara': on the
    attributes of the five provinces 68
'The Spirit of the Nation' 206–7
'Tree of Liberty' 202

UÍ NÉILL: 68, 194
Uí Néill: as focal point of resistance to the
    Vikings 68
Uisneach: as part of the symbolic centre of
    Ireland 61–2
Ulster, Plantation of: in poems by Fear
    Flatha Ó Gnímh and Lochlainn Ó
    Dálaigh 65
United Irish Society: use of saoirseacht as a
    password 202
úr (Tamil) 'village', 'locale' 86–7

Vaterland (German) 'homeland' 97–8
Verschueren, Jeff: on pragmatics 18, 96
verbs of freeing in Irish 196
Vikings 59, 68
VOLOSHINOV V.I. 10, 12, 96
Voloshinov V. I.: the linguistic sign as socially
    multi-accented 96
Voloshinov V. I.: words as indexes of social
    and cultural change 10, 12
von Humboldt, Wilhelm 15, 134

WAGNER, HEINRICH 133, 158–9
Wagner, Heinrich: Irish dialect atlas 132
Wagner, Heinrich: on verb categories in Irish
    133
Wagner, Heinrich: on agentive and non-
    agentive constructions in Irish 158–9
Walsh, Edward 206
WATKINS, CALVERT 1, 12–13, 106
Watkins, Calvert: on the semantics of reci-
    procity in Irish poetry 106
Watkins, Calvert: on language and culture 1,
    12
Watkins, Calvert: on linguistics and philol-
    ogy 12–13
Whorf, Benjamin Lee: and linguistic relativ-
    ity 134, 165ff, 170
WIERZBICKA, ANNA 1, 2, 5, 7, 8, 27, 96, 97,
    98, 158, 165, 167, 188, 213, 222ff
Wierzbicka, Anna: lack of objective criteria
    for key words 7–8

Wierzbicka, Anna: on words for 'freedom' (English, Latin, Polish, Russian and Japanese) 7–8, 188, 222ff

Wierzbicka, Anna: on 'negative freedom' in English 213

Wierzbicka, Anna: on the cultural salience of key words 27

Wierzbicka, Anna: on agentive and non-agentive syntax in language 158, 165, 167

Wierzbicka, Anna: on words for 'homeland' (German, Polish, Russian) 5, 97–8

Wierzbicka, Anna: on 'key' words in cultures 1–2

WILLIAMS, RAYMOND 5, 9

Williams, Raymond: on his Keywords 5

Williams, Raymond: on the word culture 9

wolność, (Polish) 'freedom': compared to Irish saoirse and contrasted with English freedom 213–14, 224

Index of Poems by First Line

A mhic Uí Dhálaigh is sásta an bheatha dhuit (Caithréim Thaidhg) 33–4

A BHANBHA BHOG-OMH DHONA DHUAIBHSEACH 129–30

A Bhanbha bhog-omh dhona dhuaibhseach: on the prostitution of Ireland 129–30

A Bhanbha bhog-omh dhona dhuaibhseach: on the concepts of dual, gnáth and iongnadh 129–30

A MHIC NÁ MEBHRAIG ÉIGSI 95–6, 110, 161–2

A mhic ná mebhraig éigsi: on the use of the imperative mood 161–2

A mhic ná mebhraig éigsi: on the threat to the hereditary order of poets 95–6, 110, 161–2

A mhic ná mebhraig éigsi: on the change in literary fashion 95–6, 110, 161–2

A mbeidh ar dtír mhocht áluinn saor go deo?: critique of late nineteenth-century notions of saoirse 218

A FHIR THÉID GO FIADH bhFUINIDH 80–1

A fhir théid go Fiadh bhFuinidh: as an example of sixteenth-century patriotism 80–1

A fhir théid go Fiadh bhFuinidh: on faith and fatherland ideology 80–1

A shaoi is a shagairt atá ag seasamh go síorchróga 199

Ag seinnim duit dánta chun suain, a mhic (Mamma, am I a repealer?): the idea of saoirse as 'translated' from 'The Spirit

of the Nation' 206–7

ANOCHT IS UAIGNEACH ÉIRE 128–9

Anocht is uaigneach Éire: on the concept of dual 128–9

Anocht is uaigneach Éire: effects of the Flight of the Earls 128–9

Ar Maidin indé cois céidh na slimbharc: on the relationship between saoirse, réim and sealbh 198

Atá an fhuireann so thall gan amhras díleas 199–200

CÁIT AR GHABHADAR GAOIDHIL? 67, 129

Cáit ar ghabhadar Gaoidhil?: on the concept of iongnadh 129

Cáit ar ghabhadar Gaoidhil?: on the Plantation of Ulster 67, 129

CRÉACHT DO DHÁIL MÉ IM ARTHACH GALAIR 127–8

Créacht do dháil mé im arthach galair: on the aftermath of the Cromwellian wars 127–8

Créacht do dháil mé im arthach galair: on the rhetorical effect of the past habitual 127–8

CRÉD FUARAIS ORAM, A AOIDH? 108–10

Créd fuarais oram, a Aoidh?: on the concept of dualgas 108–10

Créd fuarais oram, a Aoidh?: a poet protests his treatment 108–10

D'FHIOR CHOGAIDH COMHAILTEAR SÍOTHCHÁIN 62–3

D'fhior chogaidh comhailtear síothcháin: on an ethnic Gaelic nationalism 62–3

D'fhior chogaidh comhailtear síothcháin: on the symbolic centre of Ireland 62–3

DIA LIBH A LAOCHRUIDH GAOIDHIOL 40–1, 60, 63–5

Dia libh a laochruidh Gaoidhiol: on the symbolic centre of Ireland 40–1, 60, 63–5

Dia libh a laochruidh Gaoidhiol: on an ethnic Gaelic nationalism 40–1, 60, 63–5

Diombáidh triall ó thulchaibh Fáil: as an example of sixteenth-century patriotism 39, 79

DO ROINNEADH RÍGHE CONNACHT 71–3

Do roinneadh ríghe Connacht: on the relationship between right and force 71–3

Do roinneadh ríghe Connacht: on the relationship between dúthaigh and dúchas and the foreign charter 71–3

Druididh suas a chuaine an chaointe 30–1

Fada cóir Fhódla ar Albain 27–8
FADA I n-ÉAGMAIS INSE FÁIL 39, 79–80
Fada i n-éagmais Inse Fáil: as an example of sixteenth-century patriotism 39, 79–80
Fada i n-éagmais Inse Fáil: on the internalization of *dúchas* 39, 79–80
FEARANN CLOIDHIMH CRÍOCH BHANBHA 28, 69, 73–7
Fearann cloidhimh críoch Bhanbha: on the relationship of *dúthaigh* and *fearann cloidhimh* 69, 73–7
Fearann cloidhimh críoch Bhanbha: on the rights of the Old English in Ireland 73–7
Fearann cloidhimh críoch Bhanbha: on the relationship between right and force 28
Fiu a bheatha bás tighearna: on *dual* and *dualgas* 112–3
FÚARUS IONGNADH A FHIR CHUMAINN 122–3
Fúarus iongnadh a fhir chumainn: on the concepts of *dual*, *gnáth* and *iongnadh* 122–3
Fúarus iongnadh a fhir chumainn: on the change in literary fashion 122–3
Fúarus iongnadh a fhir chumainn: the rhetorical effect of the past habitual 122–3

Is díth liom na Gaeil-se a bheith tláith lag fann 202–3
Iomchair th'atuirse, a Aoidh Ruaidh 109–10
IONMHOLTA MALAIRT BHISIGH 126–7
Ionmholta malairt bhisigh: on the concept *gnáth* 126–7
Ionmholta malairt bhisigh: the rhetorical effect of the past habitual 126–7
Ionmholta malairt bhisigh: on the change in literary fashion 126–7
IS MAIRG NÁR CHREAN RE MAITHEAS SAOGHALTA 128
Is mairg nár chrean re maitheas saoghalta: the rhetorical effect of the past habitual 128–9
Is mairg nár chrean re maitheas saoghalta: on the decline of the poetic order 128
IS FADA ATÁ AN AINNISE AR GHAEDHLUIBH (Staid Nua na hÉireann 1697) 195–6
Is fada atá an ainnise ar Ghaedhluibh 195–6

Is fada atá an ainnise ar Ghaedhluibh: on the captivity of Ireland in the 1690s 195–6
Is fada atá an ainnise ar Ghaedhluibh: on *saoirse* and *daoirse* 195–6
IS AINM DAMH SAOIRSE 201–2
Is ainm damh Saoirse: idea of *saoirse* as 'enlightenment' 201–2
Is ainm damh Saoirse: idea of *saoirse* as originating in France 201–2
Is ainm damh Saoirse: idea of *saoirse* as coming to Ireland 201–2
Is ainm damh Saoirse: idea of *saoirse* as opposed to the Orange order 201–2

Mairg rug ar an aimsirsi: on *tearmann*, *comairce* and the social order 193
MAIRG DO-CHUAIDH RE CEIRD nDÚTHCHAIS 95, 110, 159–61
Mairg do-chuaidh re ceird ndúthchais: on the change in literary fashion 95, 110, 159–61
Mairg do-chuaidh re ceird ndúthchais: on the threat to the hereditary order of poets 95, 110, 159–61
Mairg do-chuaidh re ceird ndúthchais: on the use of the verbal of necessity 159–61
MO THRUAIGHE MAR TÁID GAOIDHIL 65–6
Mo thruaighe mar táid Gaoidhil: on *dúchas* and the symbolic centre 65–6
Mo thruaighe mar táid Gaoidhil: on the Plantation of Ulster 65–6
Mór theasda dh'obair Óivid: on the use of the loanword *libheirte* 211

Senchas cía lín non-iarfaig: on the concept of *dualgas* 111–3

T'aire riot, a Riocaird Óig 123–7, 162–4, 173–4
TÁ NA FRANNCAIGH SAN AM SO CUR CÉIM AR gCÚL 220
Tá na Franncaigh san am so cur céim ar gcúl: on the French Revolution 220
Tá na Franncaigh san am so cur céim ar gcúl: on the Irish *toil shaor* 220
Táid cléir ag guí 's ag agall: as critique of 'Seán Ó Duibhir an Ghleanna' 209
Taoim cásmhar a' machtnamh am aonar 208
Tig fuacht i ngaoth gheimhridh: idea of *saoirse* as coming to Ireland 203
Tógaibh eadrad is Éire 28

Tomhais cia mise, a Mhurchaidh 37

Tráth indé is mé tnáidhte i bpéin: on the relationship between *saoirse, réim* and *sealbh* 199

Trí coróna i gcairt Shéamais: on the crown of Ireland as due (*dú*) to James I 113

Truagh ceas na gcarad anocht 27

Urra oc oighreacht Éiremhóin 37